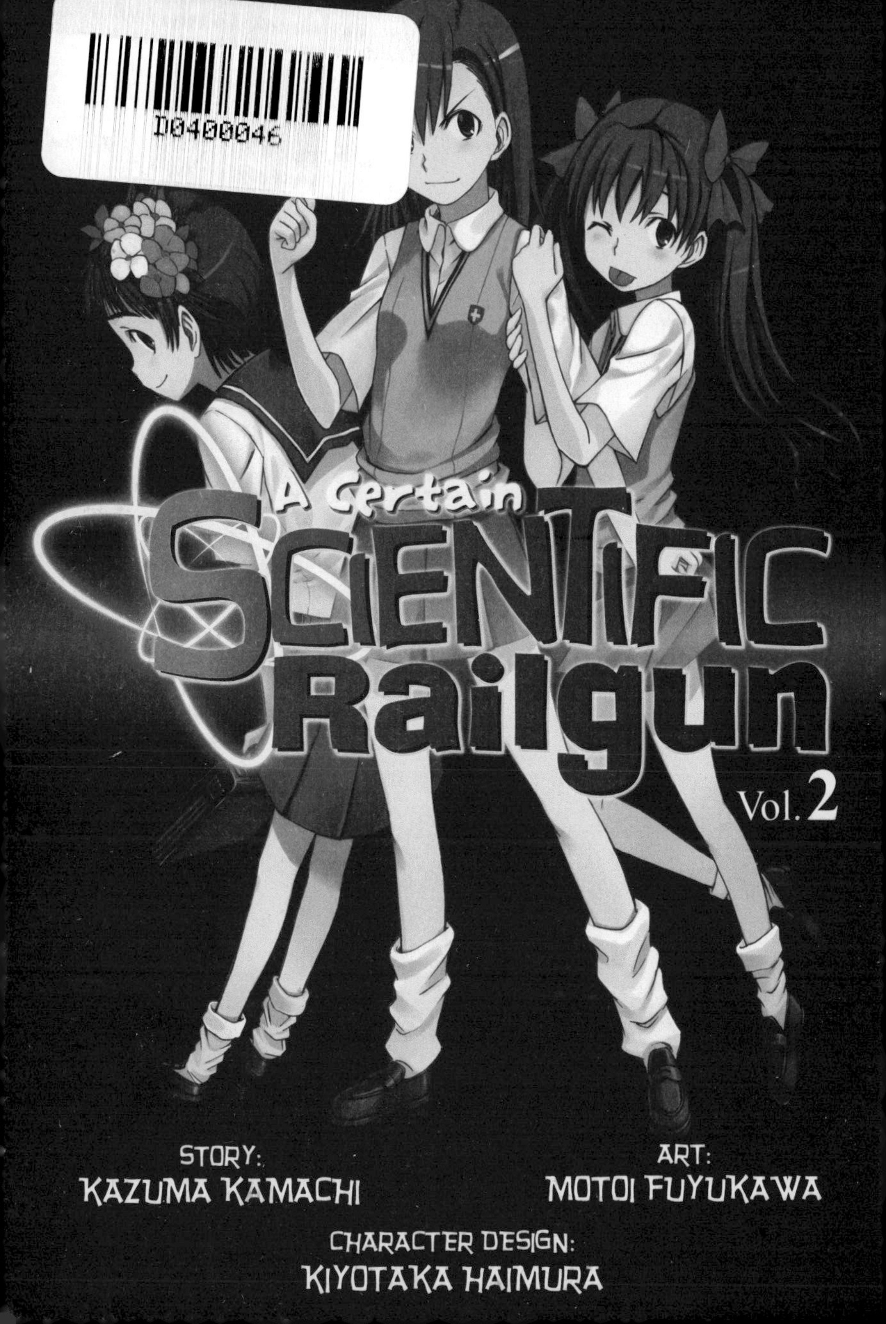
A Certain
SCIENTIFIC
Railgun
Vol. 2

STORY:
KAZUMA KAMACHI

ART:
MOTOI FUYUKAWA

CHARACTER DESIGN:
KIYOTAKA HAIMURA

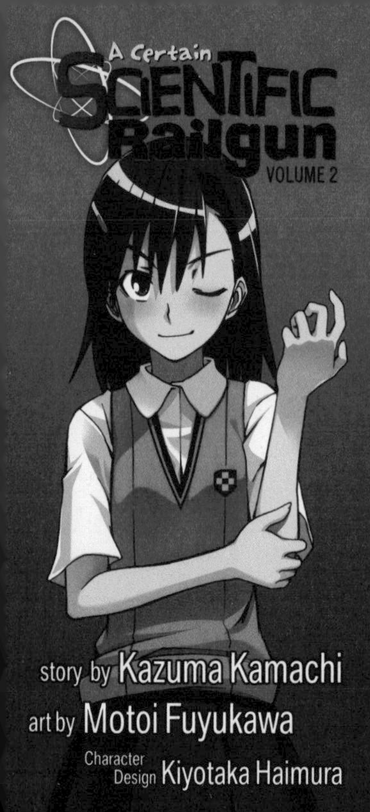
A Certain
SCIENTIFIC
Railgun
VOLUME 2
story by Kazuma Kamachi
art by Motoi Fuyukawa
Character Design Kiyotaka Haimura

STAFF CREDITS

translation Andrew Cunningham
adaptation Janet Houck
lettering Roland Amago
layout Bambi Eloriaga-Amago
cover design Nicky Lim
copy editor Shanti Whitesides
editor Adam Arnold

publisher Jason DeAngelis
Seven Seas Entertainment

A CERTAIN SCIENTIFIC RAILGUN VOL. 2

ISBN: 978-1-935934-02-8

Printed in the USA

First Printing: October 2011

10 9 8 7 6 5 4 3 2

FOLLOW US ONLINE: *www.gomanga.com*

READING DIRECTIONS

This book reads from *right to left*, Japanese style. If this is your first time reading manga, you start reading from the top right panel on each page and take it from there. If you get lost, just follow the numbered diagram here. It may seem backwards at first, but you'll get the hang of it! Have fun!!

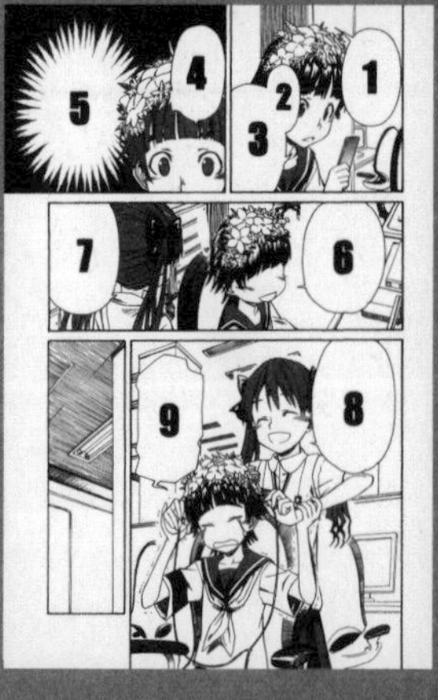
1
2
3
4
5
6
7
8
9

CONTENTS

CHAPTER 8: JULY 20

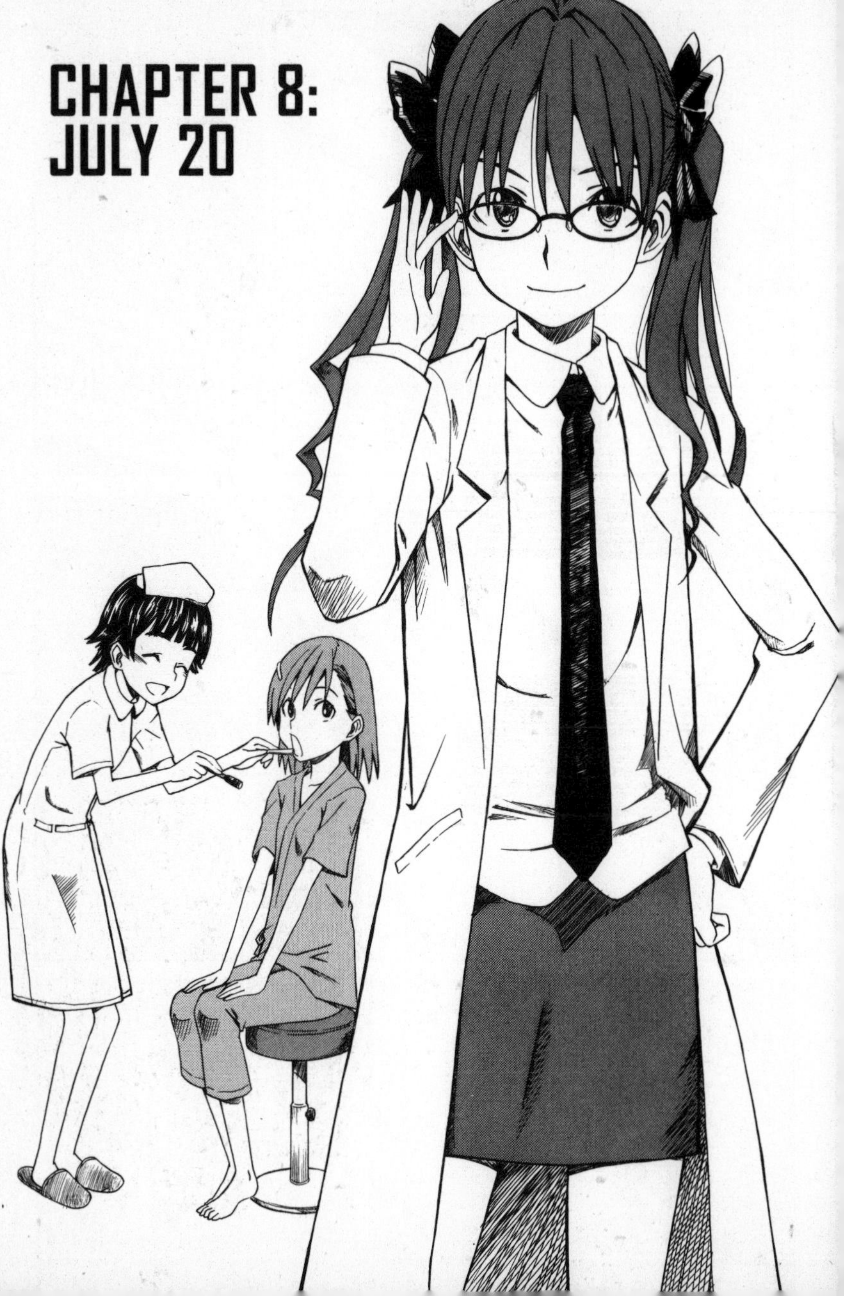

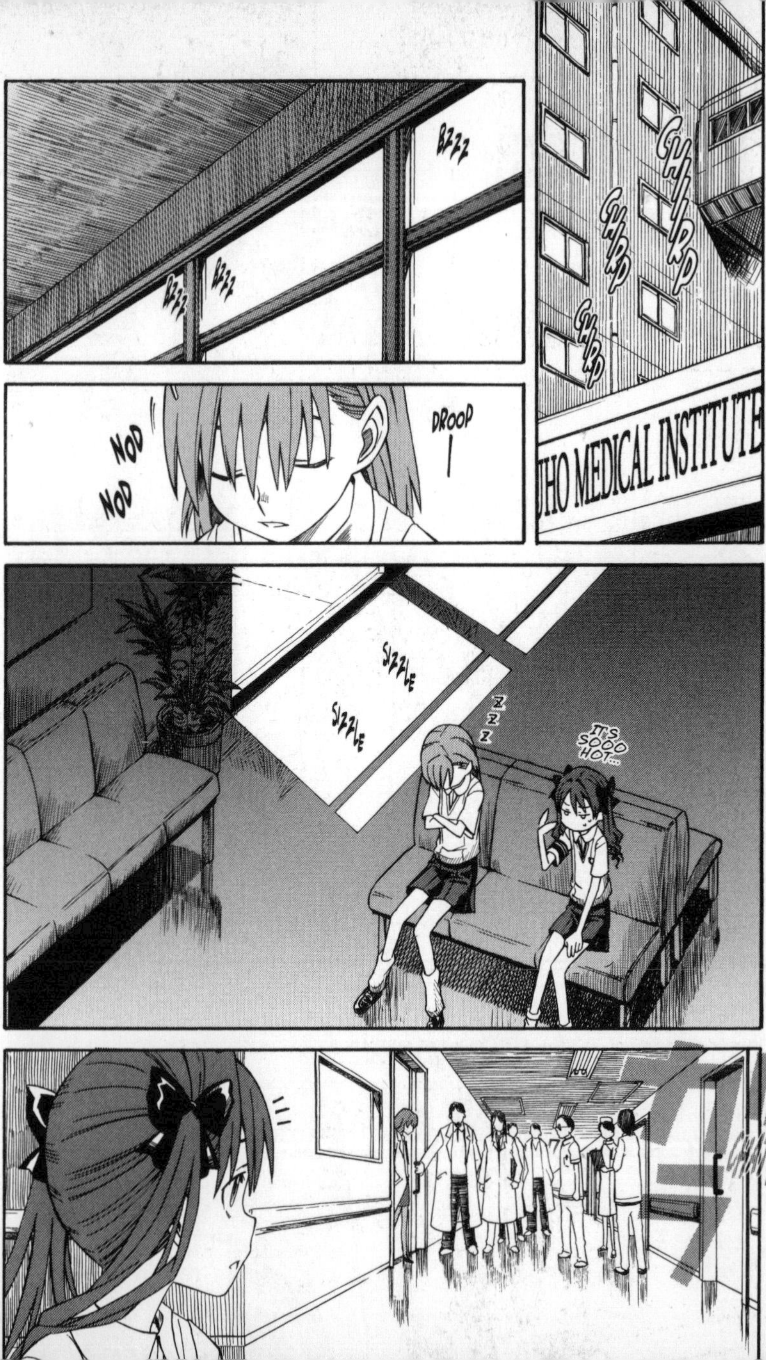
CHIRP
CHIRP
CHIRP
CHIRP
UHO MEDICAL INSTITUTE
BZZZ
BZZZ
BZZZ
DROOP
NOD
NOD
SIZZLE
SIZZLE
Z Z Z
IT'S SOOO HOT...
CHATTER

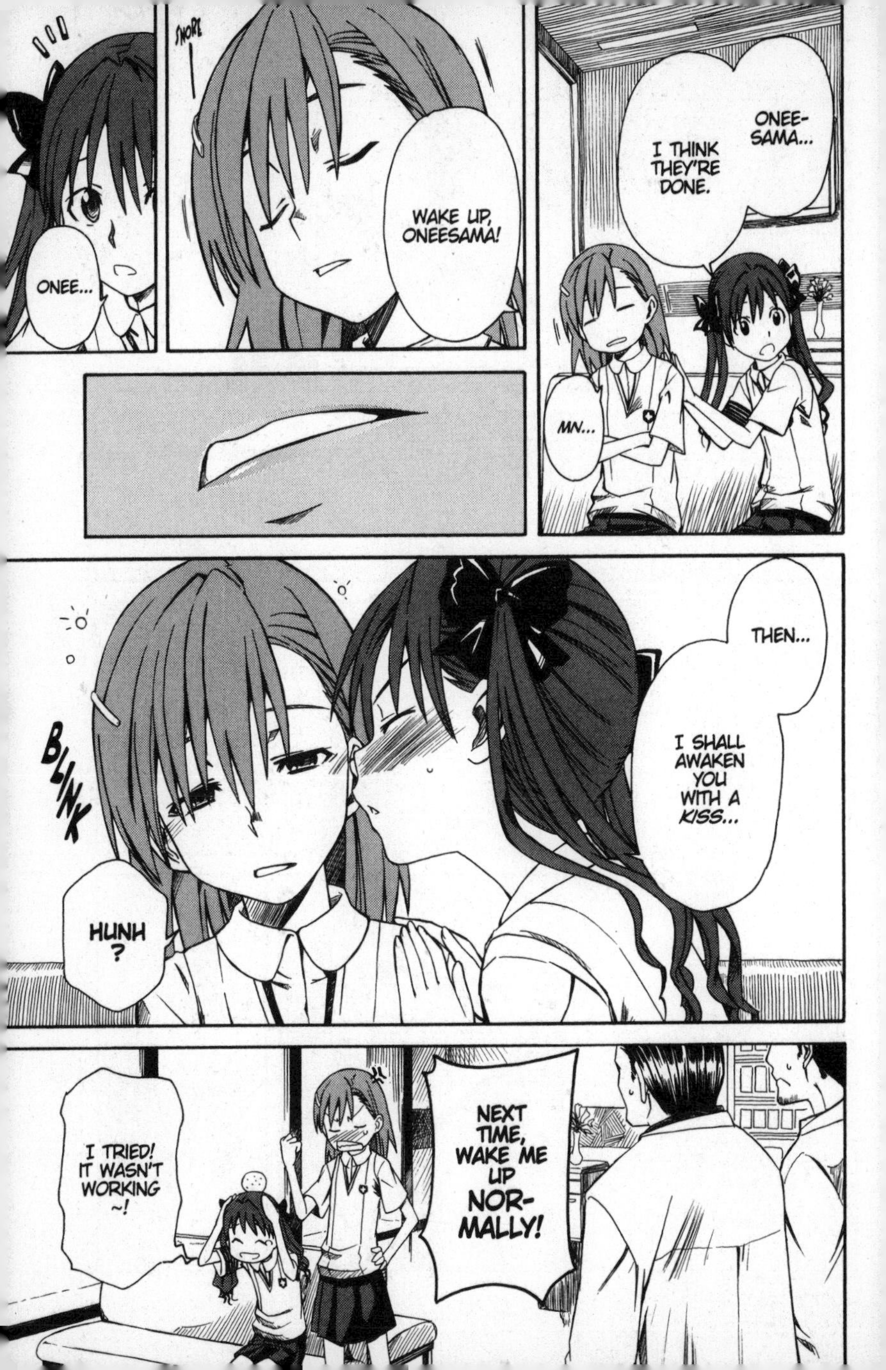
ONEE-SAMA...
I THINK THEY'RE DONE.
MN...
SNORE
WAKE UP, ONEESAMA!
ONEE...
THEN...
I SHALL AWAKEN YOU WITH A KISS...
BLINK
HUNH ?
NEXT TIME, WAKE ME UP NOR-MALLY!
I TRIED! IT WASN'T WORKING ~!

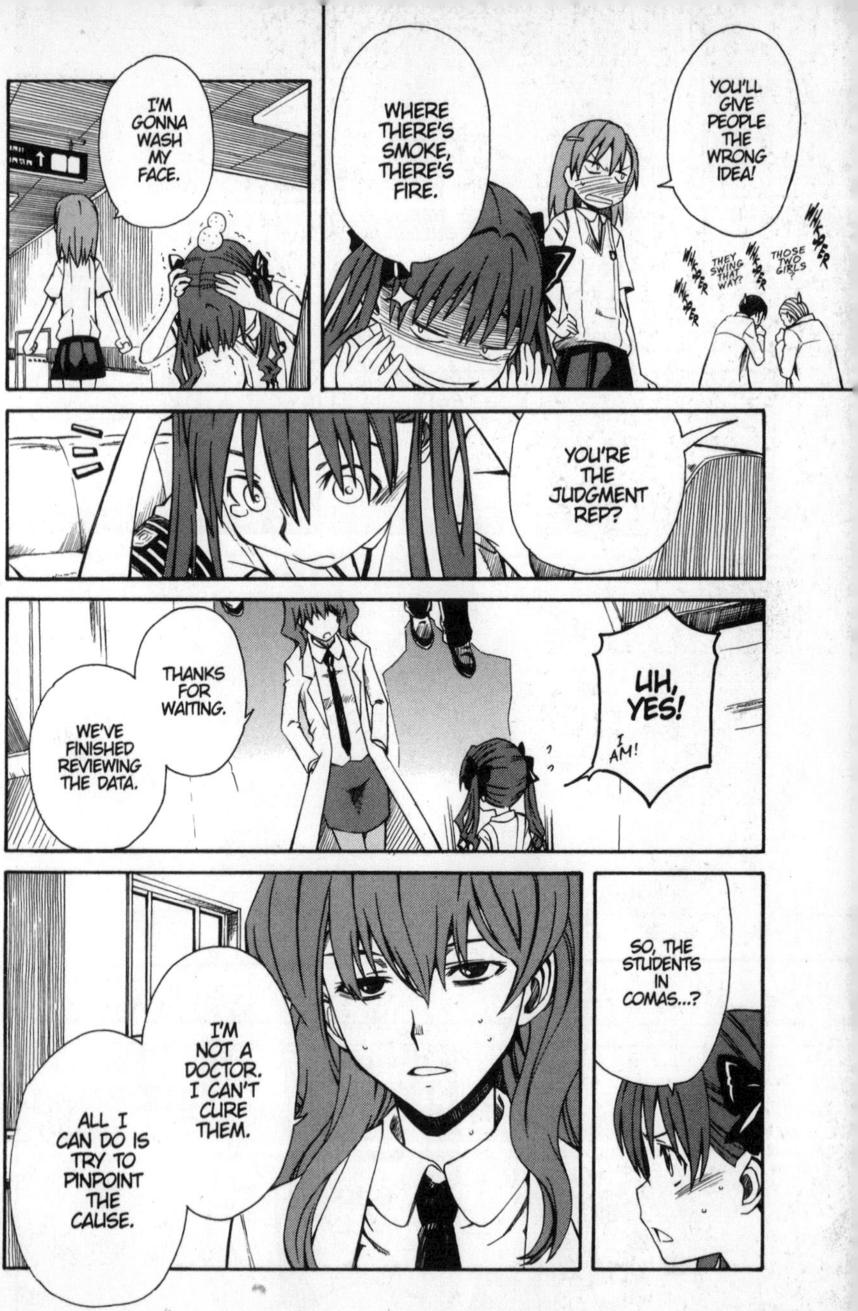
YOU'LL GIVE PEOPLE THE WRONG IDEA!
WHISPER
THOSE TWO GIRLS?
WHISPER
THEY SWING THAT WAY?
WHISPER
WHISPER
WHERE THERE'S SMOKE, THERE'S FIRE.
I'M GONNA WASH MY FACE.
YOU'RE THE JUDGMENT REP?
UH, YES!
I AM!
THANKS FOR WAITING.
WE'VE FINISHED REVIEWING THE DATA.
SO, THE STUDENTS IN COMAS...?
I'M NOT A DOCTOR. I CAN'T CURE THEM.
ALL I CAN DO IS TRY TO PINPOINT THE CAUSE.

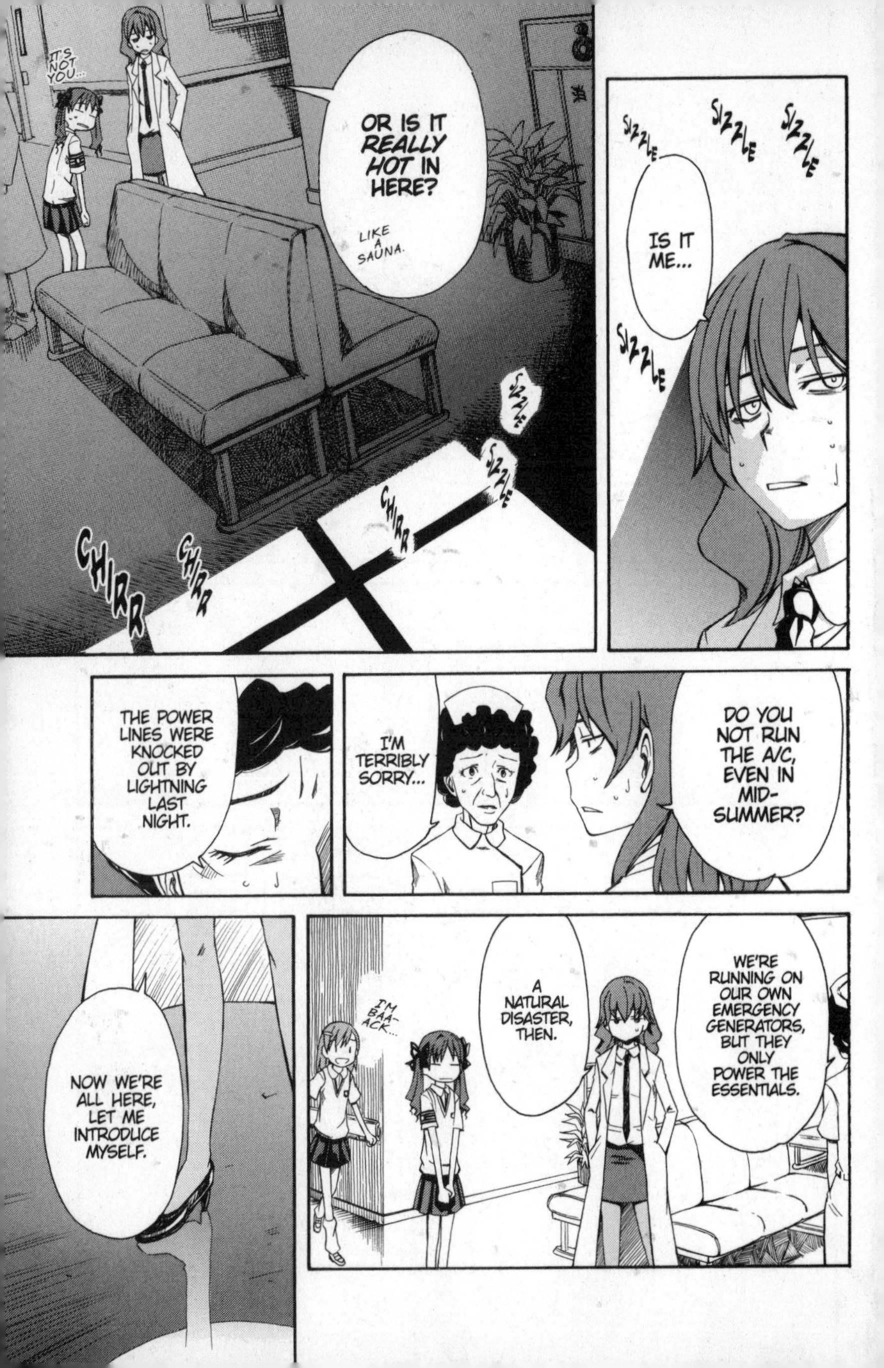
SIZZLE
SIZZLE
SIZZLE
IS IT ME...
SIZZLE
OR IS IT REALLY HOT IN HERE?
LIKE A SAUNA.
IT'S NOT YOU...
SIZZLE
SIZZLE
CHIRR
CHIRR
CHIRR
DO YOU NOT RUN THE A/C, EVEN IN MID-SUMMER?
I'M TERRIBLY SORRY...
THE POWER LINES WERE KNOCKED OUT BY LIGHTNING LAST NIGHT.
WE'RE RUNNING ON OUR OWN EMERGENCY GENERATORS, BUT THEY ONLY POWER THE ESSENTIALS.
A NATURAL DISASTER, THEN.
I'M BAA-ACK...
NOW WE'RE ALL HERE, LET ME INTRODUCE MYSELF.

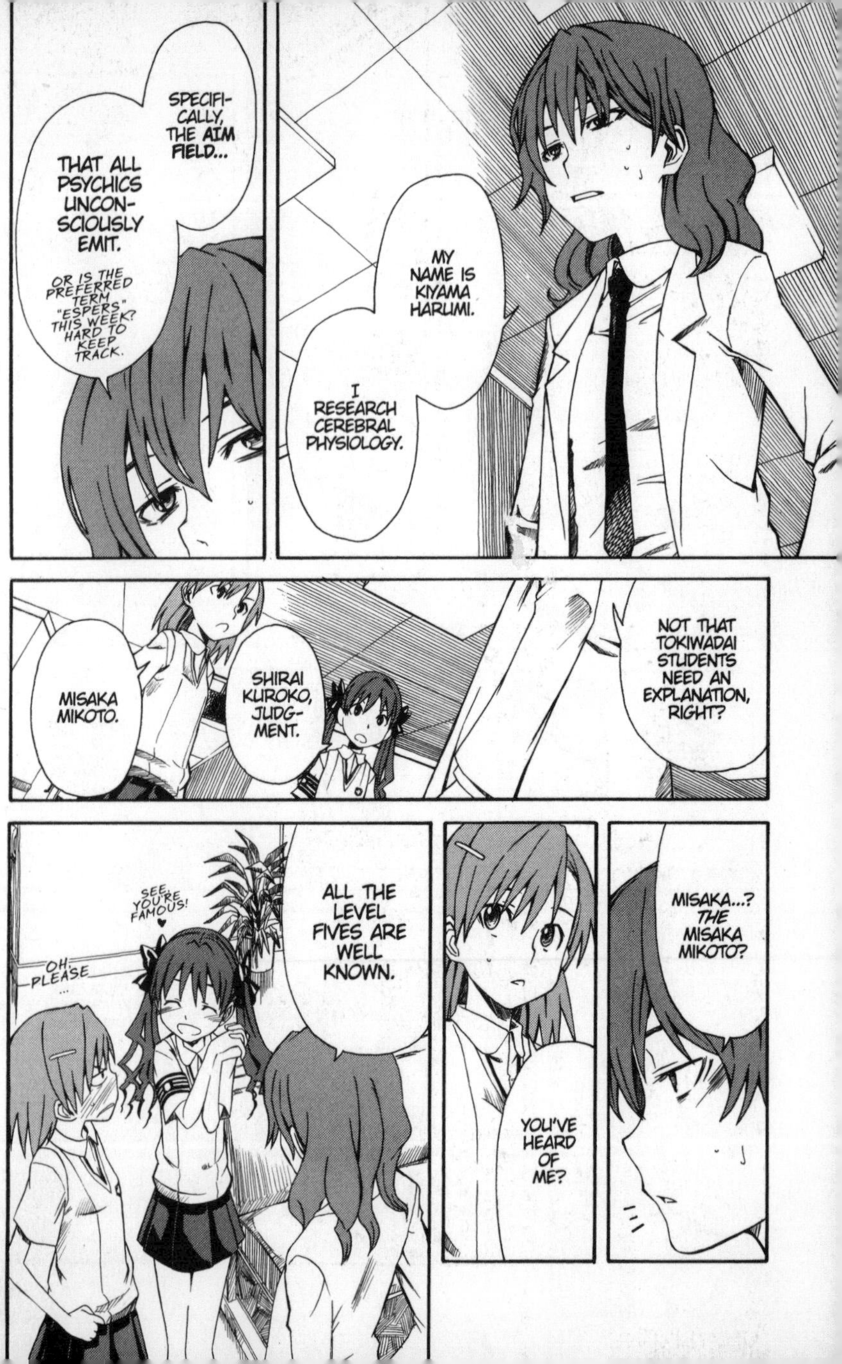
MY NAME IS KIYAMA HARUMI.
I RESEARCH CEREBRAL PHYSIOLOGY.
SPECIFICALLY, THE AIM FIELD...
THAT ALL PSYCHICS UNCONSCIOUSLY EMIT.
OR IS THE PREFERRED TERM "ESPERS" THIS WEEK? HARD TO KEEP TRACK.
NOT THAT TOKIWADAI STUDENTS NEED AN EXPLANATION, RIGHT?
SHIRAI KUROKO, JUDGMENT.
MISAKA MIKOTO.
MISAKA...? *THE* MISAKA MIKOTO?
YOU'VE HEARD OF ME?
ALL THE LEVEL FIVES ARE WELL KNOWN.
SEE, YOU'RE FAMOUS! ♥
OH, PLEASE...

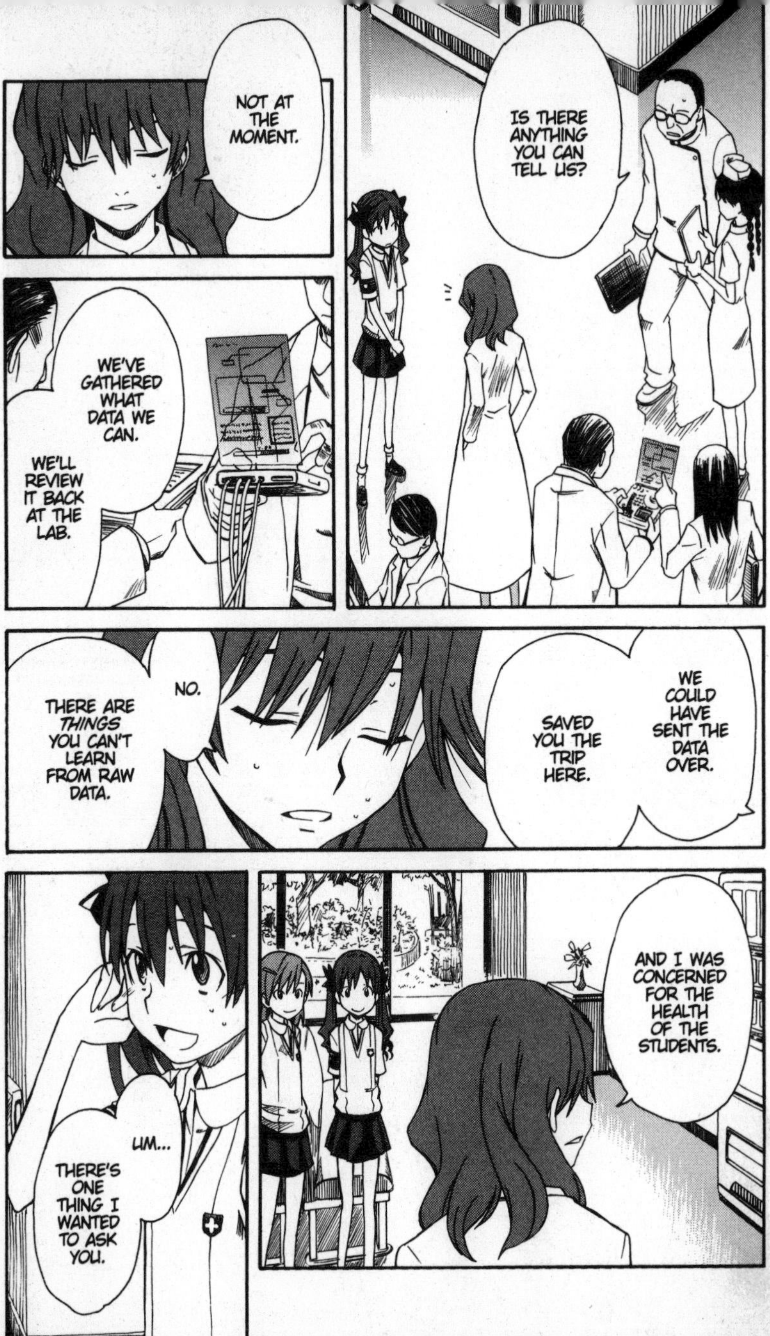
IS THERE ANYTHING YOU CAN TELL US?
NOT AT THE MOMENT.
WE'VE GATHERED WHAT DATA WE CAN.
WE'LL REVIEW IT BACK AT THE LAB.
WE COULD HAVE SENT THE DATA OVER.
SAVED YOU THE TRIP HERE.
NO.
THERE ARE *THINGS* YOU CAN'T LEARN FROM RAW DATA.
AND I WAS CONCERNED FOR THE HEALTH OF THE STUDENTS.
UM...
THERE'S ONE THING I WANTED TO ASK YOU.

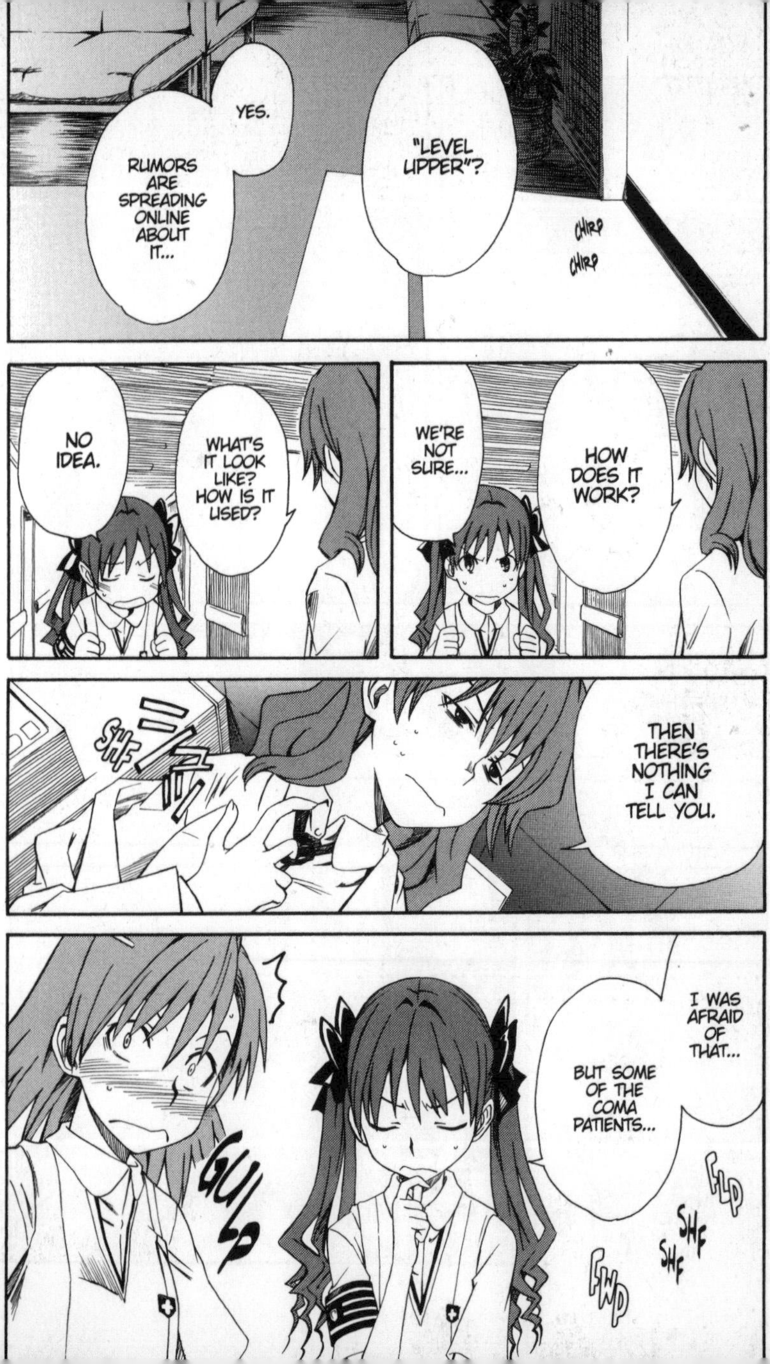
"LEVEL UPPER"?
CHIRP
CHIRP
YES.
RUMORS ARE SPREADING ONLINE ABOUT IT...
HOW DOES IT WORK?
WE'RE NOT SURE...
WHAT'S IT LOOK LIKE? HOW IS IT USED?
NO IDEA.
THEN THERE'S NOTHING I CAN TELL YOU.
SHF
I WAS AFRAID OF THAT...
BUT SOME OF THE COMA PATIENTS...
FLP
SHF
SHF
FWD
GULP

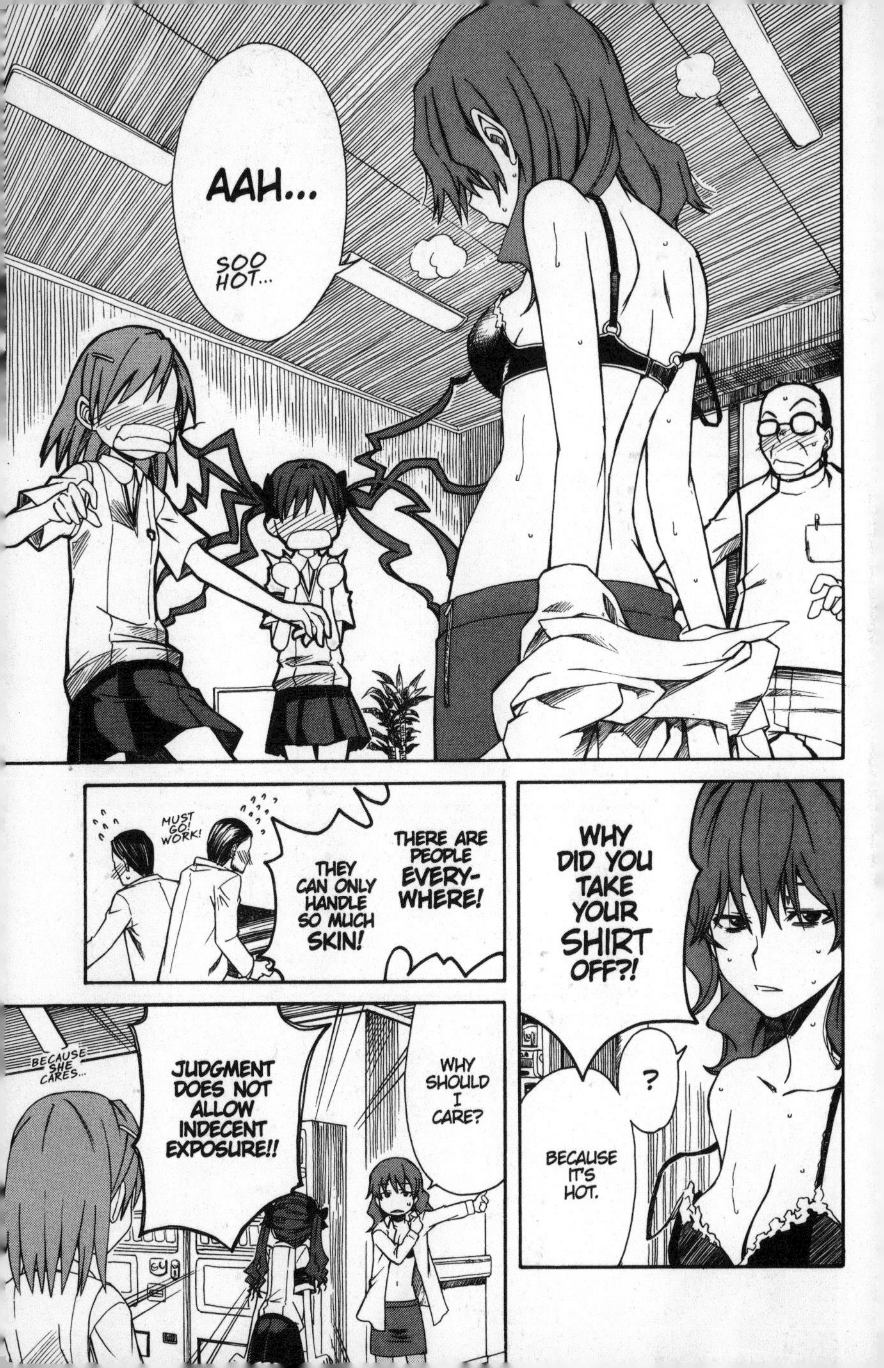
AAH...
SOO HOT...
WHY DID YOU TAKE YOUR SHIRT OFF?!
?
BECAUSE IT'S HOT.
THERE ARE PEOPLE EVERYWHERE!
THEY CAN ONLY HANDLE SO MUCH SKIN!
MUST GO! WORK!
WHY SHOULD I CARE?
JUDGMENT DOES NOT ALLOW INDECENT EXPOSURE!!
BECAUSE SHE CARES...

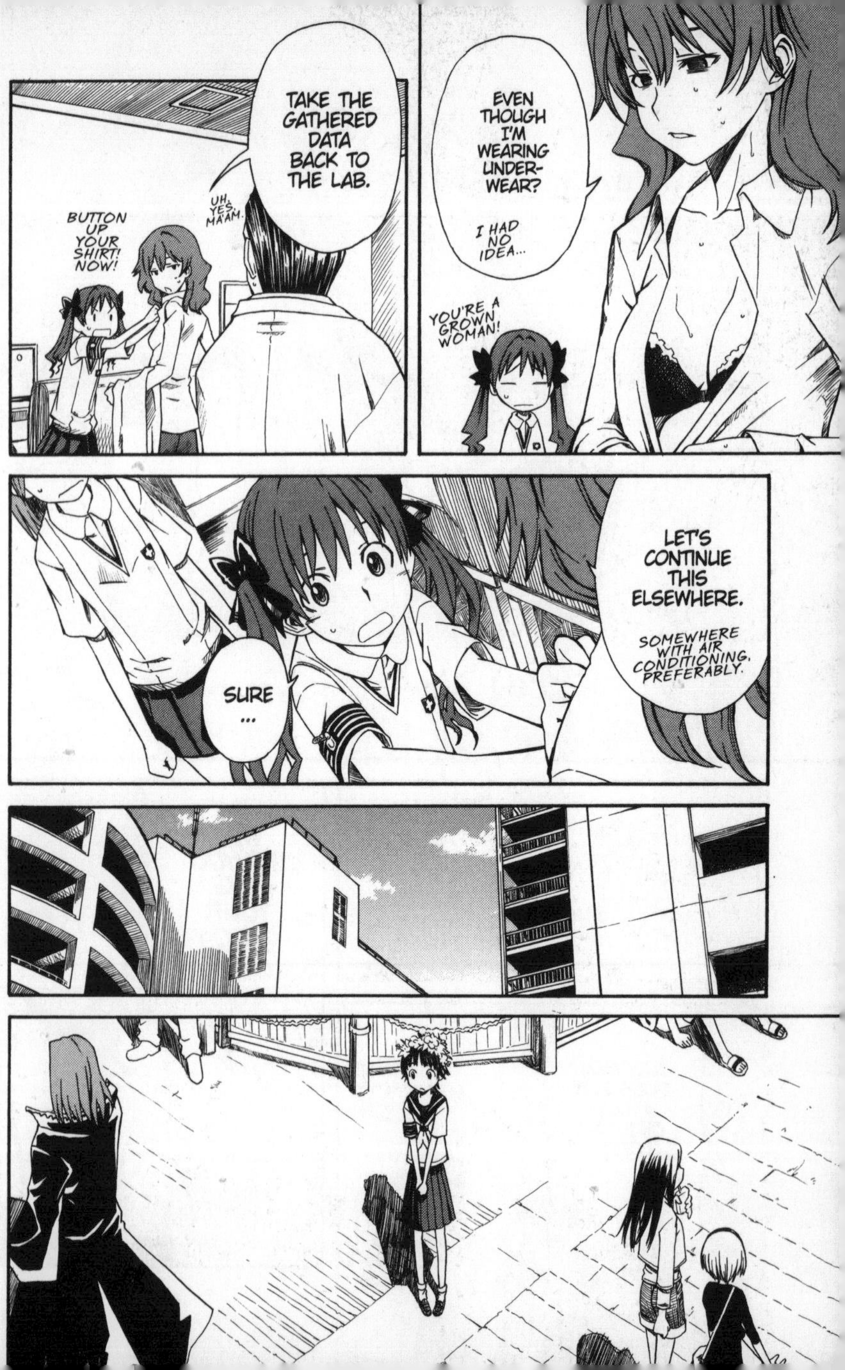
EVEN THOUGH I'M WEARING UNDER-WEAR?
I HAD NO IDEA...
YOU'RE A GROWN WOMAN!
TAKE THE GATHERED DATA BACK TO THE LAB.
UH, YES, MA'AM.
BUTTON UP YOUR SHIRT! NOW!
LET'S CONTINUE THIS ELSEWHERE.
SOMEWHERE WITH AIR CONDITIONING, PREFERABLY.
SURE ...

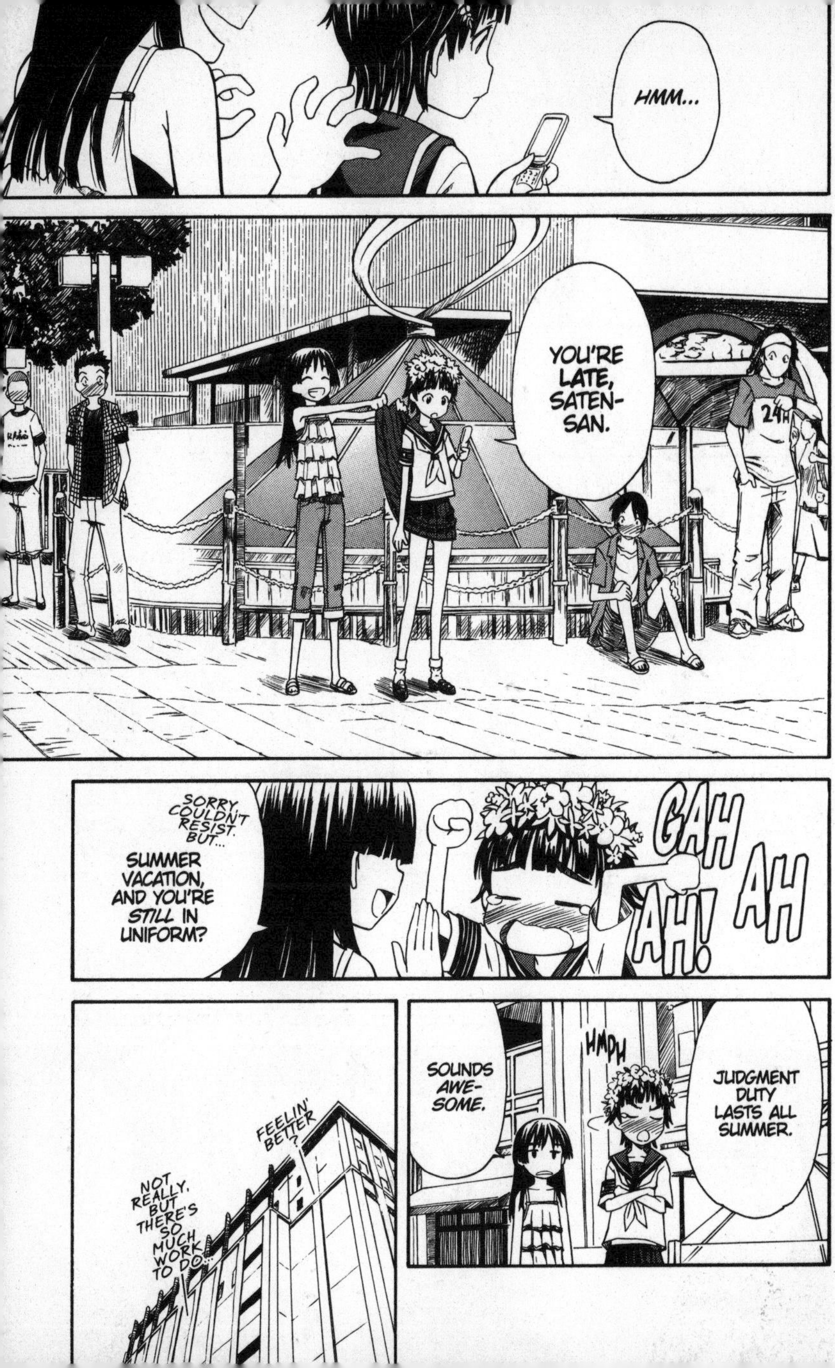
HMM...
YOU'RE LATE, SATEN-SAN.
GAH AH AH!
SORRY, COULDN'T RESIST. BUT...
SUMMER VACATION, AND YOU'RE *STILL* IN UNIFORM?
JUDGMENT DUTY LASTS ALL SUMMER.
HMPH
SOUNDS AWE-SOME.
FEELIN' BETTER?
NOT REALLY, BUT THERE'S SO MUCH WORK TO DO...

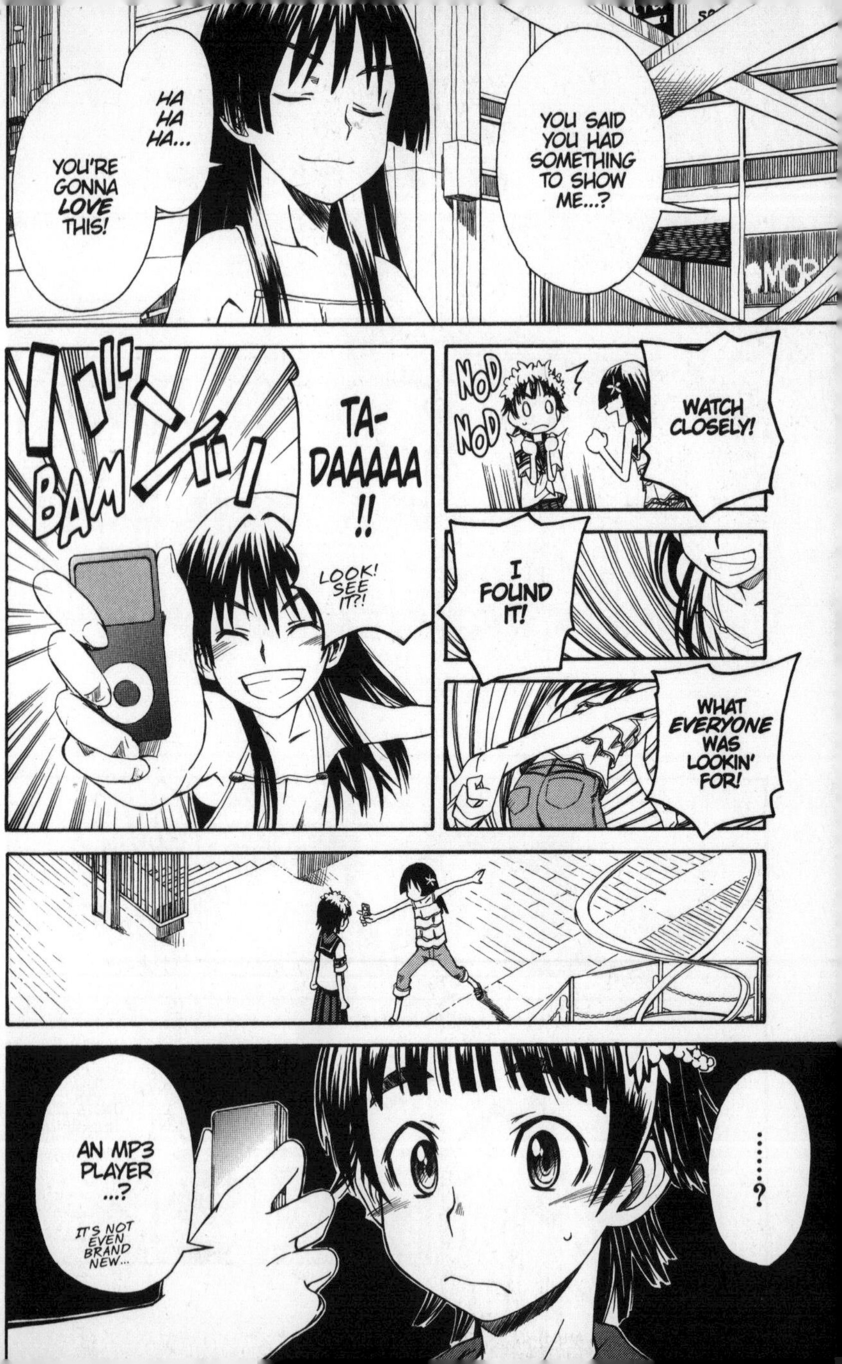
YOU SAID YOU HAD SOMETHING TO SHOW ME...?
HA HA HA...
YOU'RE GONNA LOVE THIS!
WATCH CLOSELY!
NOD NOD
I FOUND IT!
WHAT EVERYONE WAS LOOKIN' FOR!
TA-DAAAAA!!
LOOK! SEE IT?!
BAM
......?
AN MP3 PLAYER...?
IT'S NOT EVEN BRAND NEW...

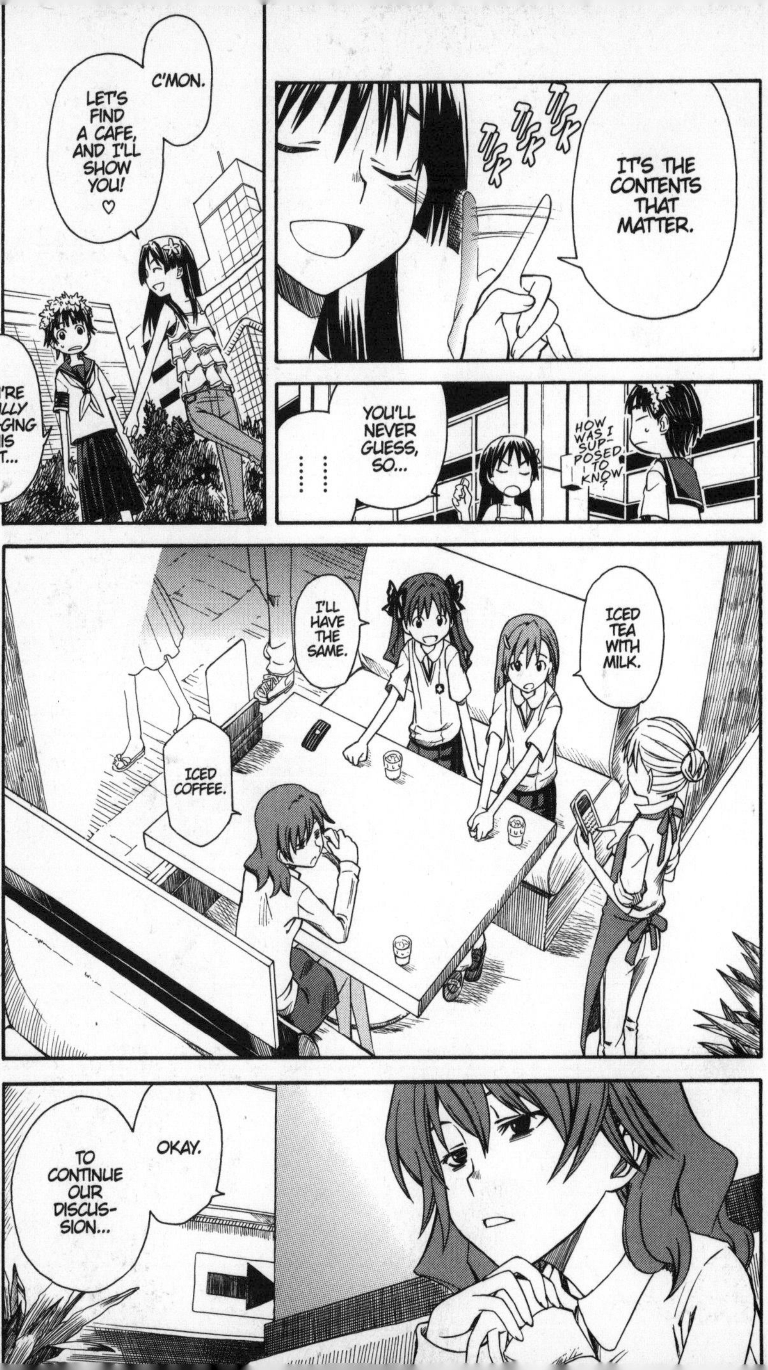
TIK TIK TIK
IT'S THE CONTENTS THAT MATTER.
HOW WAS I SUP-POSED TO KNOW?
YOU'LL NEVER GUESS, SO...
......
C'MON.
LET'S FIND A CAFE, AND I'LL SHOW YOU! ♡
YOU'RE *REALLY* DRAGGING THIS OUT...
ICED TEA WITH MILK.
I'LL HAVE THE SAME.
ICED COFFEE.
OKAY.
TO CONTINUE OUR DISCUS-SION...

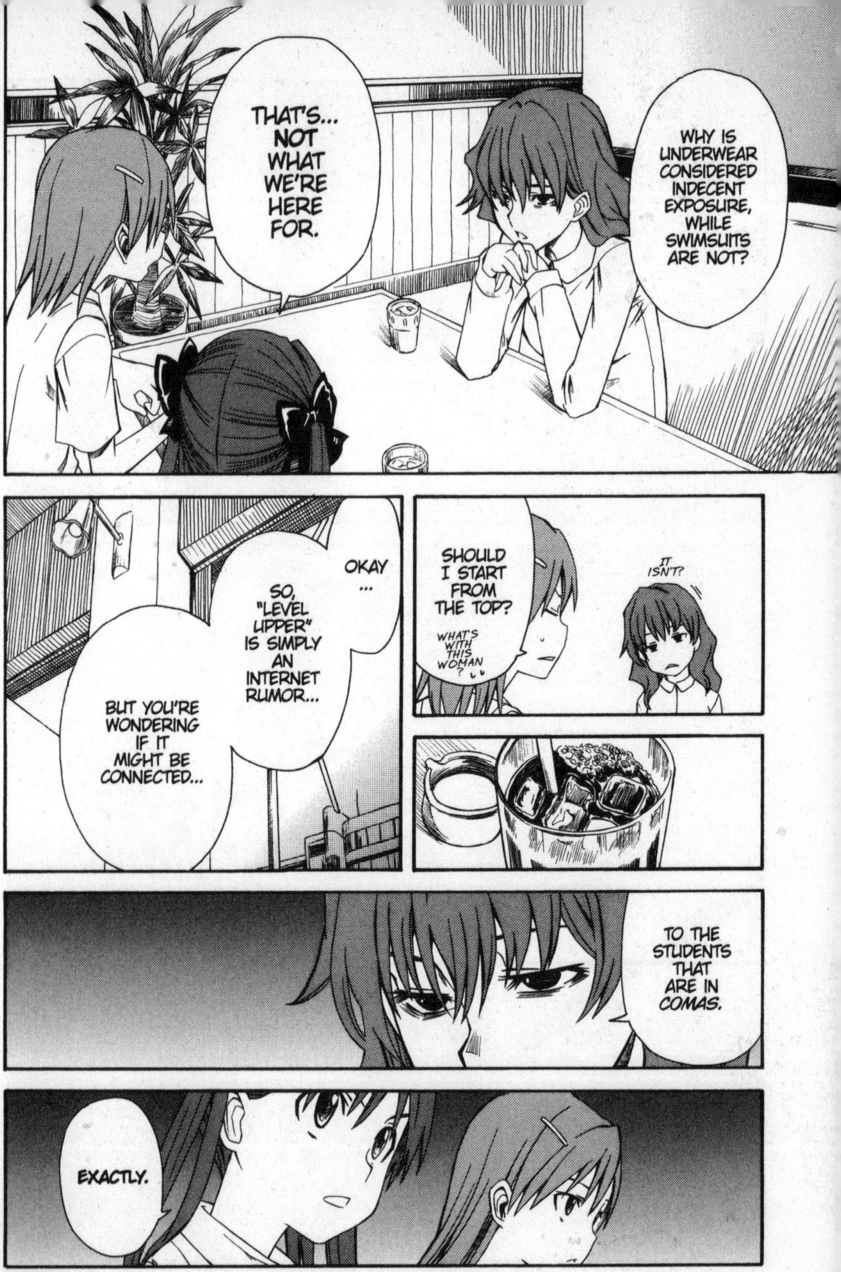
WHY IS UNDERWEAR CONSIDERED INDECENT EXPOSURE, WHILE SWIMSUITS ARE NOT?
THAT'S... NOT WHAT WE'RE HERE FOR.
IT ISN'T?
SHOULD I START FROM THE TOP?
WHAT'S WITH THIS WOMAN?
OKAY ...
SO, "LEVEL UPPER" IS SIMPLY AN INTERNET RUMOR...
BUT YOU'RE WONDERING IF IT MIGHT BE CONNECTED...
TO THE STUDENTS THAT ARE IN COMAS.
EXACTLY.

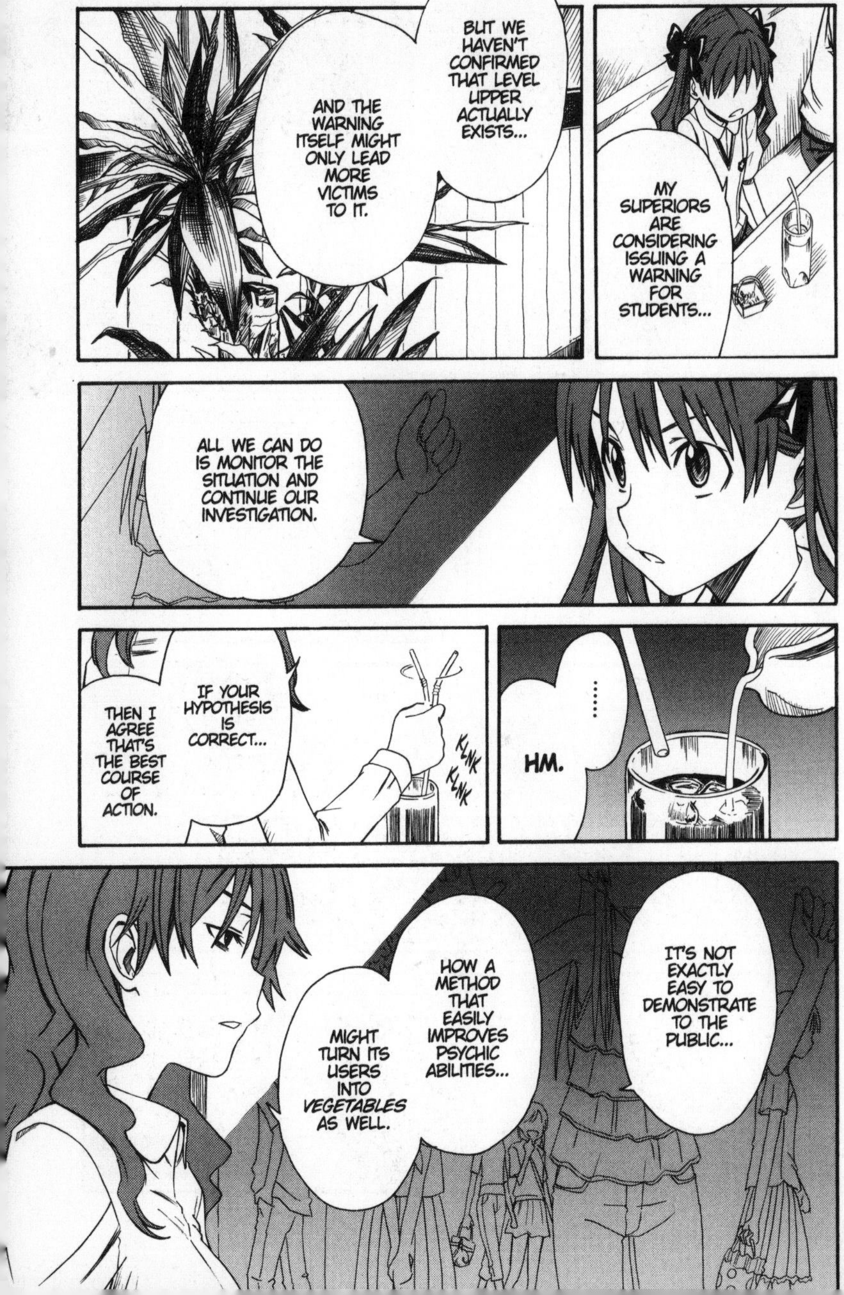
MY SUPERIORS ARE CONSIDERING ISSUING A WARNING FOR STUDENTS...
BUT WE HAVEN'T CONFIRMED THAT LEVEL UPPER ACTUALLY EXISTS...
AND THE WARNING ITSELF MIGHT ONLY LEAD MORE VICTIMS TO IT.
ALL WE CAN DO IS MONITOR THE SITUATION AND CONTINUE OUR INVESTIGATION.
......
HM.
IF YOUR HYPOTHESIS IS CORRECT...
THEN I AGREE THAT'S THE BEST COURSE OF ACTION.
KLNK KLNK
IT'S NOT EXACTLY EASY TO DEMONSTRATE TO THE PUBLIC...
HOW A METHOD THAT EASILY IMPROVES PSYCHIC ABILITIES...
MIGHT TURN ITS USERS INTO *VEGETABLES* AS WELL.

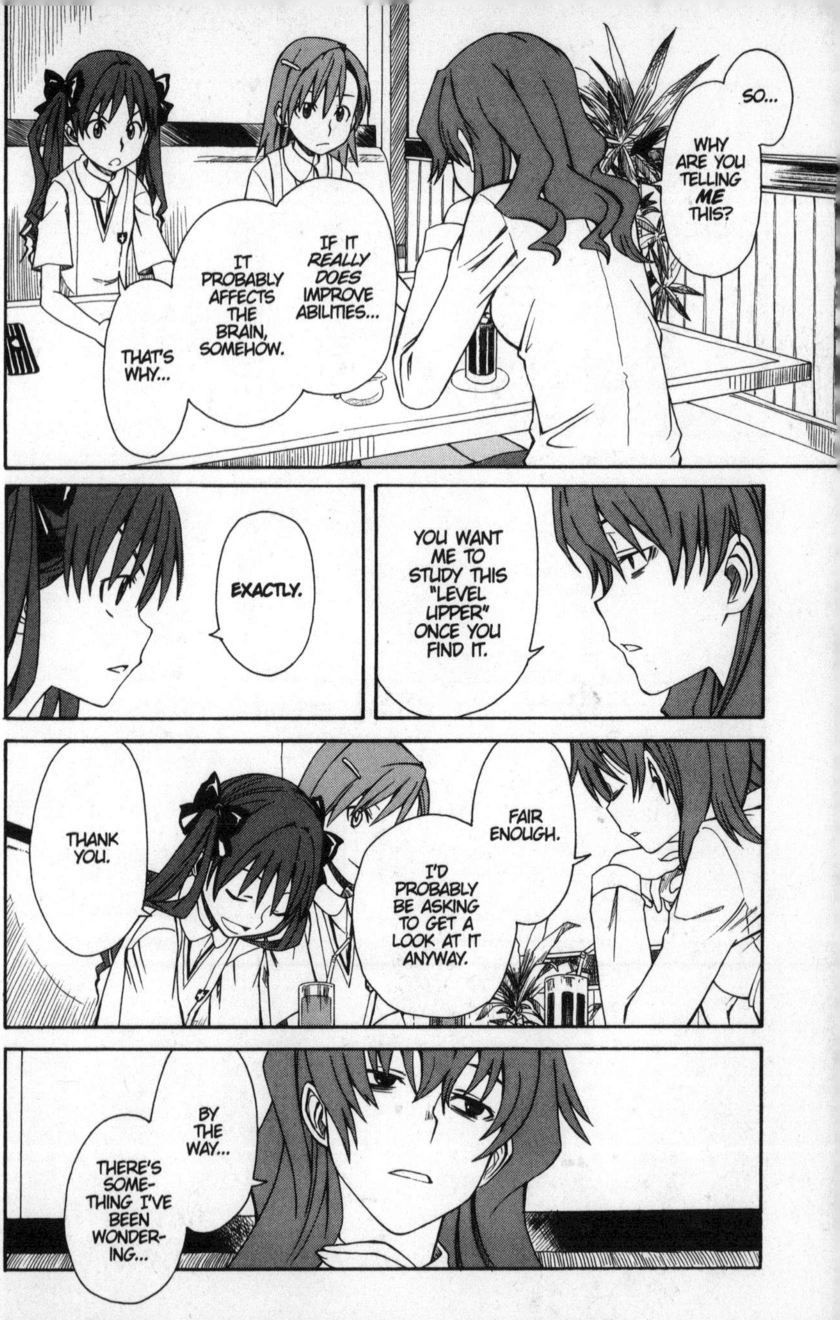
SO...
WHY ARE YOU TELLING *ME* THIS?
IF IT *REALLY DOES* IMPROVE ABILITIES...
IT PROBABLY AFFECTS THE BRAIN, SOMEHOW.
THAT'S WHY...
YOU WANT ME TO STUDY THIS "LEVEL UPPER" ONCE YOU FIND IT.
EXACTLY.
FAIR ENOUGH.
I'D PROBABLY BE ASKING TO GET A LOOK AT IT ANYWAY.
THANK YOU.
BY THE WAY...
THERE'S SOME-THING I'VE BEEN WONDER-ING...

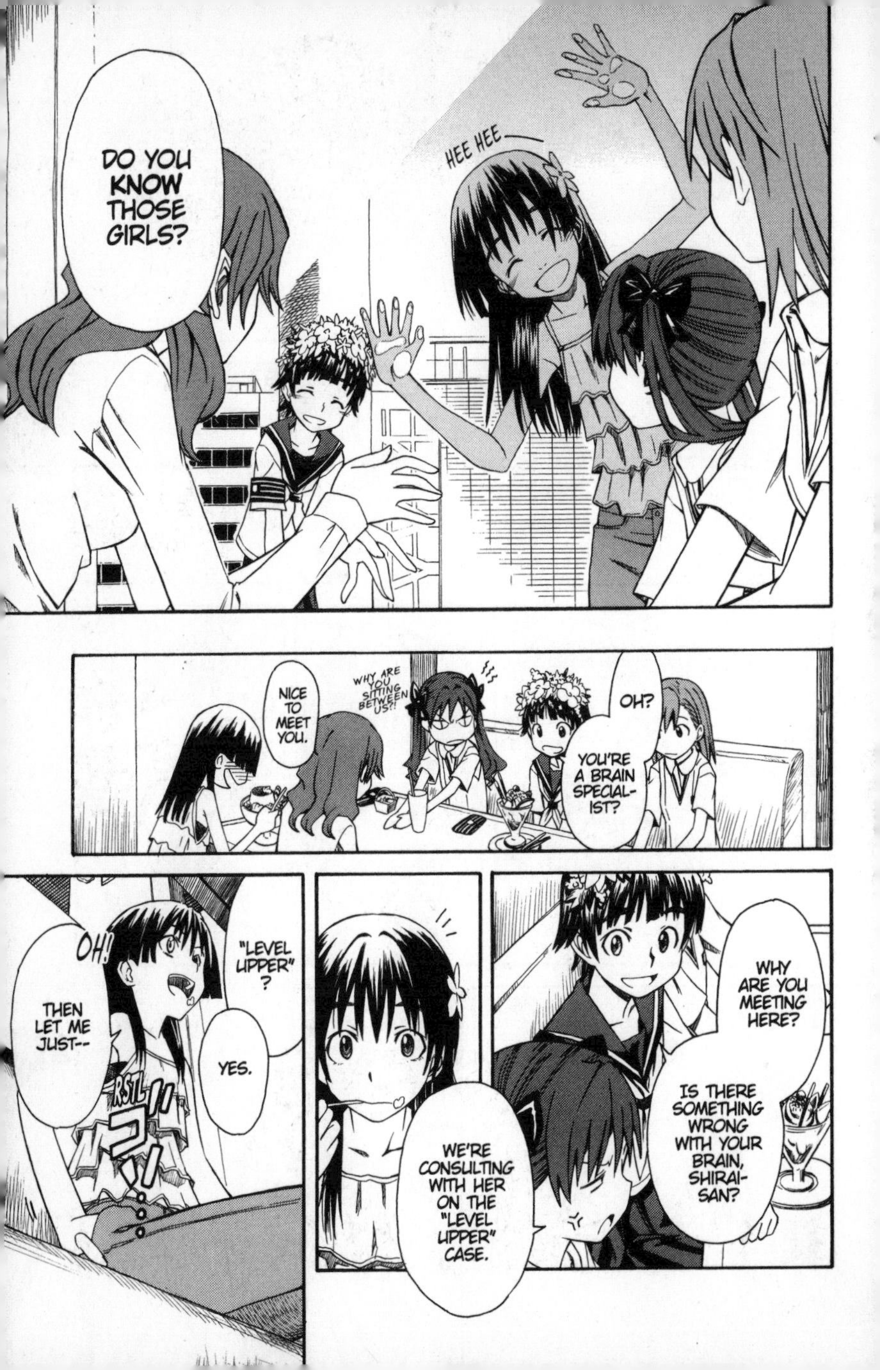
HEE HEE—
DO YOU KNOW THOSE GIRLS?
OH?
YOU'RE A BRAIN SPECIAL-IST?
WHY ARE YOU SITTING BETWEEN US?!
NICE TO MEET YOU.
WHY ARE YOU MEETING HERE?
IS THERE SOMETHING WRONG WITH YOUR BRAIN, SHIRAI-SAN?
WE'RE CONSULTING WITH HER ON THE "LEVEL UPPER" CASE.
"LEVEL UPPER"?
YES.
OH!
THEN LET ME JUST--
RSTL

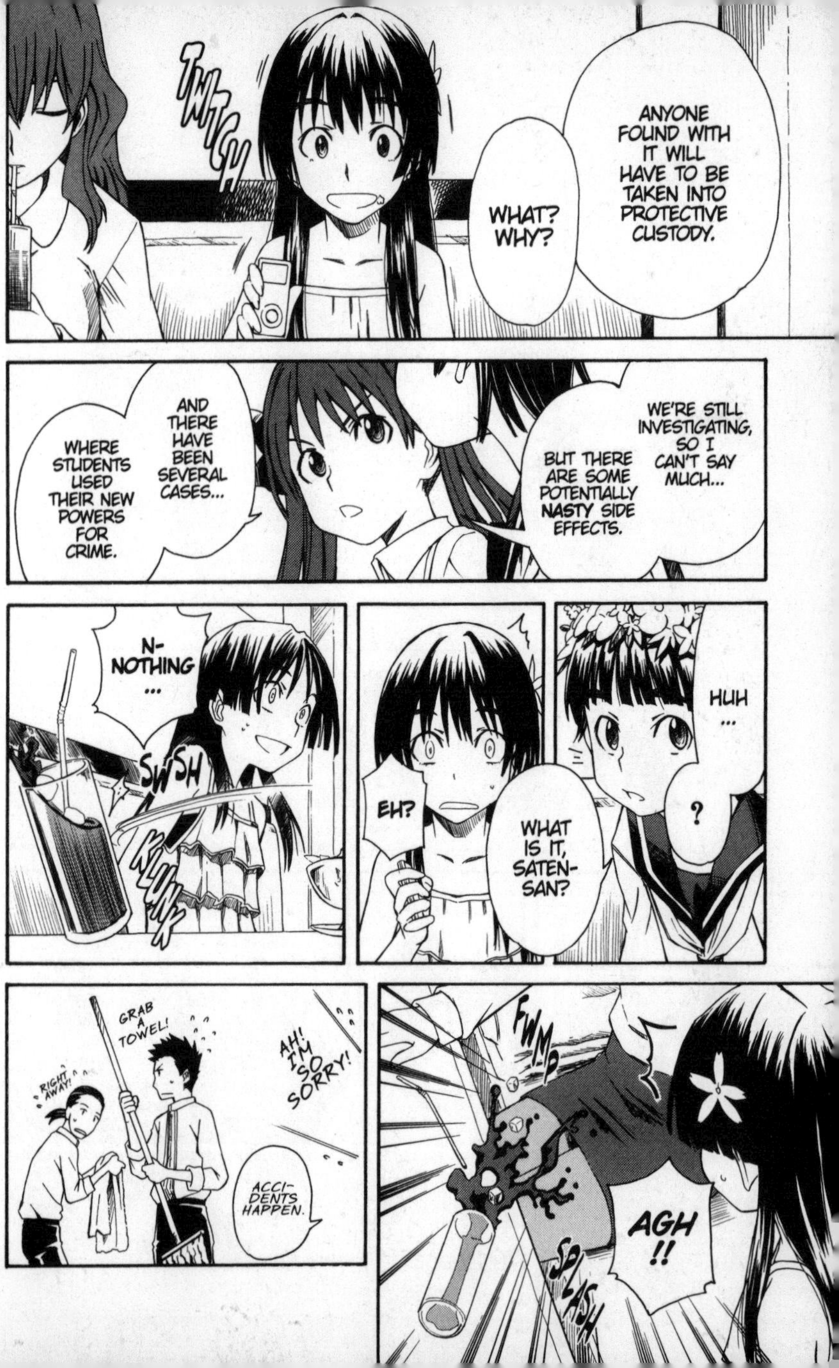
ANYONE FOUND WITH IT WILL HAVE TO BE TAKEN INTO PROTECTIVE CUSTODY.
WHAT? WHY?
TWITCH
WE'RE STILL INVESTIGATING, SO I CAN'T SAY MUCH...
BUT THERE ARE SOME POTENTIALLY NASTY SIDE EFFECTS.
AND THERE HAVE BEEN SEVERAL CASES...
WHERE STUDENTS USED THEIR NEW POWERS FOR CRIME.
HUH...
?
EH?
WHAT IS IT, SATEN-SAN?
N-NOTHING...
SWSH
KLUNK
FWMP
AGH!!
SPLASH
AH! I'M SO SORRY!
GRAB A TOWEL!
ACCIDENTS HAPPEN.
RIGHT AWAY!

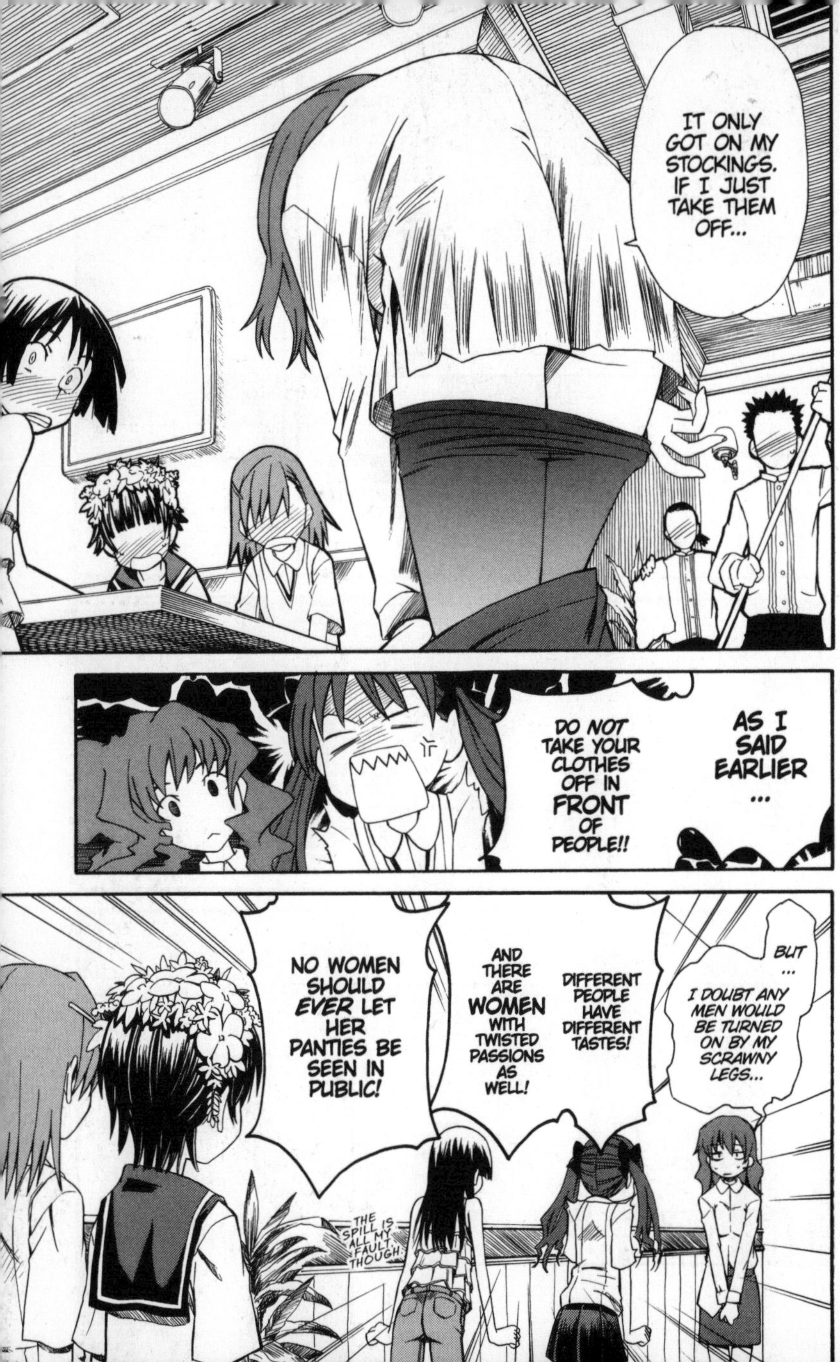
IT ONLY GOT ON MY STOCKINGS. IF I JUST TAKE THEM OFF...
AS I SAID EARLIER...
DO NOT TAKE YOUR CLOTHES OFF IN FRONT OF PEOPLE!!
BUT... I DOUBT ANY MEN WOULD BE TURNED ON BY MY SCRAWNY LEGS...
DIFFERENT PEOPLE HAVE DIFFERENT TASTES!
AND THERE ARE WOMEN WITH TWISTED PASSIONS AS WELL!
NO WOMEN SHOULD EVER LET HER PANTIES BE SEEN IN PUBLIC!
THE SPILL IS ALL MY FAULT, THOUGH.

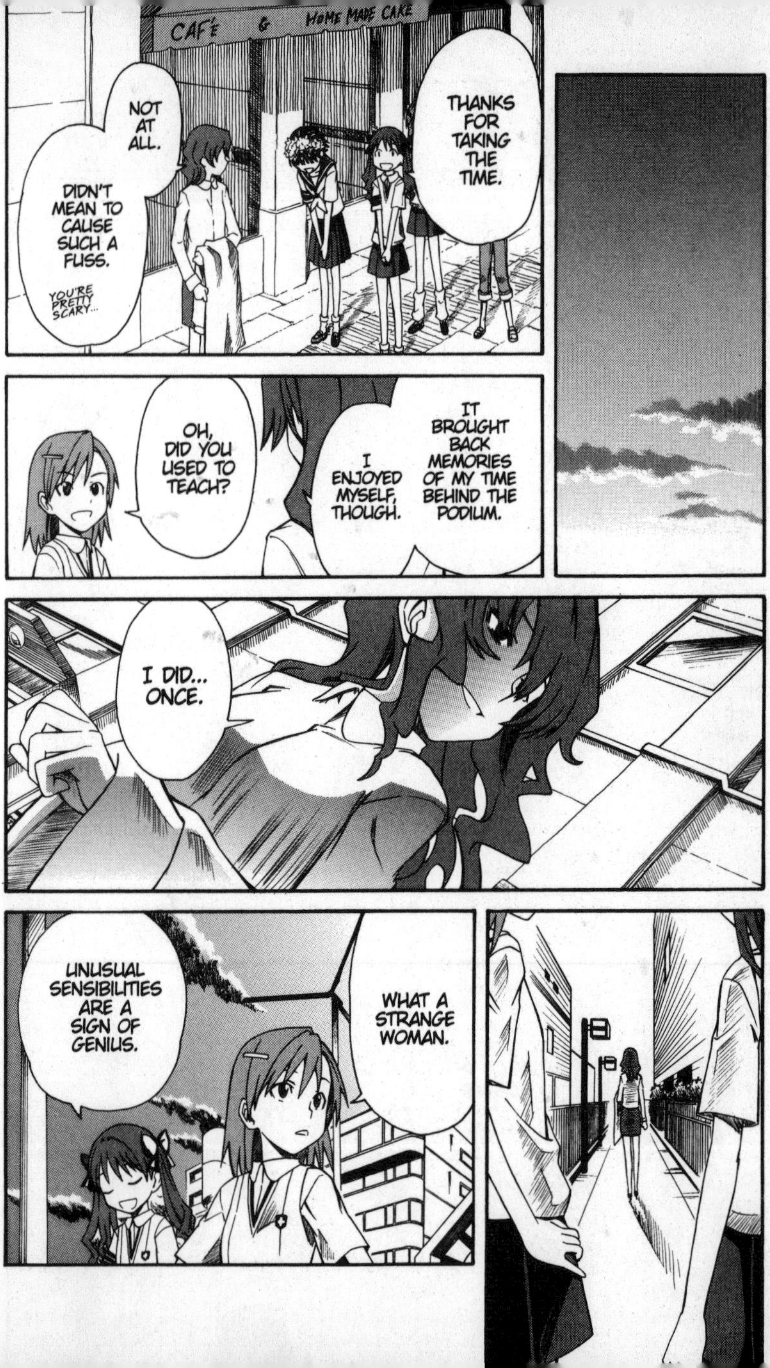
CAF'E & HOME MADE CAKE
THANKS FOR TAKING THE TIME.
NOT AT ALL.
DIDN'T MEAN TO CAUSE SUCH A FUSS.
YOU'RE PRETTY SCARY...
IT BROUGHT BACK MEMORIES OF MY TIME BEHIND THE PODIUM.
I ENJOYED MYSELF, THOUGH.
OH, DID YOU USED TO TEACH?
I DID... ONCE.
WHAT A STRANGE WOMAN.
UNUSUAL SENSIBILITIES ARE A SIGN OF GENIUS.

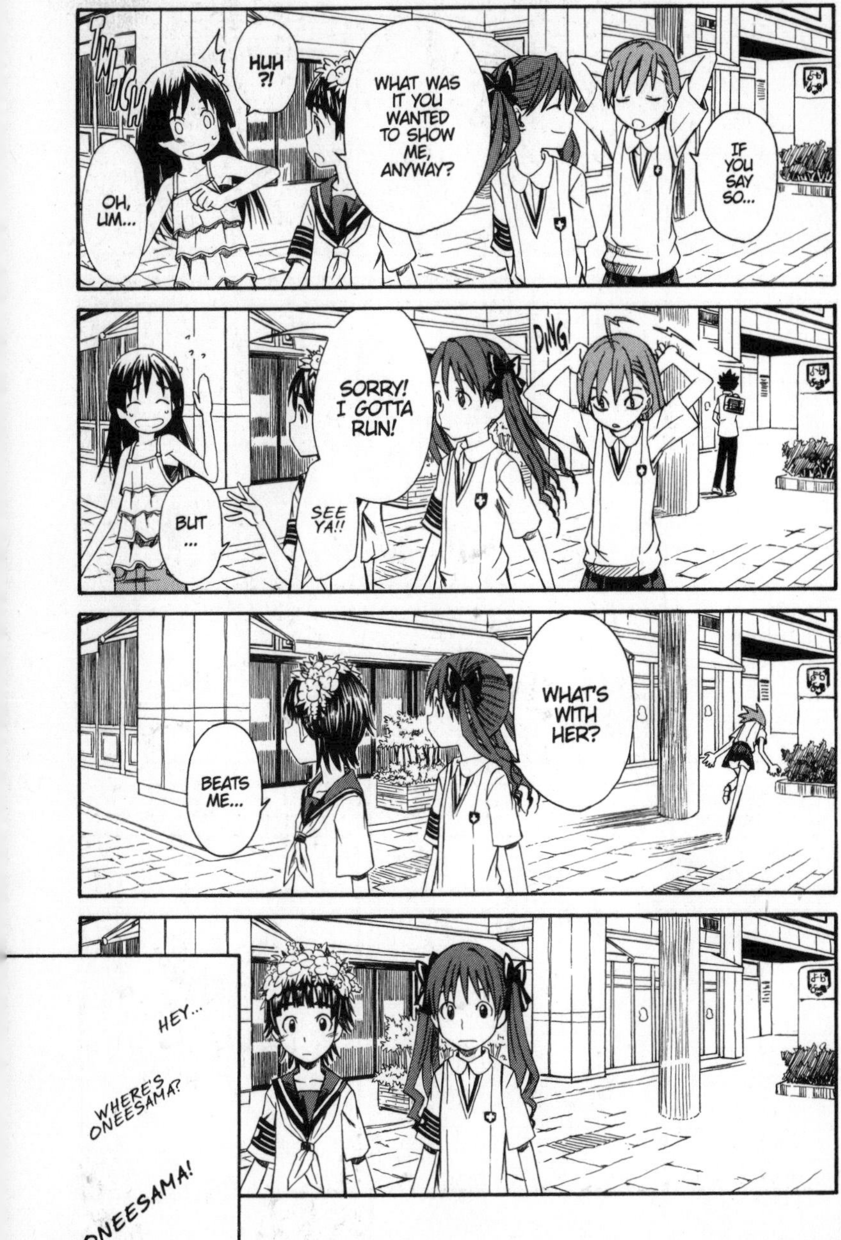
IF YOU SAY SO...
WHAT WAS IT YOU WANTED TO SHOW ME, ANYWAY?
HUH ?!
TWITCH
OH, UM...
DING
SORRY! I GOTTA RUN!
SEE YA!!
BUT ...
WHAT'S WITH HER?
BEATS ME...
HEY...
WHERE'S ONEESAMA?
ONEESAMA!

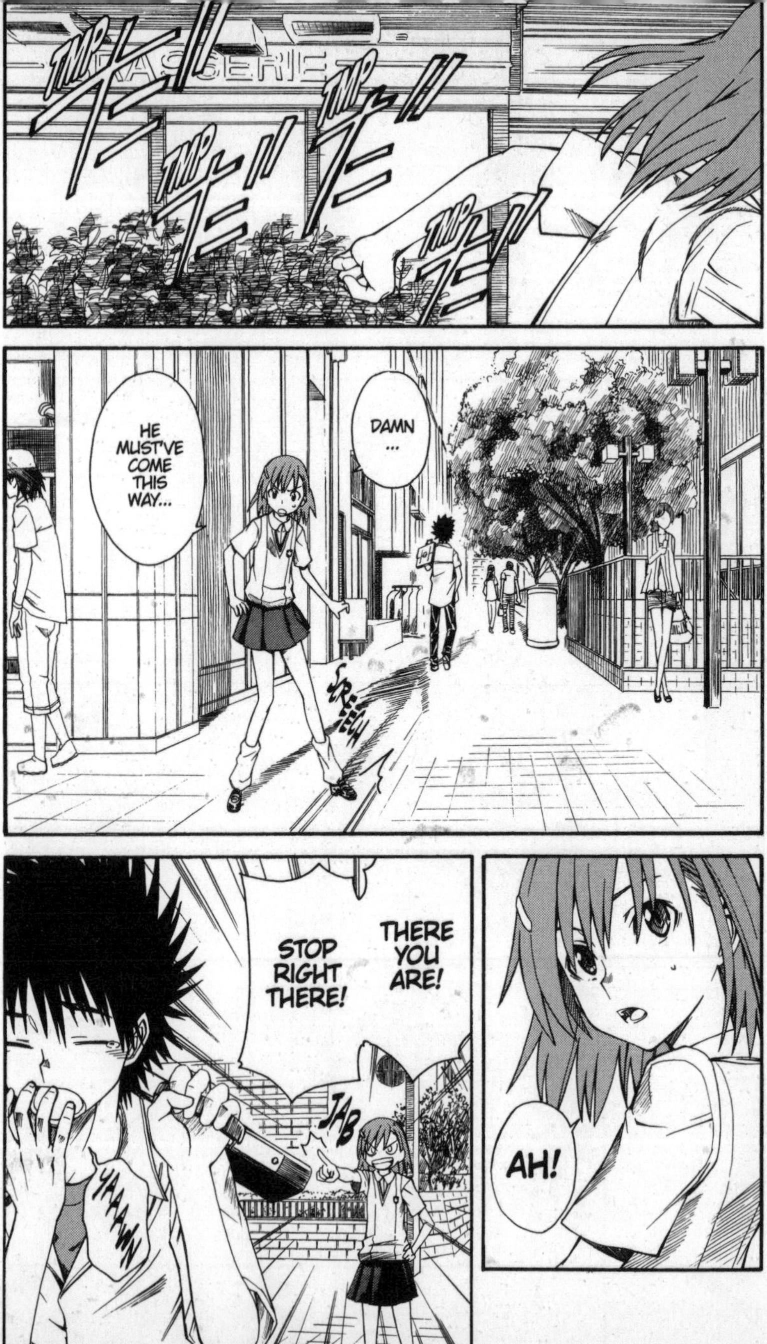
TMP
TMP
TMP
TMP
TMP
DAMN ...
HE MUST'VE COME THIS WAY...
SCREECH
AH!
THERE YOU ARE!
STOP RIGHT THERE!
JAB
YAAAWN

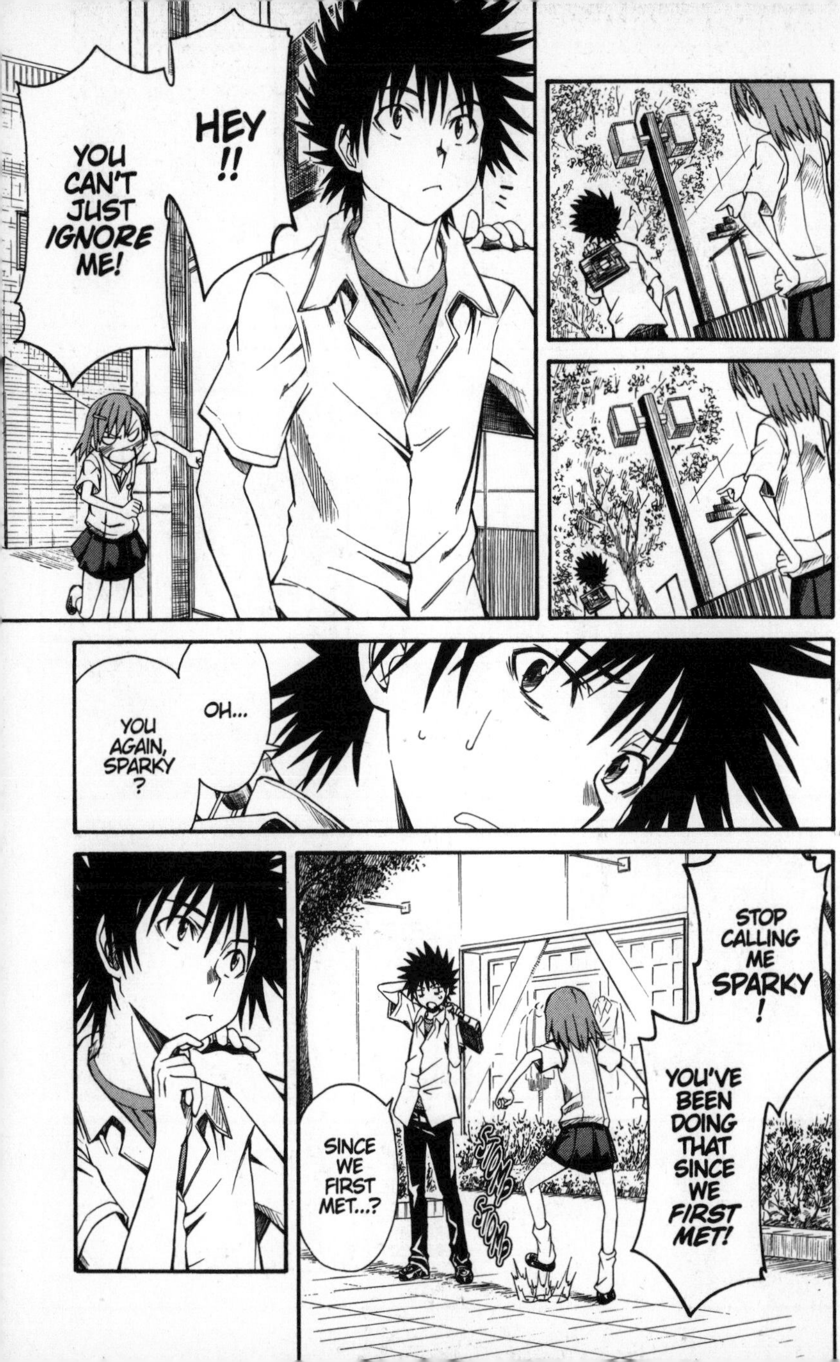
HEY!!
YOU CAN'T JUST IGNORE ME!
OH...
YOU AGAIN, SPARKY?
STOP CALLING ME SPARKY!
YOU'VE BEEN DOING THAT SINCE WE FIRST MET!
STOMP STOMP
SINCE WE FIRST MET...?

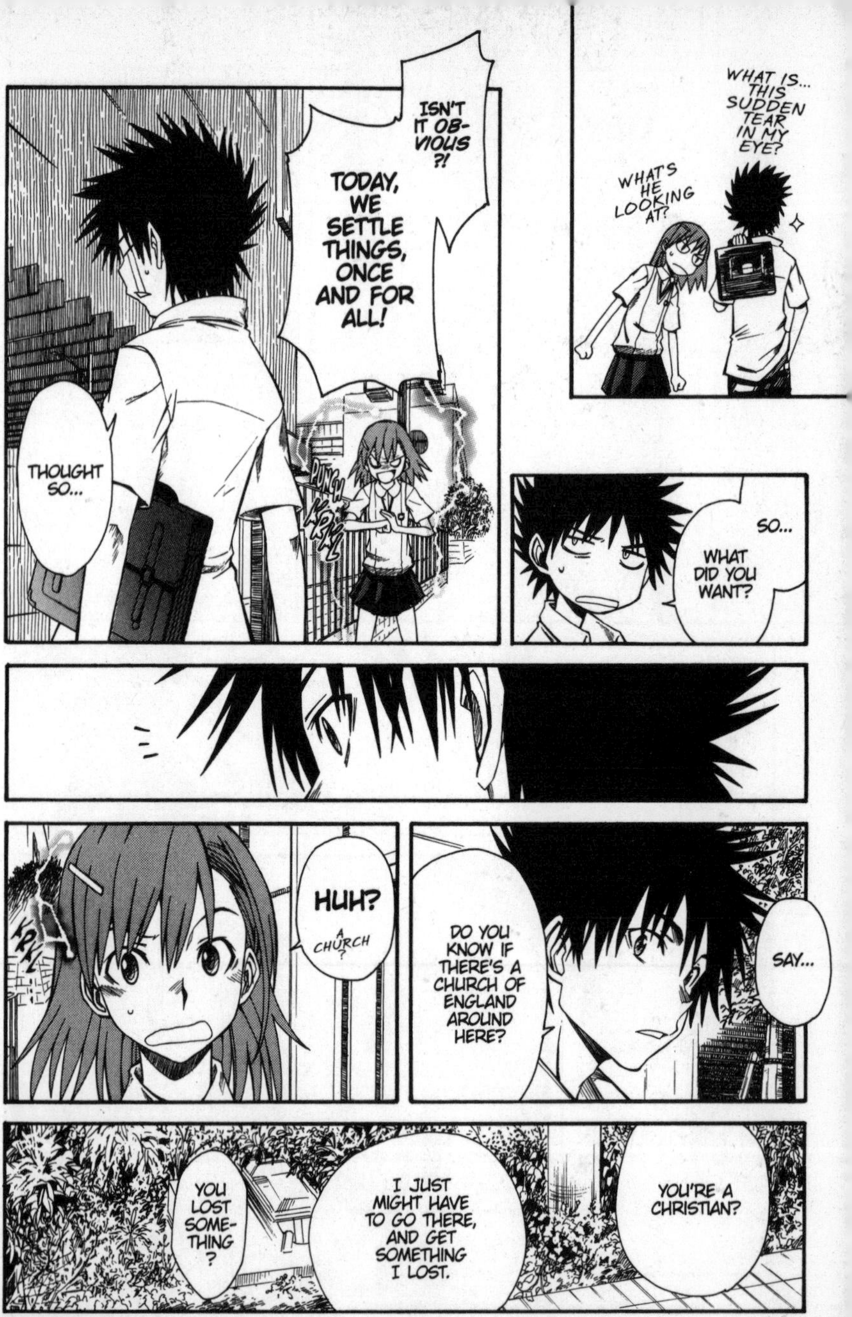
WHAT IS... THIS SUDDEN TEAR IN MY EYE?
WHAT'S HE LOOKING AT?
SO...
WHAT DID YOU WANT?
ISN'T IT OBVIOUS?!
TODAY, WE SETTLE THINGS, ONCE AND FOR ALL!
PUNCH
KRKL
THOUGHT SO...
SAY...
DO YOU KNOW IF THERE'S A CHURCH OF ENGLAND AROUND HERE?
HUH?
A CHURCH?
KRKL
YOU'RE A CHRISTIAN?
I JUST MIGHT HAVE TO GO THERE, AND GET SOMETHING I LOST.
YOU LOST SOMETHING?

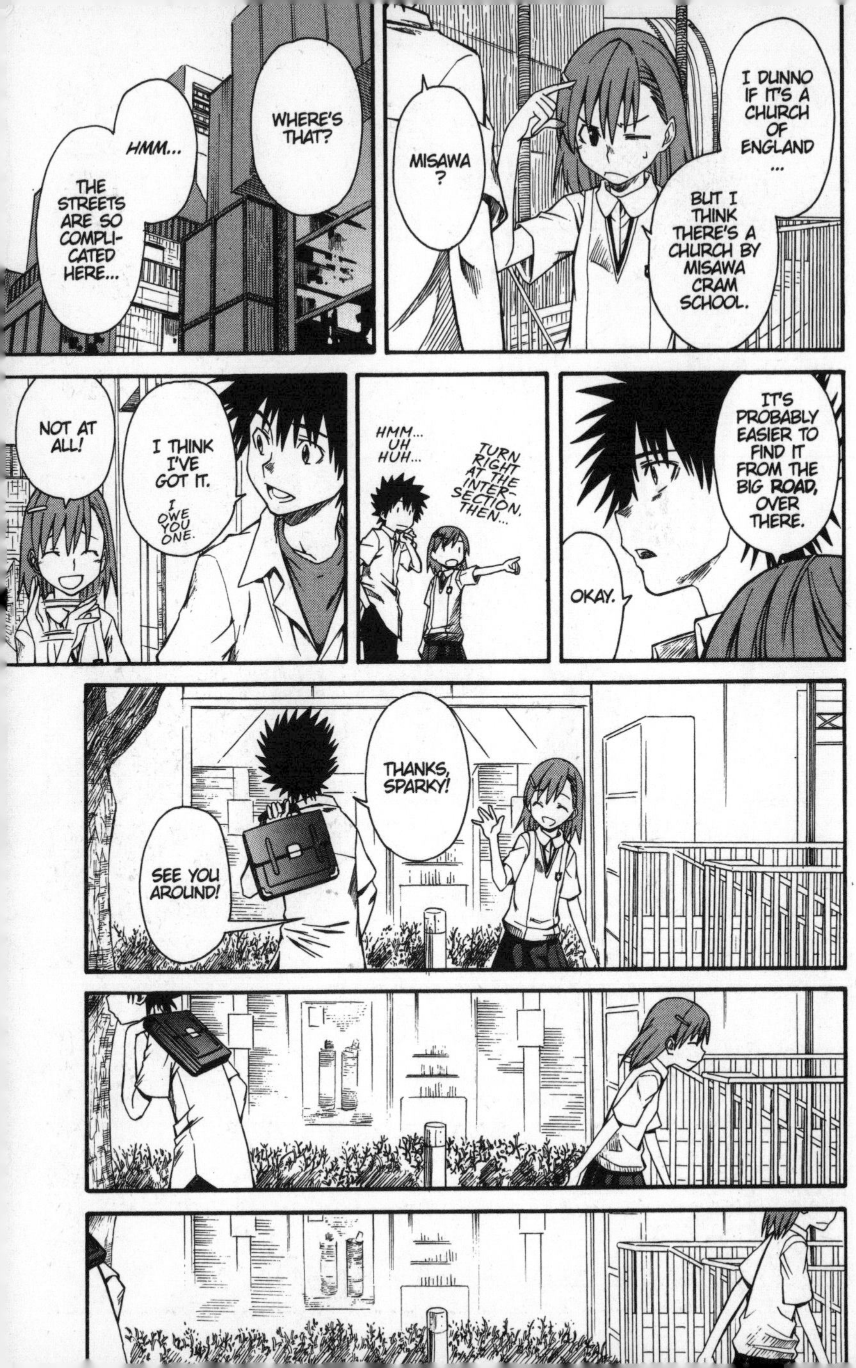
I DUNNO IF IT'S A CHURCH OF ENGLAND ...
BUT I THINK THERE'S A CHURCH BY MISAWA CRAM SCHOOL.
MISAWA?
WHERE'S THAT?
HMM...
THE STREETS ARE SO COMPLICATED HERE...
IT'S PROBABLY EASIER TO FIND IT FROM THE BIG ROAD, OVER THERE.
OKAY.
TURN RIGHT AT THE INTERSECTION, THEN...
HMM... UH HUH...
I THINK I'VE GOT IT.
I OWE YOU ONE.
NOT AT ALL!
THANKS, SPARKY!
SEE YOU AROUND!

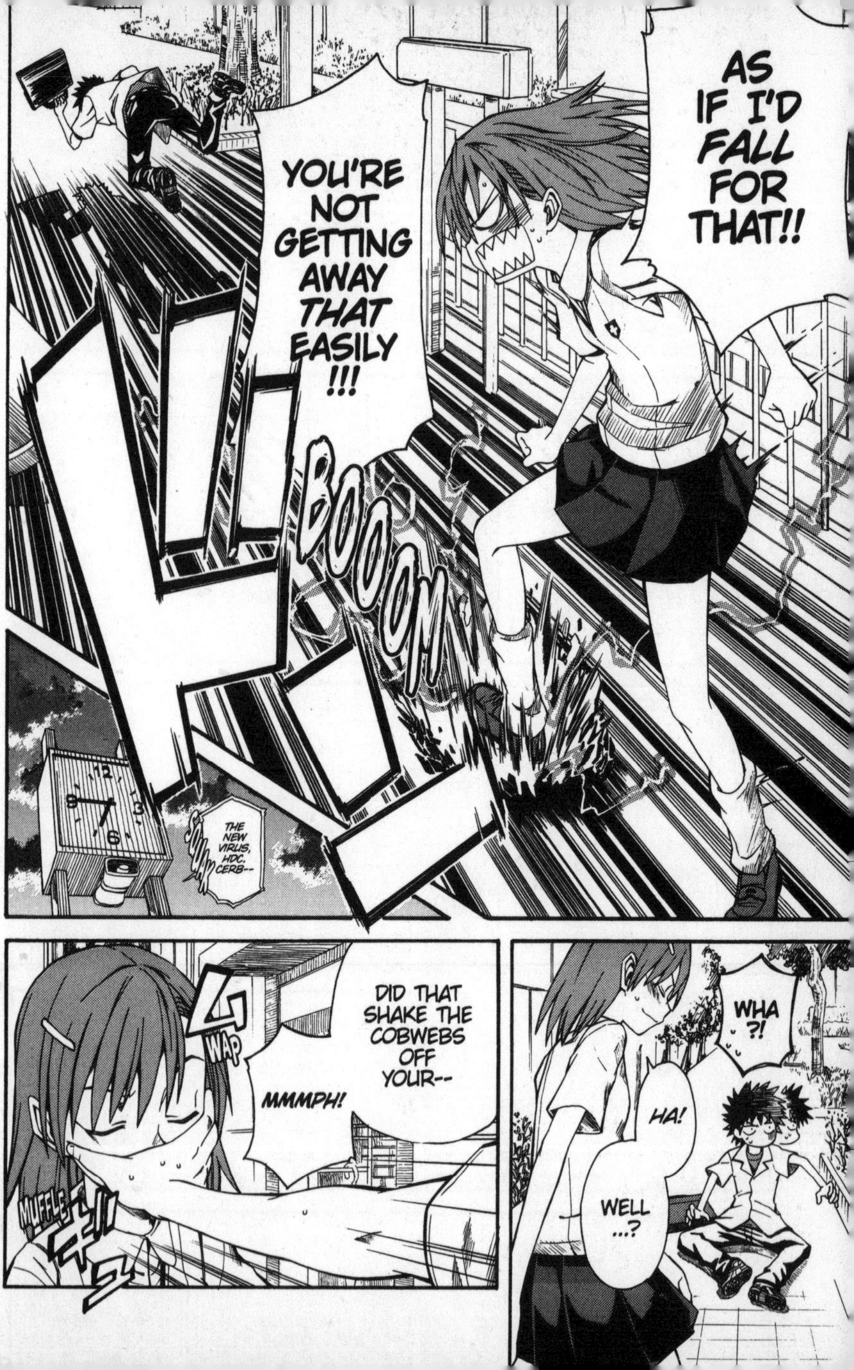
AS IF I'D FALL FOR THAT!!
YOU'RE NOT GETTING AWAY THAT EASILY!!!
BOOOOM
THE NEW VIRUS, HDC, CERB--
WHA?!
HA!
WELL...?
DID THAT SHAKE THE COBWEBS OFF YOUR--
WAP
MMMPH!
MUFFLE

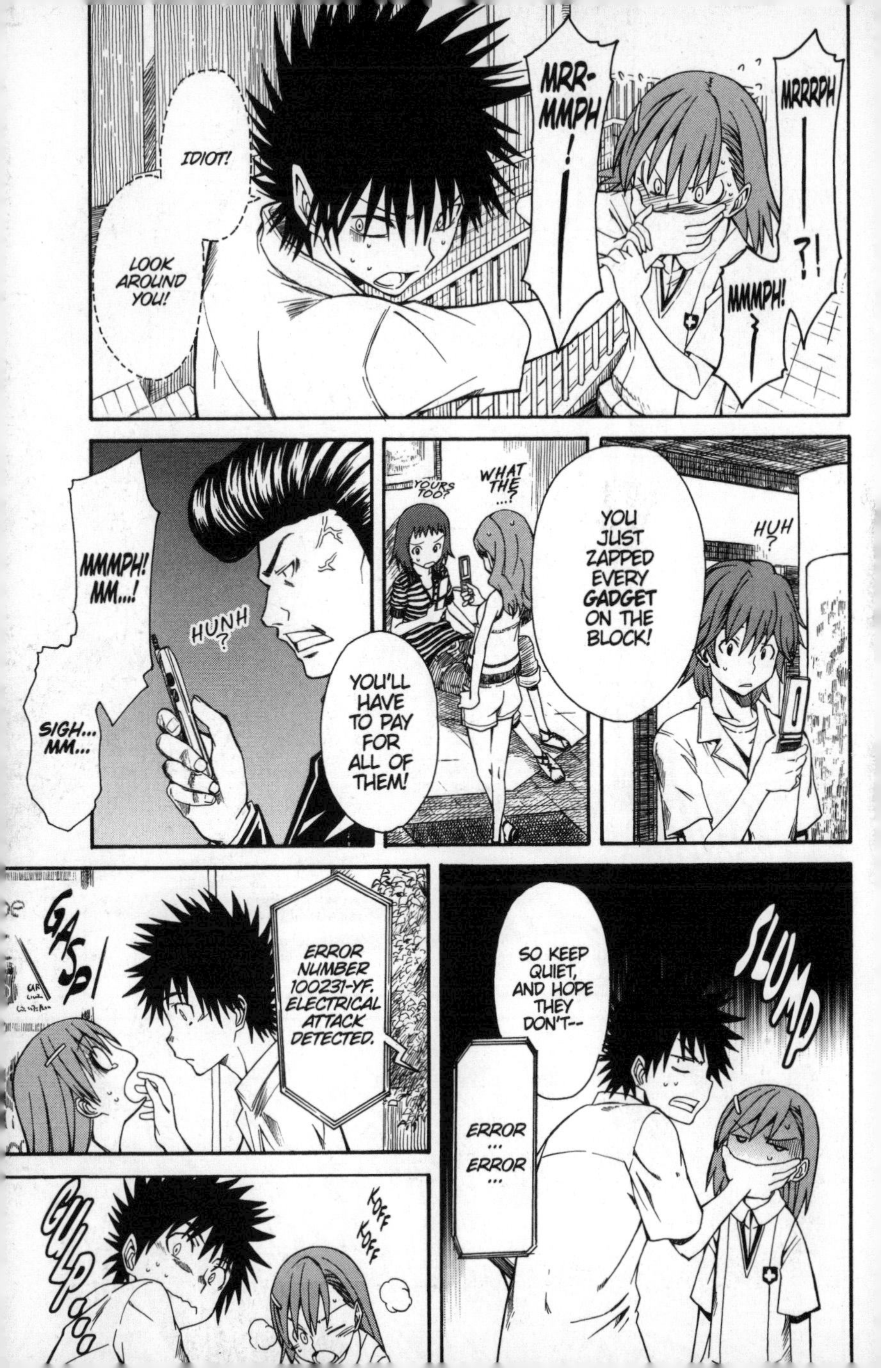
MRRRPH —?!
MRR-MMPH!
MMMPH!
IDIOT!
LOOK AROUND YOU!
HUH?
YOU JUST ZAPPED EVERY GADGET ON THE BLOCK!
WHAT THE...?
YOURS TOO?
YOU'LL HAVE TO PAY FOR ALL OF THEM!
MMMPH! MM...!
HUNH?
SIGH... MM...
SLUMP
SO KEEP QUIET, AND HOPE THEY DON'T--
ERROR... ERROR...
ERROR NUMBER 100231-YF. ELECTRICAL ATTACK DETECTED.
GASP!
KOFF KOFF
GULP

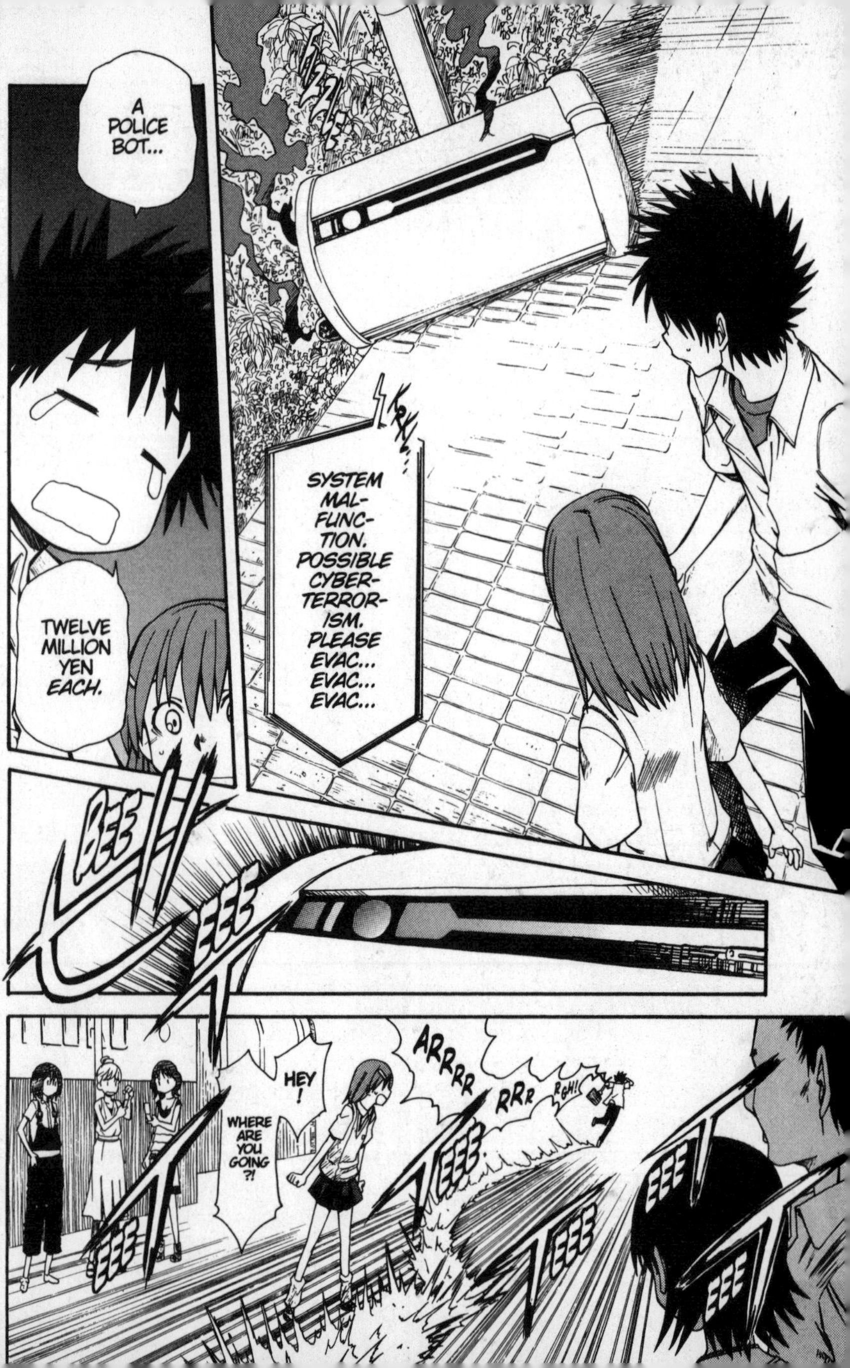
SYSTEM MALFUNCTION. POSSIBLE CYBER-TERRORISM. PLEASE EVAC... EVAC... EVAC...
A POLICE BOT...
TWELVE MILLION YEN EACH.
BEEE
EEE
EEE
TEEE
ARRRR
RRR
RGH!
HEY!
WHERE ARE YOU GOING?!
TEEE
EEE
TEEE
EEE
EEE

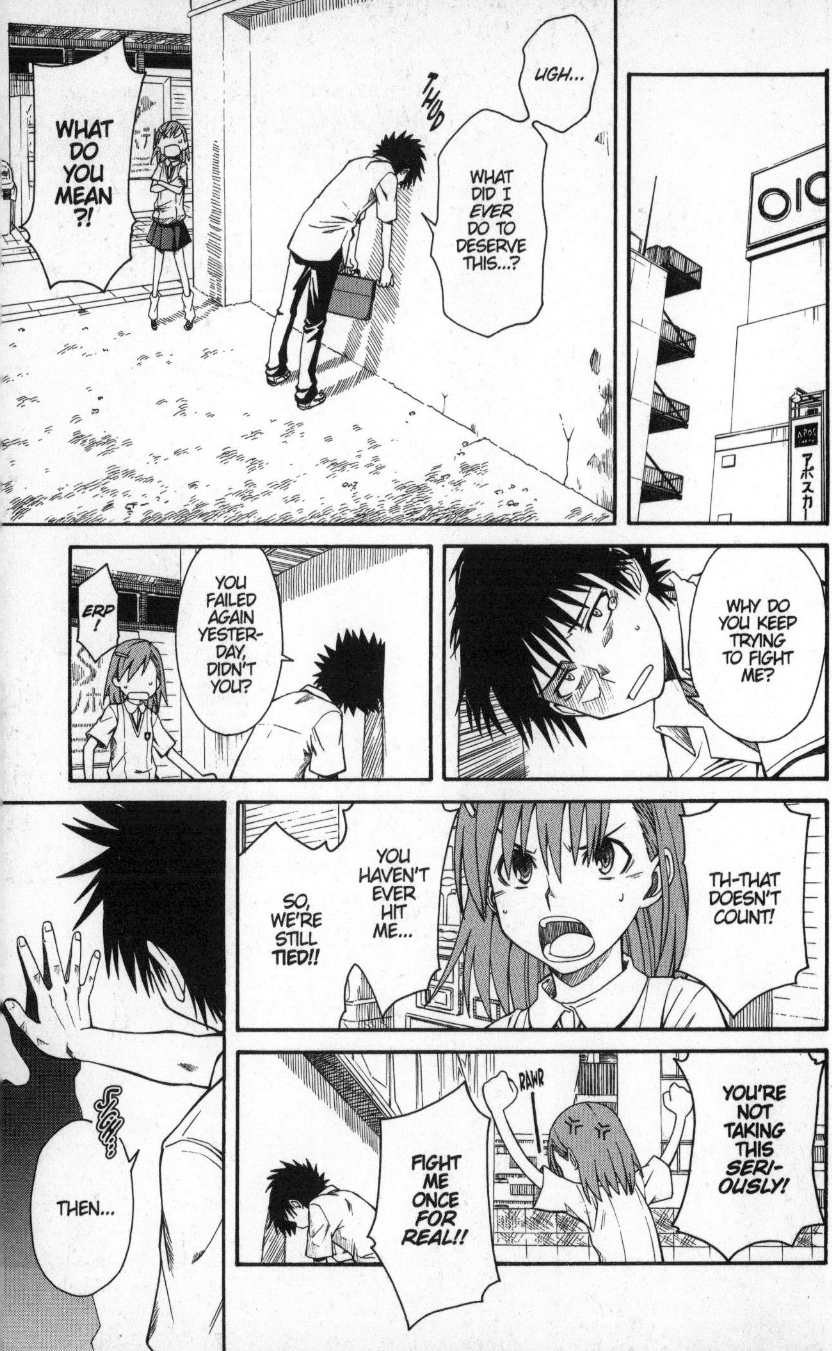
UGH...
THUD
WHAT DID I EVER DO TO DESERVE THIS...?
WHAT DO YOU MEAN ?!
WHY DO YOU KEEP TRYING TO FIGHT ME?
YOU FAILED AGAIN YESTER-DAY, DIDN'T YOU?
ERP!
TH-THAT DOESN'T COUNT!
YOU HAVEN'T EVER HIT ME...
SO, WE'RE STILL TIED!!
YOU'RE NOT TAKING THIS SERI-OUSLY!
RAWR
FIGHT ME ONCE FOR REAL!!
SIGH...
THEN...

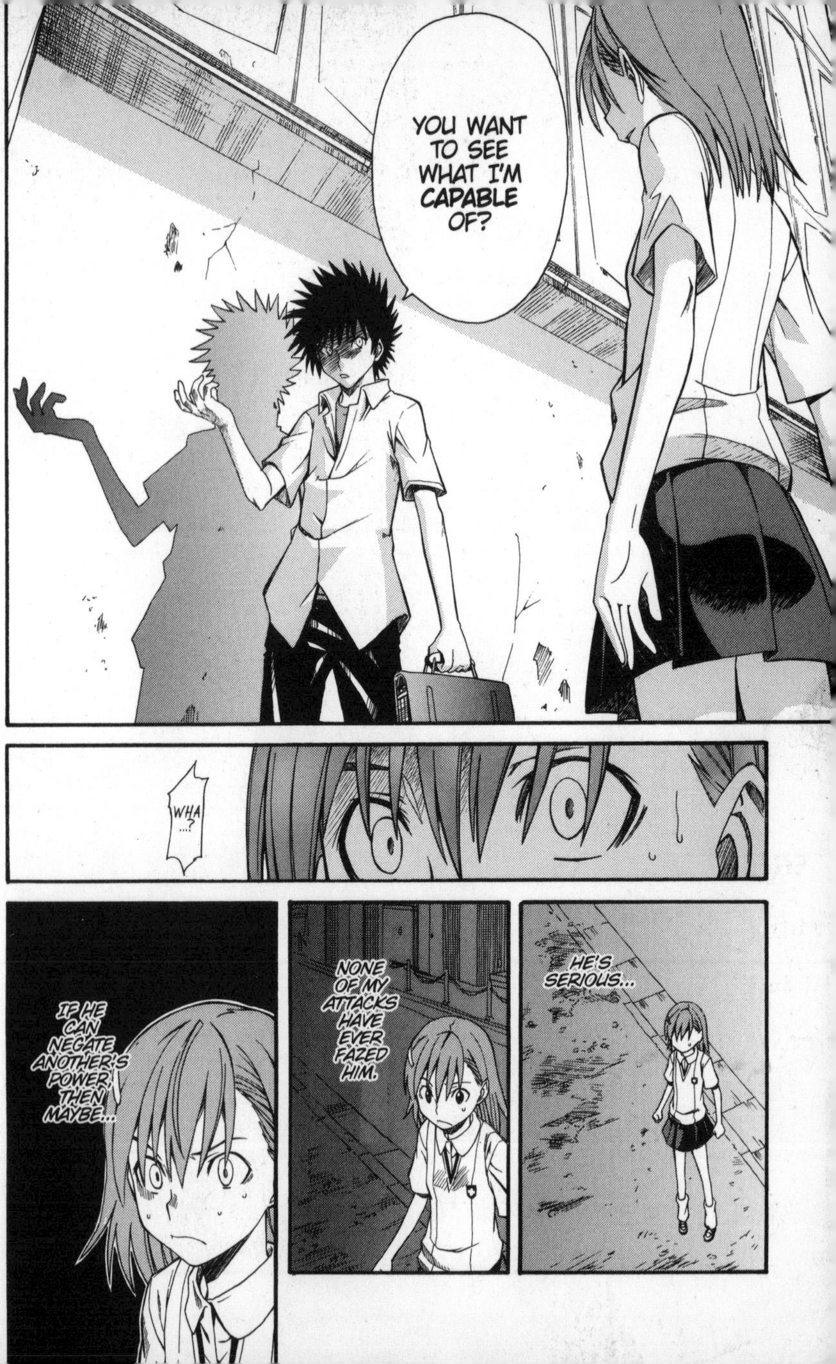
YOU WANT TO SEE WHAT I'M CAPABLE OF?
WHA ...?
HE'S SERIOUS...
NONE OF MY ATTACKS HAVE EVER FAZED HIM.
IF HE CAN NEGATE ANOTHER'S POWER, THEN MAYBE...

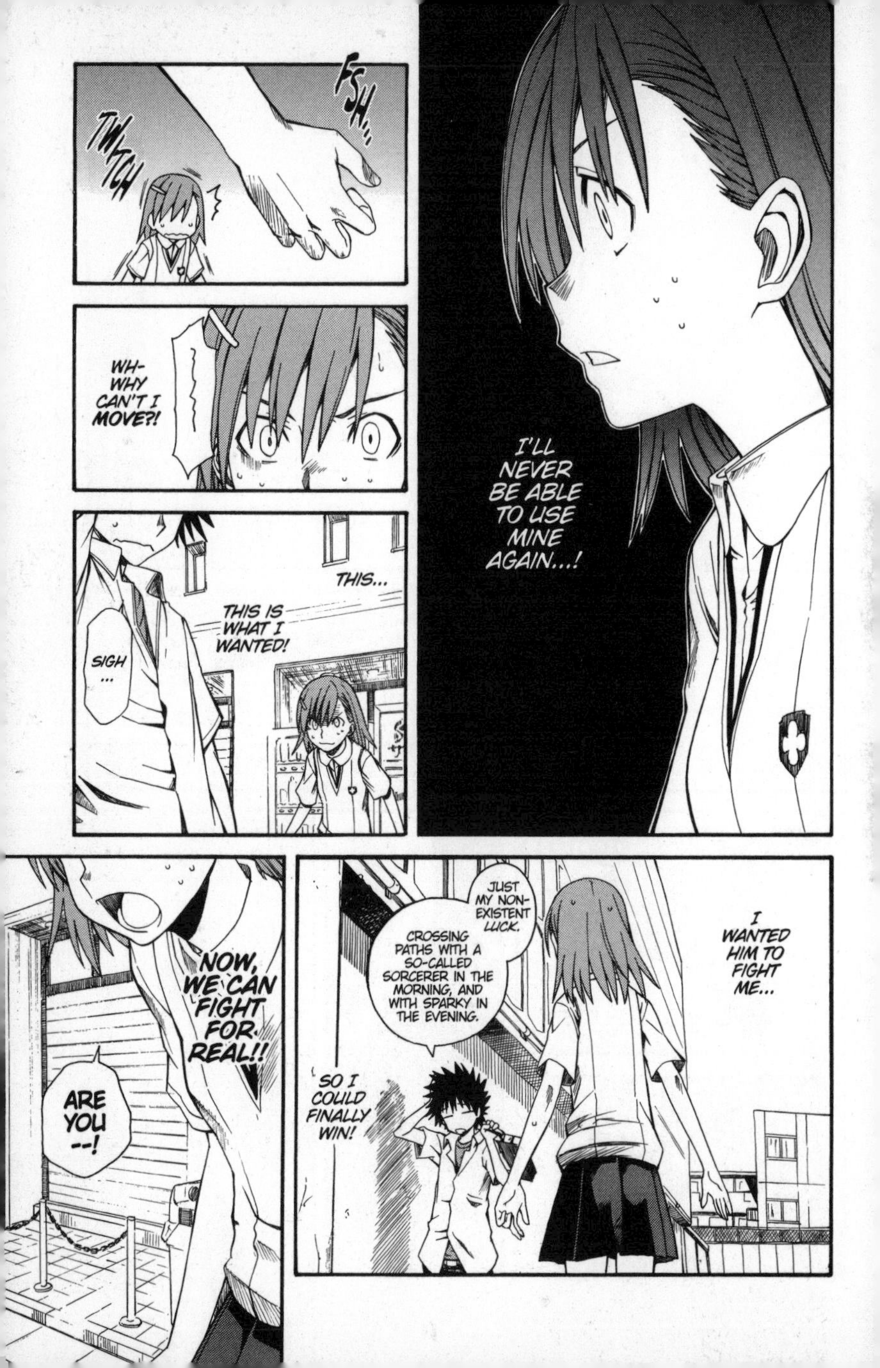
I'LL NEVER BE ABLE TO USE MINE AGAIN...!
FSH..
TWITCH
WH-WHY CAN'T I MOVE?!
THIS...
THIS IS WHAT I WANTED!
SIGH...
JUST MY NON-EXISTENT LUCK.
I WANTED HIM TO FIGHT ME...
CROSSING PATHS WITH A SO-CALLED SORCERER IN THE MORNING, AND WITH SPARKY IN THE EVENING.
SO I COULD FINALLY WIN!
NOW, WE CAN FIGHT FOR REAL!!
ARE YOU --!

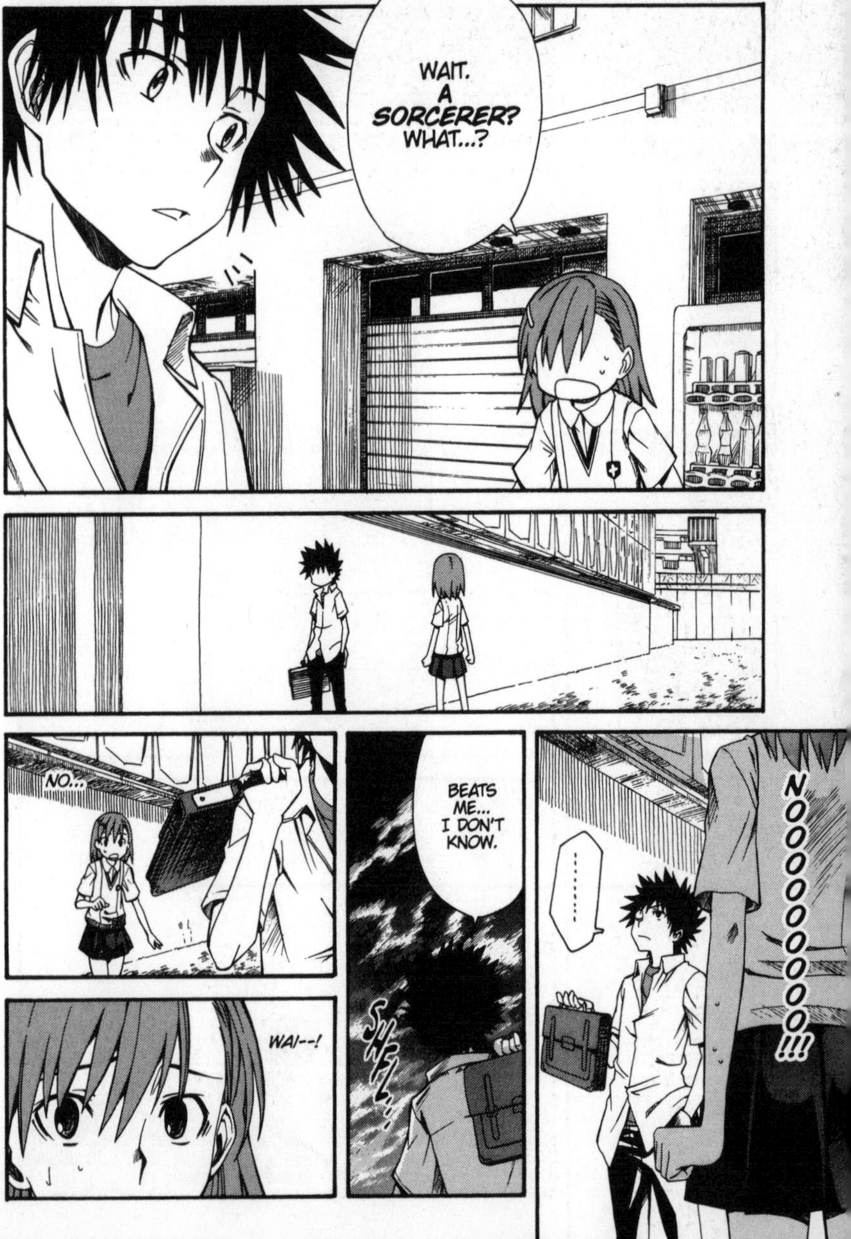
WAIT. A SORCERER? WHAT...?
......
NOOOOOOOOOOO!!!
BEATS ME... I DON'T KNOW.
SHFL..
NO...
WAI--!

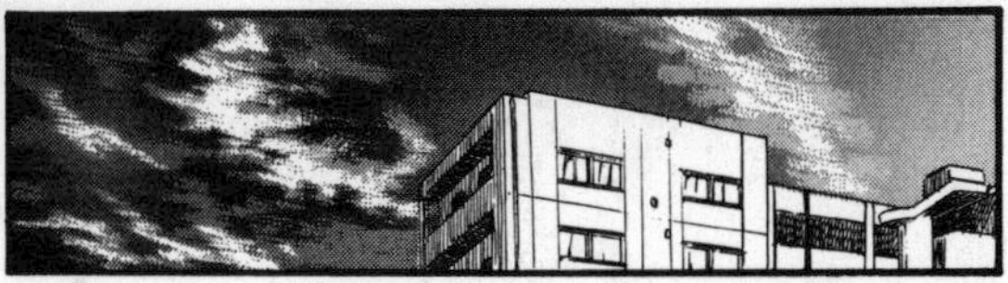

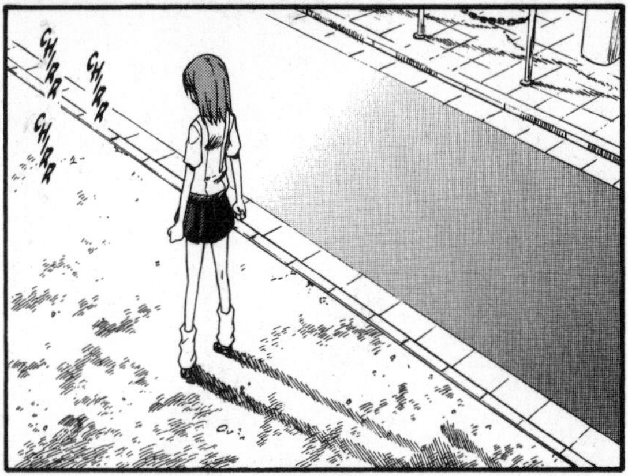
CHIRR
CHIRR
CHIRR

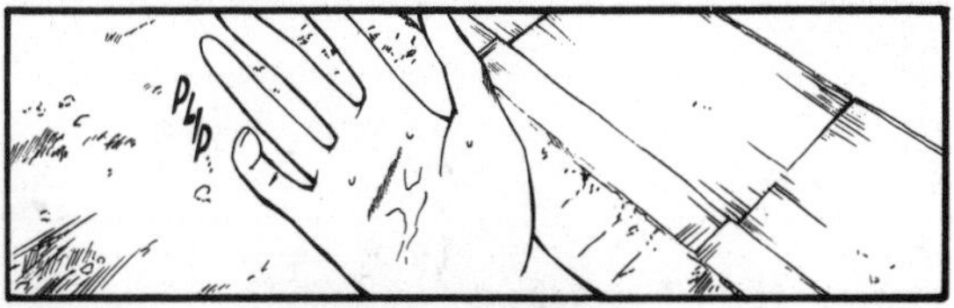
PLIP

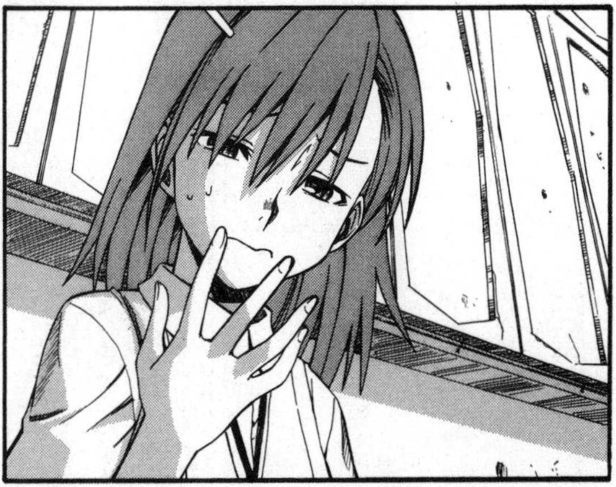

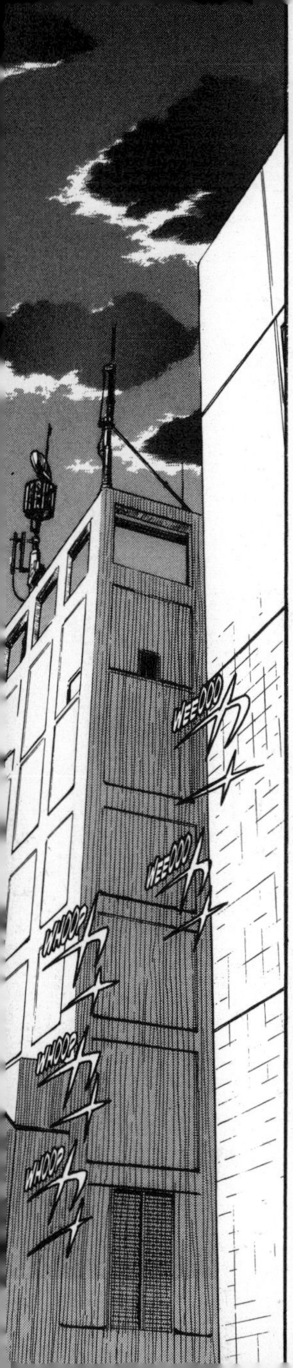
WEEOOO
WEEOOO
WHOOP
WHOOP
WHOOP

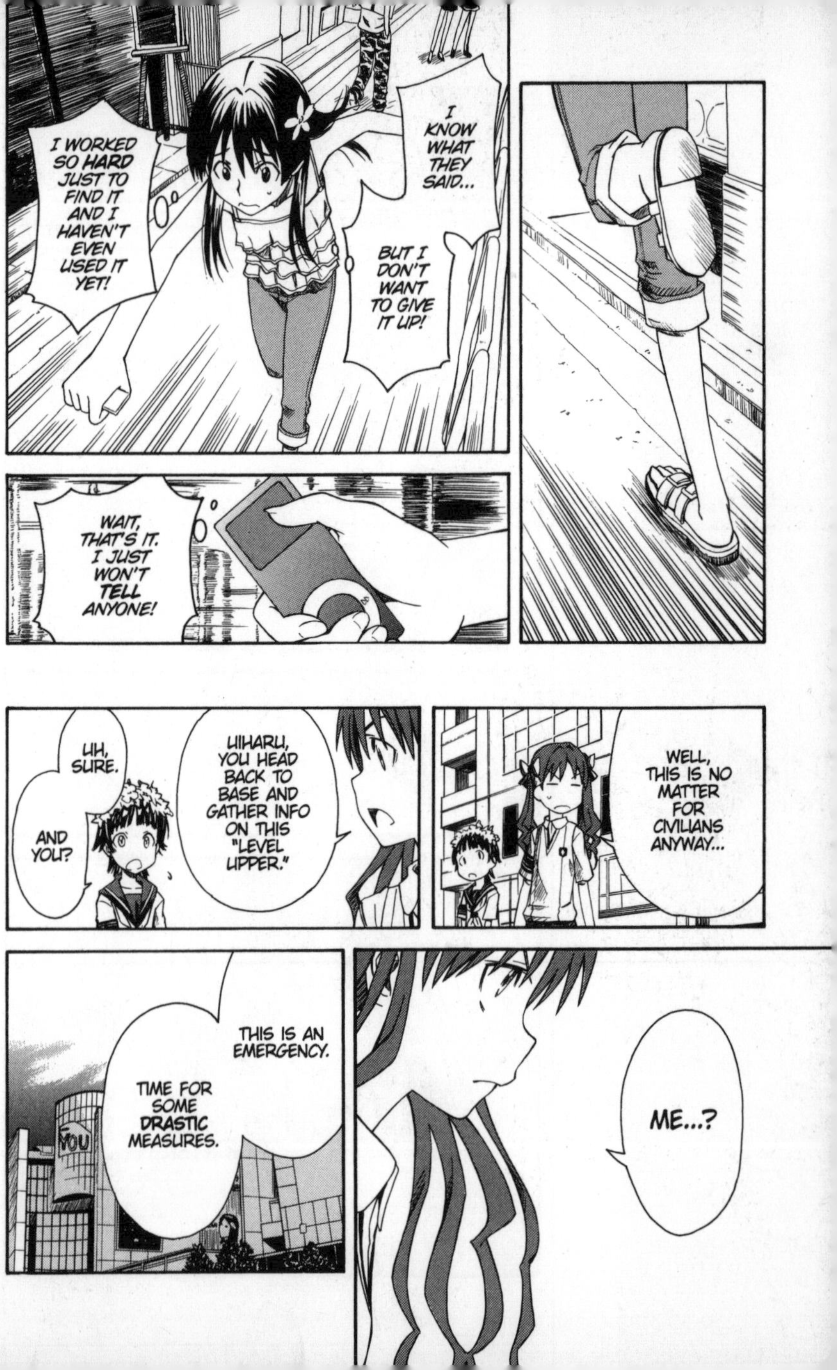
I KNOW WHAT THEY SAID...
BUT I DON'T WANT TO GIVE IT UP!
I WORKED SO HARD JUST TO FIND IT AND I HAVEN'T EVEN USED IT YET!
WAIT, THAT'S IT. I JUST WON'T TELL ANYONE!
WELL, THIS IS NO MATTER FOR CIVILIANS ANYWAY...
UIHARU, YOU HEAD BACK TO BASE AND GATHER INFO ON THIS "LEVEL UPPER."
UH, SURE.
AND YOU?
ME...?
THIS IS AN EMERGENCY.
TIME FOR SOME DRASTIC MEASURES.
YOU

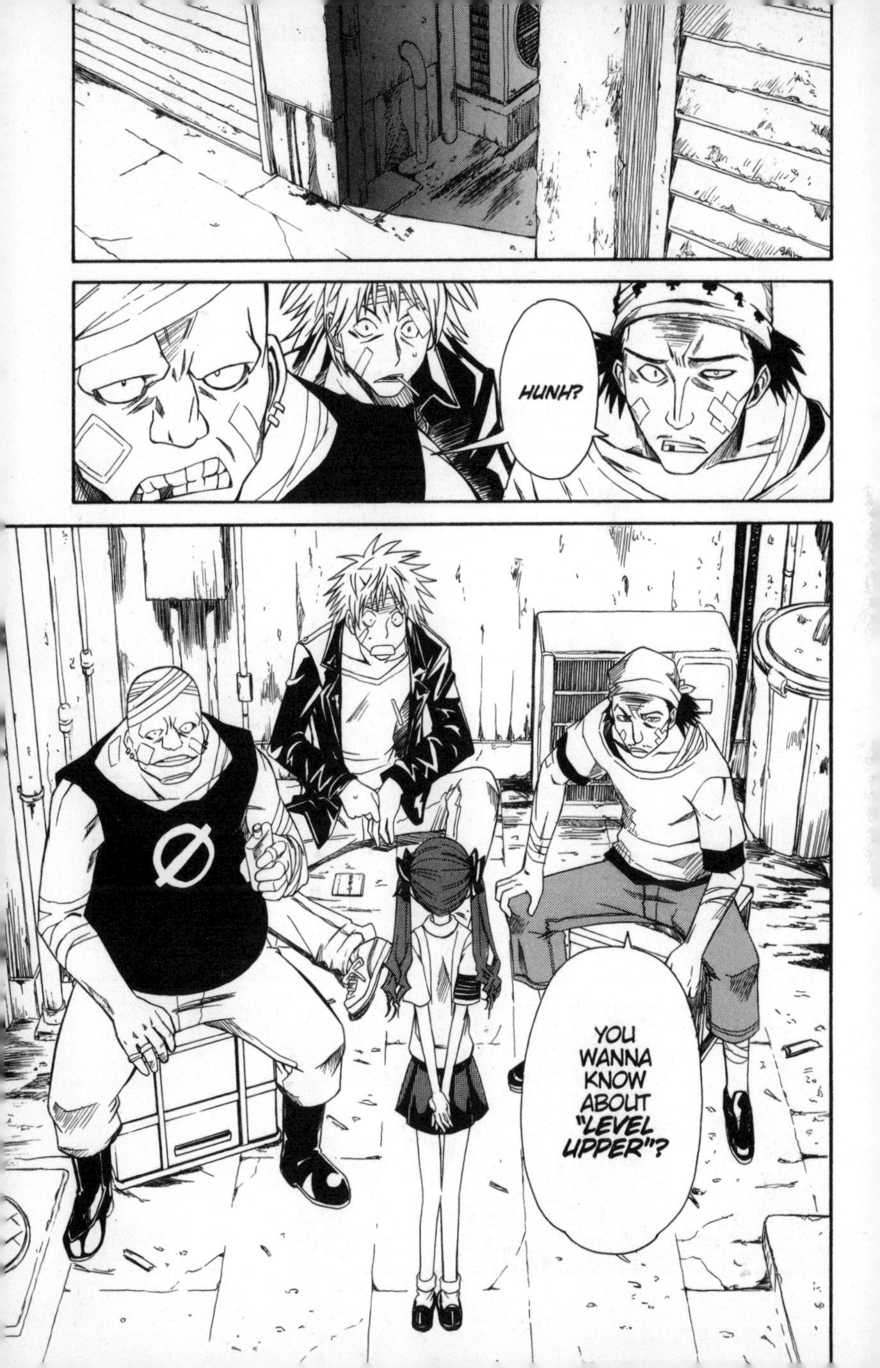
HUNH?
YOU WANNA KNOW ABOUT "LEVEL UPPER"?

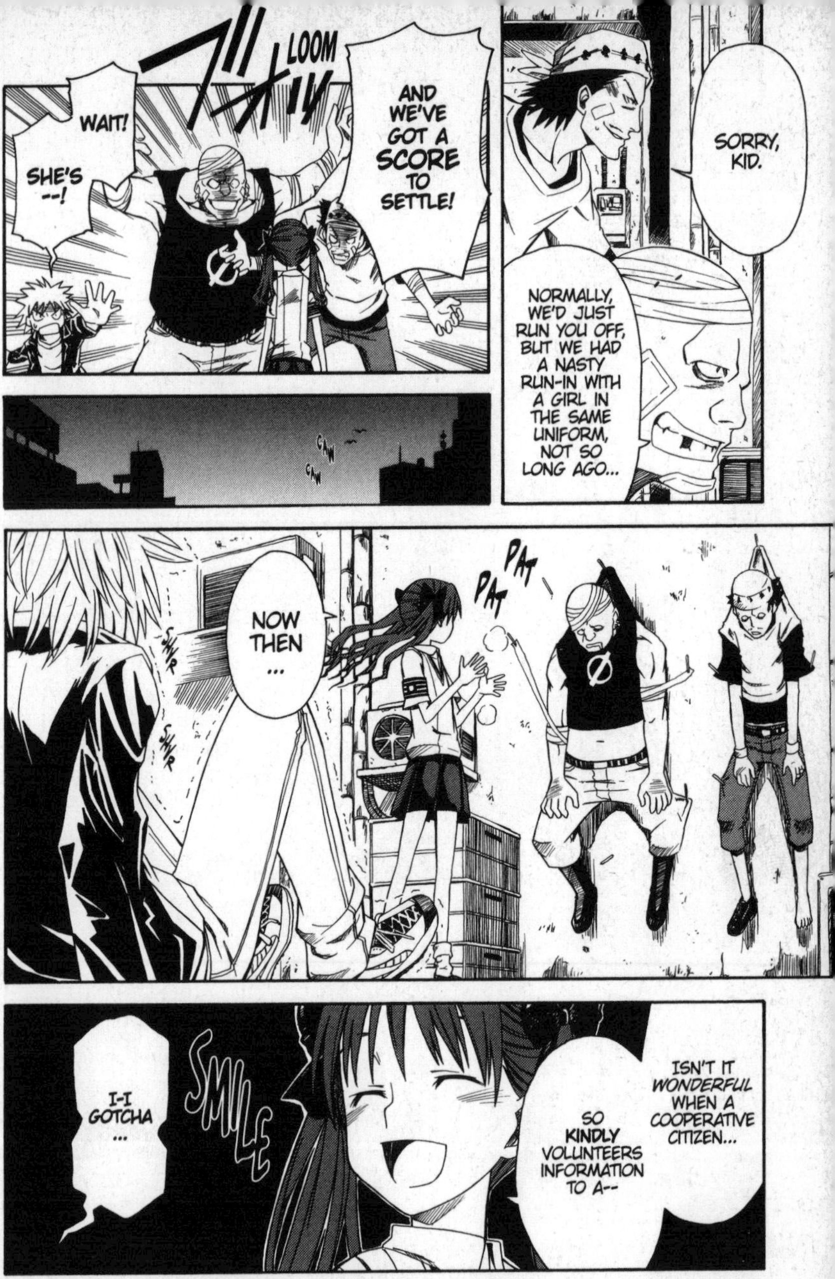
SORRY, KID.
NORMALLY, WE'D JUST RUN YOU OFF, BUT WE HAD A NASTY RUN-IN WITH A GIRL IN THE SAME UNIFORM, NOT SO LONG AGO...
LOOM
AND WE'VE GOT A SCORE TO SETTLE!
WAIT!
SHE'S --!
CAW
CAW
PAT
PAT
NOW THEN ...
SHVR
SHVR
ISN'T IT *WONDERFUL* WHEN A COOPERATIVE CITIZEN...
SO **KINDLY** VOLUNTEERS INFORMATION TO A--
SMILE
I-I GOTCHA ...

A Certain SCIENTIFIC Railgun

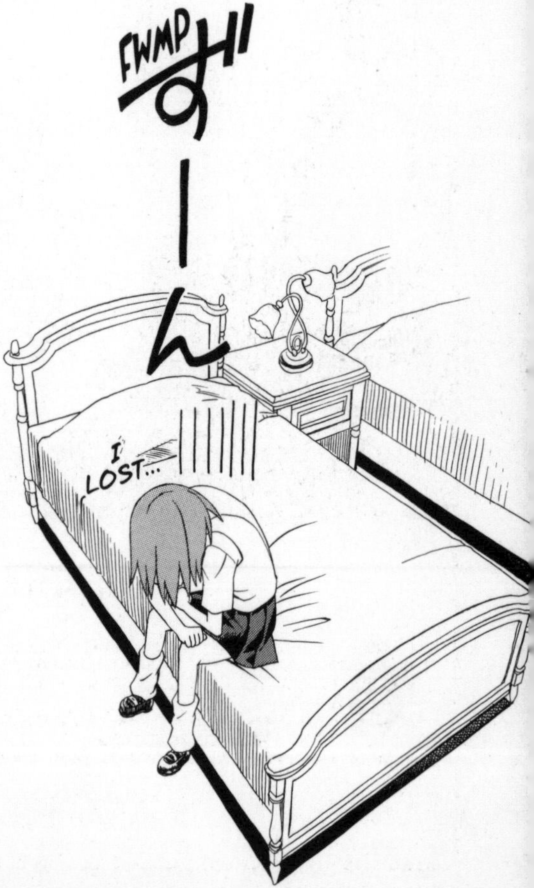
FWMP
ずーん
I LOST...

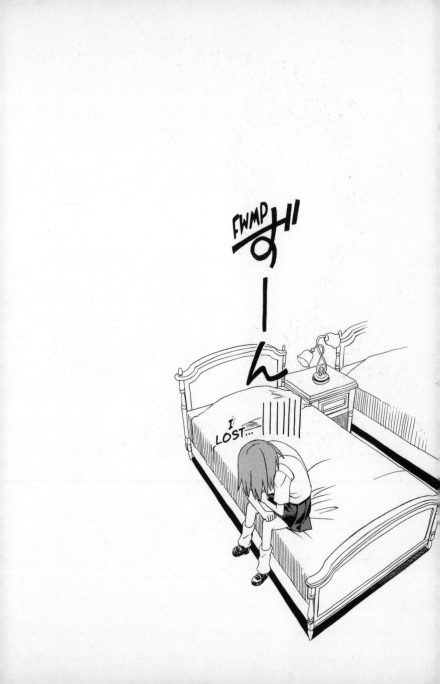

CHAPTER 9: JULY 21 (1)

JUDGMENT

* COMPRISED OF STUDENTS WITH PSYCHIC POWERS, THEY ARE RESPONSIBLE FOR ALL MATTERS OF DISCIPLINE IN ACADEMY CITY. SHIRAI KUROKO AND UIHARU KAZARI ARE BOTH MEMBERS.
* EACH SCHOOL HAS THEIR OWN JUDGMENT TEAM, AND ANYTHING THAT OCCURS ON CAMPUS IS IN THEIR JURISDICTION.
* APPLICANTS TO JUDGMENT MUST SIGN NINE CONTRACTS, PASS THIRTEEN APTITUDE TESTS, AND UNDERGO A FOUR-MONTH PROBATION PERIOD.
* JUDGMENT MEMBERS ARE RECOGNIZED BY THE SHIELD INSIGNIA ON THEIR ARMBANDS.

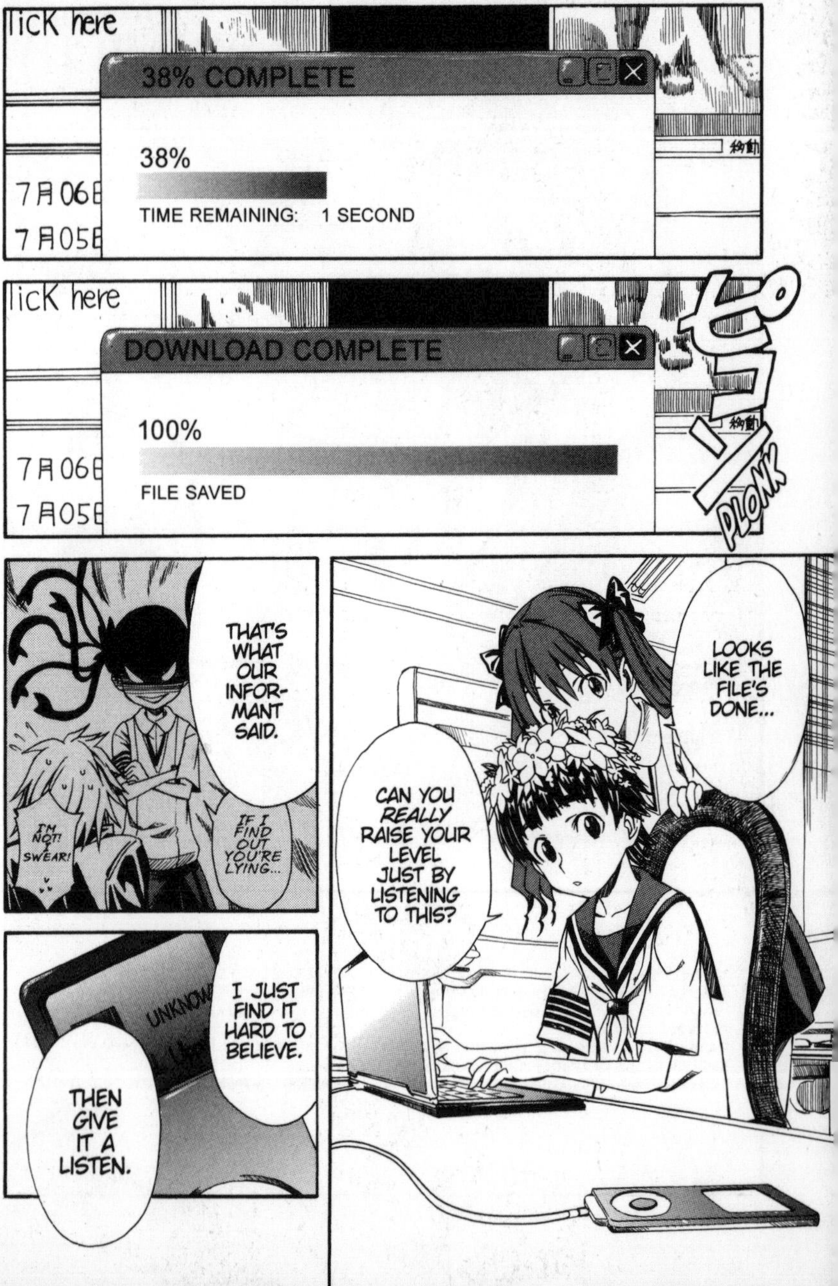
38% COMPLETE
38%
TIME REMAINING: 1 SECOND
DOWNLOAD COMPLETE
100%
FILE SAVED
ピコン
PLONK
LOOKS LIKE THE FILE'S DONE...
CAN YOU REALLY RAISE YOUR LEVEL JUST BY LISTENING TO THIS?
THAT'S WHAT OUR INFORMANT SAID.
IF I FIND OUT YOU'RE LYING...
I'M NOT! I SWEAR!
I JUST FIND IT HARD TO BELIEVE.
THEN GIVE IT A LISTEN.

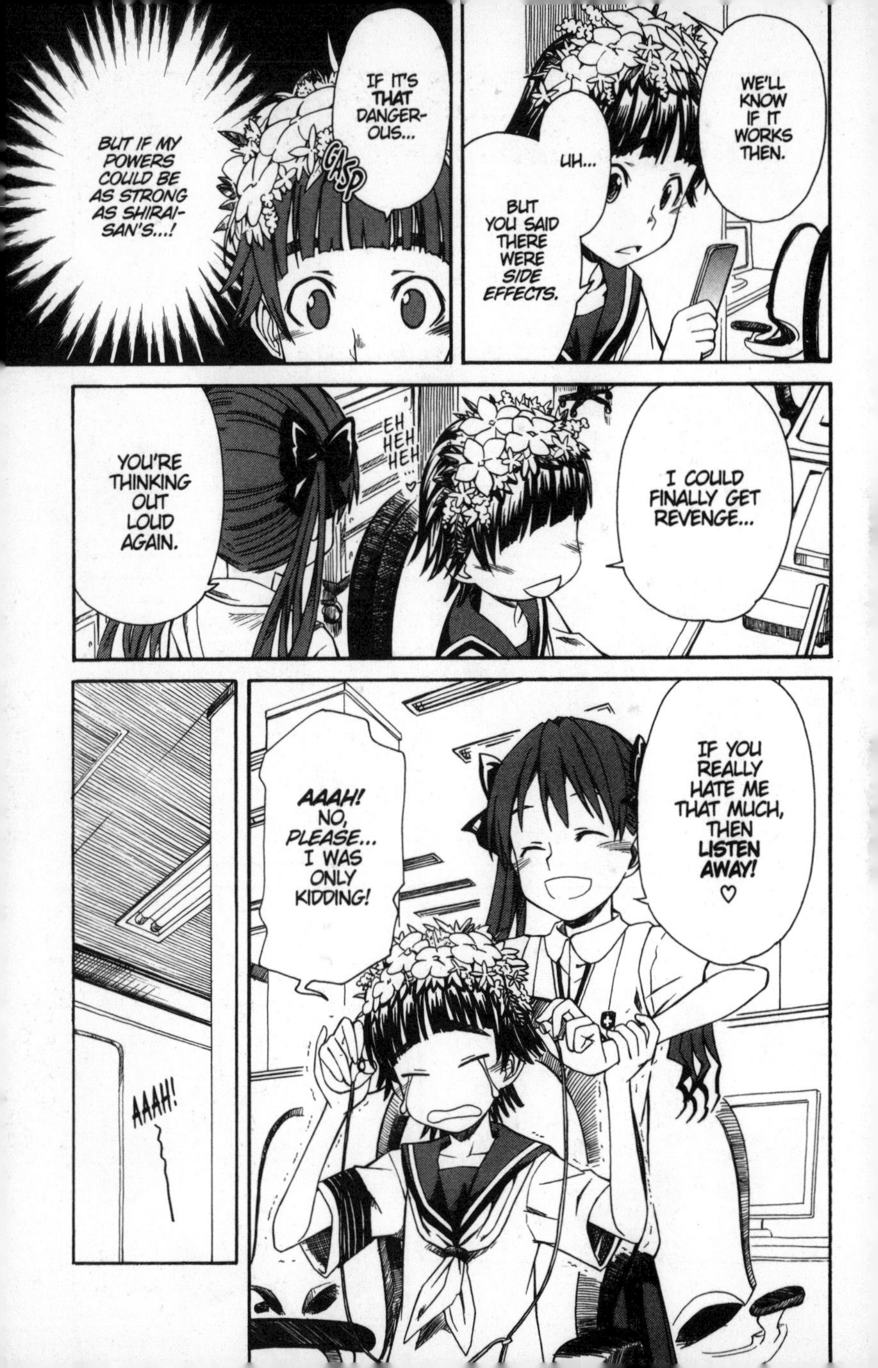
WE'LL KNOW IF IT WORKS THEN.
UH...
BUT YOU SAID THERE WERE SIDE EFFECTS.
IF IT'S **THAT** DANGER-OUS...
GASP
BUT IF MY POWERS COULD BE AS STRONG AS SHIRAI-SAN'S...!
I COULD FINALLY GET REVENGE...
EH HEH HEH... ♡
YOU'RE THINKING OUT LOUD AGAIN.
IF YOU REALLY HATE ME THAT MUCH, THEN **LISTEN AWAY!** ♡
AAAH! NO, ***PLEASE...*** I WAS ONLY KIDDING!
AAAH!

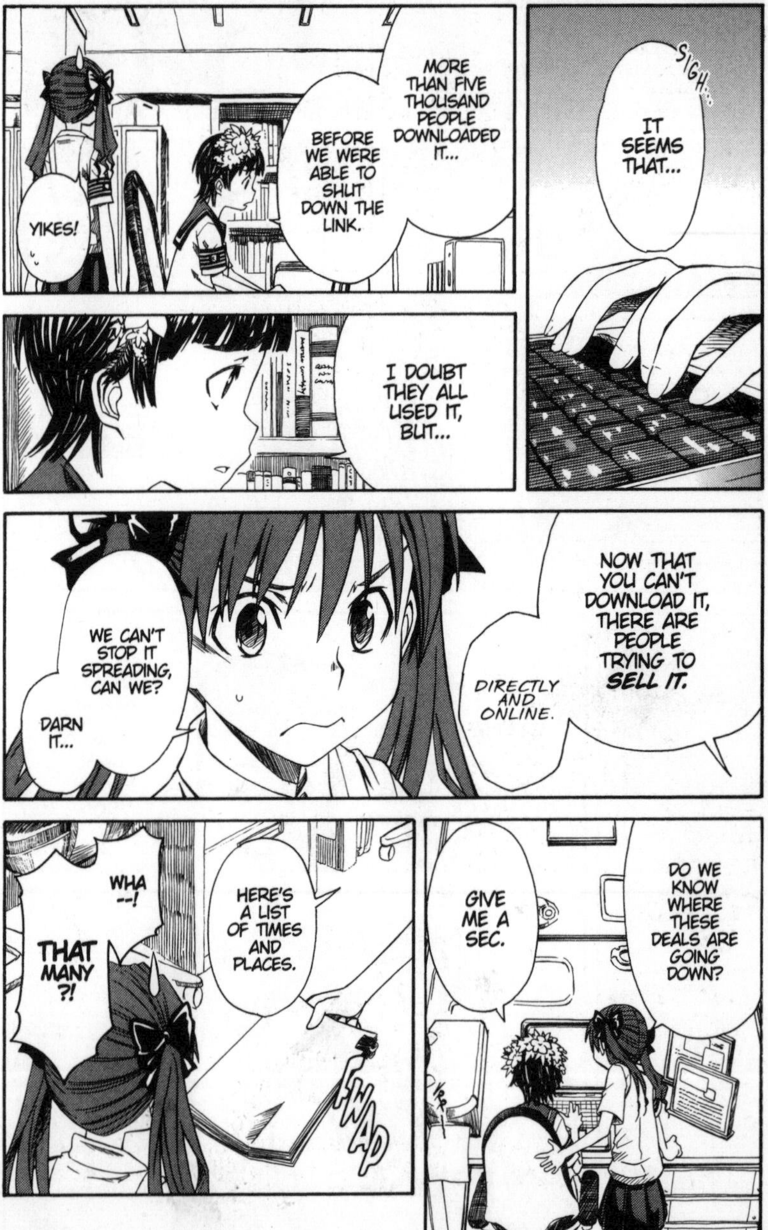
SIGH...
IT SEEMS THAT...
MORE THAN FIVE THOUSAND PEOPLE DOWNLOADED IT...
BEFORE WE WERE ABLE TO SHUT DOWN THE LINK.
YIKES!
I DOUBT THEY ALL USED IT, BUT...
NOW THAT YOU CAN'T DOWNLOAD IT, THERE ARE PEOPLE TRYING TO **SELL IT.**
DIRECTLY AND ONLINE.
WE CAN'T STOP IT SPREADING, CAN WE?
DARN IT...
DO WE KNOW WHERE THESE DEALS ARE GOING DOWN?
GIVE ME A SEC.
HERE'S A LIST OF TIMES AND PLACES.
WHA--!
THAT MANY?!
FWAP

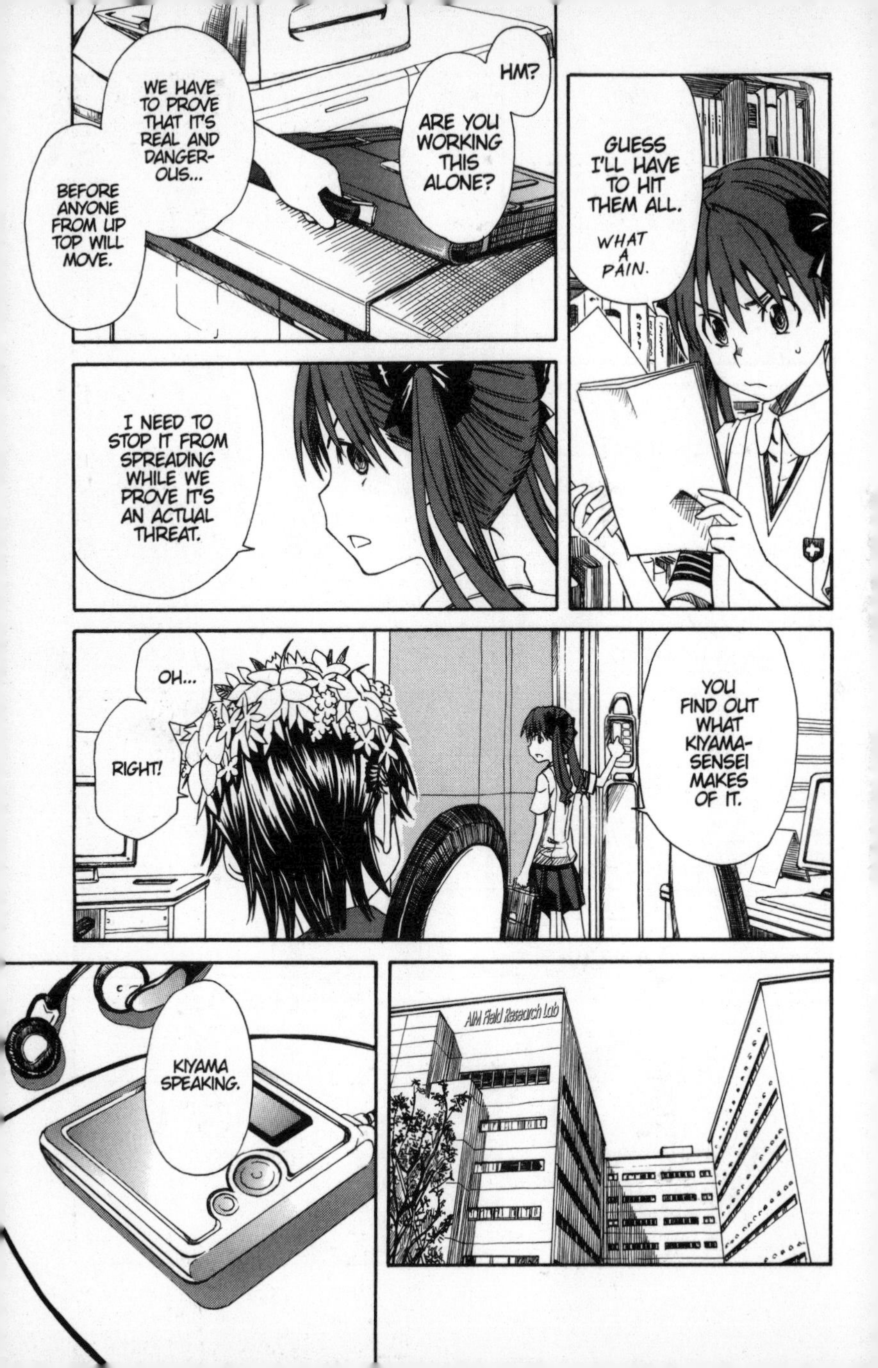
GUESS I'LL HAVE TO HIT THEM ALL.
WHAT A PAIN.
HM?
ARE YOU WORKING THIS ALONE?
WE HAVE TO PROVE THAT IT'S REAL AND DANGER-OUS...
BEFORE ANYONE FROM UP TOP WILL MOVE.
I NEED TO STOP IT FROM SPREADING WHILE WE PROVE IT'S AN ACTUAL THREAT.
YOU FIND OUT WHAT KIYAMA-SENSEI MAKES OF IT.
OH...
RIGHT!
AIM Field Research Lab
KIYAMA SPEAKING.

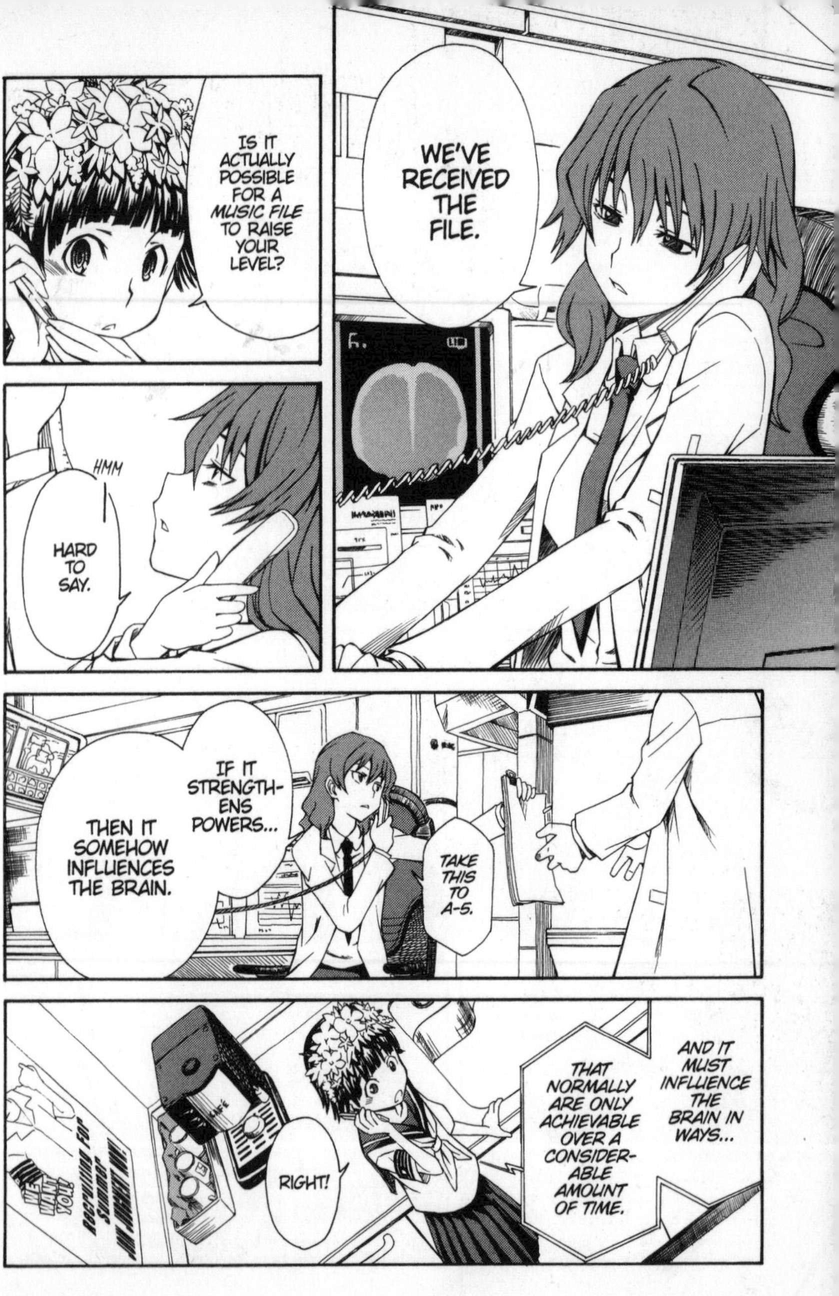
WE'VE RECEIVED THE FILE.
IS IT ACTUALLY POSSIBLE FOR A *MUSIC FILE* TO RAISE YOUR LEVEL?
HMM
HARD TO SAY.
IF IT STRENGTH-ENS POWERS...
THEN IT SOMEHOW INFLUENCES THE BRAIN.
TAKE THIS TO A-5.
AND IT MUST INFLUENCE THE BRAIN IN WAYS...
THAT NORMALLY ARE ONLY ACHIEVABLE OVER A CONSIDER-ABLE AMOUNT OF TIME.
RIGHT!

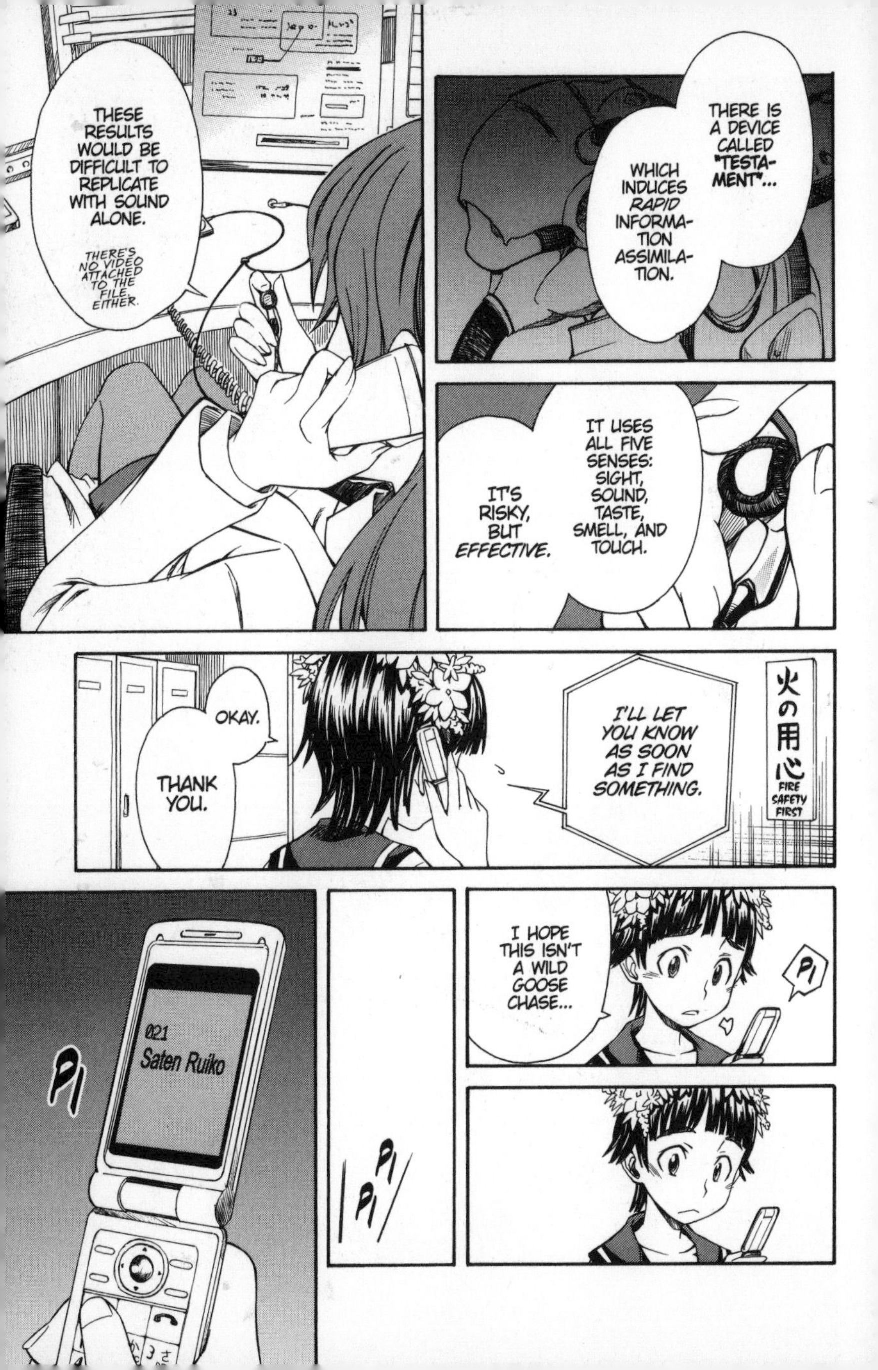
THERE IS A DEVICE CALLED "TESTAMENT"...
WHICH INDUCES RAPID INFORMATION ASSIMILATION.
IT USES ALL FIVE SENSES: SIGHT, SOUND, TASTE, SMELL, AND TOUCH.
IT'S RISKY, BUT EFFECTIVE.
THESE RESULTS WOULD BE DIFFICULT TO REPLICATE WITH SOUND ALONE.
THERE'S NO VIDEO ATTACHED TO THE FILE, EITHER.
火の用心
FIRE SAFETY FIRST
I'LL LET YOU KNOW AS SOON AS I FIND SOMETHING.
OKAY.
THANK YOU.
PI
I HOPE THIS ISN'T A WILD GOOSE CHASE...
PI PI
021
Saten Ruiko
PI

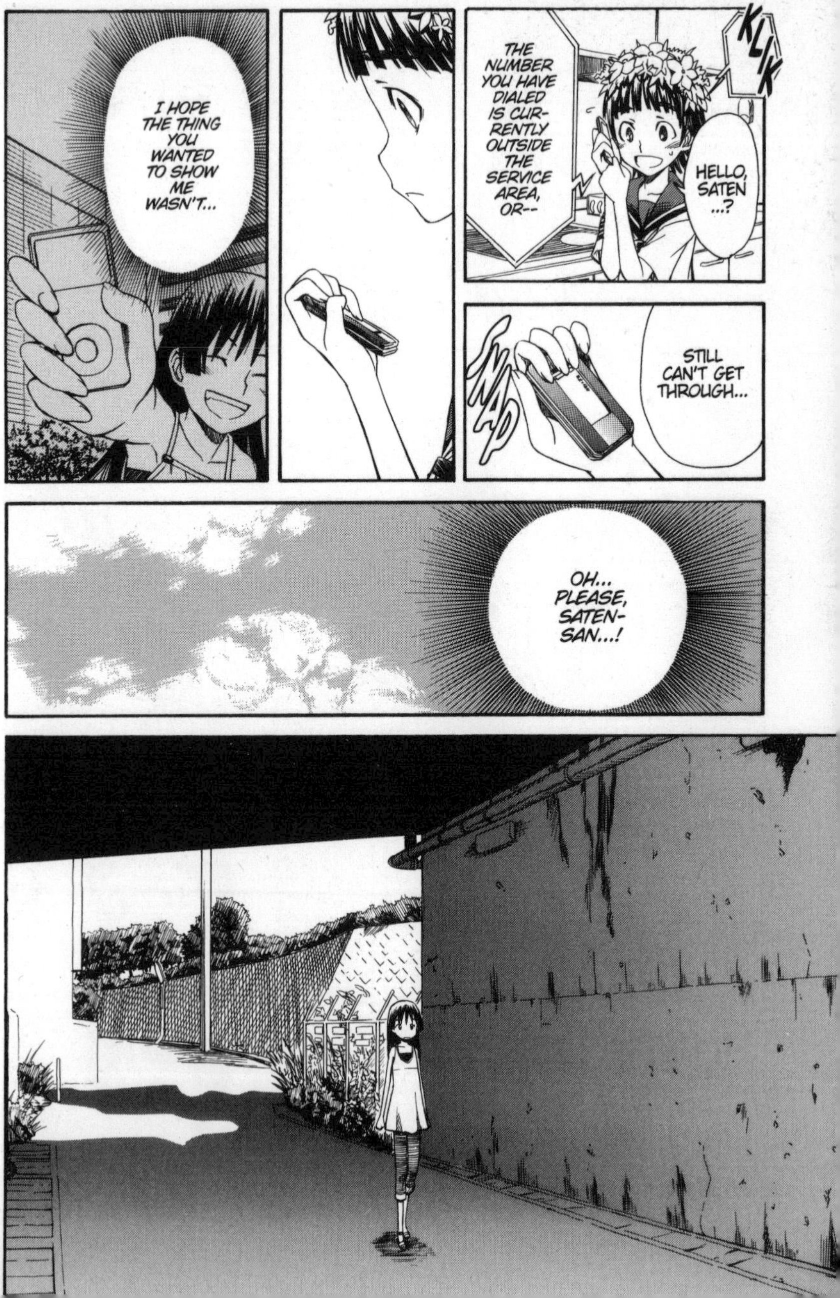
KLIK
HELLO, SATEN ...?
THE NUMBER YOU HAVE DIALED IS CURRENTLY OUTSIDE THE SERVICE AREA, OR--
STILL CAN'T GET THROUGH...
SNAP
I HOPE THE THING YOU WANTED TO SHOW ME WASN'T...
OH... PLEASE, SATEN-SAN...!

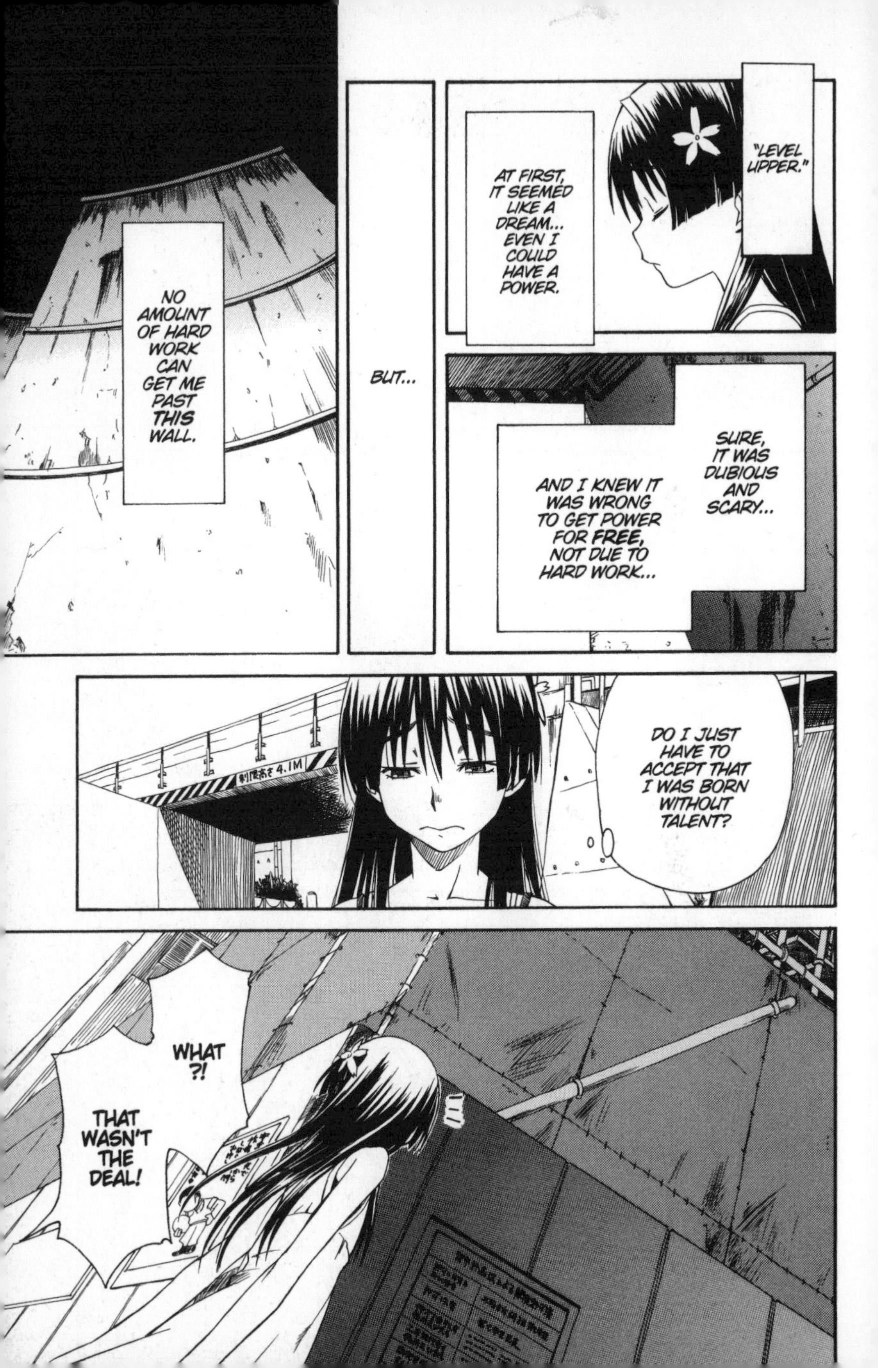
"LEVEL UPPER."
AT FIRST, IT SEEMED LIKE A DREAM... EVEN I COULD HAVE A POWER.
SURE, IT WAS DUBIOUS AND SCARY...
AND I KNEW IT WAS WRONG TO GET POWER FOR FREE, NOT DUE TO HARD WORK...
BUT...
NO AMOUNT OF HARD WORK CAN GET ME PAST THIS WALL.
DO I JUST HAVE TO ACCEPT THAT I WAS BORN WITHOUT TALENT?
制限高さ4.1M
WHAT?!
THAT WASN'T THE DEAL!

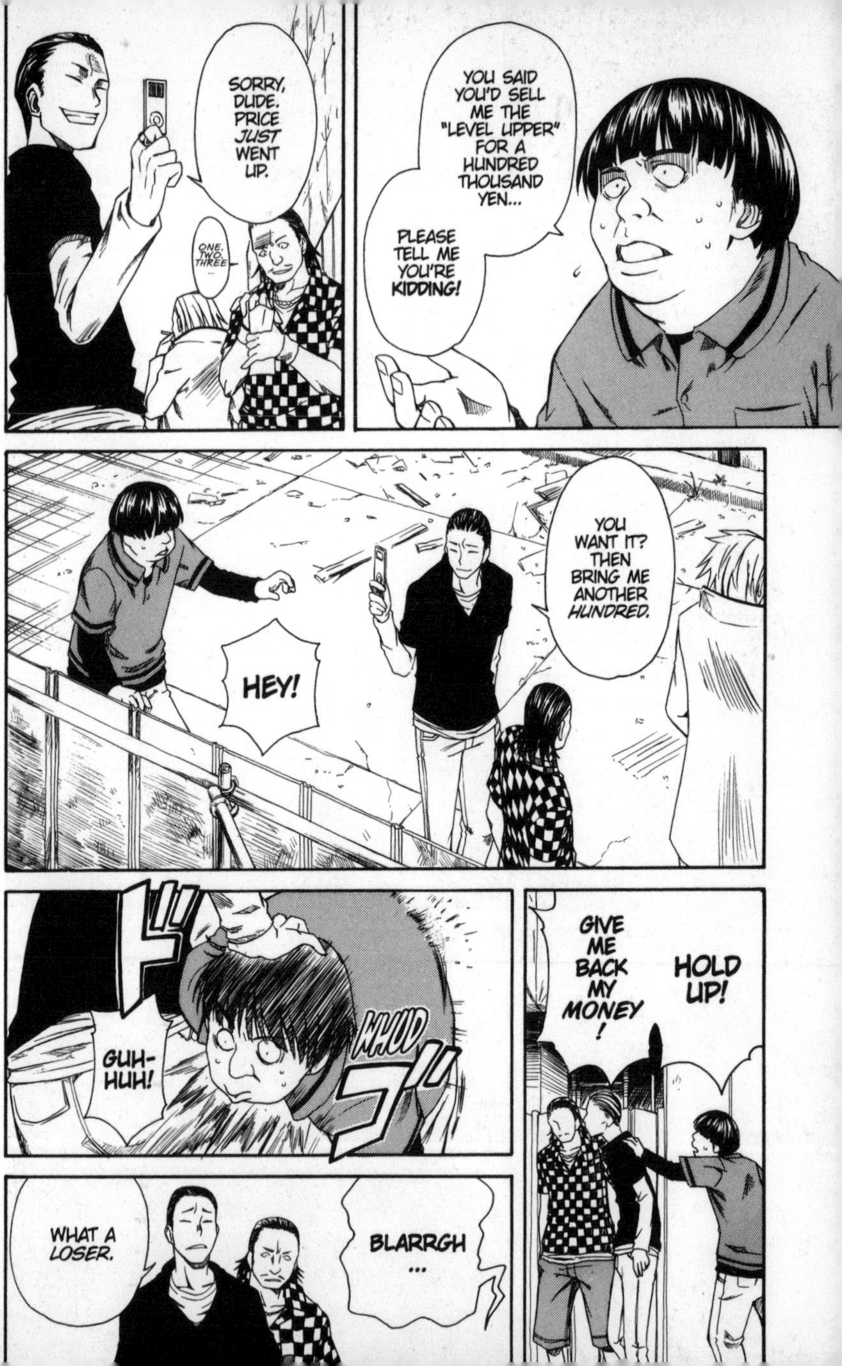
YOU SAID YOU'D SELL ME THE "LEVEL UPPER" FOR A HUNDRED THOUSAND YEN...
PLEASE TELL ME YOU'RE KIDDING!
SORRY, DUDE. PRICE JUST WENT UP.
ONE, TWO, THREE ...
YOU WANT IT? THEN BRING ME ANOTHER HUNDRED.
HEY!
HOLD UP!
GIVE ME BACK MY MONEY!
WHUD
GUH-HUH!
BLARRGH ...
WHAT A LOSER.

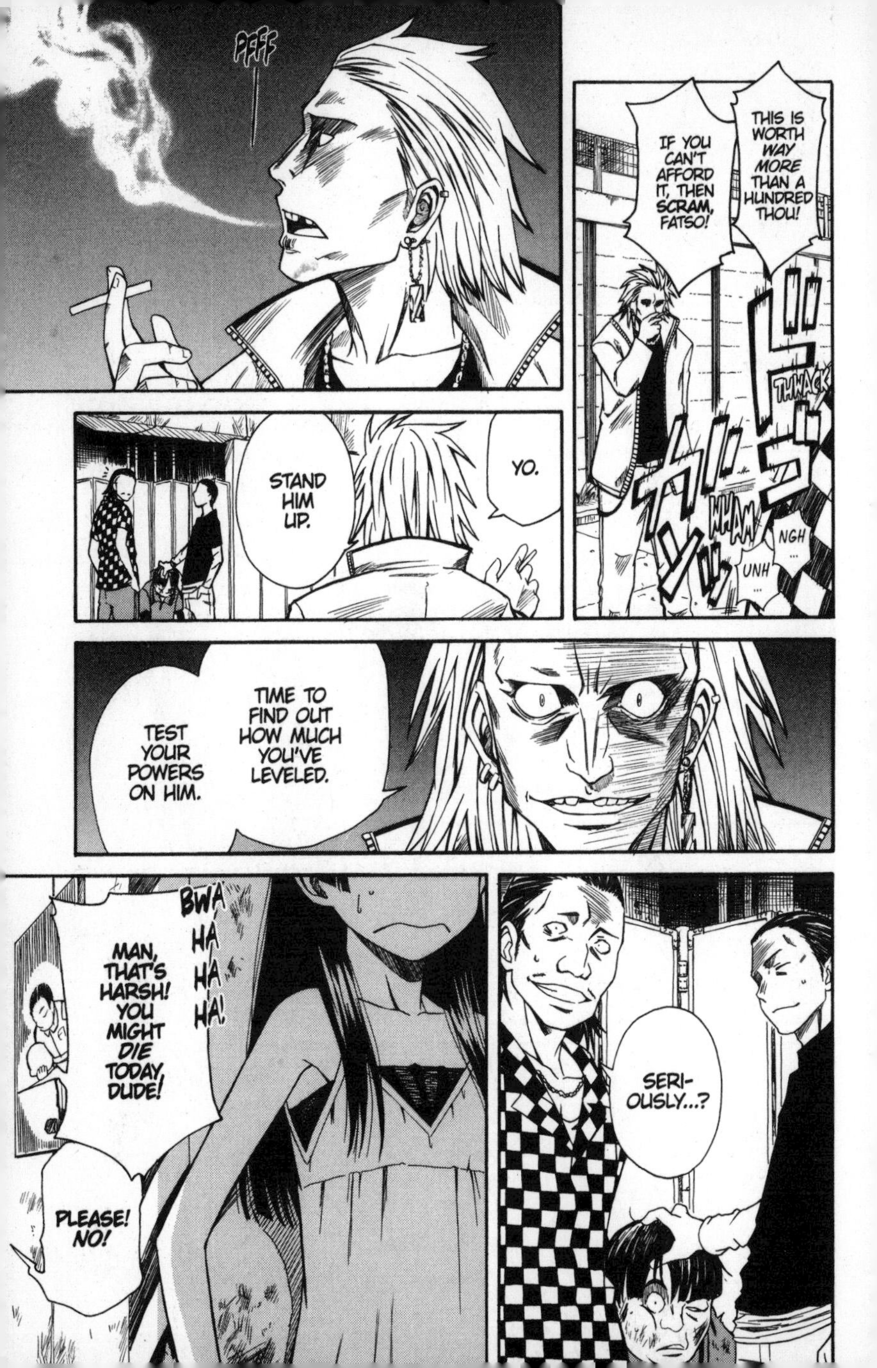
THIS IS WORTH WAY MORE THAN A HUNDRED THOU!
IF YOU CAN'T AFFORD IT, THEN SCRAM, FATSO!
THWACK
WHAM
NGH...
UNH...
PFFF
YO.
STAND HIM UP.
TIME TO FIND OUT HOW MUCH YOU'VE LEVELED.
TEST YOUR POWERS ON HIM.
SERI-OUSLY...?
BWA HA HA HA!
MAN, THAT'S HARSH! YOU MIGHT DIE TODAY, DUDE!
PLEASE! NO!

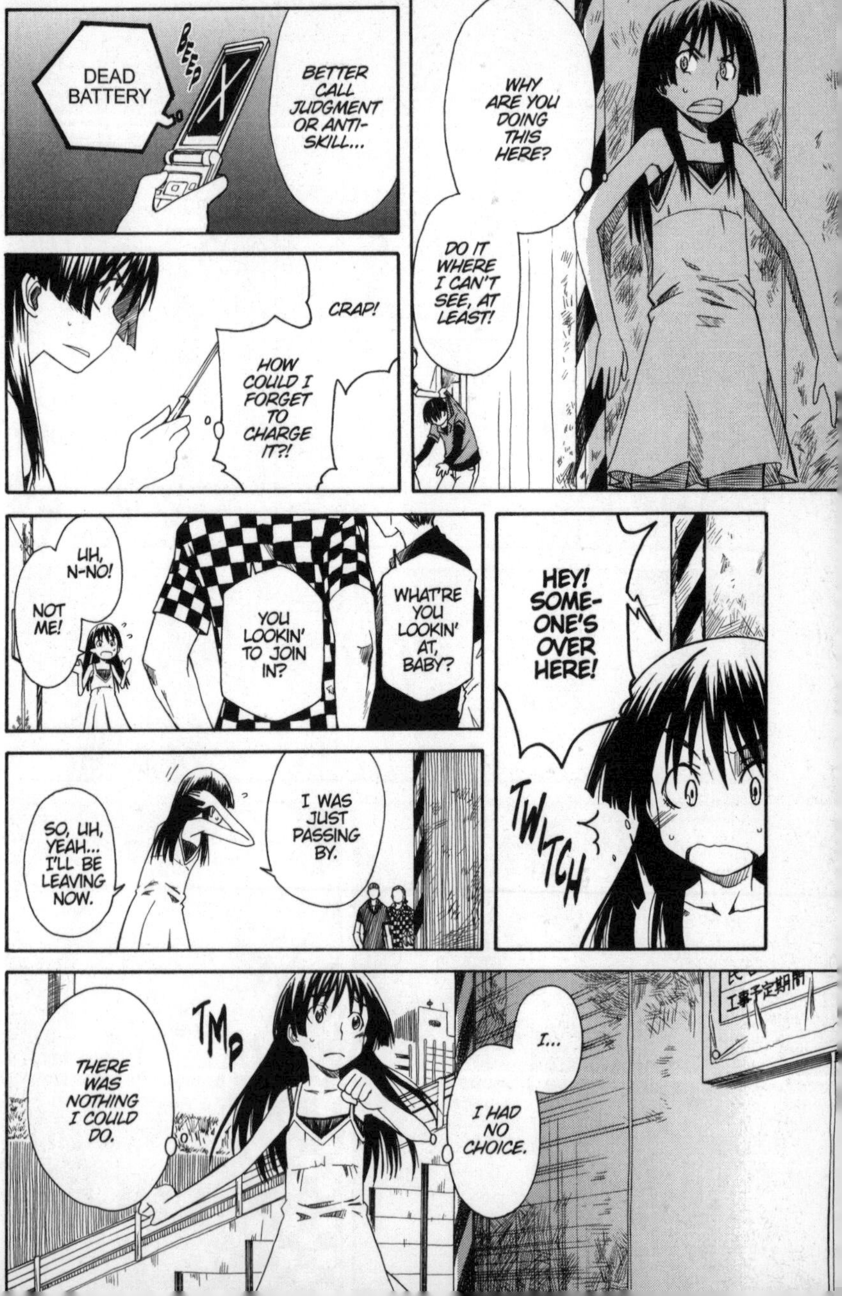
WHY ARE YOU DOING THIS HERE?
DO IT WHERE I CAN'T SEE, AT LEAST!
BETTER CALL JUDGMENT OR ANTI-SKILL...
BEEP
DEAD BATTERY
CRAP!
HOW COULD I FORGET TO CHARGE IT?!
HEY! SOMEONE'S OVER HERE!
TWITCH
WHAT'RE YOU LOOKIN' AT, BABY?
YOU LOOKIN' TO JOIN IN?
UH, N-NO!
NOT ME!
I WAS JUST PASSING BY.
SO, UH, YEAH... I'LL BE LEAVING NOW.
I...
I HAD NO CHOICE.
TMP
THERE WAS NOTHING I COULD DO.

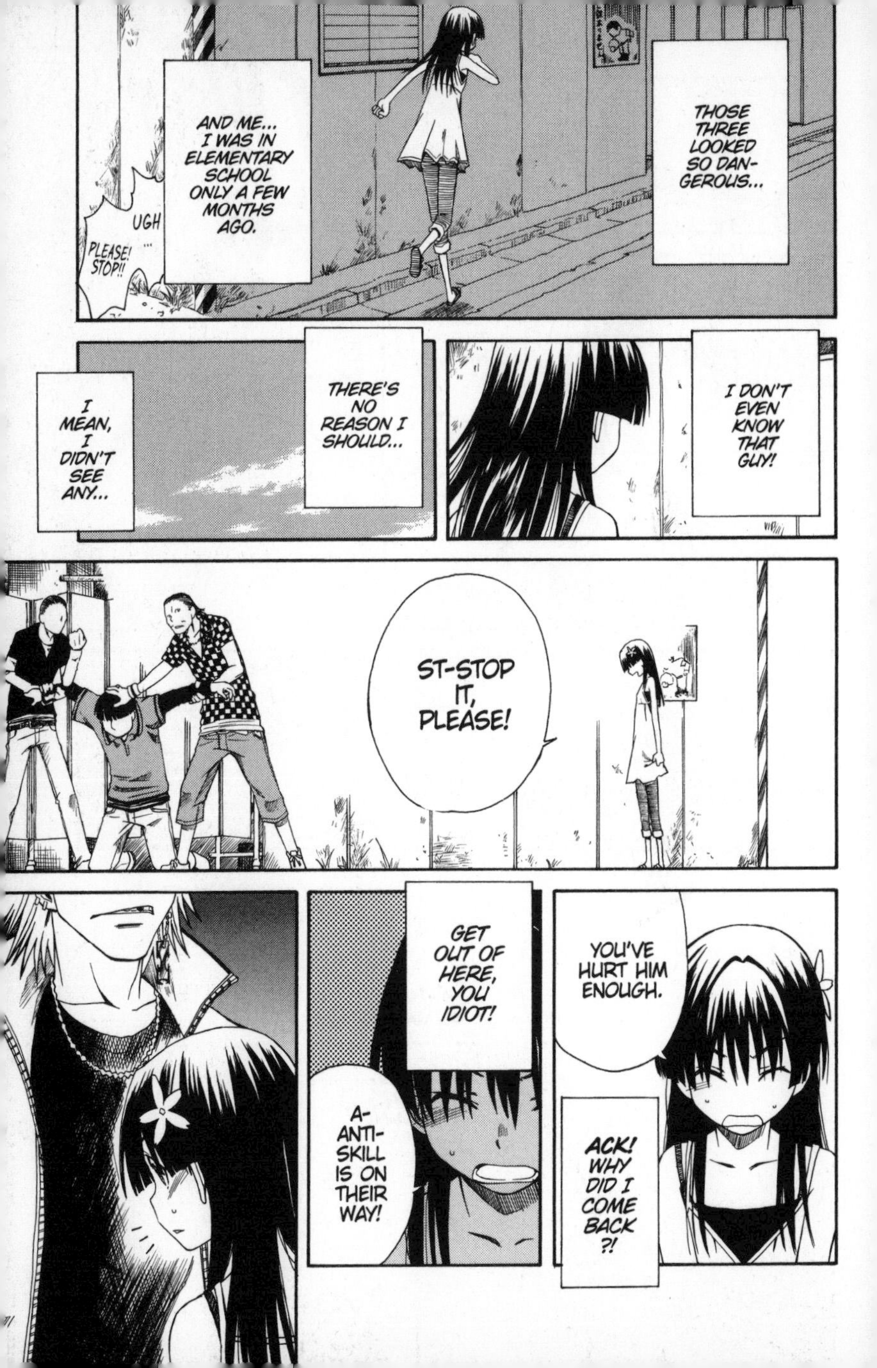
THOSE THREE LOOKED SO DANGEROUS...
AND ME... I WAS IN ELEMENTARY SCHOOL ONLY A FEW MONTHS AGO.
UGH ...
PLEASE! STOP!!
I DON'T EVEN KNOW THAT GUY!
THERE'S NO REASON I SHOULD...
I MEAN, I DIDN'T SEE ANY...
ST-STOP IT, PLEASE!
YOU'VE HURT HIM ENOUGH.
ACK! WHY DID I COME BACK?!
GET OUT OF HERE, YOU IDIOT!
A-ANTI-SKILL IS ON THEIR WAY!

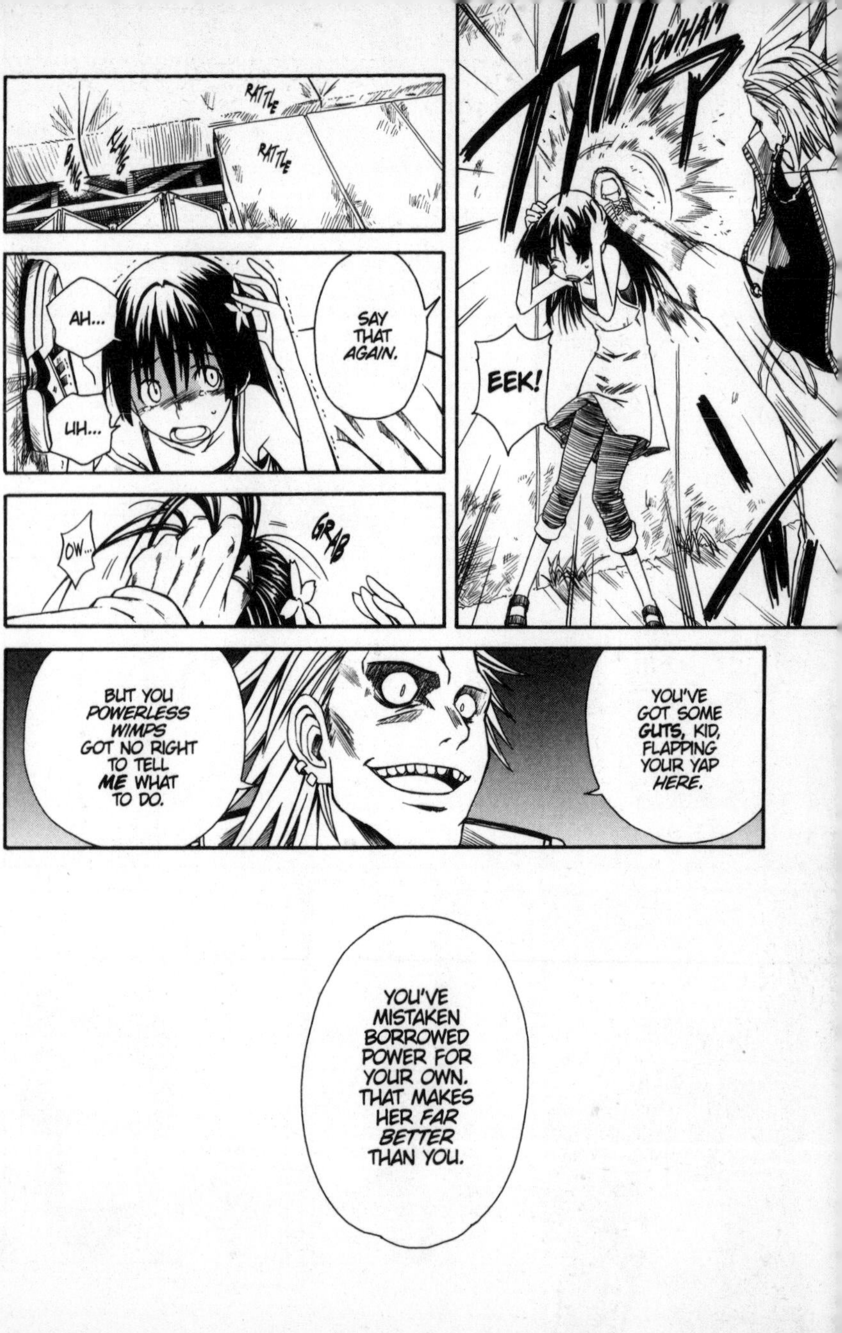
KWHAM
EEK!
RATTLE
RATTLE
KLANG
BANG
SAY THAT AGAIN.
AH...
UH...
GRAB
OW...
YOU'VE GOT SOME GUTS, KID, FLAPPING YOUR YAP HERE.
BUT YOU POWERLESS WIMPS GOT NO RIGHT TO TELL ME WHAT TO DO.
YOU'VE MISTAKEN BORROWED POWER FOR YOUR OWN. THAT MAKES HER FAR BETTER THAN YOU.

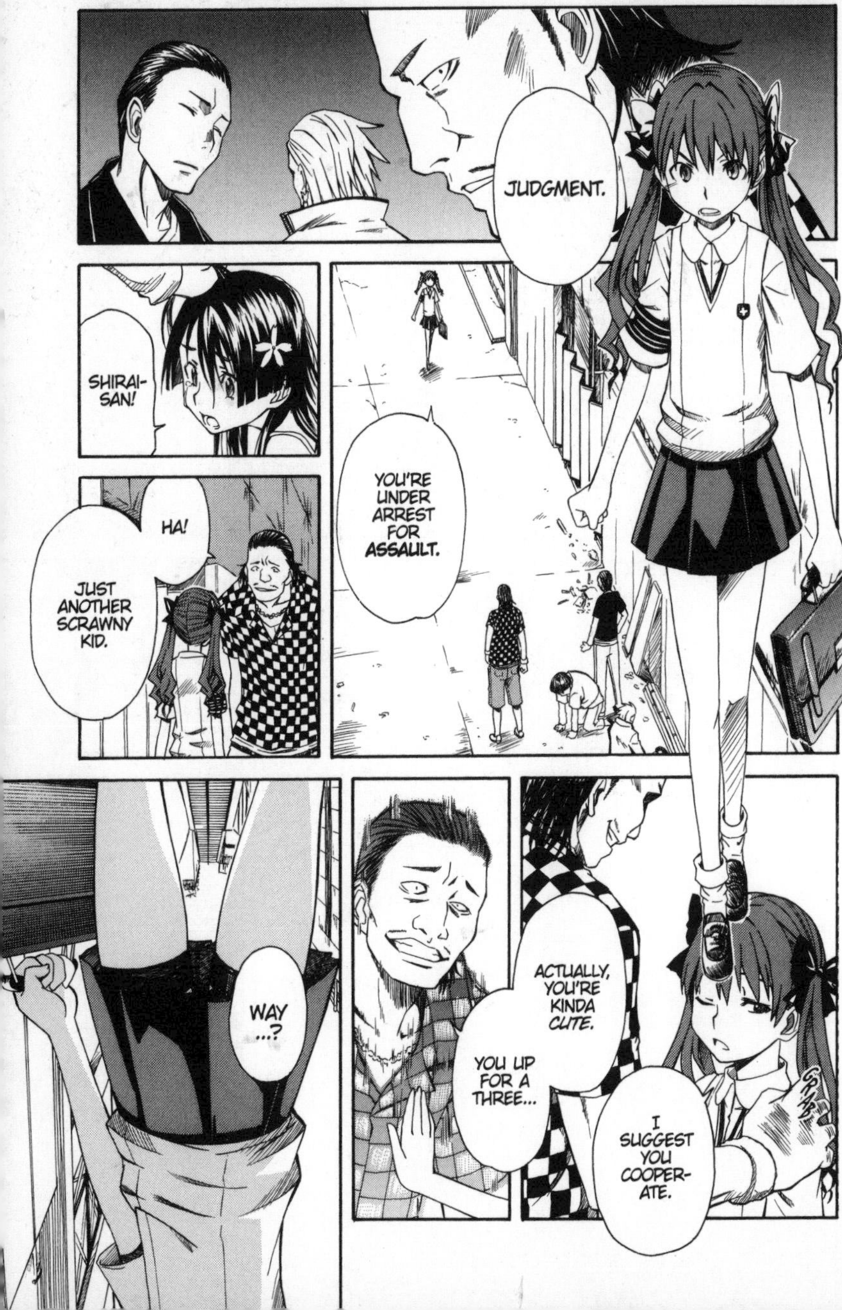
JUDGMENT.
YOU'RE UNDER ARREST FOR ASSAULT.
SHIRAI-SAN!
HA!
JUST ANOTHER SCRAWNY KID.
ACTUALLY, YOU'RE KINDA CUTE.
YOU UP FOR A THREE...
I SUGGEST YOU COOPER-ATE.
GRAB
WAY ...?

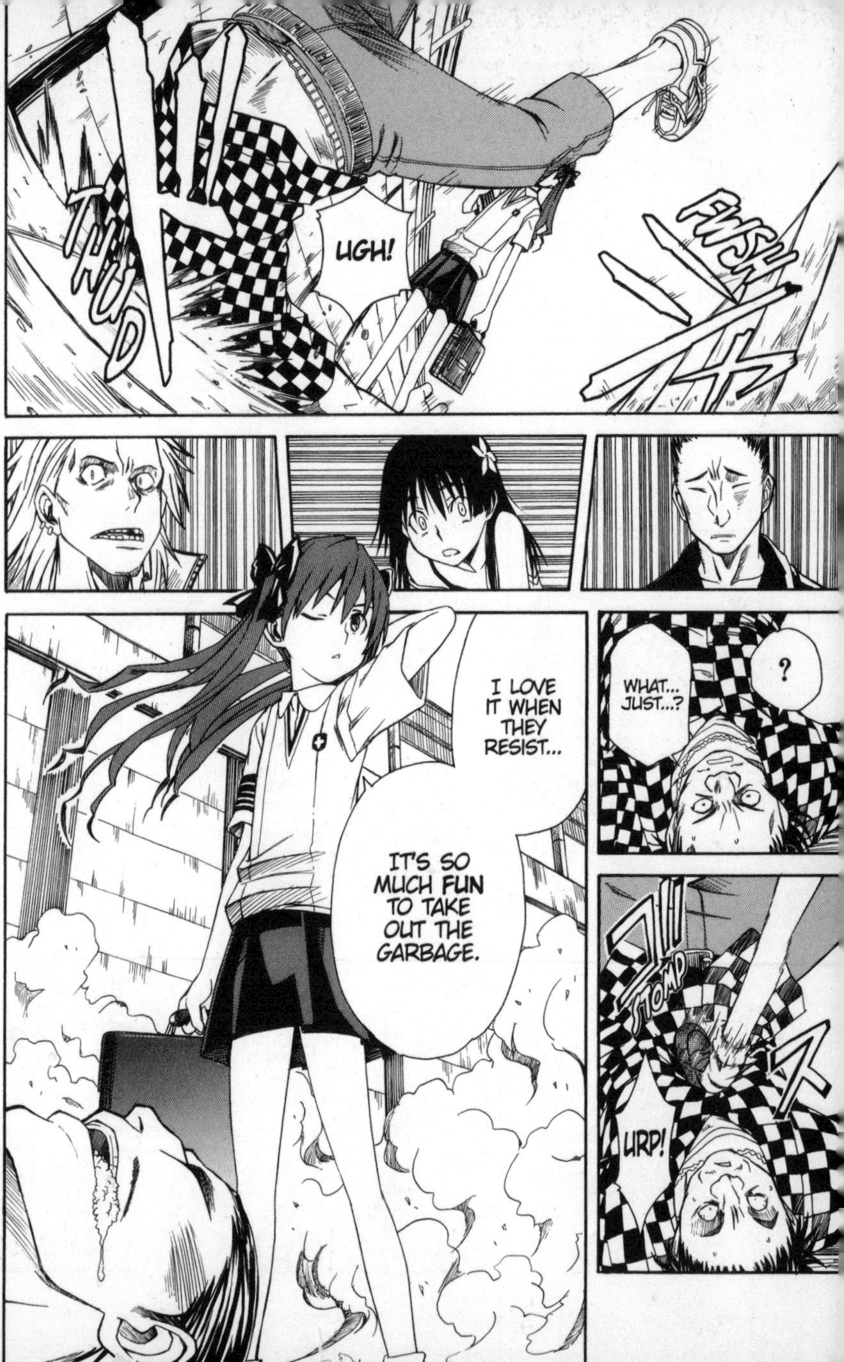
FWSH
UGH!
THUD
?
WHAT... JUST...?
STOMP
URP!
I LOVE IT WHEN THEY RESIST...
IT'S SO MUCH FUN TO TAKE OUT THE GARBAGE.

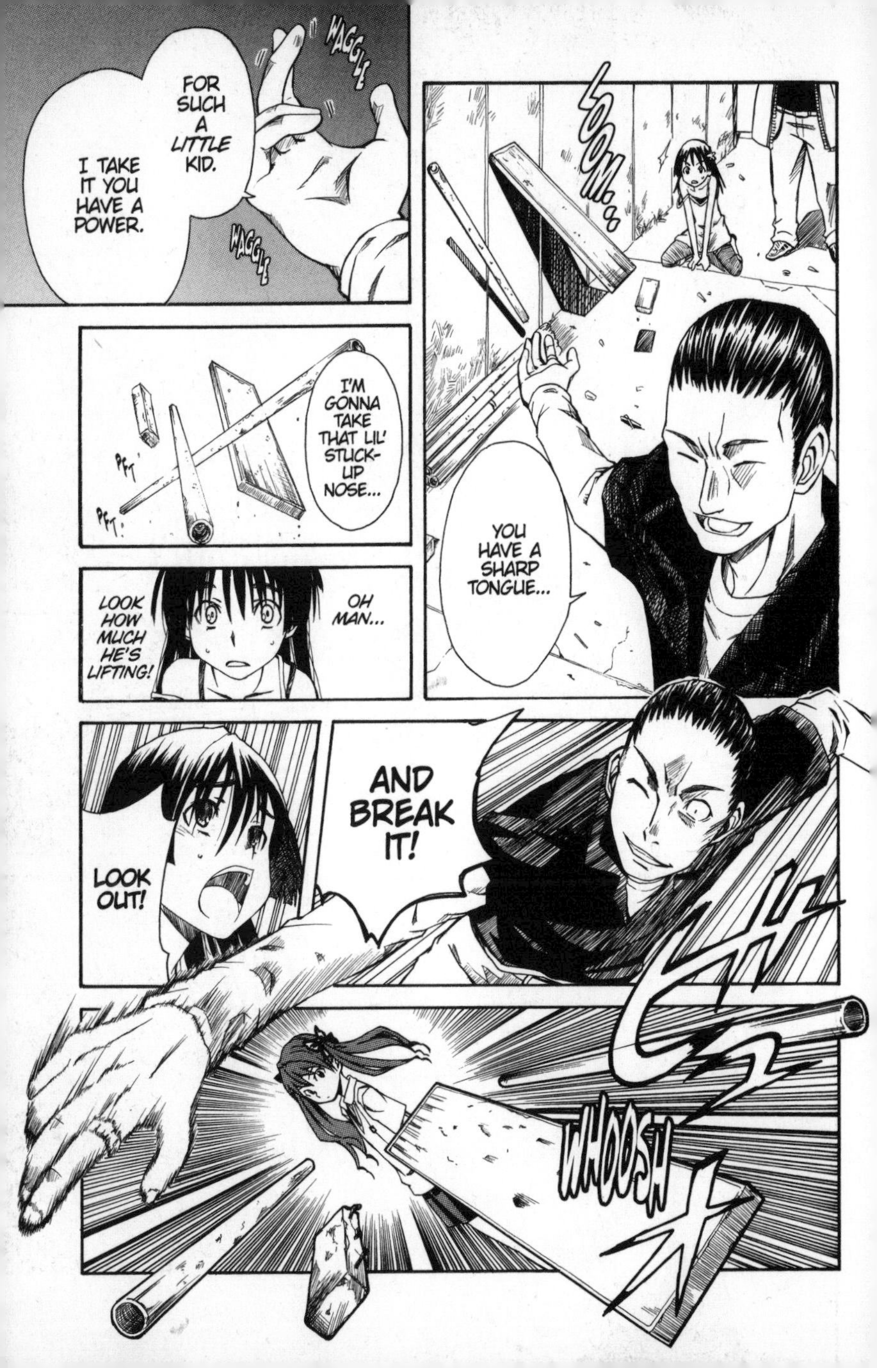
WAGGLE
FOR SUCH A LITTLE KID.
I TAKE IT YOU HAVE A POWER.
WAGGLE
LOOM
YOU HAVE A SHARP TONGUE...
I'M GONNA TAKE THAT LIL' STUCK-UP NOSE...
PFFT
PFFT
OH MAN...
LOOK HOW MUCH HE'S LIFTING!
AND BREAK IT!
LOOK OUT!
WHOOSH

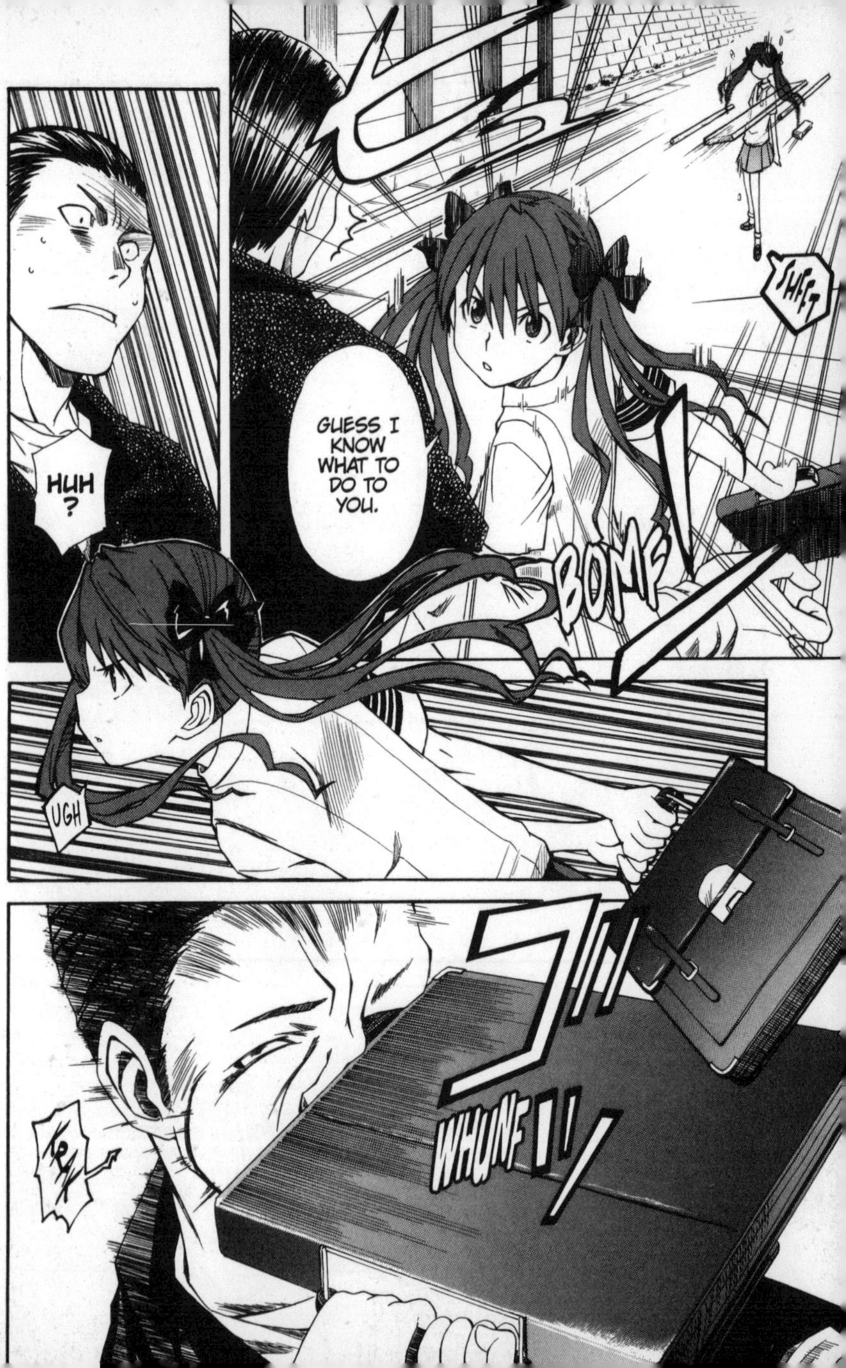
SHEFT
GUESS I KNOW WHAT TO DO TO YOU.
BOMF
HUH ?
UGH
WHUNF
KRAK

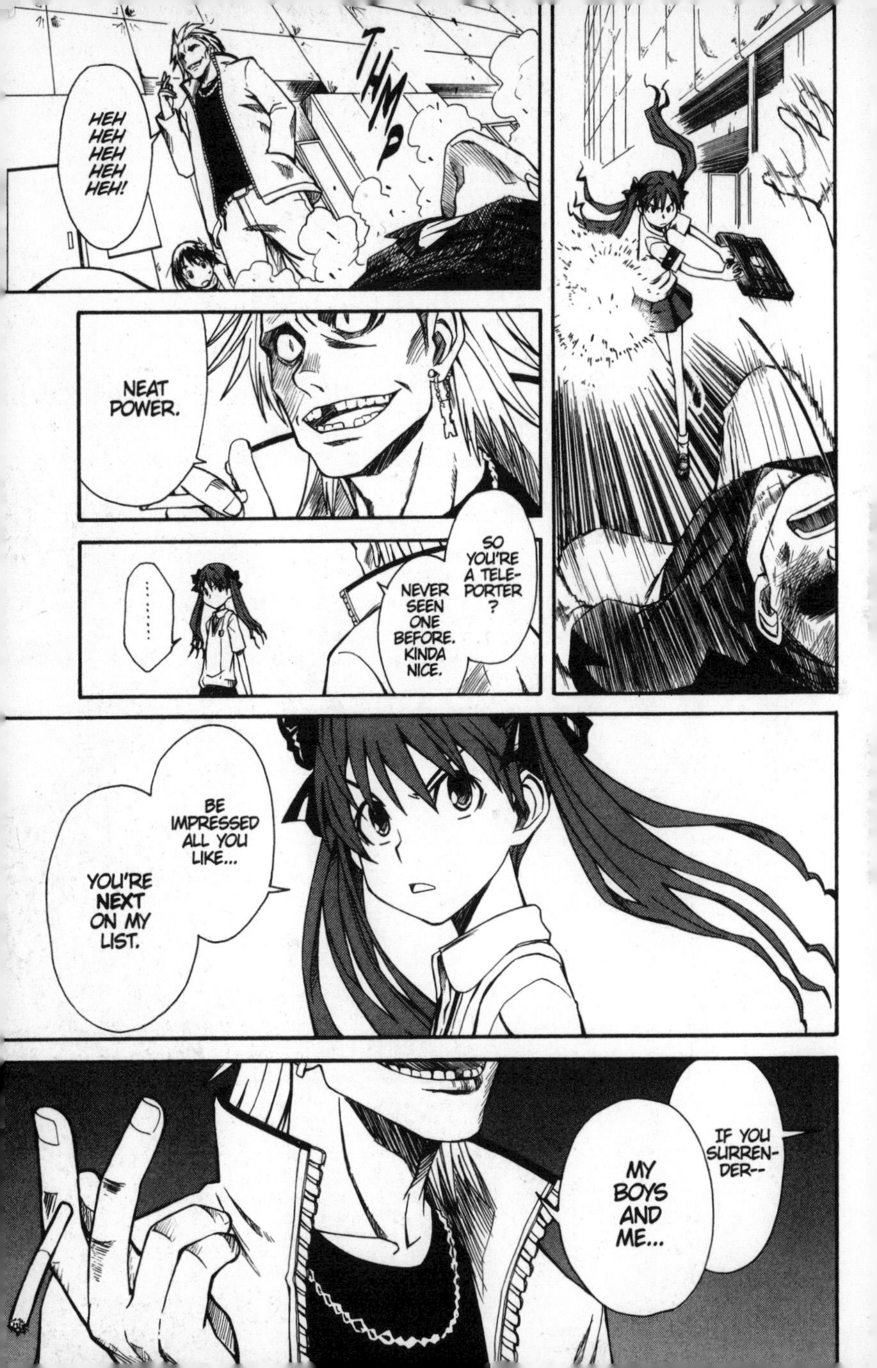
THMP
HEH HEH HEH HEH HEH!
NEAT POWER.
SO YOU'RE A TELEPORTER?
NEVER SEEN ONE BEFORE. KINDA NICE.
......
BE IMPRESSED ALL YOU LIKE...
YOU'RE NEXT ON MY LIST.
IF YOU SURRENDER--
MY BOYS AND ME...

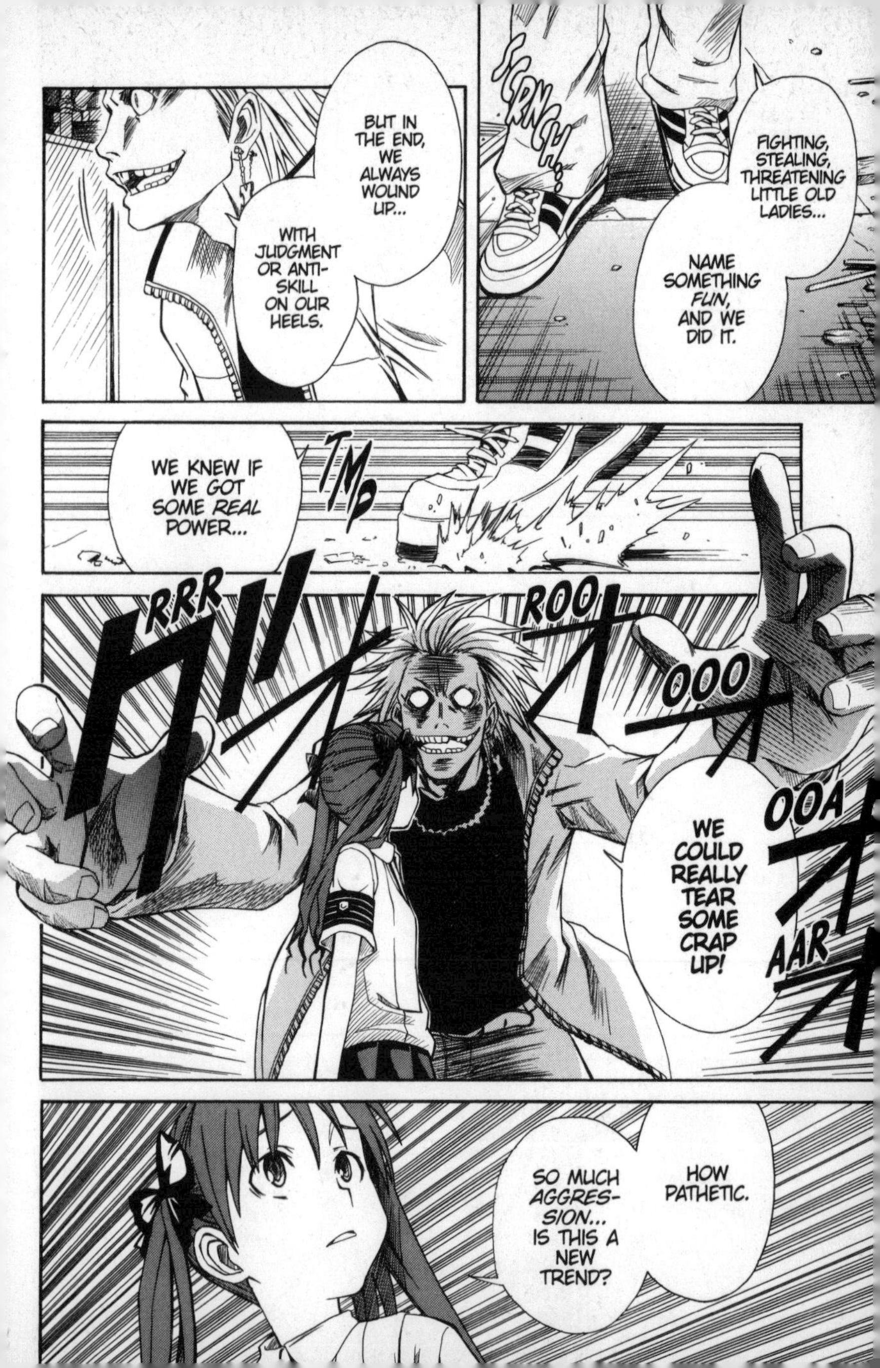
SCRNCH...
FIGHTING, STEALING, THREATENING LITTLE OLD LADIES...
NAME SOMETHING *FUN*, AND WE DID IT.
BUT IN THE END, WE ALWAYS WOUND UP...
WITH JUDGMENT OR ANTI-SKILL ON OUR HEELS.
TMP
WE KNEW IF WE GOT SOME *REAL* POWER...
RRR
ROO
OOO
OOA
AAR
WE COULD REALLY TEAR SOME CRAP UP!
HOW PATHETIC.
SO MUCH AGGRES-SION... IS THIS A NEW TREND?

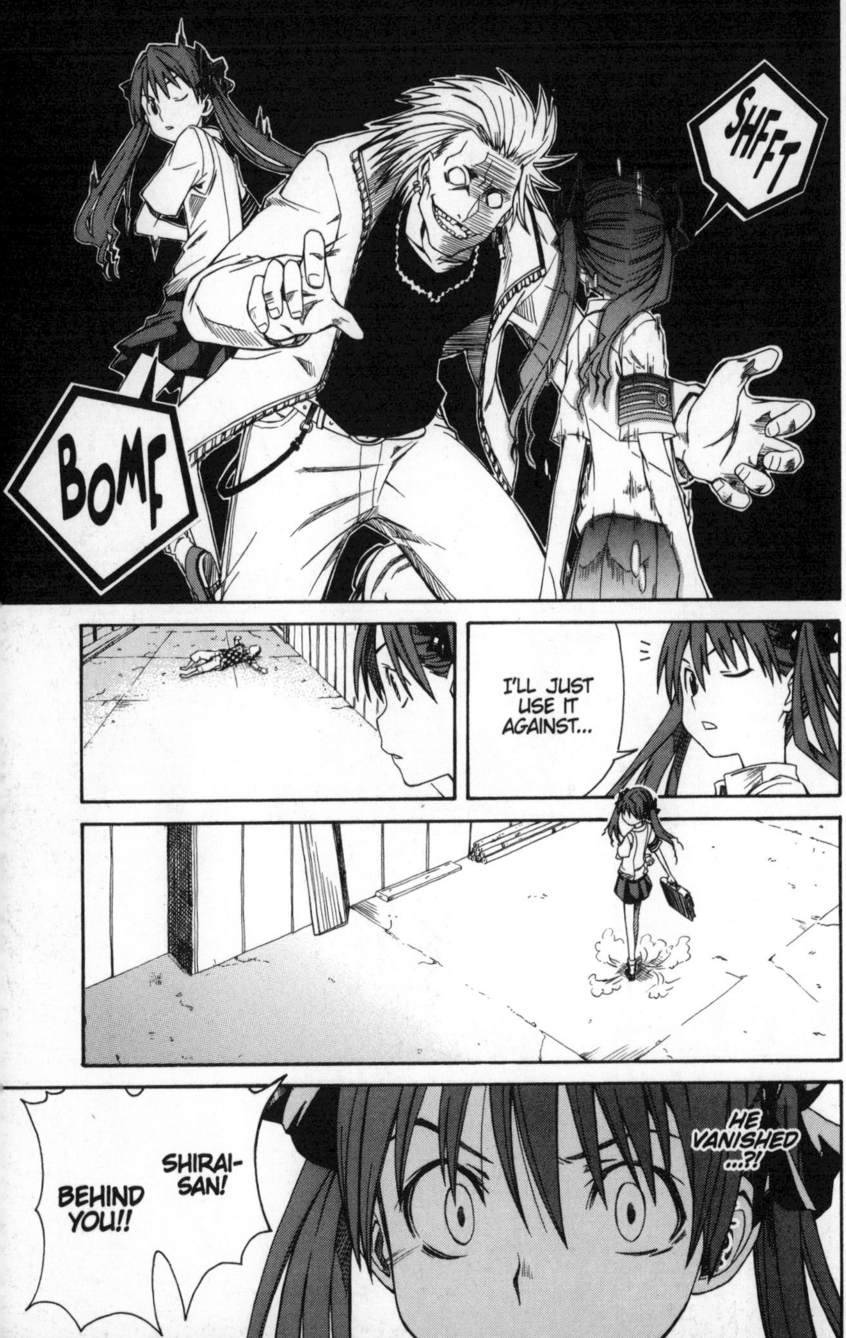
SHFFT
BOMF
I'LL JUST USE IT AGAINST...
HE VANISHED ...?!
SHIRAI-SAN! BEHIND YOU!!

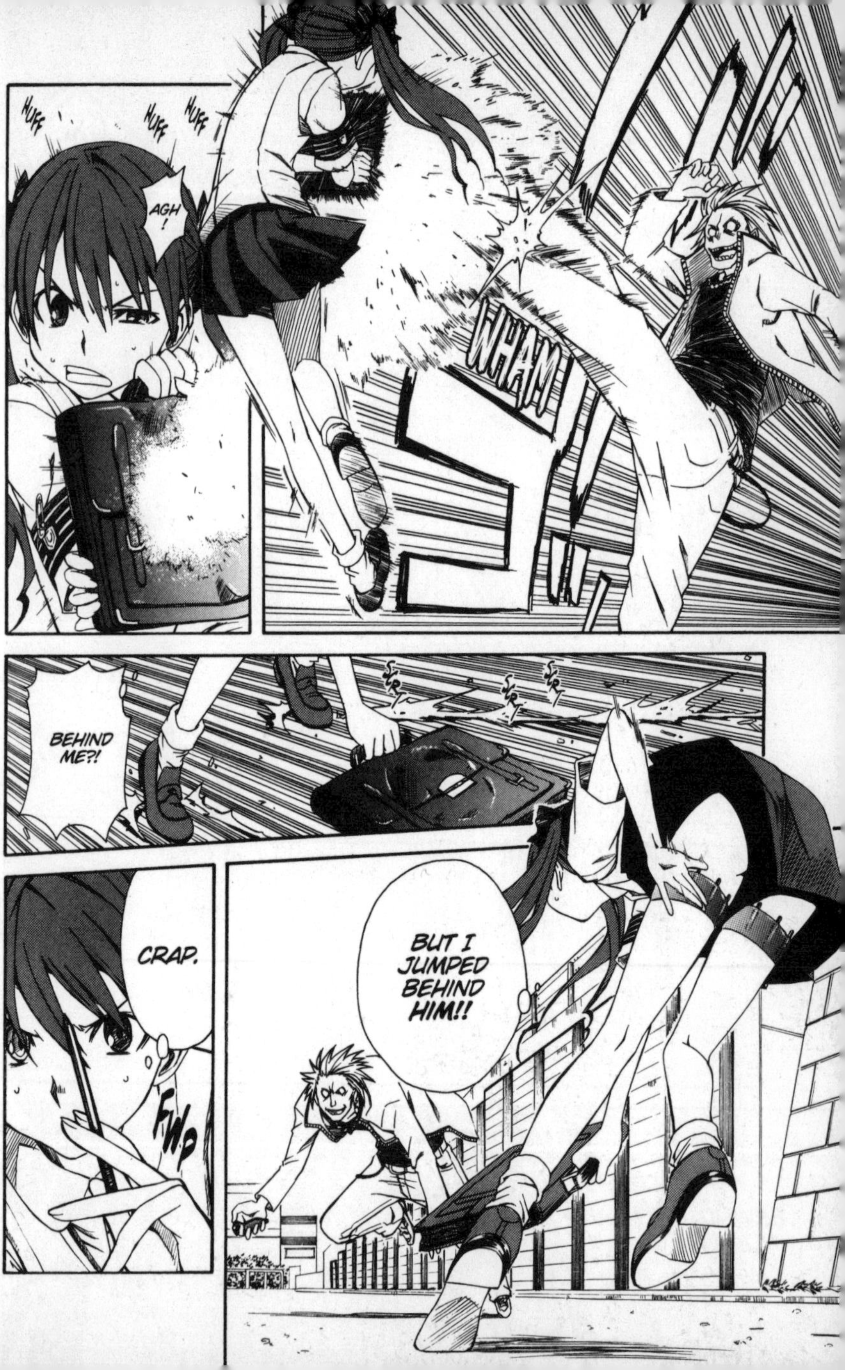
WHAM
AGH!
HUFF
HUFF
HUFF
BEHIND ME?!
BUT I JUMPED BEHIND HIM!!
CRAP.
FWIP

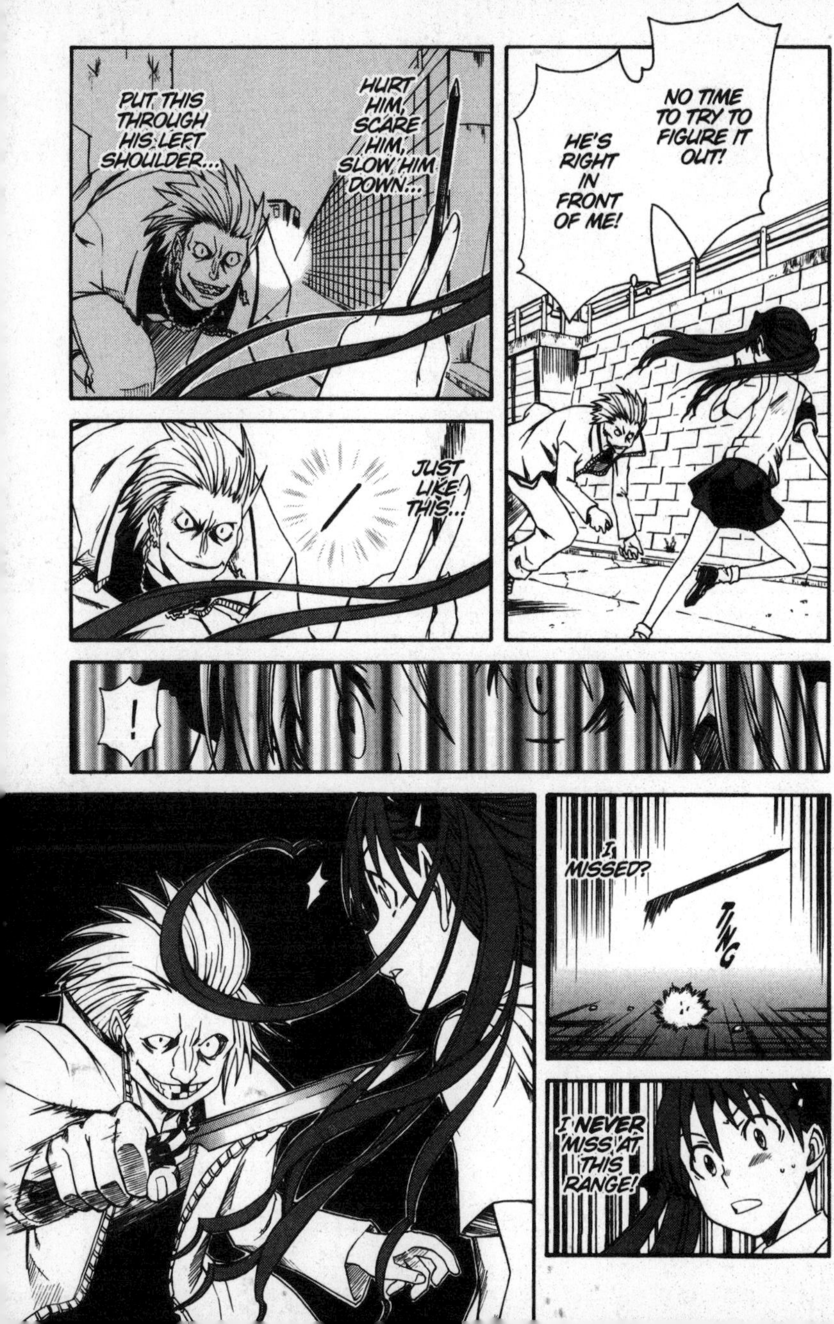
NO TIME TO TRY TO FIGURE IT OUT!
HE'S RIGHT IN FRONT OF ME!
HURT HIM, SCARE HIM, SLOW HIM DOWN...
PUT THIS THROUGH HIS LEFT SHOULDER...
JUST LIKE THIS...
!
I MISSED?
TING
I NEVER MISS AT THIS RANGE!

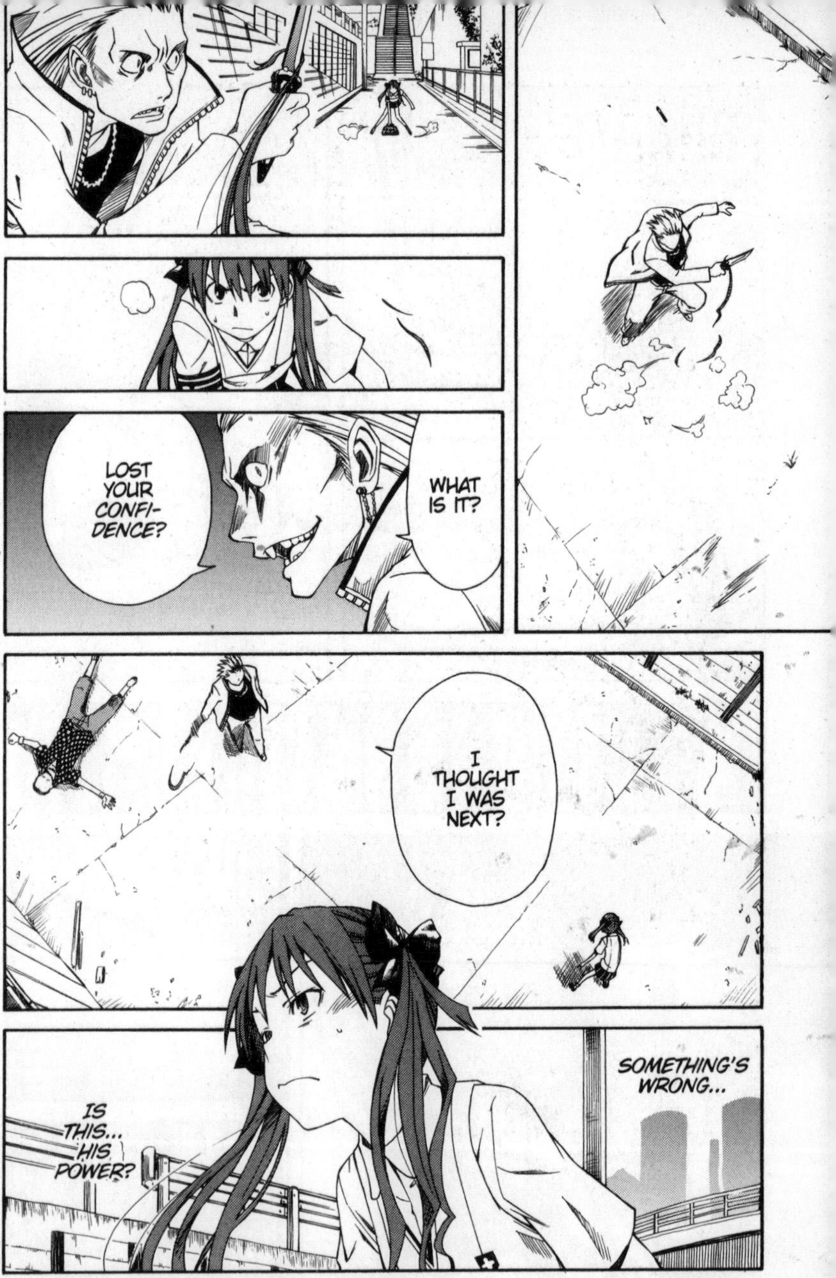
WHAT IS IT?
LOST YOUR CONFI-DENCE?
I THOUGHT I WAS NEXT?
SOMETHING'S WRONG...
IS THIS... HIS POWER?

CHAPTER 10: JULY 21 (2)

ANTI-SKILL

* THE EQUIVALENT OF A POLICE FORCE IN ACADEMY CITY.
* COMPOSED PRIMARILY OF UNPAID VOLUNTEERS FROM THE VARIOUS SCHOOL FACULTIES, THEIR JURISDICTION IS ALL OFF-CAMPUS CRIME.
* ADDITIONALLY, THEY HANDLE INCIDENTS DEEMED TOO DANGEROUS FOR THE PSYCHIC STUDENTS IN JUDGMENT, AND THEIR AUTHORITY TRUMPS JUDGMENT'S.
* THEY ARE HEAVILY ARMED, WITH ARMOR AND WEAPONS DESIGNED FOR FIGHTING PSYCHICS.
* ANTI-SKILL'S LOGO IS A STYLIZED TRIDENT.

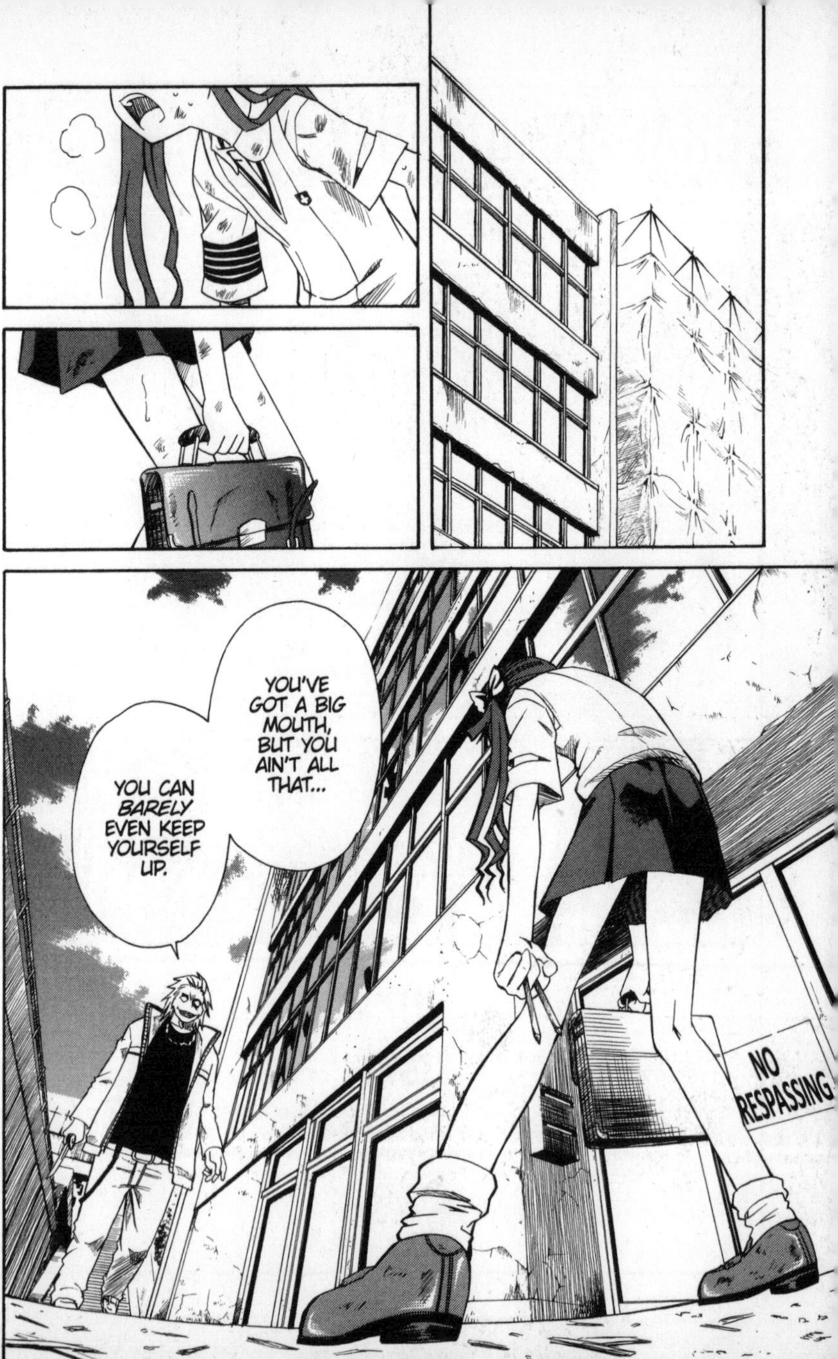
YOU'VE GOT A BIG MOUTH, BUT YOU AIN'T ALL THAT...
YOU CAN BARELY EVEN KEEP YOURSELF UP.
NO RESPASSING

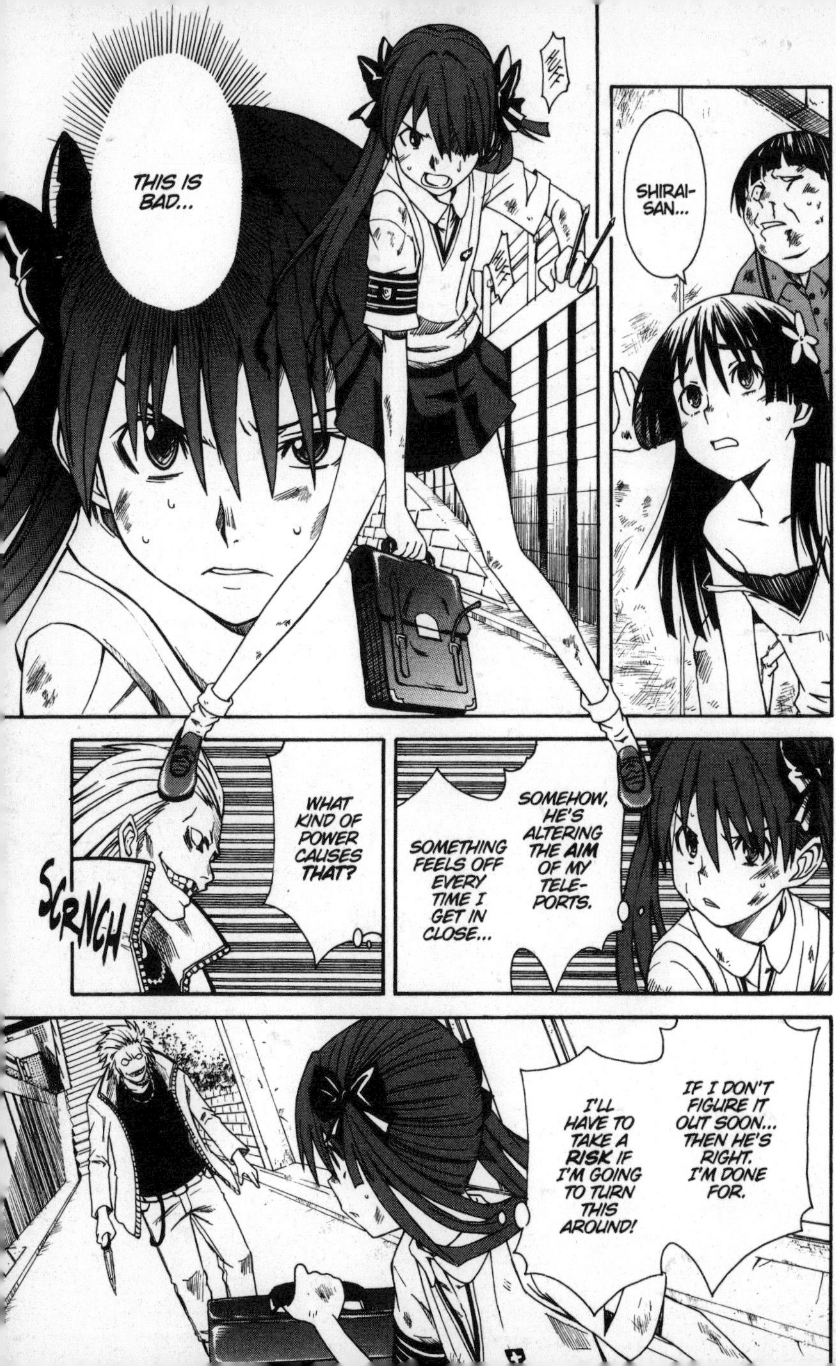
SHIRAI-SAN...
HUFF
HUFF
THIS IS BAD...
SOMEHOW, HE'S ALTERING THE AIM OF MY TELE-PORTS.
SOMETHING FEELS OFF EVERY TIME I GET IN CLOSE...
WHAT KIND OF POWER CAUSES THAT?
SCRNCH
IF I DON'T FIGURE IT OUT SOON... THEN HE'S RIGHT. I'M DONE FOR.
I'LL HAVE TO TAKE A RISK IF I'M GOING TO TURN THIS AROUND!

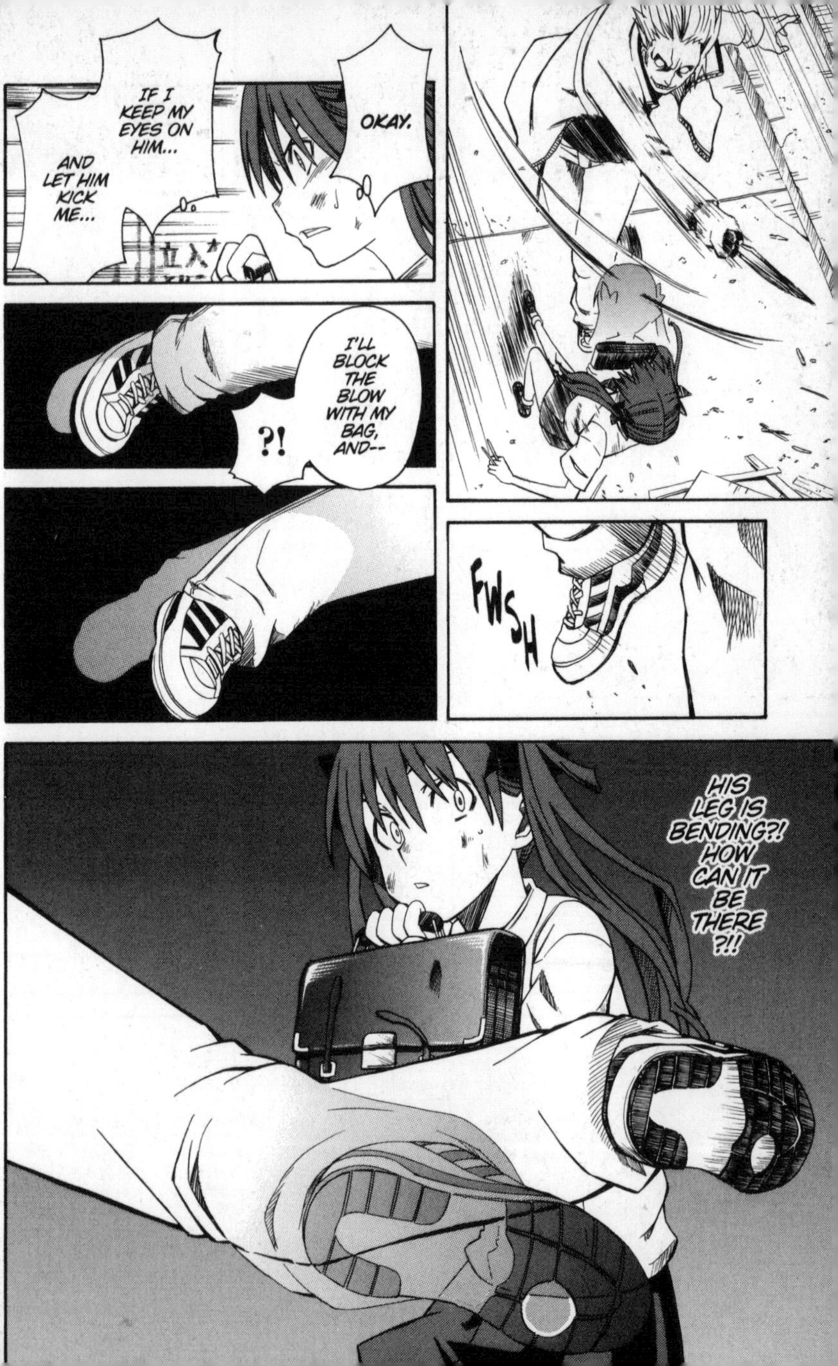
OKAY.
IF I KEEP MY EYES ON HIM...
AND LET HIM KICK ME...
I'LL BLOCK THE BLOW WITH MY BAG, AND--
?!
FWSH
HIS LEG IS BENDING?! HOW CAN IT BE THERE?!!

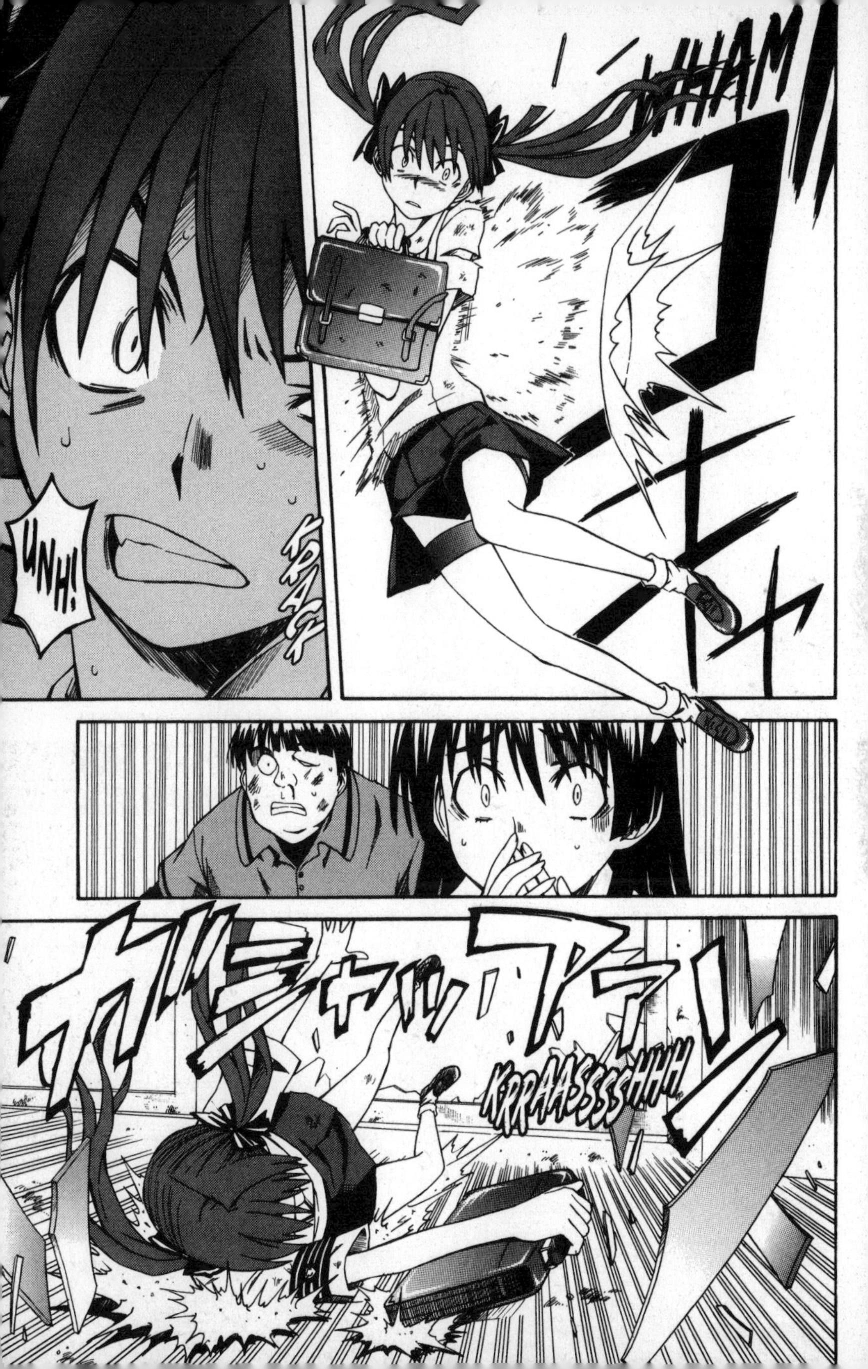
WHAM
UNH!
KRACK
KRRAASSSSHHH

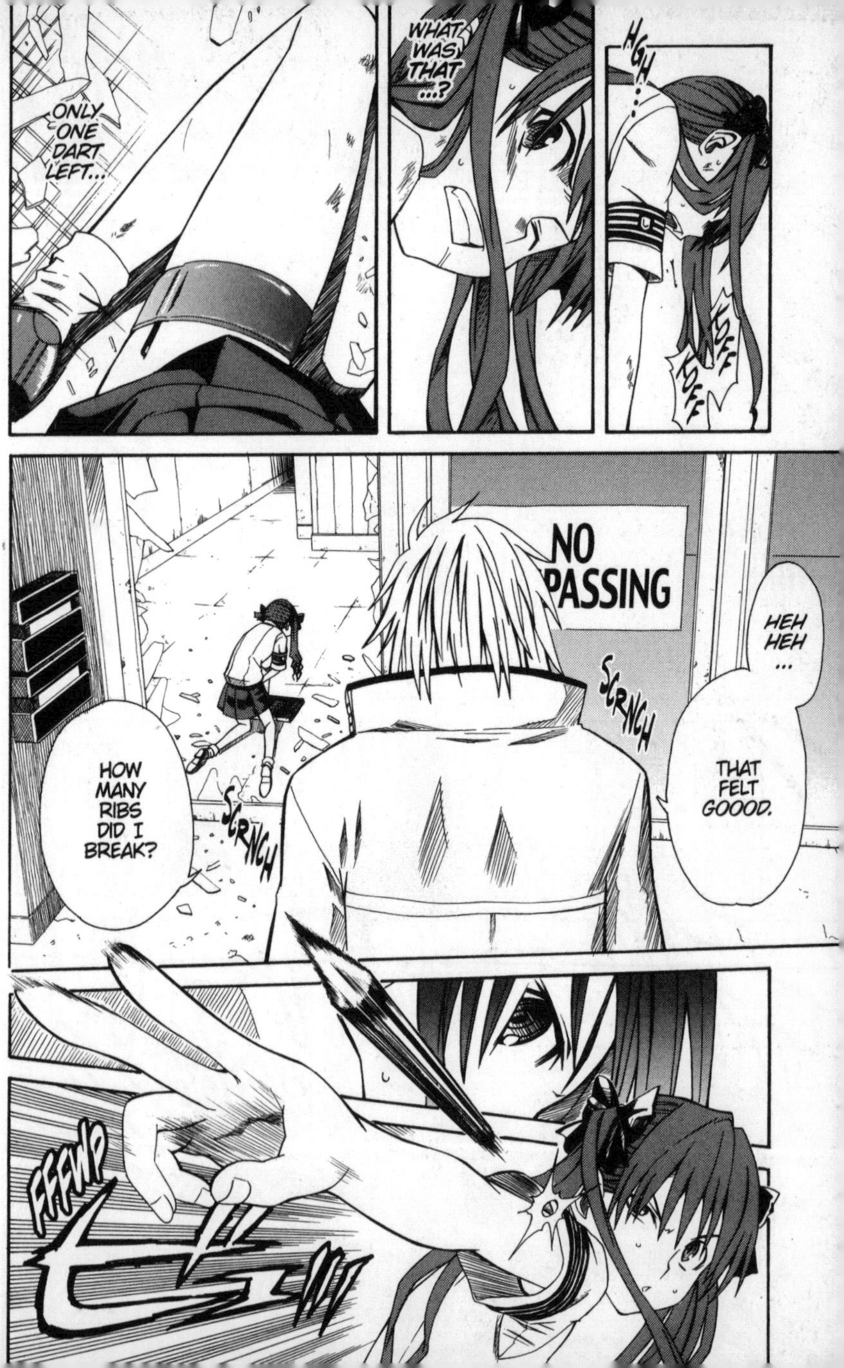
HGH...
KOFF
KOFF
WHAT WAS THAT ...?
ONLY ONE DART LEFT...
HEH HEH ...
THAT FELT GOOOD.
SCRNCH
NO PASSING
HOW MANY RIBS DID I BREAK?
SCRNCH
FFFWP

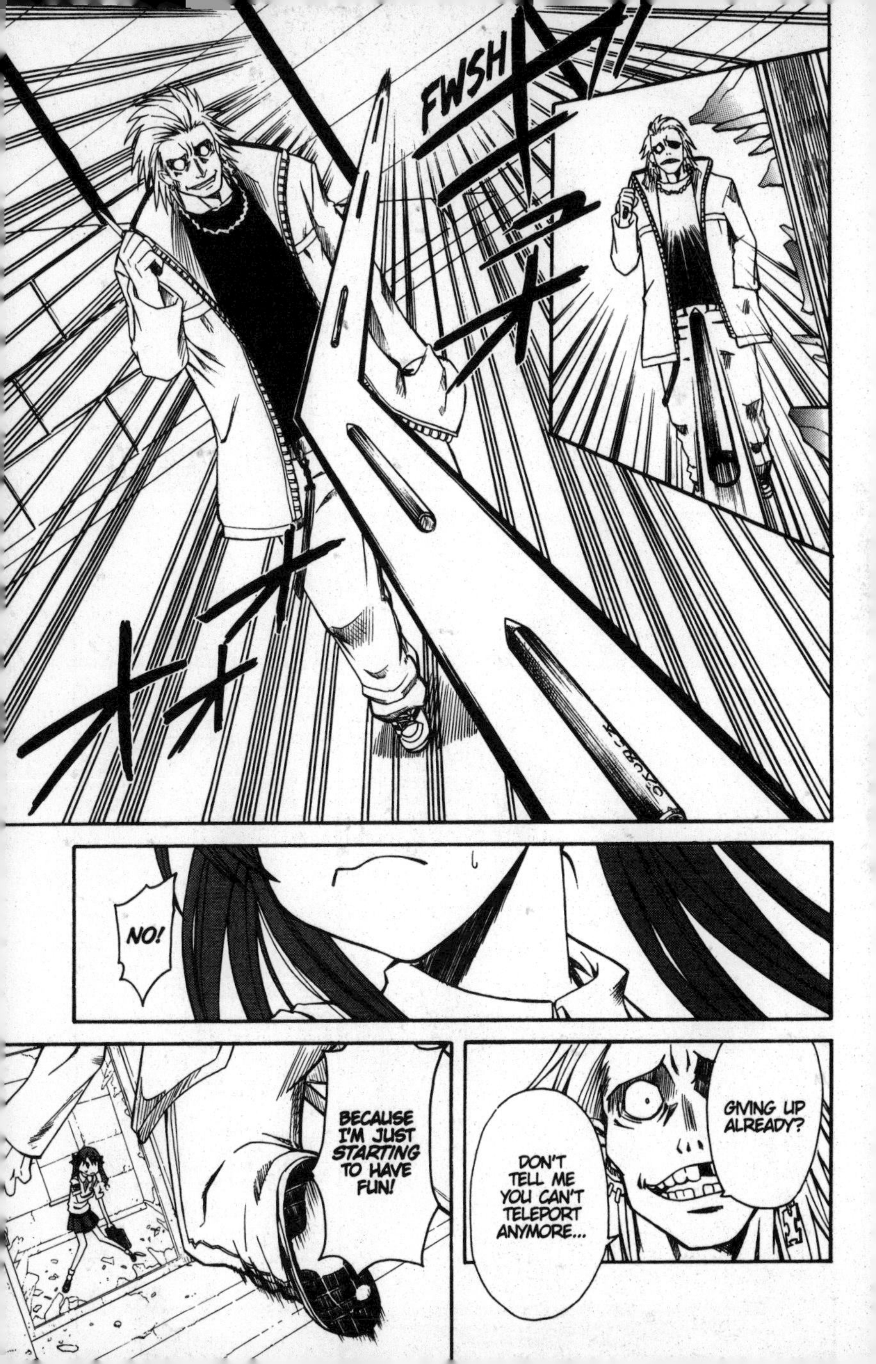
FWSH
NO!
GIVING UP ALREADY?
DON'T TELL ME YOU CAN'T TELEPORT ANYMORE...
BECAUSE I'M JUST STARTING TO HAVE FUN!

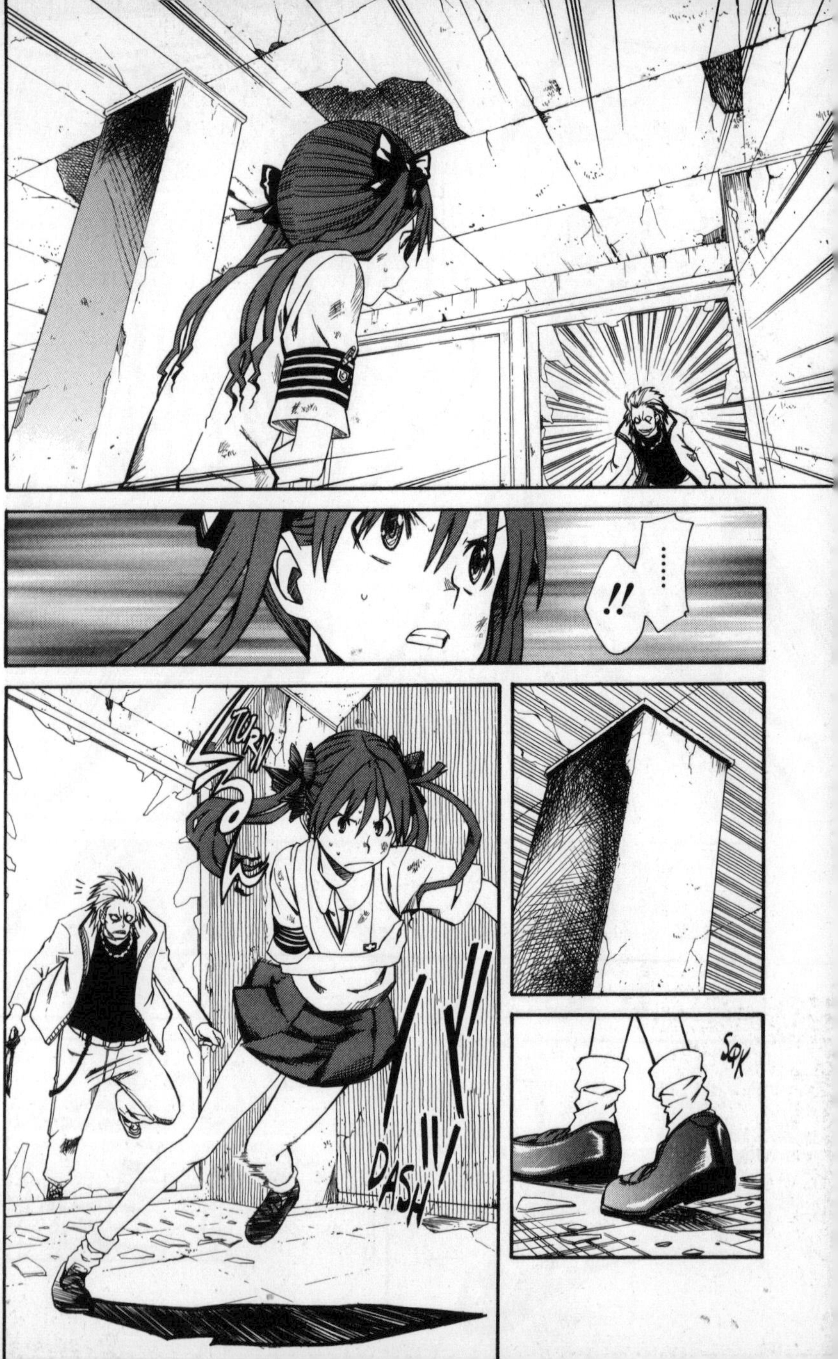
......!!
SQK
TURN
DASH

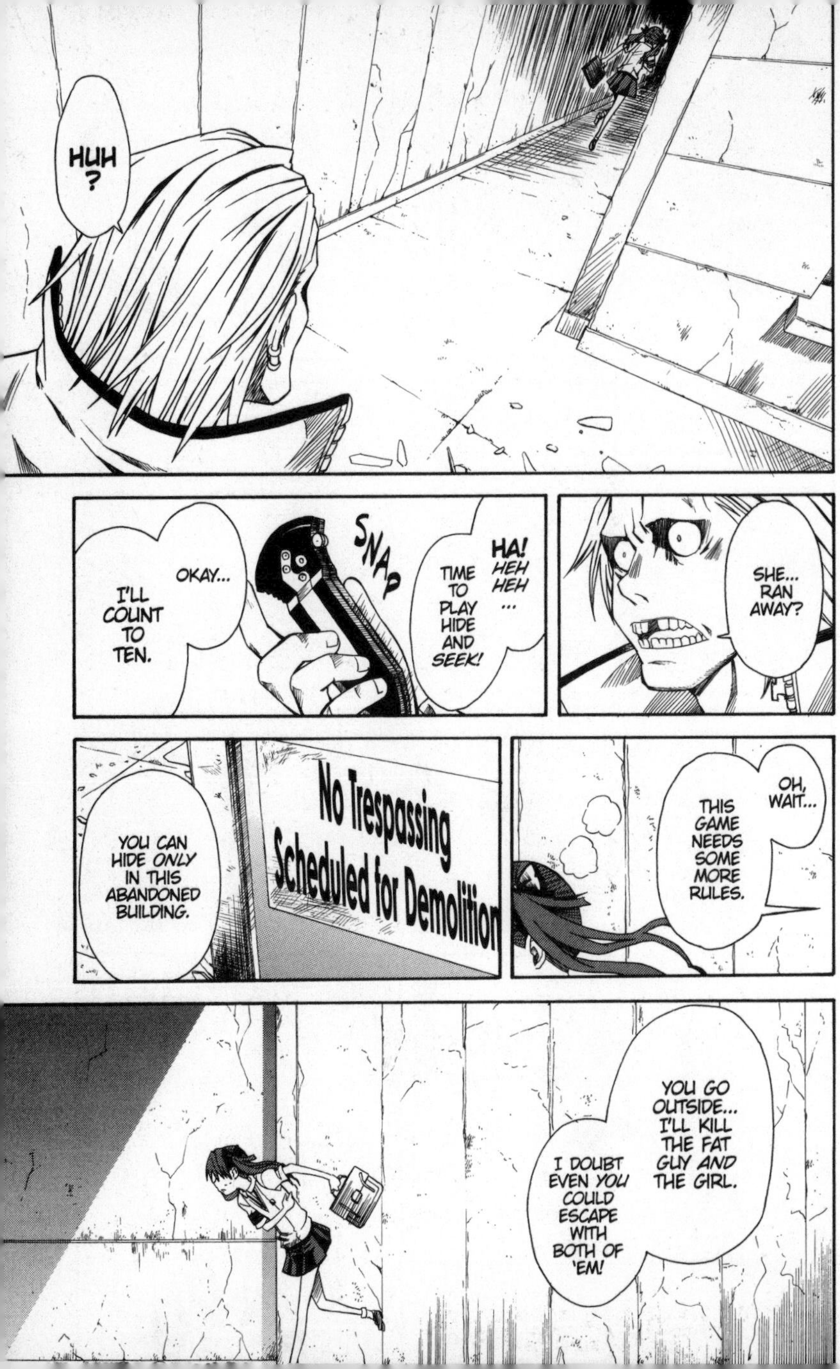
HUH?
SHE... RAN AWAY?
HA! HEH HEH... TIME TO PLAY HIDE AND SEEK!
SNAP
OKAY... I'LL COUNT TO TEN.
OH, WAIT... THIS GAME NEEDS SOME MORE RULES.
No Trespassing Scheduled for Demolition
YOU CAN HIDE ONLY IN THIS ABANDONED BUILDING.
YOU GO OUTSIDE... I'LL KILL THE FAT GUY AND THE GIRL.
I DOUBT EVEN YOU COULD ESCAPE WITH BOTH OF 'EM!

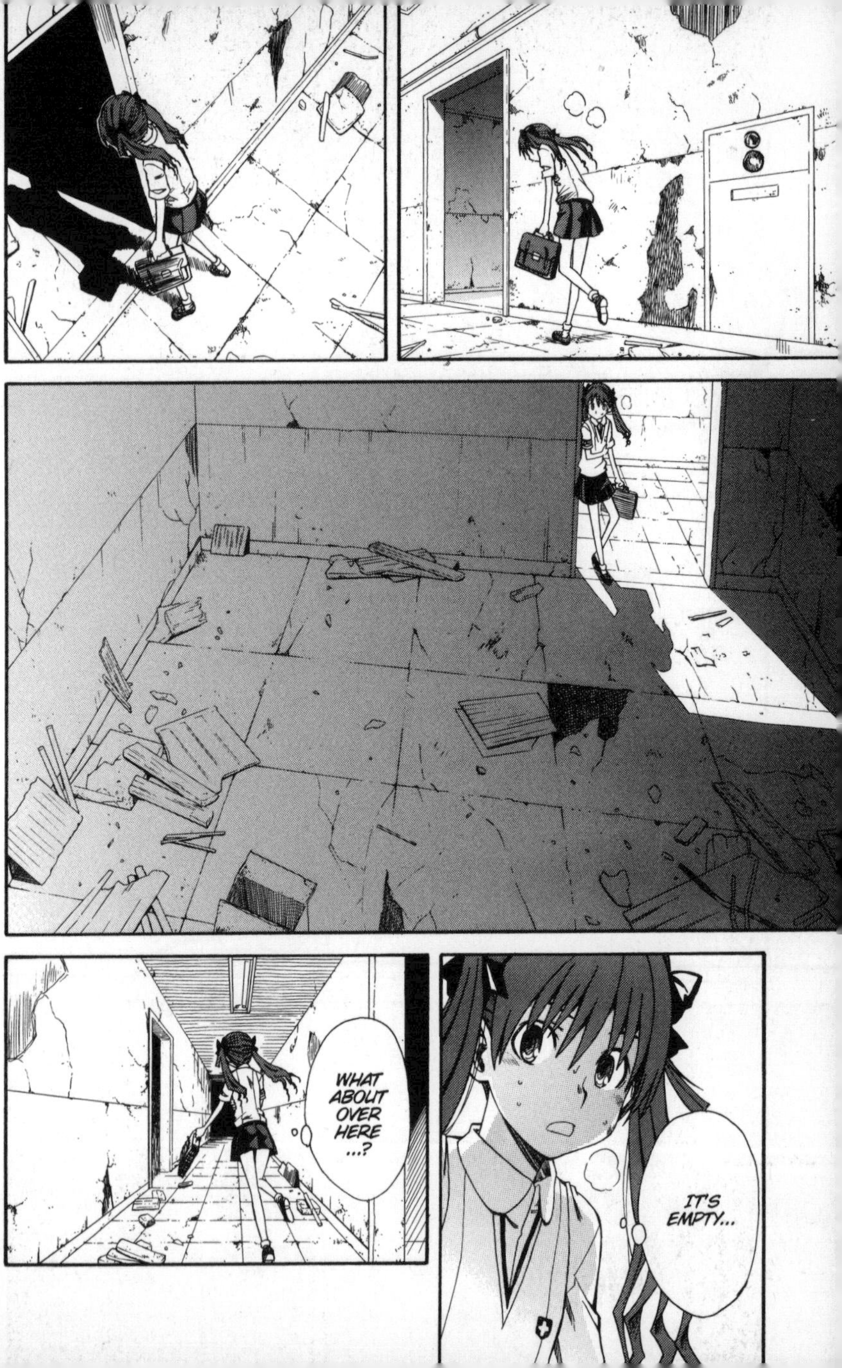
IT'S EMPTY...
WHAT ABOUT OVER HERE ...?

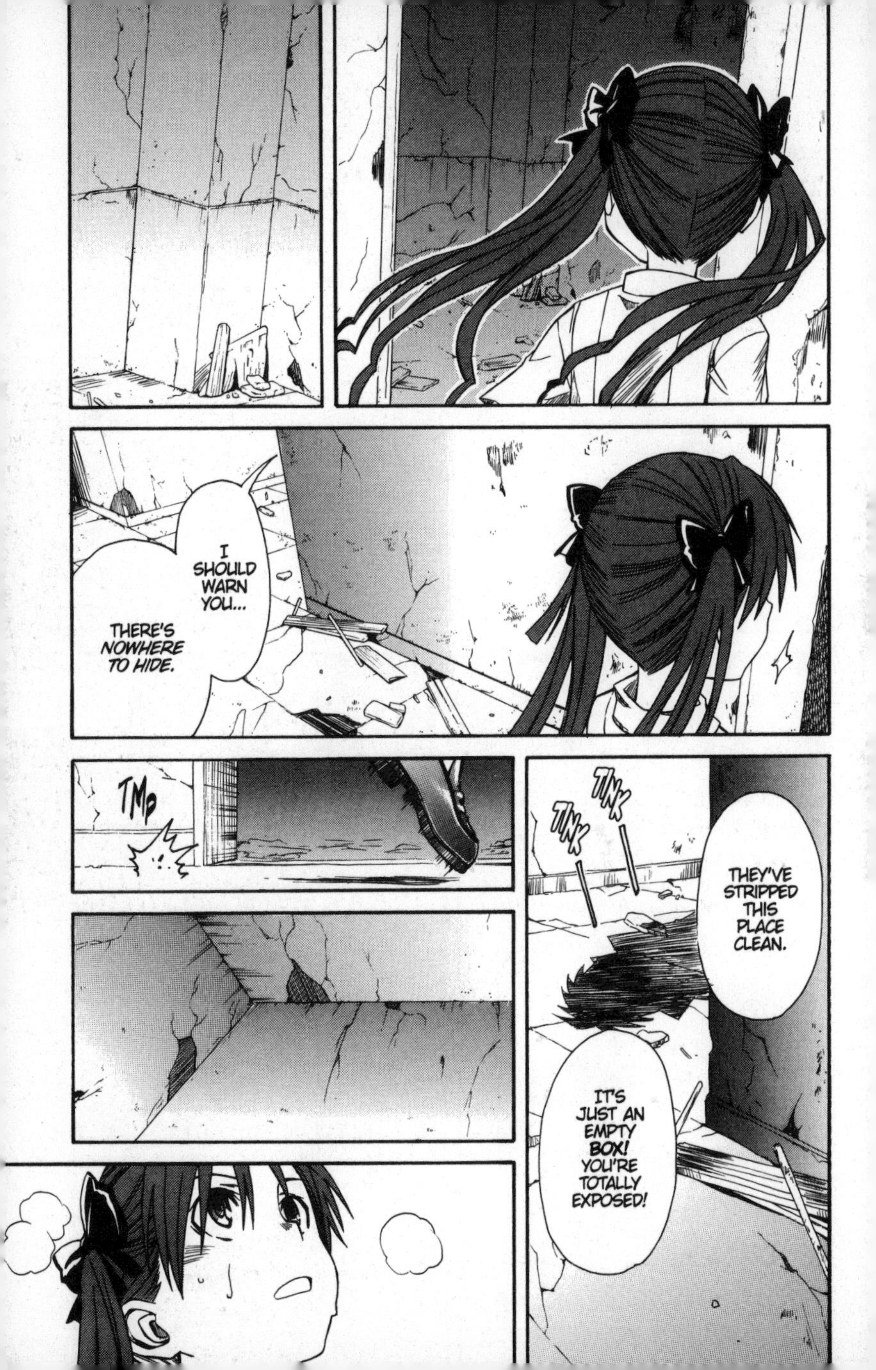
I SHOULD WARN YOU...
THERE'S NOWHERE TO HIDE.
TINK
TINK
THEY'VE STRIPPED THIS PLACE CLEAN.
IT'S JUST AN EMPTY BOX! YOU'RE TOTALLY EXPOSED!
TMP

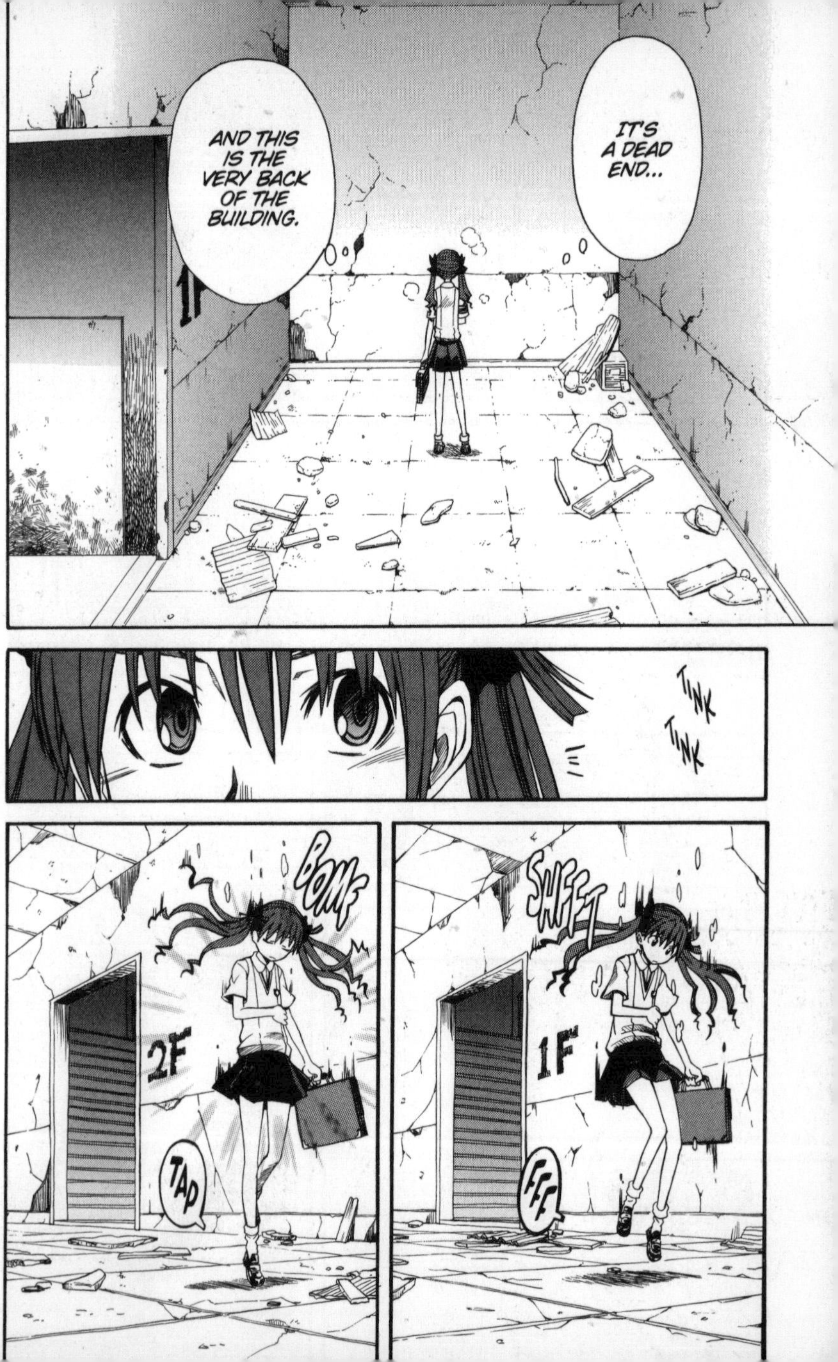
IT'S A DEAD END...
AND THIS IS THE VERY BACK OF THE BUILDING.
1F
TINK
TINK
SHFFT
1F
FFF
BONK
2F
TAP

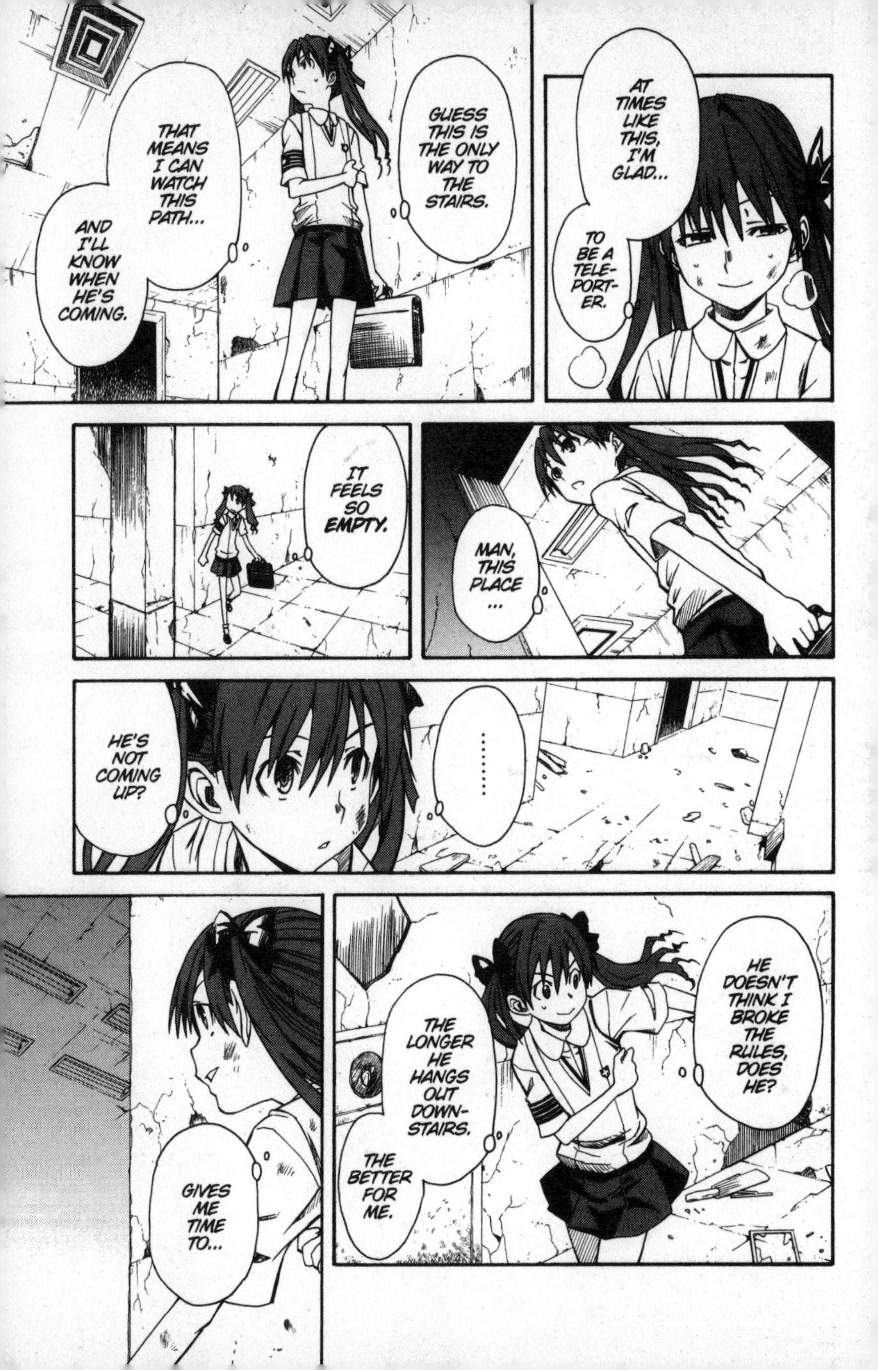
AT TIMES LIKE THIS, I'M GLAD...
TO BE A TELEPORTER.
GUESS THIS IS THE ONLY WAY TO THE STAIRS.
THAT MEANS I CAN WATCH THIS PATH...
AND I'LL KNOW WHEN HE'S COMING.
MAN, THIS PLACE ...
IT FEELS SO EMPTY.
......
HE'S NOT COMING UP?
HE DOESN'T THINK I BROKE THE RULES, DOES HE?
THE LONGER HE HANGS OUT DOWNSTAIRS.
THE BETTER FOR ME.
GIVES ME TIME TO...

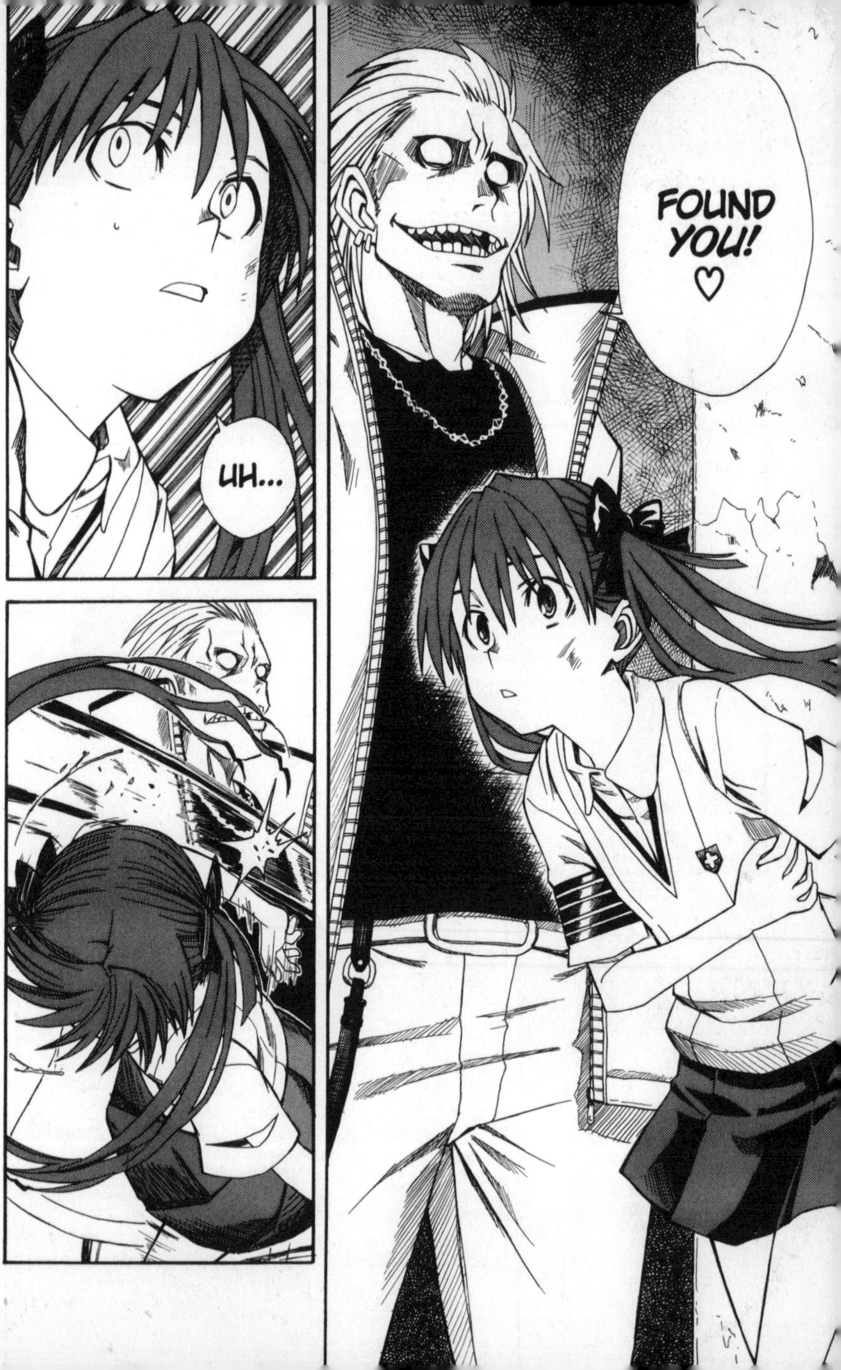
FOUND YOU! ♡
UH...

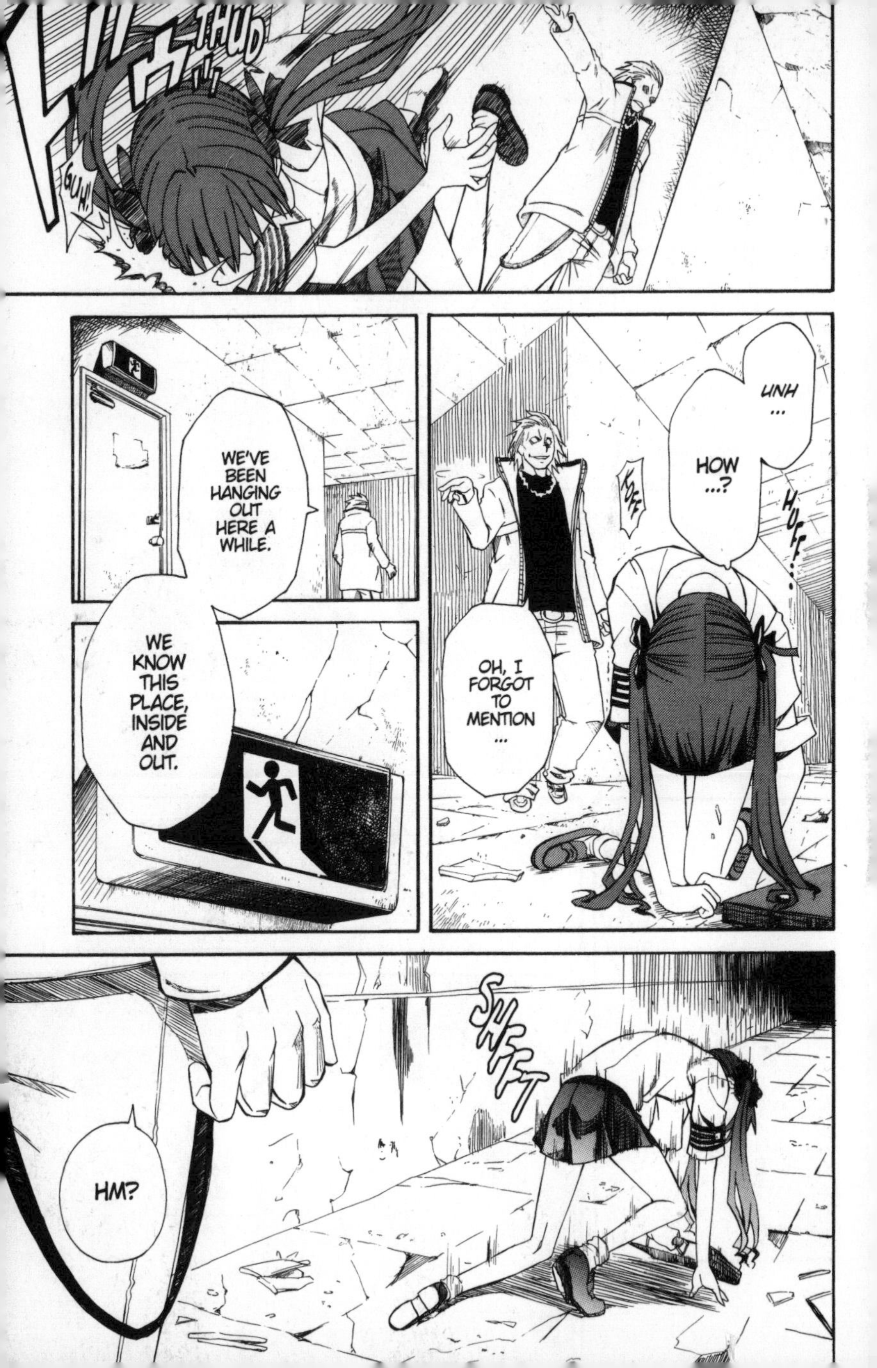

THUD
GUH!
UNH ...
HOW ...?
HUFF...
KOFF
OH, I FORGOT TO MENTION ...
WE'VE BEEN HANGING OUT HERE A WHILE.
WE KNOW THIS PLACE, INSIDE AND OUT.
SHFFT
HM?

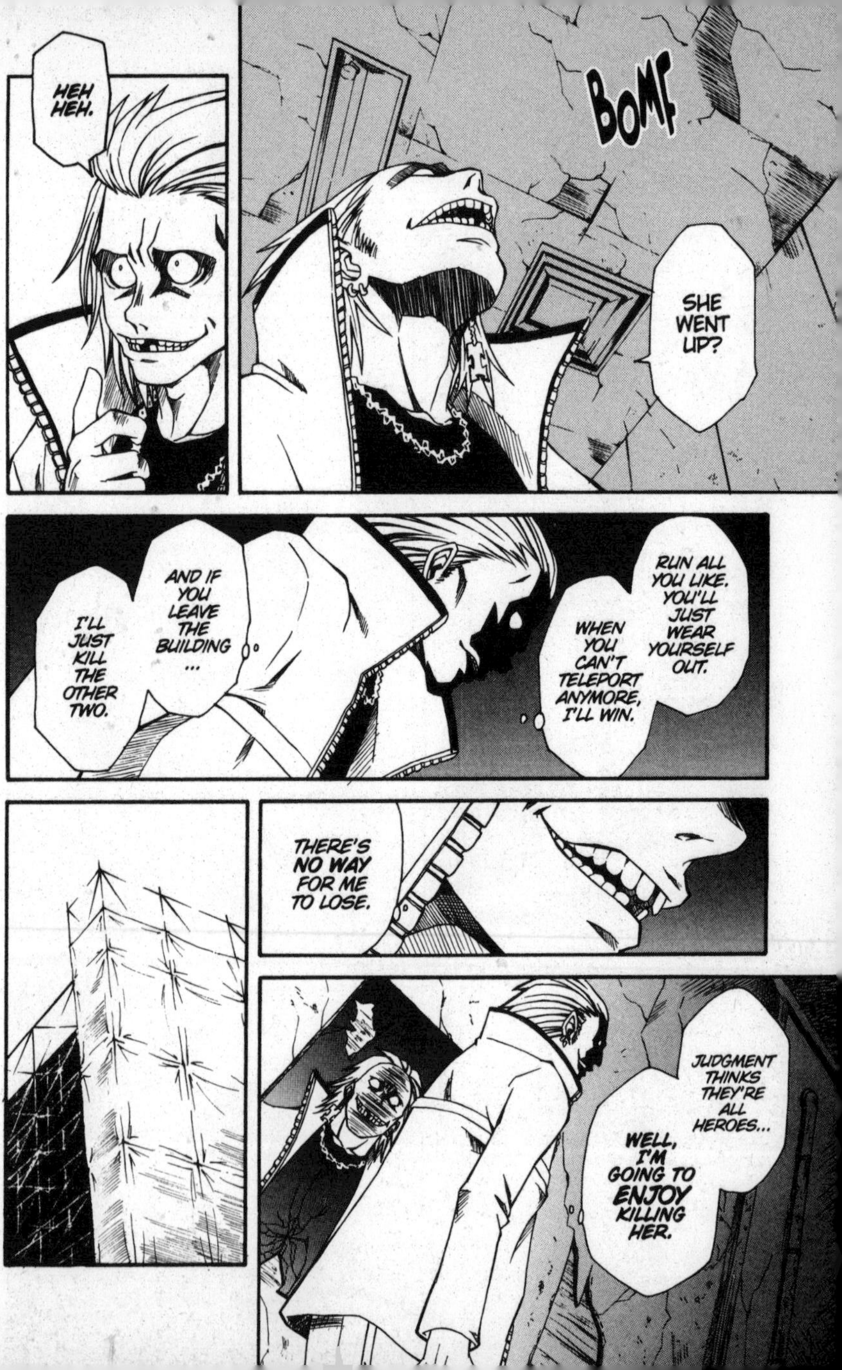
BOMF
SHE WENT UP?
HEH HEH.
RUN ALL YOU LIKE. YOU'LL JUST WEAR YOURSELF OUT.
WHEN YOU CAN'T TELEPORT ANYMORE, I'LL WIN.
AND IF YOU LEAVE THE BUILDING...
I'LL JUST KILL THE OTHER TWO.
THERE'S NO WAY FOR ME TO LOSE.
JUDGMENT THINKS THEY'RE ALL HEROES...
WELL, I'M GOING TO ENJOY KILLING HER.

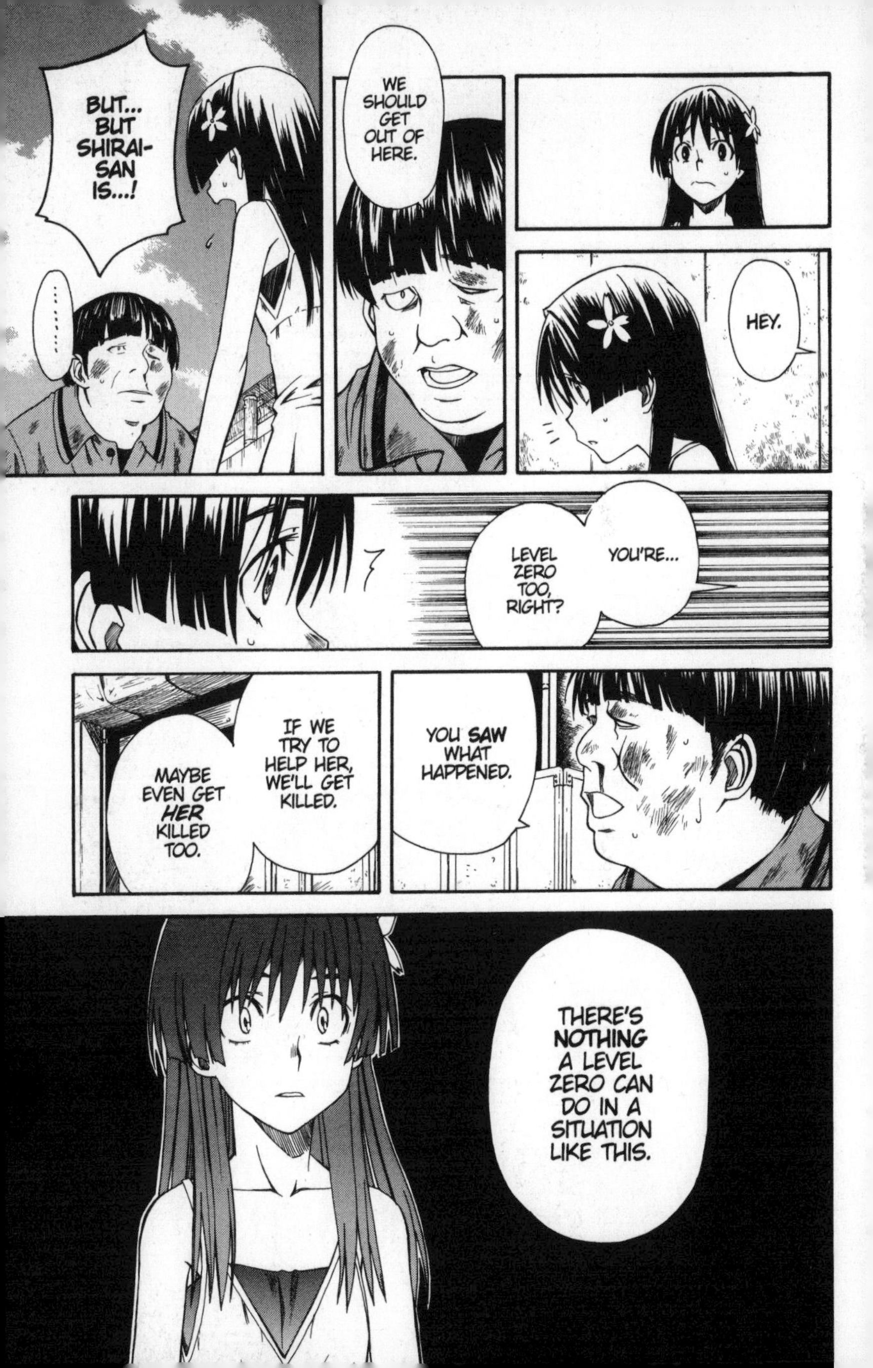
HEY.
WE SHOULD GET OUT OF HERE.
BUT... BUT SHIRAI-SAN IS...!
......
YOU'RE...
LEVEL ZERO TOO, RIGHT?
YOU SAW WHAT HAPPENED.
IF WE TRY TO HELP HER, WE'LL GET KILLED.
MAYBE EVEN GET HER KILLED TOO.
THERE'S NOTHING A LEVEL ZERO CAN DO IN A SITUATION LIKE THIS.

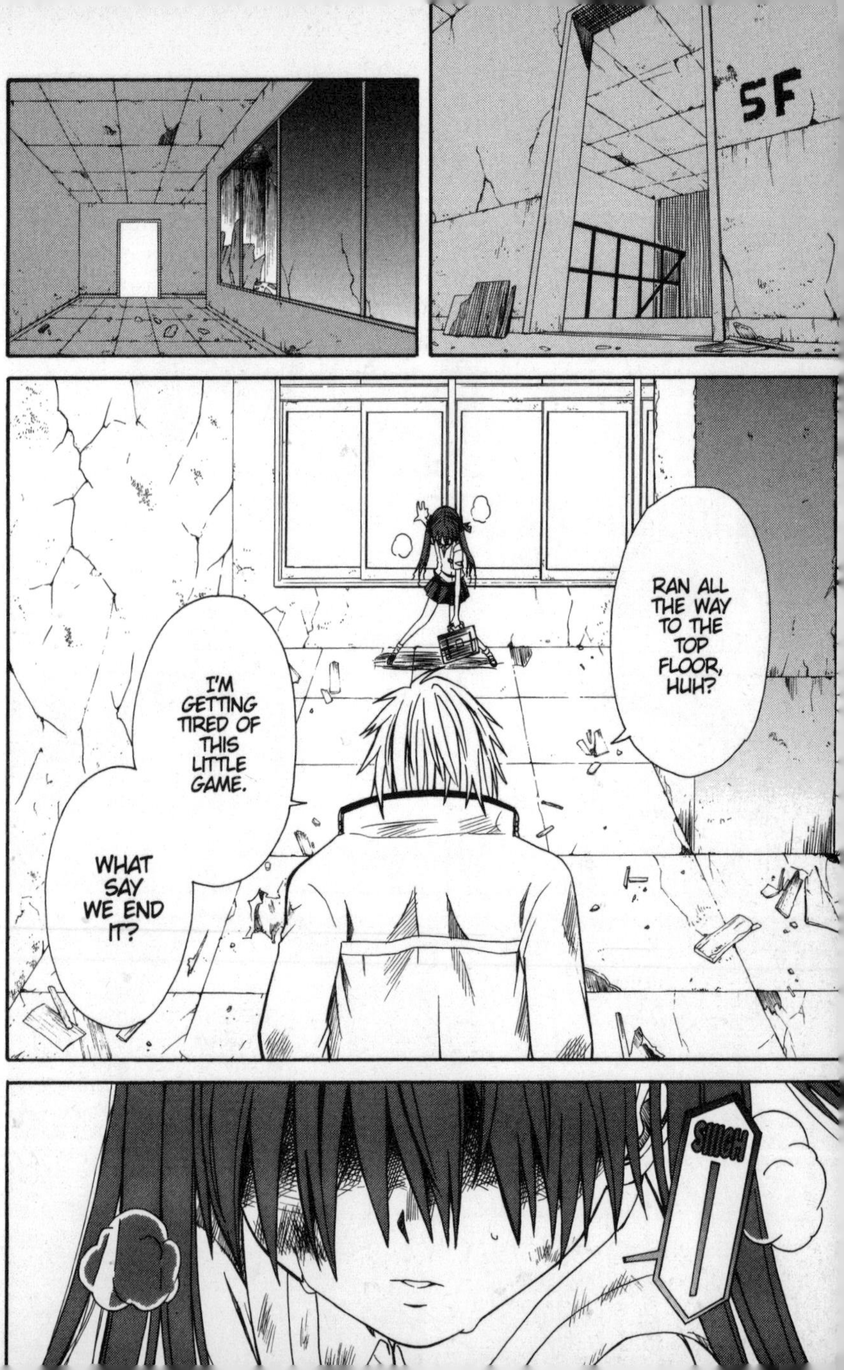
5F
RAN ALL THE WAY TO THE TOP FLOOR, HUH?
I'M GETTING TIRED OF THIS LITTLE GAME.
WHAT SAY WE END IT?
SIIGH

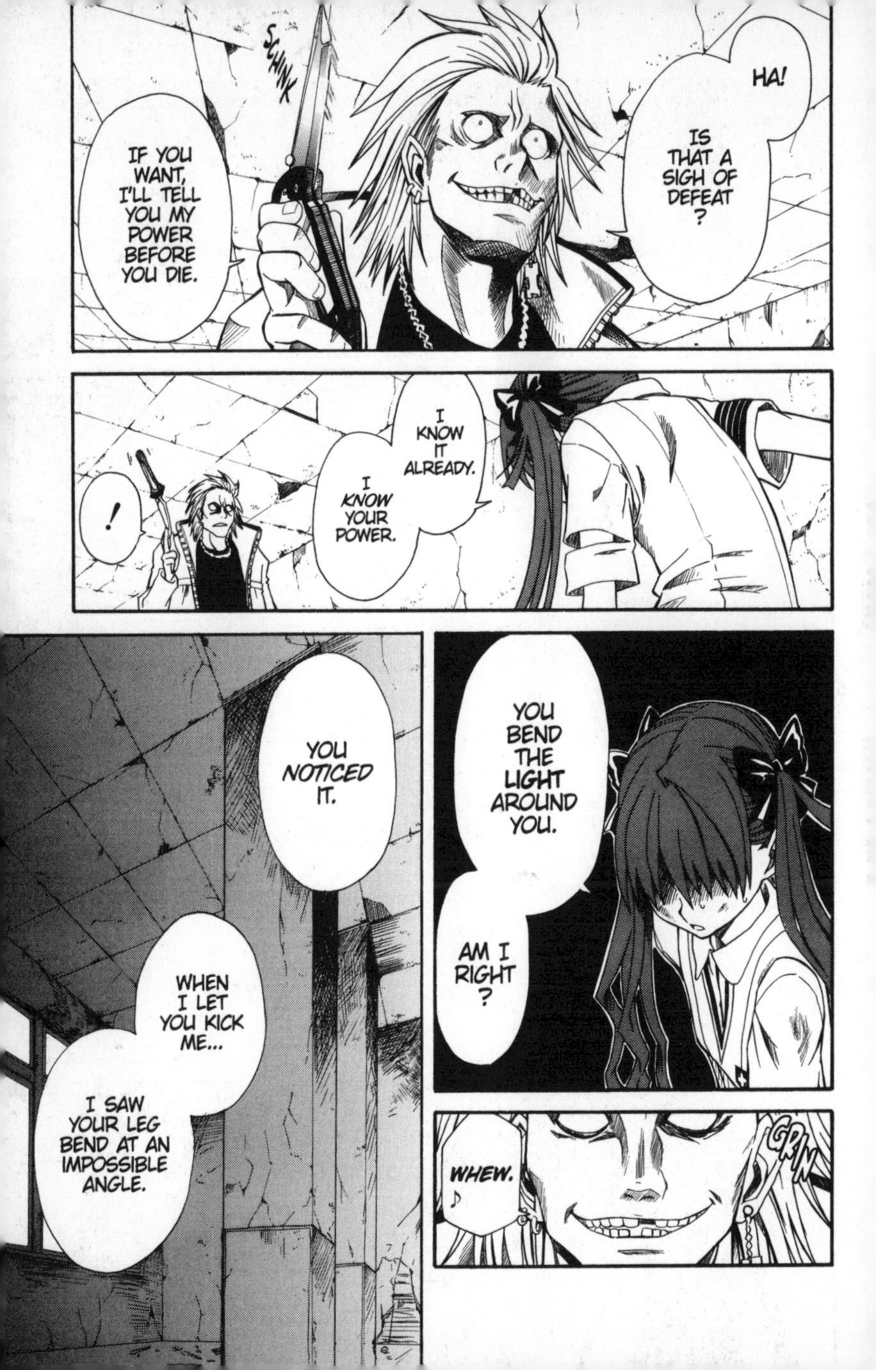
HA!
IS THAT A SIGH OF DEFEAT?
SCHINK
IF YOU WANT, I'LL TELL YOU MY POWER BEFORE YOU DIE.
I KNOW IT ALREADY.
I KNOW YOUR POWER.
!
YOU BEND THE LIGHT AROUND YOU.
AM I RIGHT?
GRIN
WHEW.
YOU NOTICED IT.
WHEN I LET YOU KICK ME...
I SAW YOUR LEG BEND AT AN IMPOSSIBLE ANGLE.

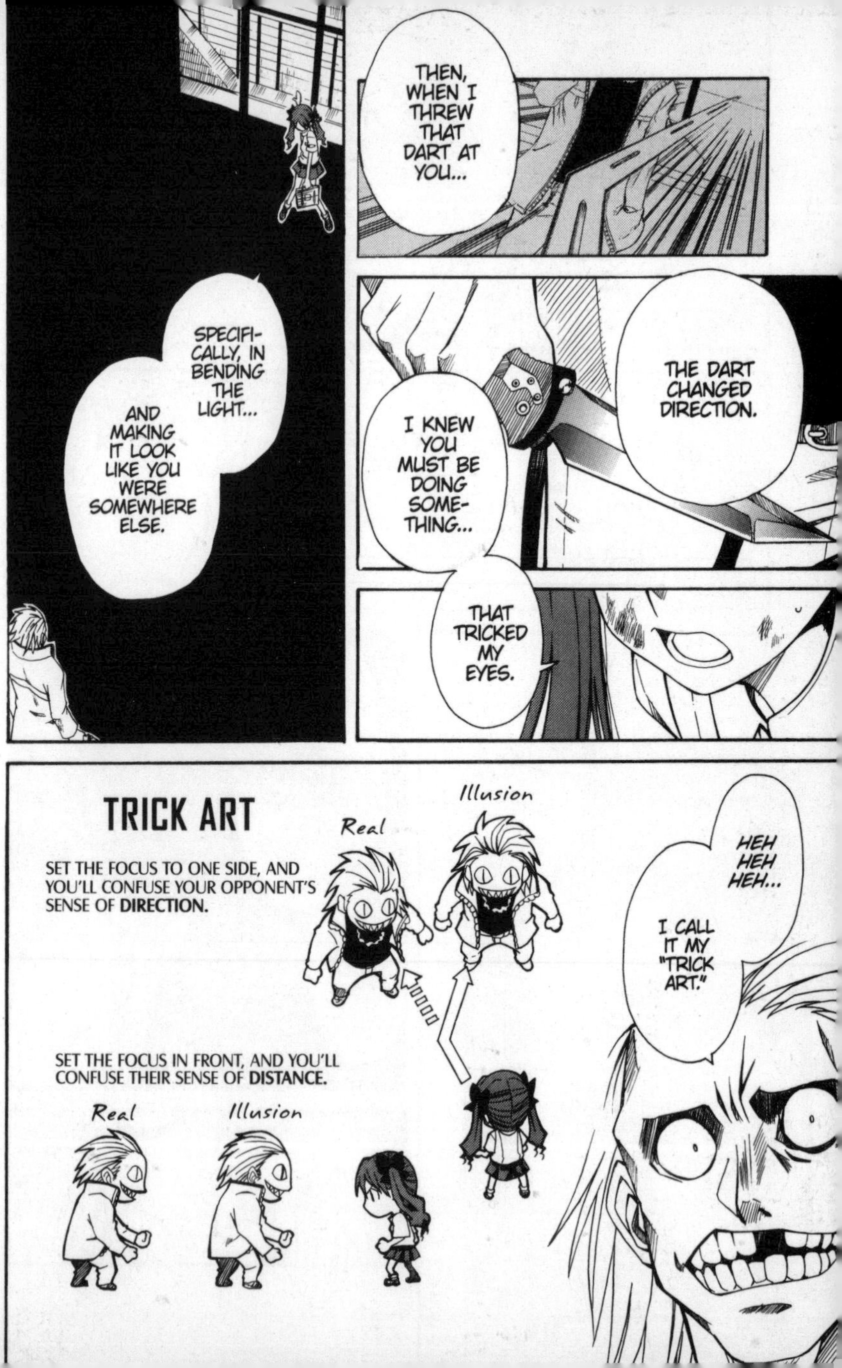
THEN, WHEN I THREW THAT DART AT YOU...
THE DART CHANGED DIRECTION.
I KNEW YOU MUST BE DOING SOME-THING...
THAT TRICKED MY EYES.
SPECIFI-CALLY, IN BENDING THE LIGHT...
AND MAKING IT LOOK LIKE YOU WERE SOMEWHERE ELSE.
HEH HEH HEH...
I CALL IT MY "TRICK ART."
TRICK ART
SET THE FOCUS TO ONE SIDE, AND YOU'LL CONFUSE YOUR OPPONENT'S SENSE OF DIRECTION.
Real
Illusion
SET THE FOCUS IN FRONT, AND YOU'LL CONFUSE THEIR SENSE OF DISTANCE.
Real
Illusion

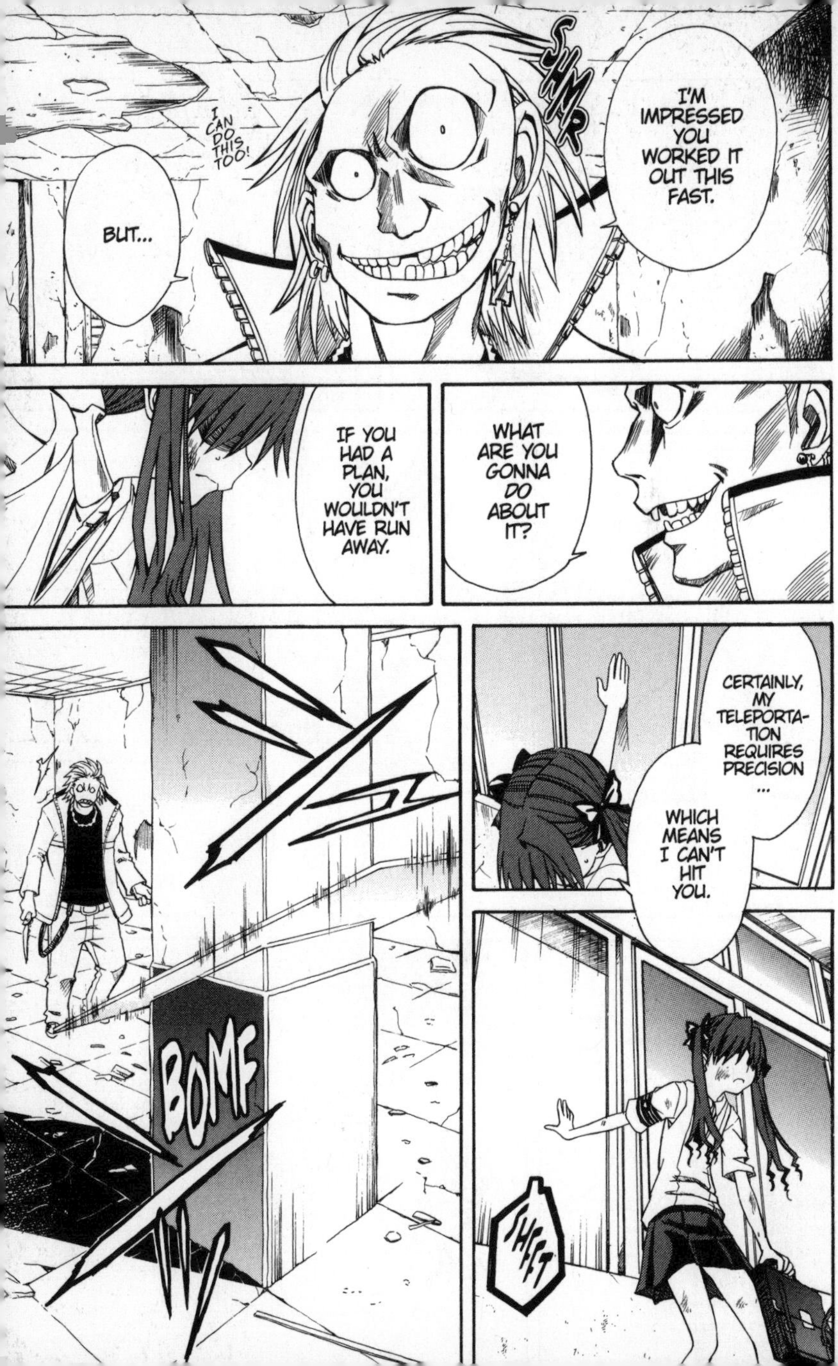
I'M IMPRESSED YOU WORKED IT OUT THIS FAST.
SHMR
I CAN DO THIS TOO!
BUT...
WHAT ARE YOU GONNA DO ABOUT IT?
IF YOU HAD A PLAN, YOU WOULDN'T HAVE RUN AWAY.
CERTAINLY, MY TELEPORTATION REQUIRES PRECISION ...
WHICH MEANS I CAN'T HIT YOU.
SHFFT
BOMF

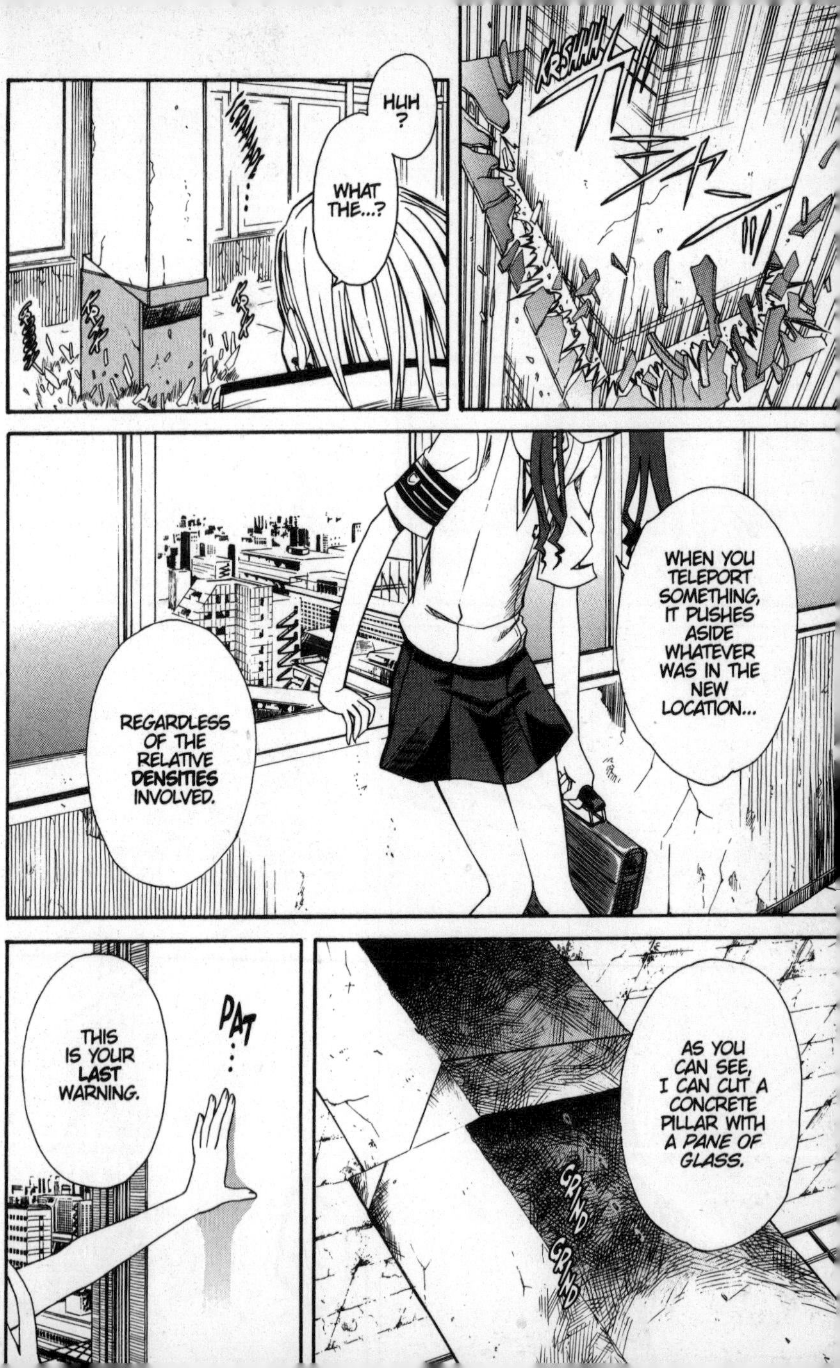
KRSHHH
HUH?
WHAT THE...?
WHEN YOU TELEPORT SOMETHING, IT PUSHES ASIDE WHATEVER WAS IN THE NEW LOCATION...
REGARDLESS OF THE RELATIVE DENSITIES INVOLVED.
AS YOU CAN SEE, I CAN CUT A CONCRETE PILLAR WITH A *PANE OF GLASS.*
GRIND GRIND
THIS IS YOUR LAST WARNING.
PAT...

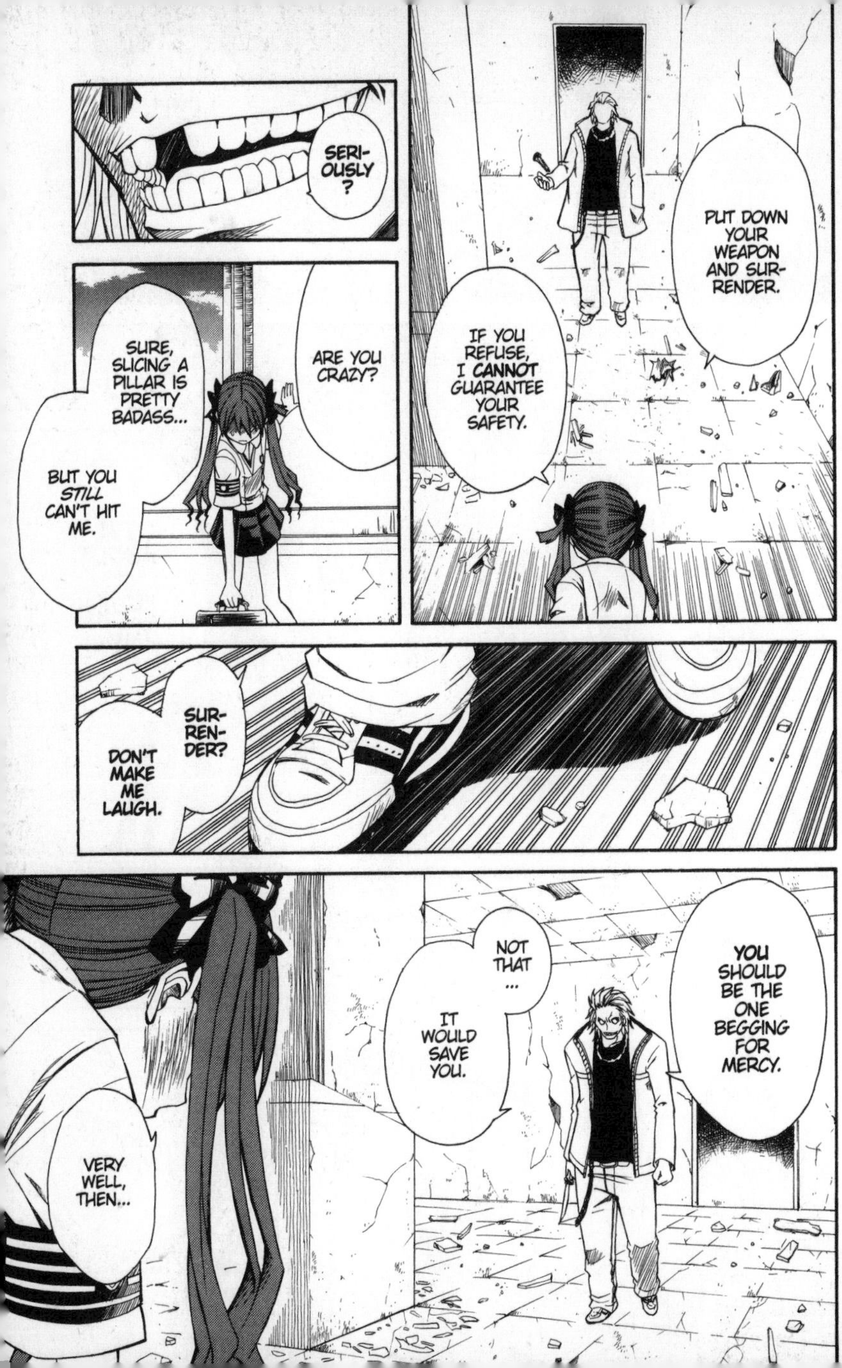
PUT DOWN YOUR WEAPON AND SURRENDER.
IF YOU REFUSE, I CANNOT GUARANTEE YOUR SAFETY.
SERIOUSLY?
ARE YOU CRAZY?
SURE, SLICING A PILLAR IS PRETTY BADASS...
BUT YOU *STILL* CAN'T HIT ME.
SURRENDER?
DON'T MAKE ME LAUGH.
YOU SHOULD BE THE ONE BEGGING FOR MERCY.
NOT THAT...
IT WOULD SAVE YOU.
VERY WELL, THEN...

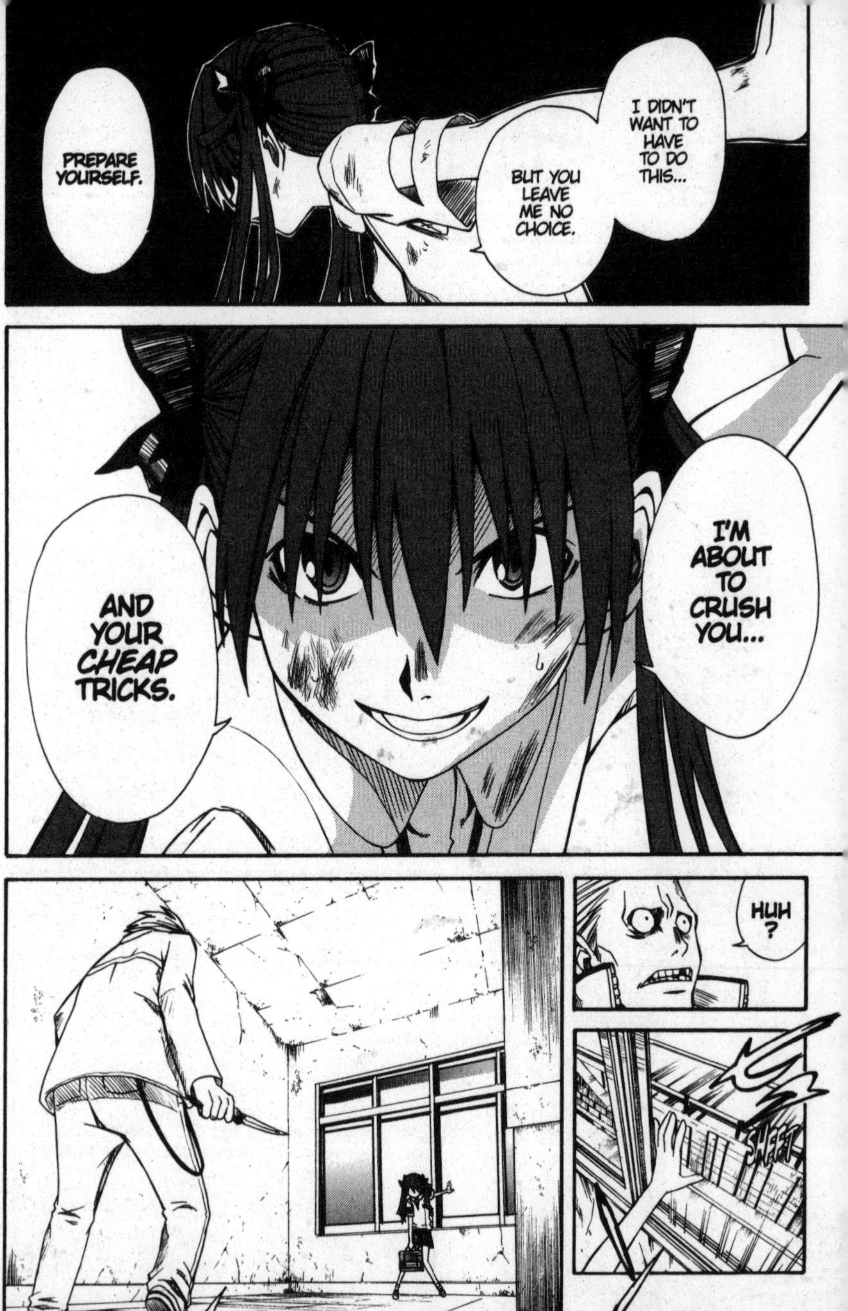
I DIDN'T WANT TO HAVE TO DO THIS...
BUT YOU LEAVE ME NO CHOICE.
PREPARE YOURSELF.
I'M ABOUT TO CRUSH YOU...
AND YOUR *CHEAP* TRICKS.
HUH ?

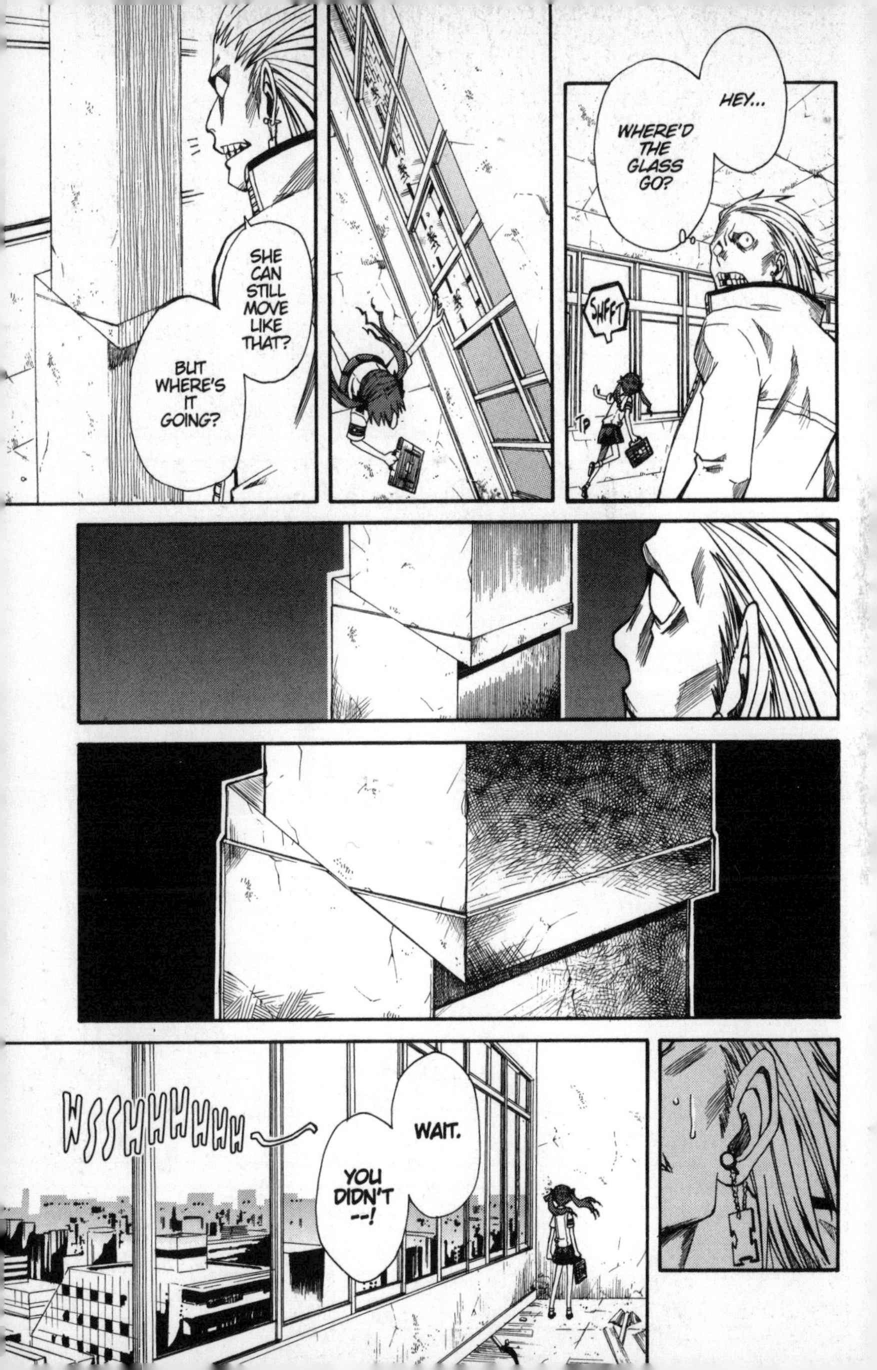
HEY... WHERE'D THE GLASS GO?
SHFFT
TP
SHE CAN STILL MOVE LIKE THAT?
BUT WHERE'S IT GOING?
WAIT. YOU DIDN'T --!
WSSHHHHHH~

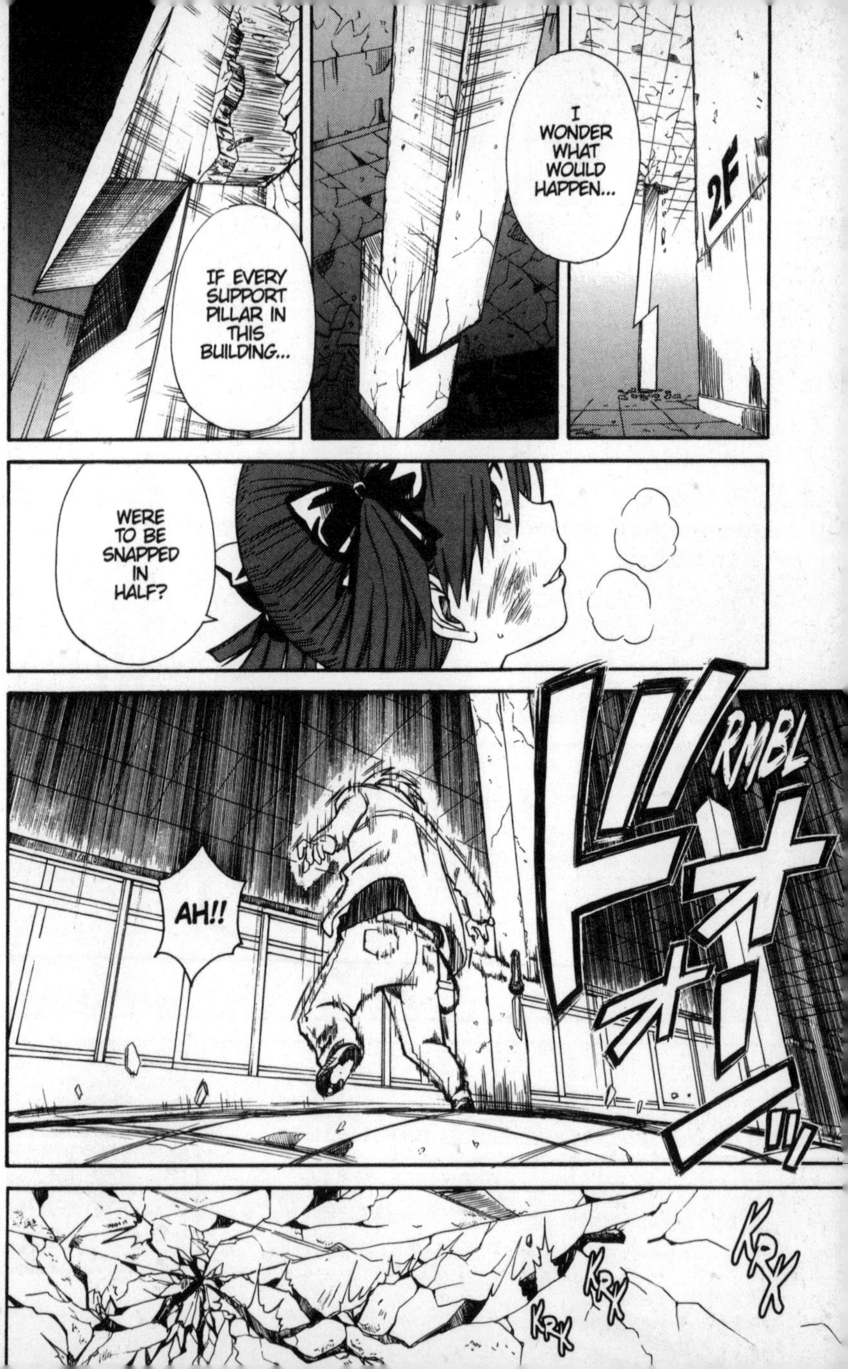
2F
I WONDER WHAT WOULD HAPPEN...
IF EVERY SUPPORT PILLAR IN THIS BUILDING...
WERE TO BE SNAPPED IN HALF?
RMBL
AH!!
KRK
KRK
KRK

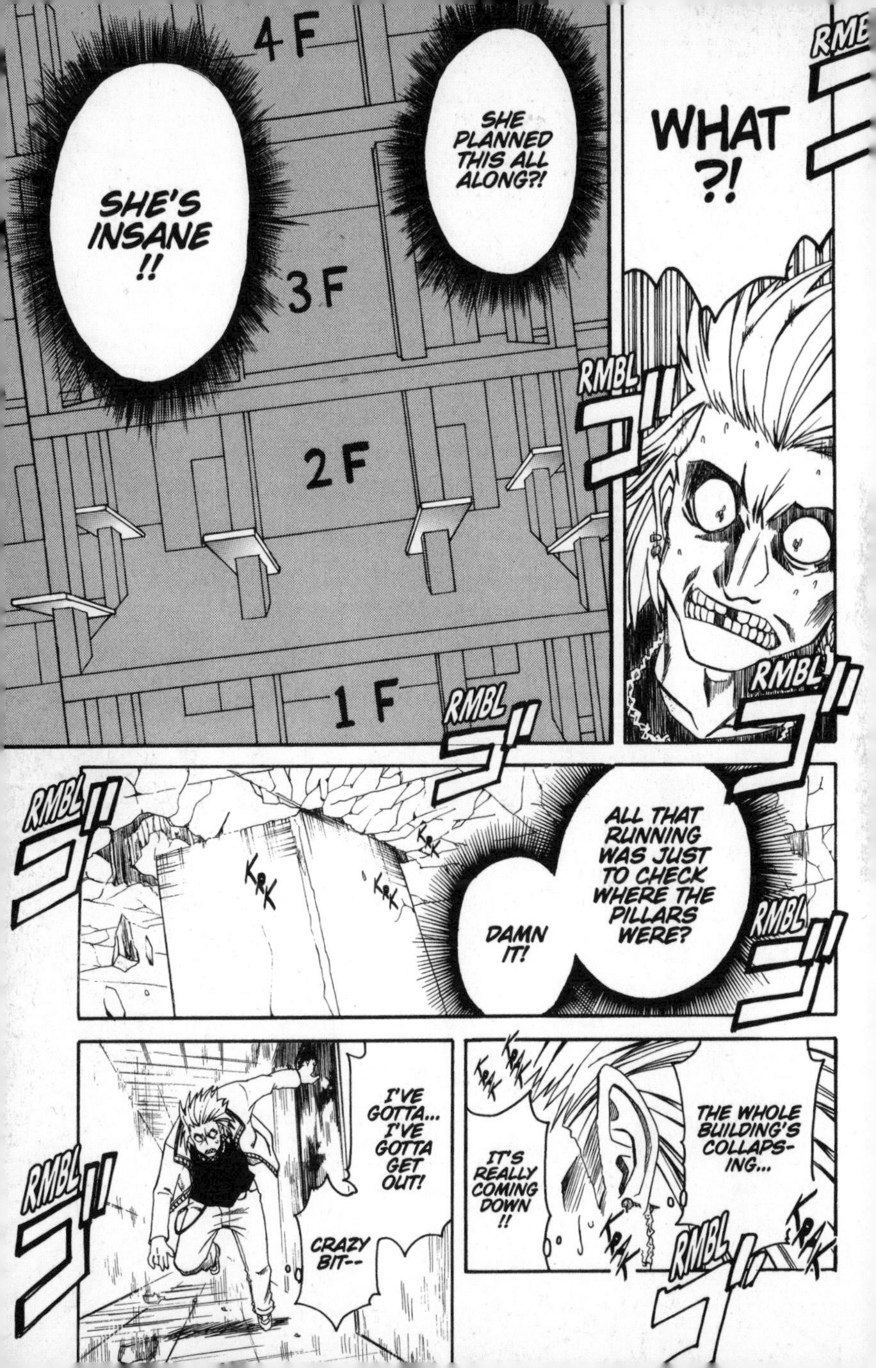
WHAT ?!
RMBL
RMBL
SHE PLANNED THIS ALL ALONG?!
SHE'S INSANE !!
4 F
3 F
2 F
1 F
RMBL
RMBL
ALL THAT RUNNING WAS JUST TO CHECK WHERE THE PILLARS WERE?
DAMN IT!
KRK
KRK
KRK
RMBL
THE WHOLE BUILDING'S COLLAPS-ING...
IT'S REALLY COMING DOWN !!
KRAK
KRAK
KRAK
KRAK
RMBL
I'VE GOTTA... I'VE GOTTA GET OUT!
CRAZY BIT--
RMBL

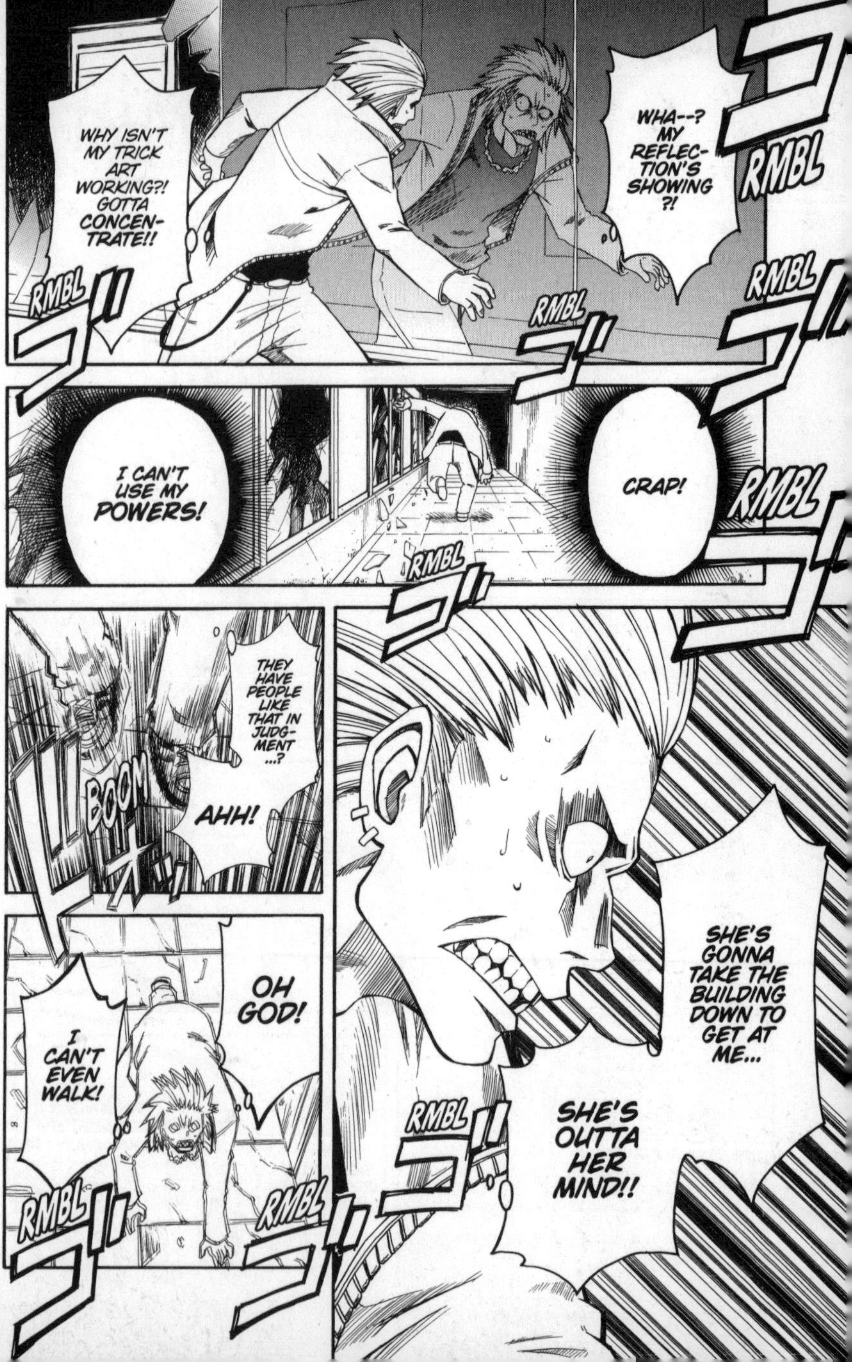

RMBL
WHA--? MY REFLECTION'S SHOWING?!
RMBL
RMBL
WHY ISN'T MY TRICK ART WORKING?! GOTTA CONCENTRATE!!
RMBL
RMBL
CRAP!
I CAN'T USE MY POWERS!
RMBL
SHE'S GONNA TAKE THE BUILDING DOWN TO GET AT ME...
SHE'S OUTTA HER MIND!!
RMBL
THEY HAVE PEOPLE LIKE THAT IN JUDGMENT...?
BOOM
AHH!
OH GOD!
I CAN'T EVEN WALK!
RMBL
RMBL

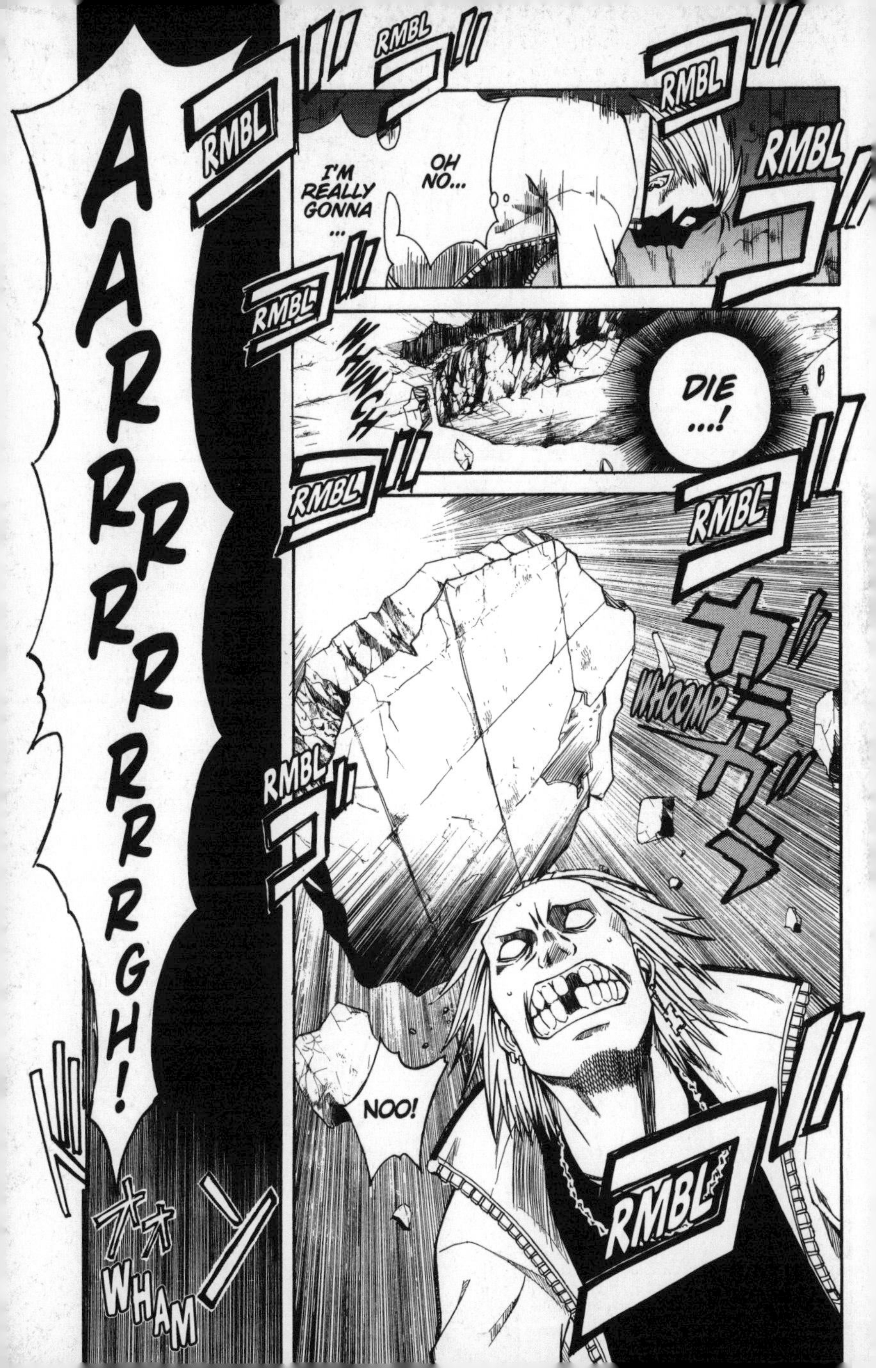
RMBL
RMBL
RMBL
OH NO...
I'M REALLY GONNA ...
RMBL
DIE ...!
RMBL
RMBL
WHOOMP
RMBL
NOO!
RMBL
RMBL
RMBL
ARRRRRRRRGH!
WHAM

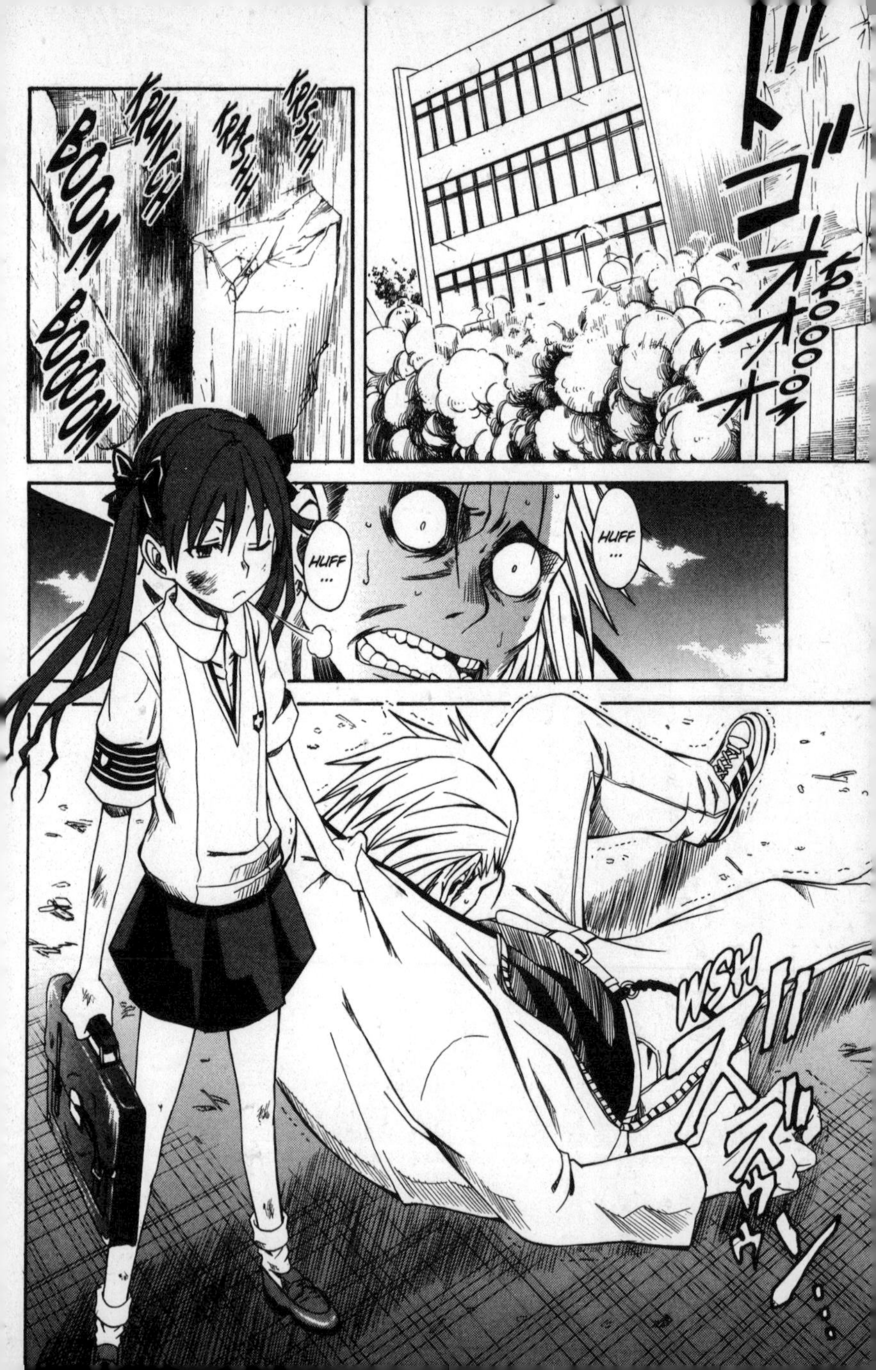
ドゴオオオ
KABOOOOM
KRISHH
KRASHH
KRUNCH
BOOM
BOOOOM
HUFF ...
HUFF ...
WSH

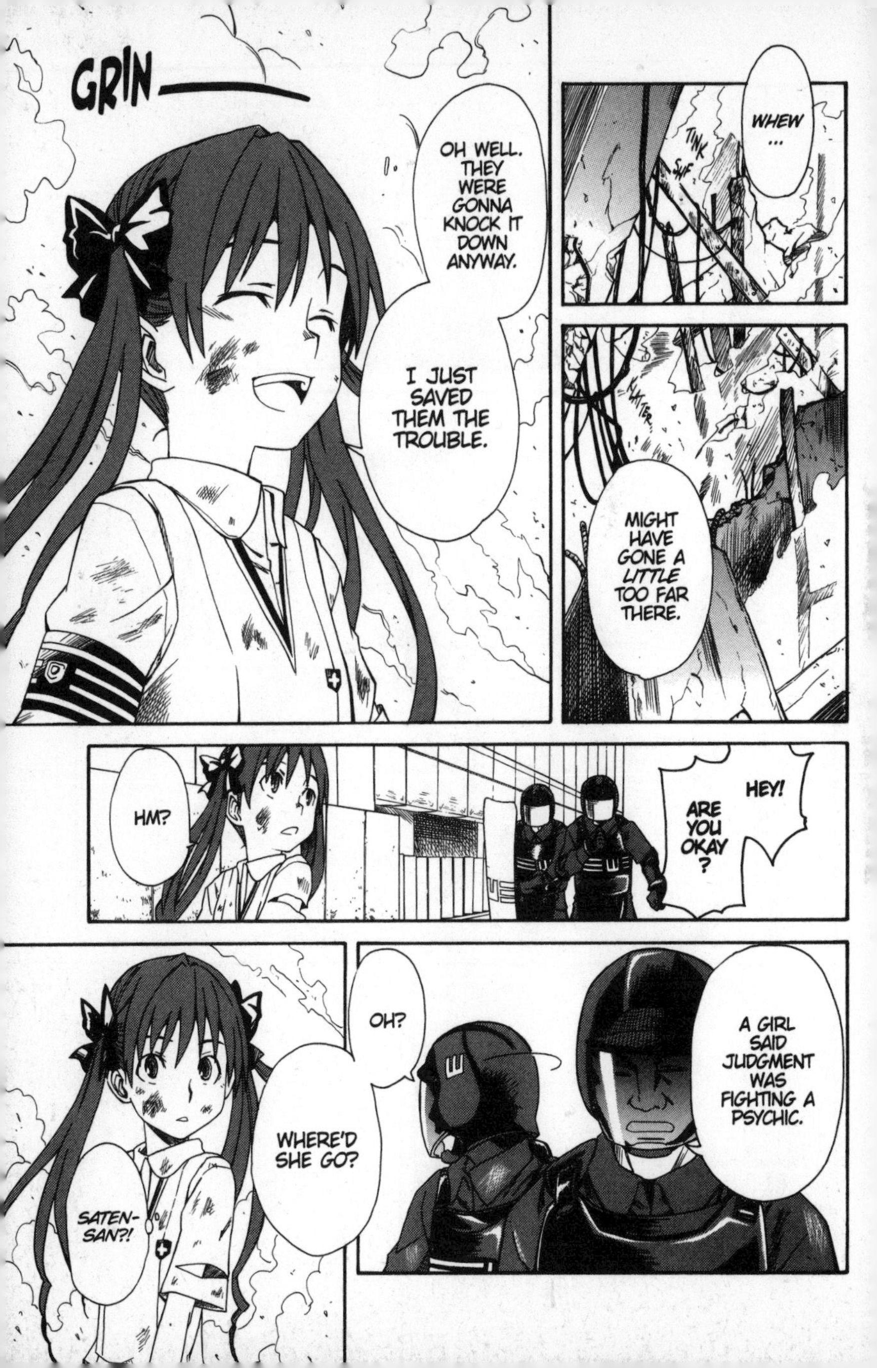
WHEW ...
TINK
SHF
KLATTER...
MIGHT HAVE GONE A LITTLE TOO FAR THERE.
GRIN___
OH WELL. THEY WERE GONNA KNOCK IT DOWN ANYWAY.
I JUST SAVED THEM THE TROUBLE.
HEY! ARE YOU OKAY?
HM?
A GIRL SAID JUDGMENT WAS FIGHTING A PSYCHIC.
OH?
WHERE'D SHE GO?
SATEN-SAN?!

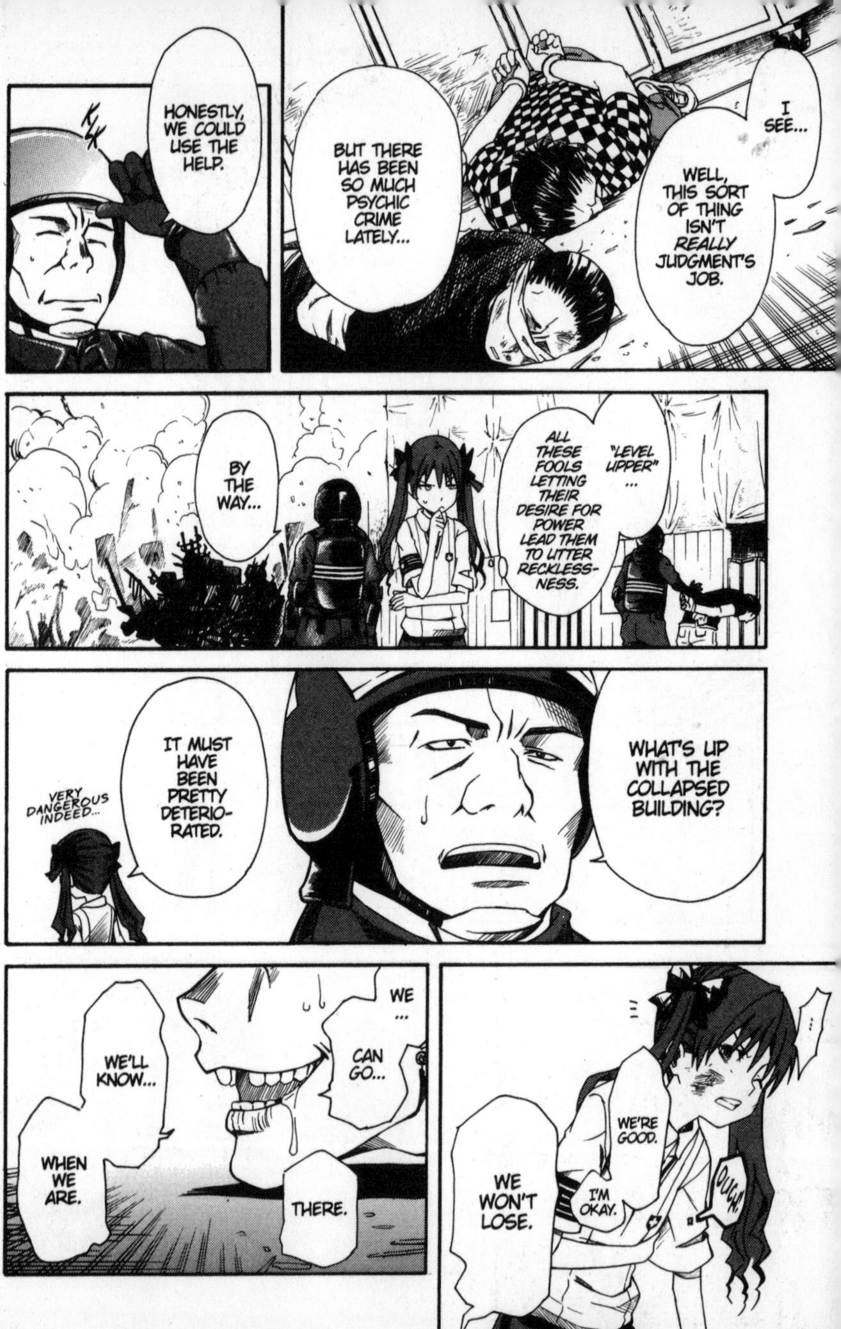
I SEE...
WELL, THIS SORT OF THING ISN'T *REALLY* JUDGMENT'S JOB.
BUT THERE HAS BEEN SO MUCH PSYCHIC CRIME LATELY...
KLIK
HONESTLY, WE COULD USE THE HELP.
"LEVEL UPPER" ...
ALL THESE FOOLS LETTING THEIR DESIRE FOR POWER LEAD THEM TO UTTER RECKLESSNESS.
BY THE WAY...
WHAT'S UP WITH THE COLLAPSED BUILDING?
IT MUST HAVE BEEN PRETTY DETERIORATED.
VERY DANGEROUS INDEED...
...
OUCH!
WE'RE GOOD.
I'M OKAY.
WE WON'T LOSE.
WE ...
CAN GO...
THERE.
WE'LL KNOW...
WHEN WE ARE.

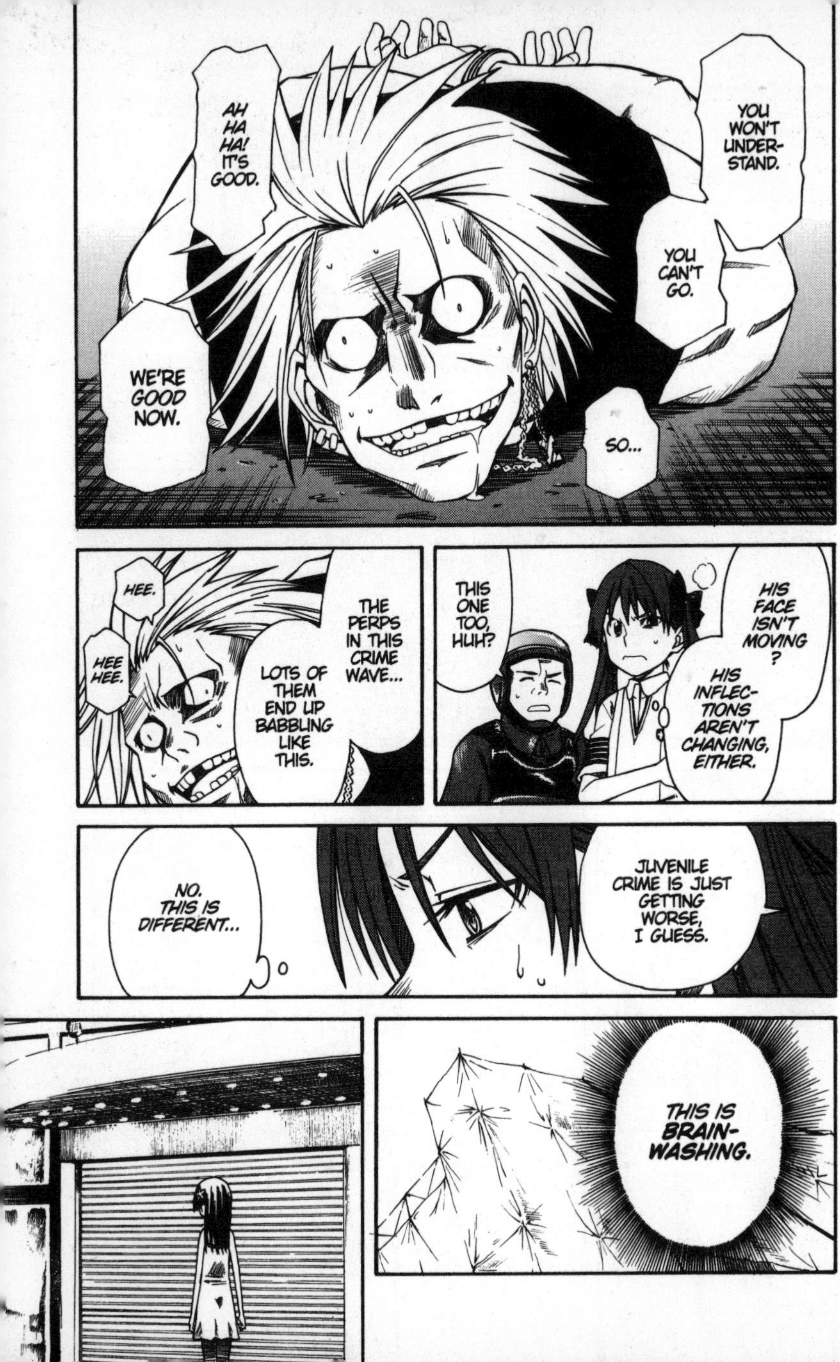
YOU WON'T UNDER-STAND.
AH HA HA! IT'S GOOD.
YOU CAN'T GO.
WE'RE GOOD NOW.
SO...
HIS FACE ISN'T MOVING?
HIS INFLEC-TIONS AREN'T CHANGING, EITHER.
THIS ONE TOO, HUH?
THE PERPS IN THIS CRIME WAVE...
LOTS OF THEM END UP BABBLING LIKE THIS.
HEE.
HEE HEE.
JUVENILE CRIME IS JUST GETTING WORSE, I GUESS.
NO. THIS IS DIFFERENT...
THIS IS BRAIN-WASHING.

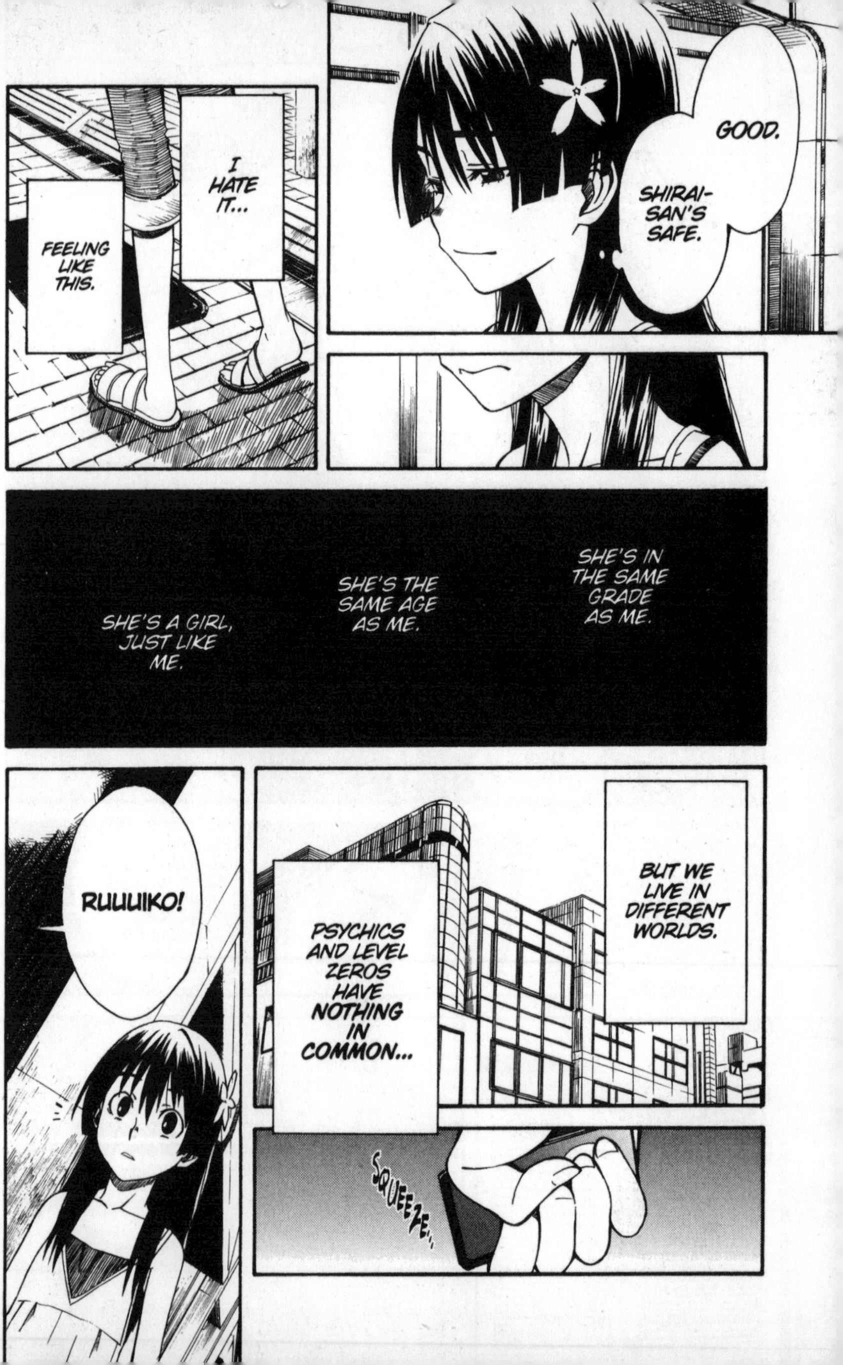
GOOD.
SHIRAI-SAN'S SAFE.
I HATE IT...
FEELING LIKE THIS.
SHE'S IN THE SAME GRADE AS ME.
SHE'S THE SAME AGE AS ME.
SHE'S A GIRL, JUST LIKE ME.
BUT WE LIVE IN DIFFERENT WORLDS.
PSYCHICS AND LEVEL ZEROS HAVE NOTHING IN COMMON...
SQUEEZE..
RUUUIKO!

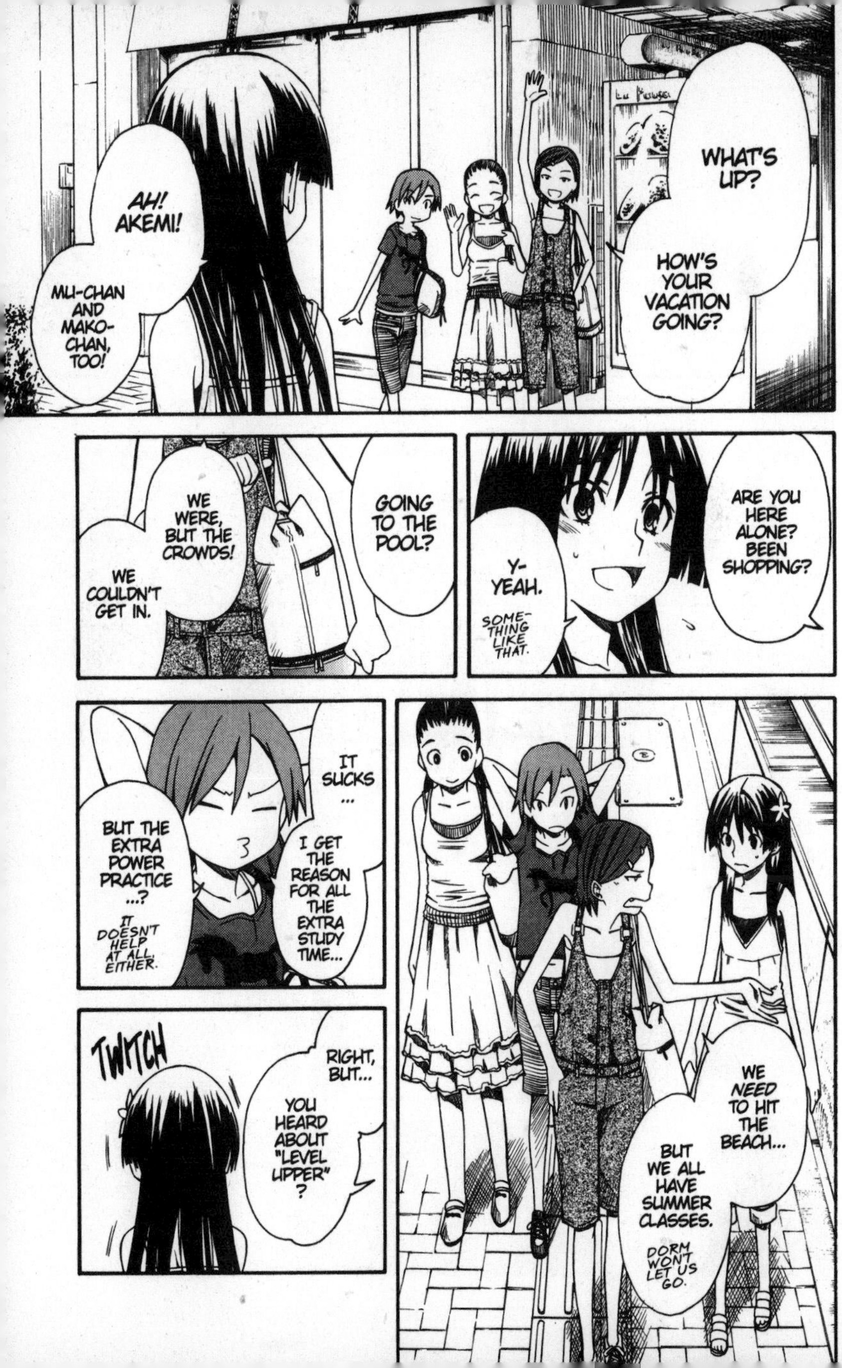
WHAT'S UP?
HOW'S YOUR VACATION GOING?
AH! AKEMI!
MU-CHAN AND MAKO-CHAN, TOO!
ARE YOU HERE ALONE? BEEN SHOPPING?
Y-YEAH.
SOMETHING LIKE THAT.
GOING TO THE POOL?
WE WERE, BUT THE CROWDS!
WE COULDN'T GET IN.
WE NEED TO HIT THE BEACH...
BUT WE ALL HAVE SUMMER CLASSES.
DORM WON'T LET US GO.
IT SUCKS...
I GET THE REASON FOR ALL THE EXTRA STUDY TIME...
BUT THE EXTRA POWER PRACTICE...?
IT DOESN'T HELP AT ALL, EITHER.
RIGHT, BUT...
YOU HEARD ABOUT "LEVEL UPPER"?
TWITCH

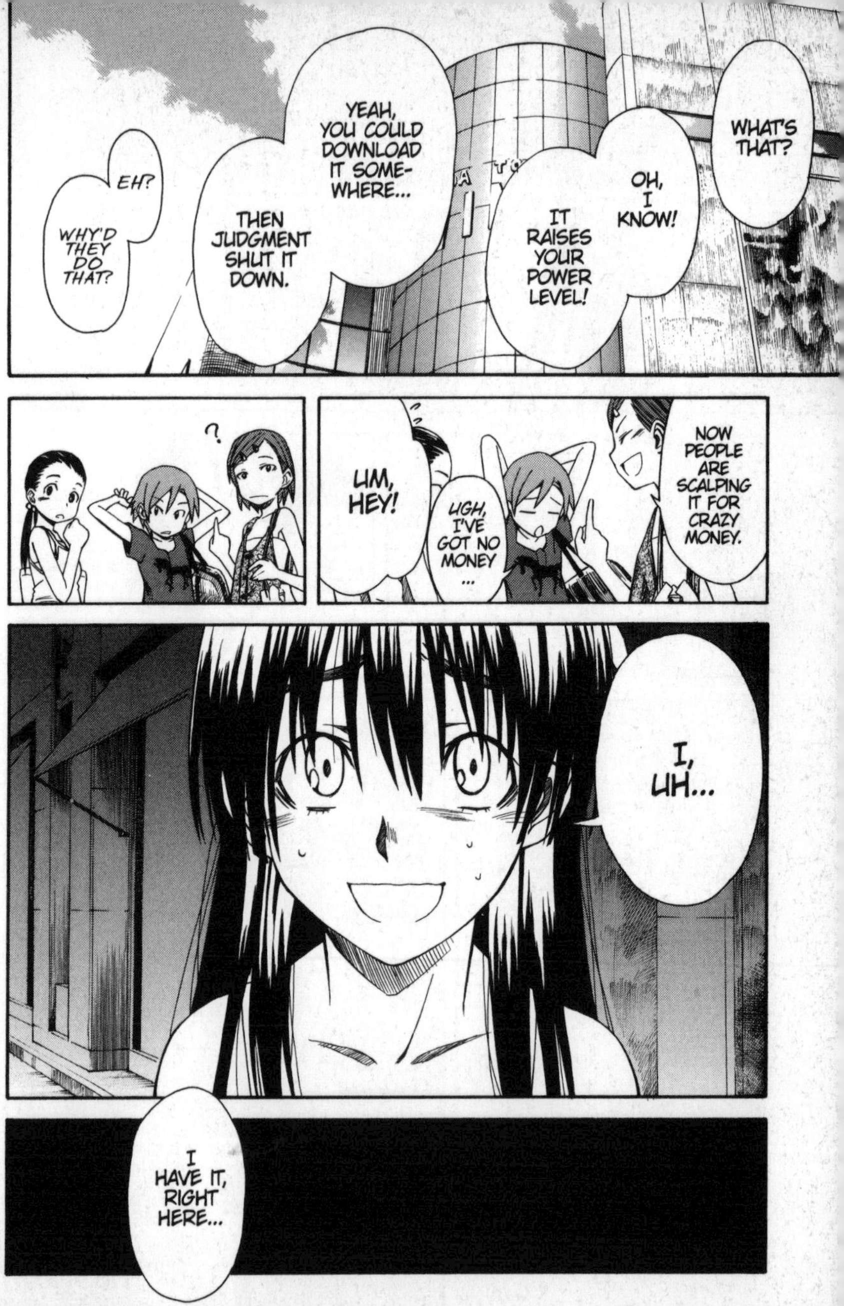
WHAT'S THAT?
OH, I KNOW!
IT RAISES YOUR POWER LEVEL!
YEAH, YOU COULD DOWNLOAD IT SOMEWHERE...
THEN JUDGMENT SHUT IT DOWN.
EH?
WHY'D THEY DO THAT?
NOW PEOPLE ARE SCALPING IT FOR CRAZY MONEY.
UGH, I'VE GOT NO MONEY ...
UM, HEY!
?
I, UH...
I HAVE IT, RIGHT HERE...

A Certain SCIENTIFIC Railgun

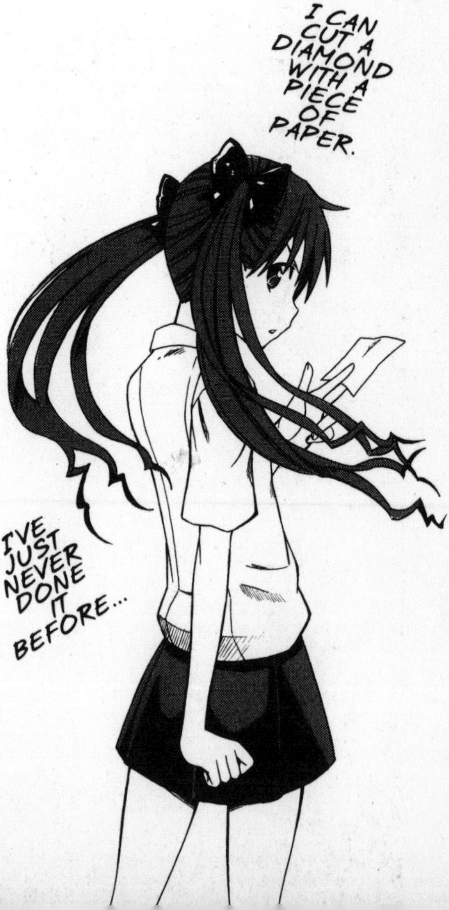
I CAN CUT A DIAMOND WITH A PIECE OF PAPER.
I'VE JUST NEVER DONE IT BEFORE...

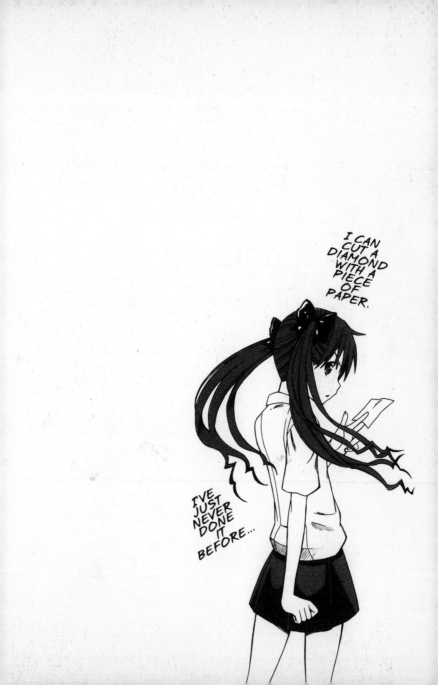

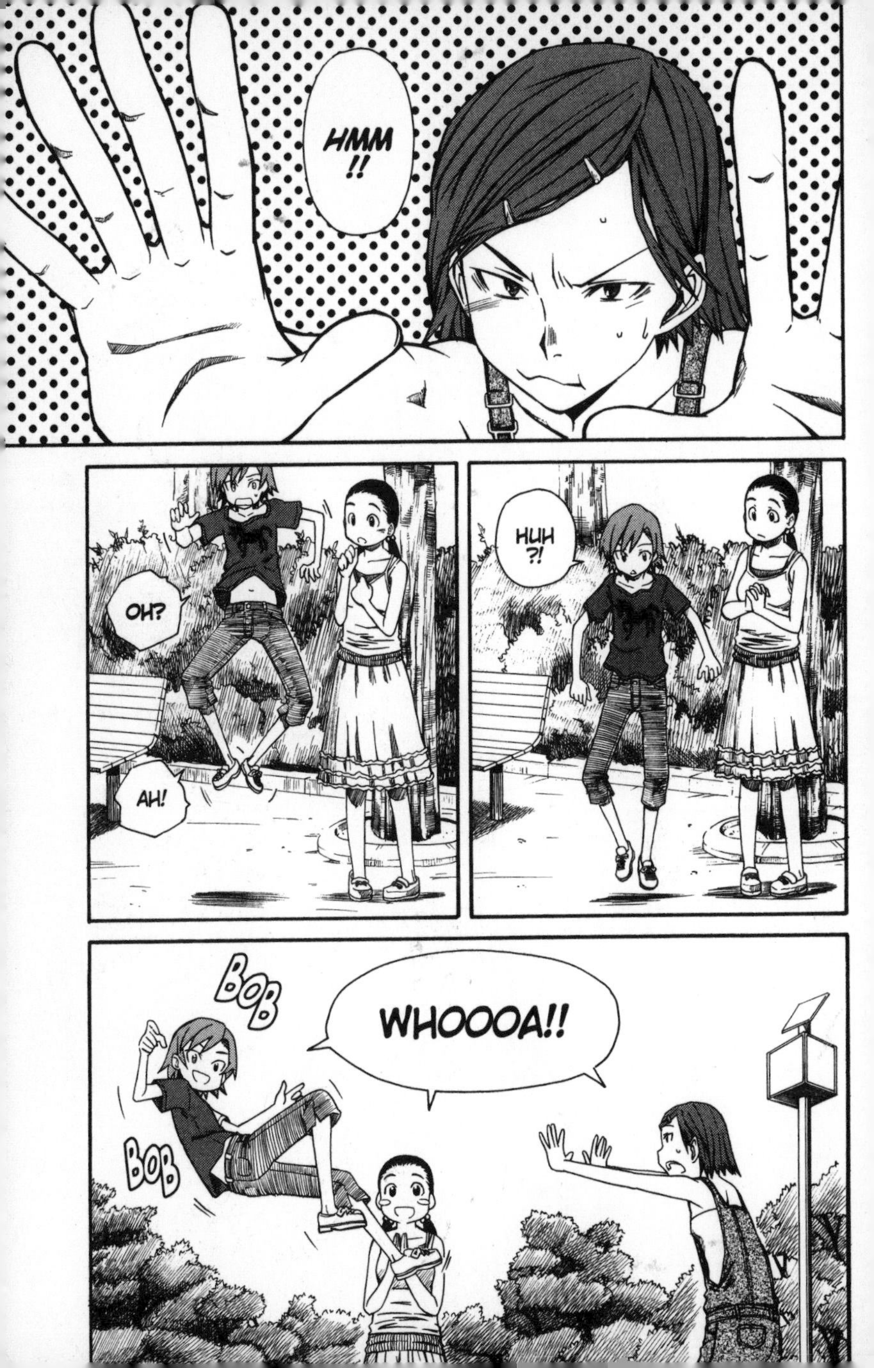
HMM !!
HUH ?!
OH?
AH!
WHOOOA!!
BOB
BOB

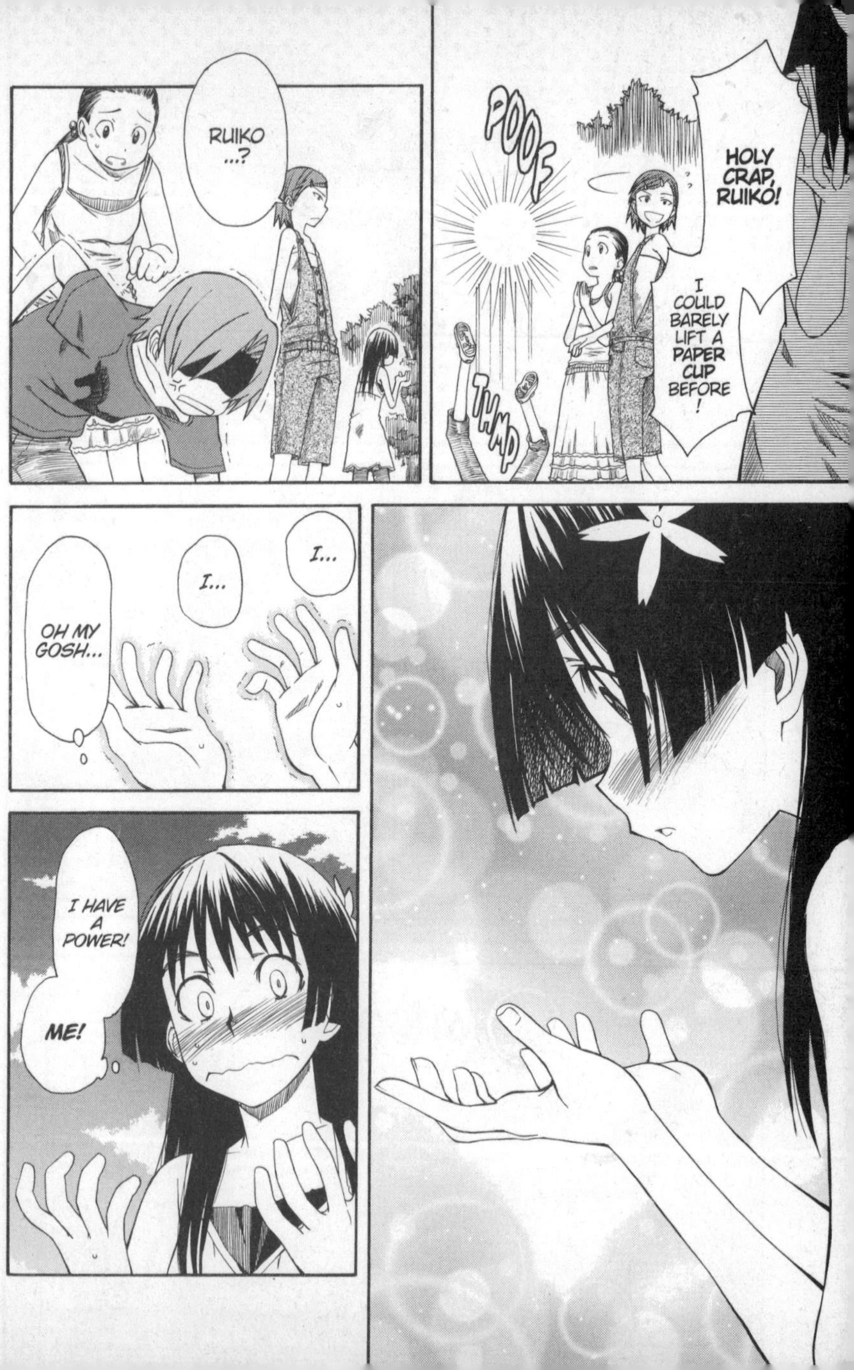
HOLY CRAP, RUIKO!
I COULD BARELY LIFT A PAPER CUP BEFORE!
POOF
THMP
RUIKO...?
I...
I...
OH MY GOSH...
I HAVE A POWER!
ME!

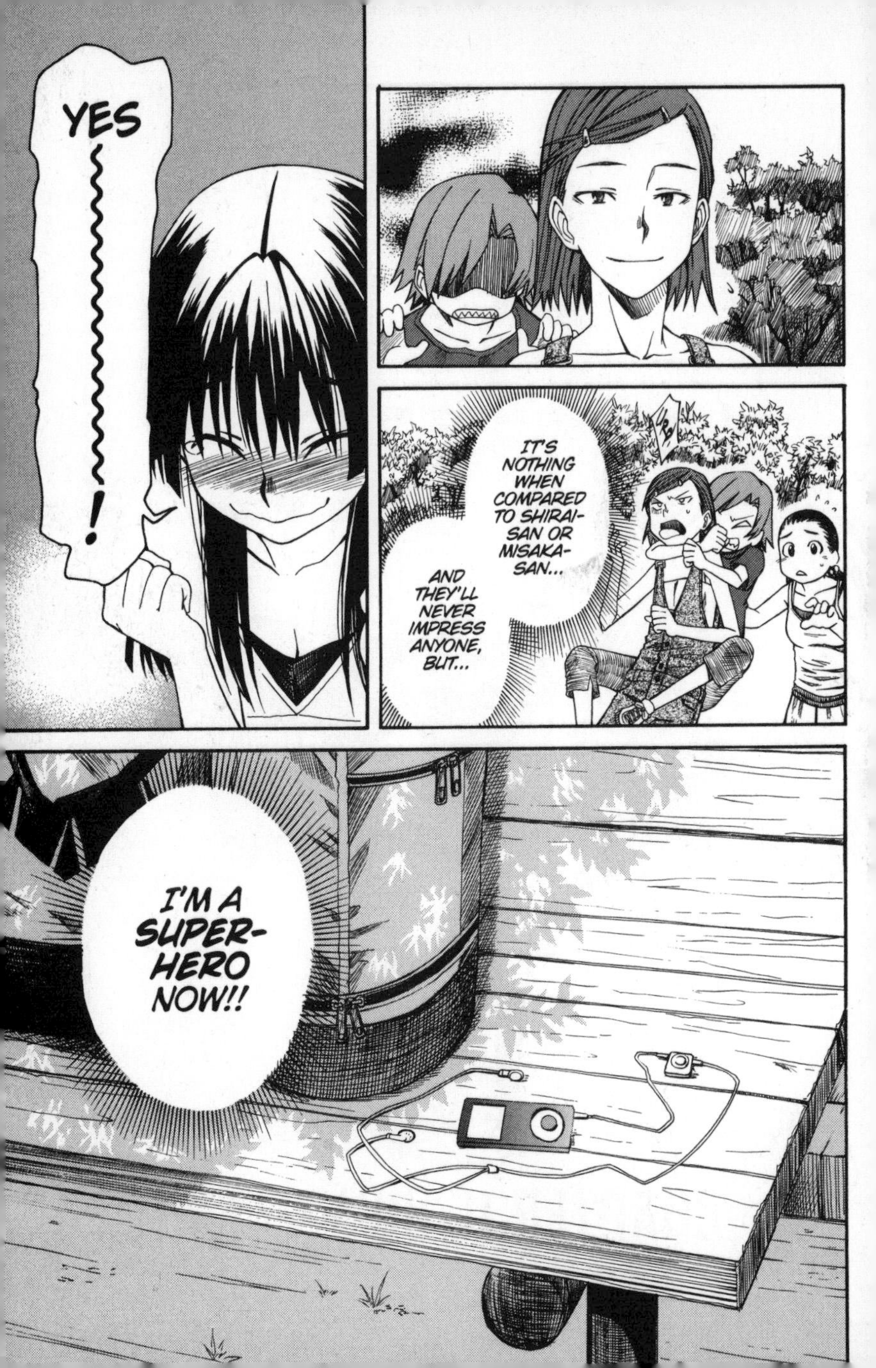
IT'S NOTHING WHEN COMPARED TO SHIRAI-SAN OR MISAKA-SAN...
AND THEY'LL NEVER IMPRESS ANYONE, BUT...
YES~~~!
I'M A SUPER-HERO NOW!!

CHAPTER 11: JULY 24TH (1)

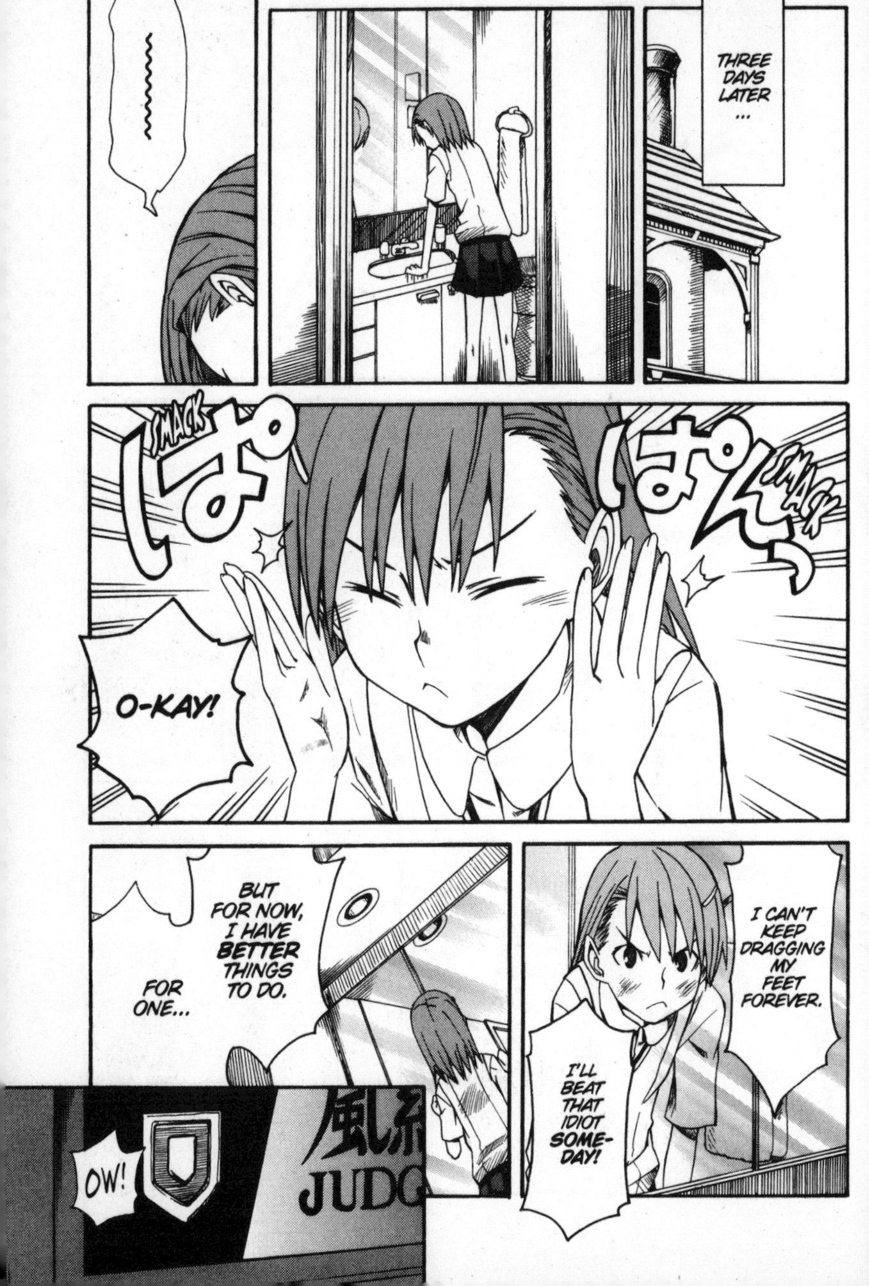
THREE DAYS LATER...
ぱん
SMACK
ぱ
SMACK
O-KAY!
I CAN'T KEEP DRAGGING MY FEET FOREVER.
I'LL BEAT THAT IDIOT SOME-DAY!
BUT FOR NOW, I HAVE **BETTER** THINGS TO DO.
FOR ONE...
OW!
JUDG

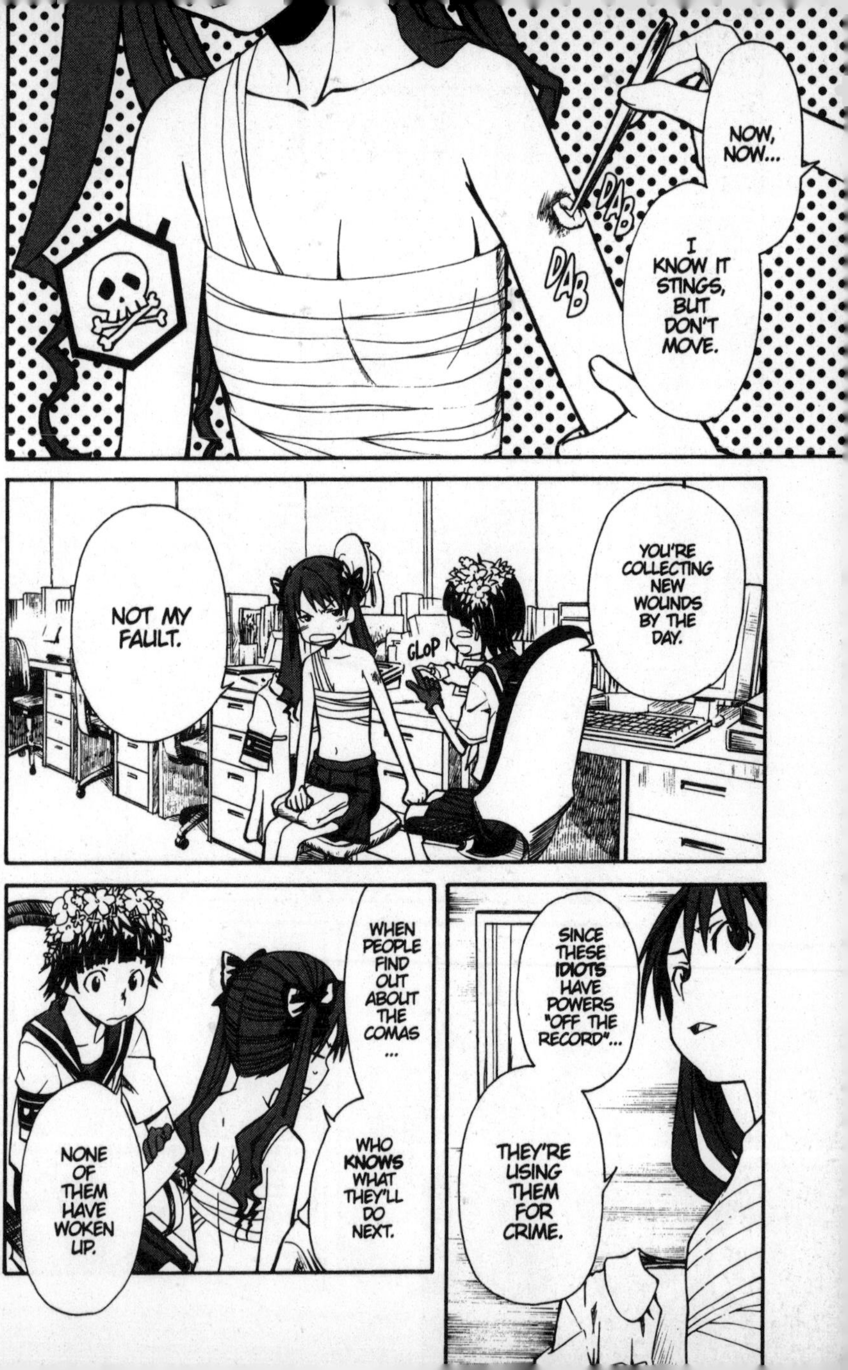
NOW, NOW...
DAB
DAB
I KNOW IT STINGS, BUT DON'T MOVE.
YOU'RE COLLECTING NEW WOUNDS BY THE DAY.
GLOP
NOT MY FAULT.
SINCE THESE IDIOTS HAVE POWERS "OFF THE RECORD"...
THEY'RE USING THEM FOR CRIME.
WHEN PEOPLE FIND OUT ABOUT THE COMAS...
WHO KNOWS WHAT THEY'LL DO NEXT.
NONE OF THEM HAVE WOKEN UP.

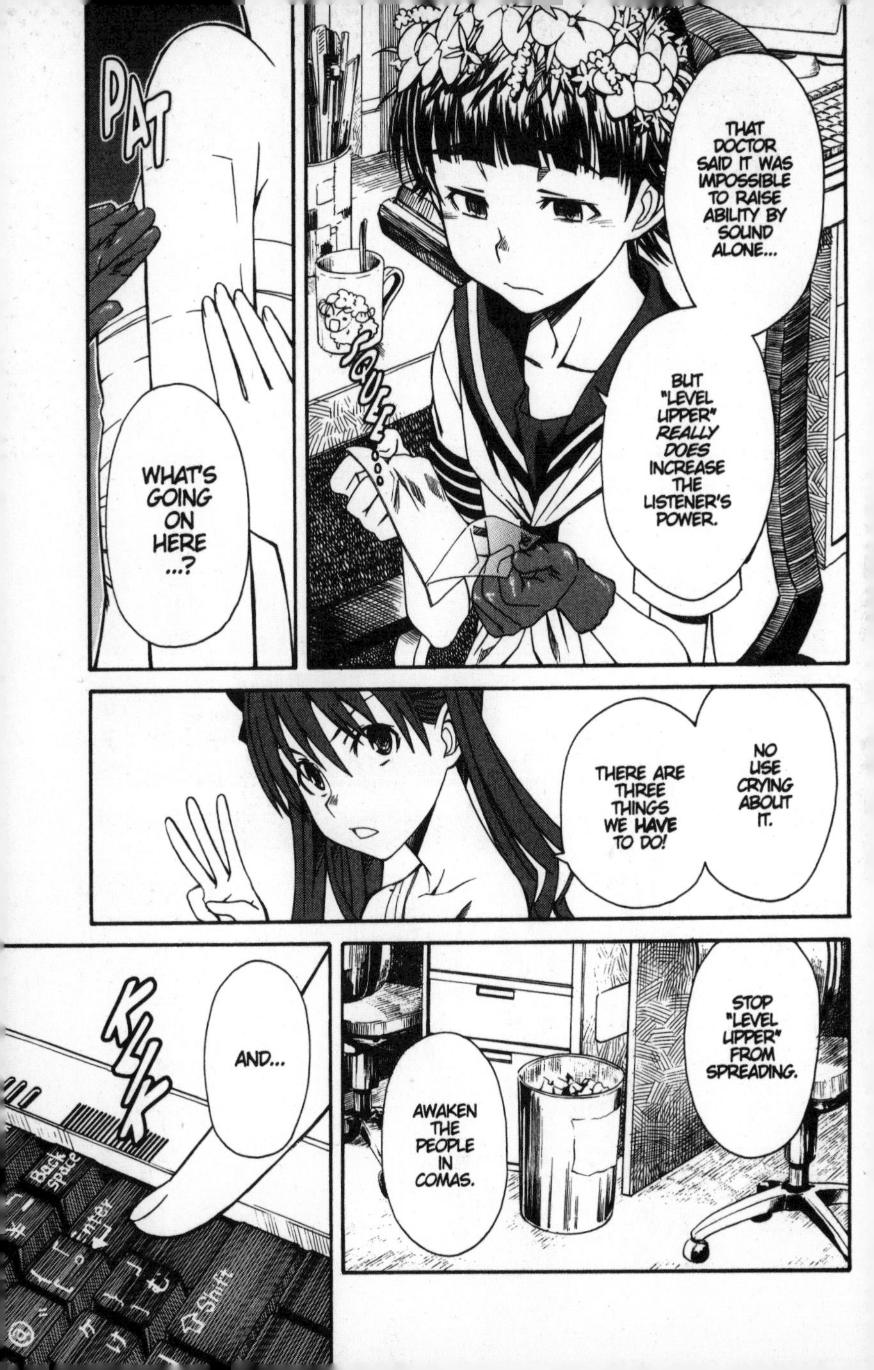
THAT DOCTOR SAID IT WAS IMPOSSIBLE TO RAISE ABILITY BY SOUND ALONE...
BUT "LEVEL UPPER" *REALLY DOES* INCREASE THE LISTENER'S POWER.
SQUEE
PAT
WHAT'S GOING ON HERE ...?
NO USE CRYING ABOUT IT.
THERE ARE THREE THINGS WE HAVE TO DO!
STOP "LEVEL UPPER" FROM SPREADING.
AWAKEN THE PEOPLE IN COMAS.
AND...
KLIK
Back space
Enter
Shift

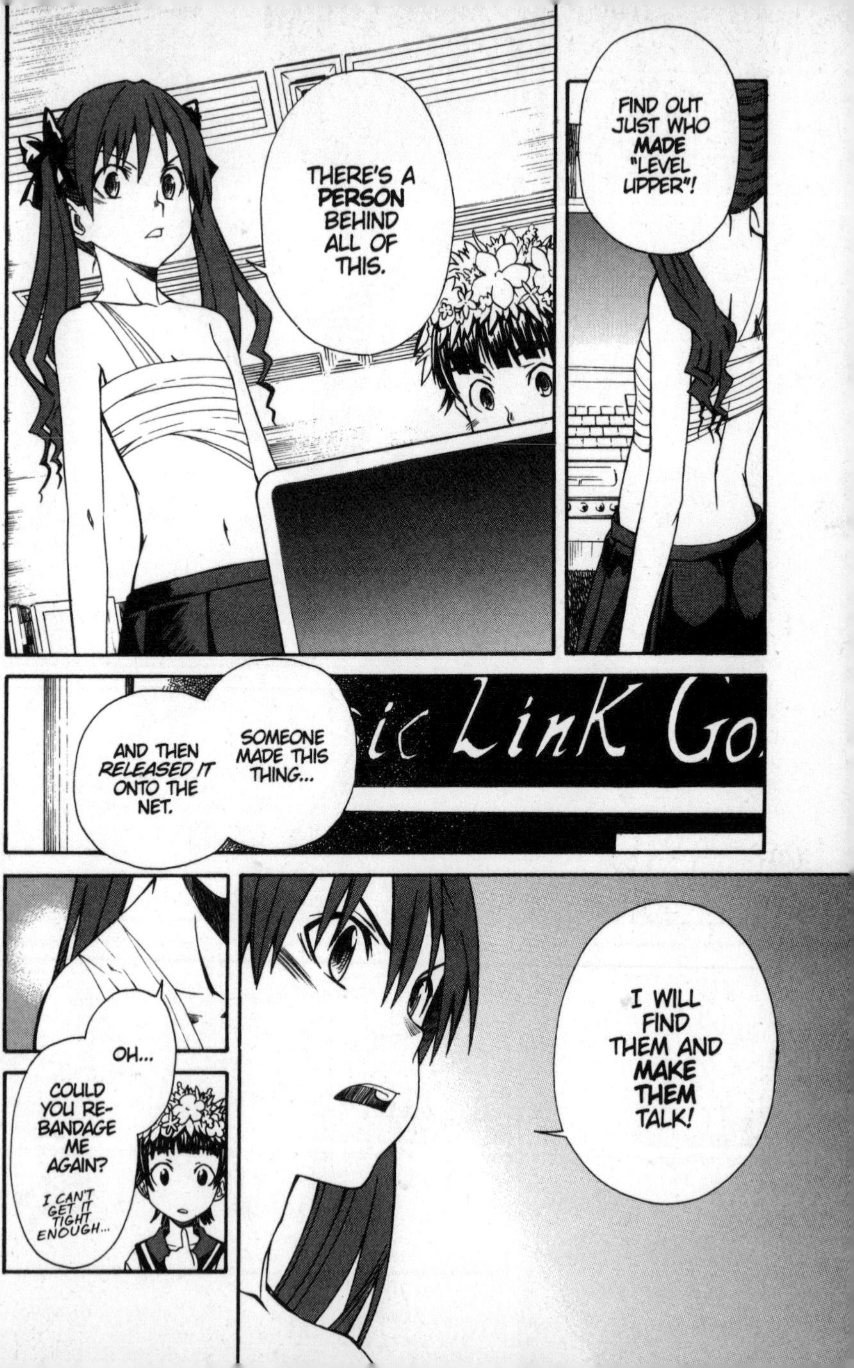
FIND OUT JUST WHO MADE "LEVEL UPPER"!
THERE'S A PERSON BEHIND ALL OF THIS.
ic LinK Go
SOMEONE MADE THIS THING...
AND THEN RELEASED IT ONTO THE NET.
I WILL FIND THEM AND MAKE THEM TALK!
OH...
COULD YOU RE-BANDAGE ME AGAIN?
I CAN'T GET IT TIGHT ENOUGH...

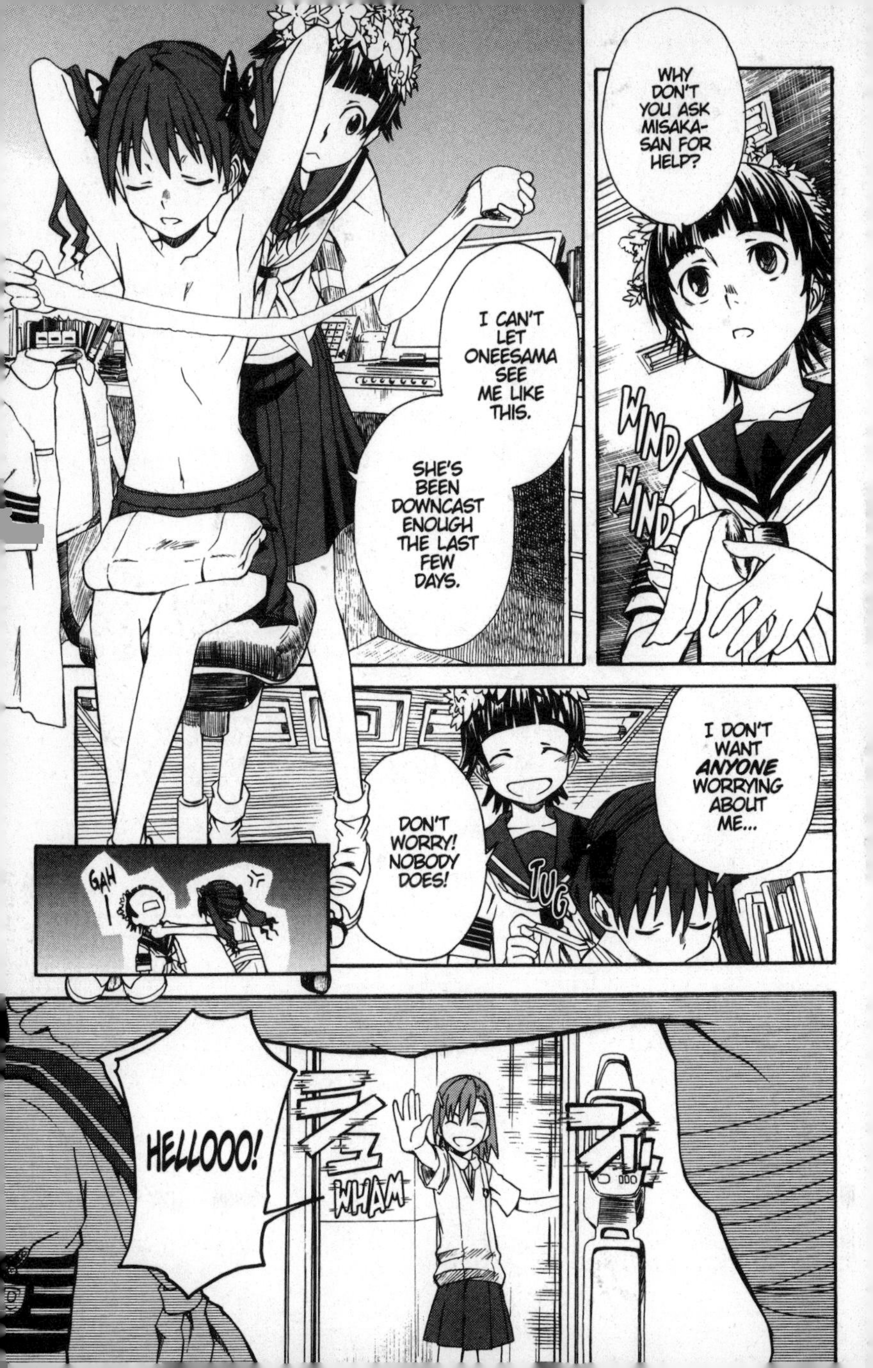
WHY DON'T YOU ASK MISAKA-SAN FOR HELP?
WIND WIND
I CAN'T LET ONEESAMA SEE ME LIKE THIS.
SHE'S BEEN DOWNCAST ENOUGH THE LAST FEW DAYS.
I DON'T WANT ANYONE WORRYING ABOUT ME...
TUG
DON'T WORRY! NOBODY DOES!
GAH
HELLOOO!
WHAM

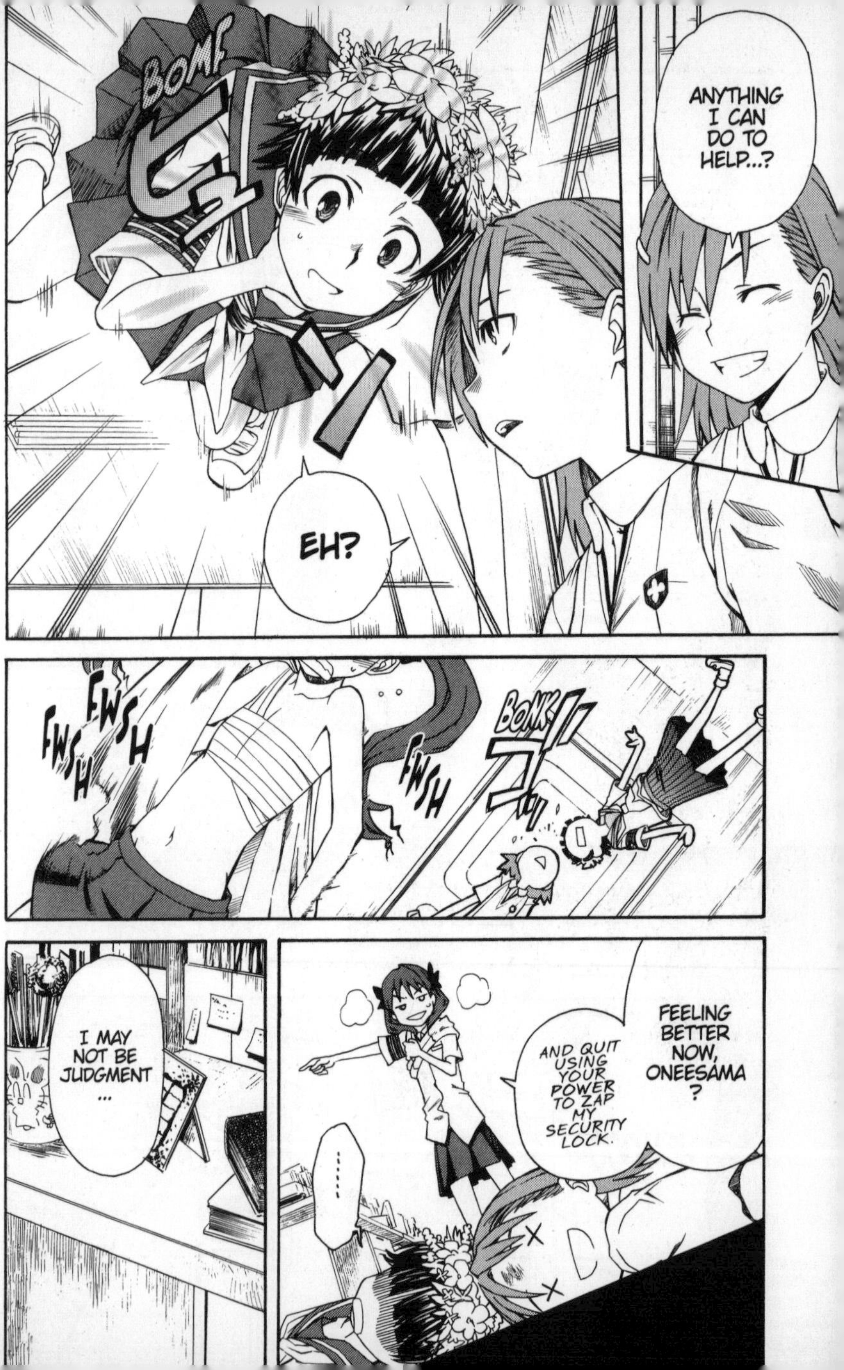
ANYTHING I CAN DO TO HELP...?
BOMF
EH?
BONK
FWSH
FWSH
FWSH
FEELING BETTER NOW, ONEESAMA?
AND QUIT USING YOUR POWER TO ZAP MY SECURITY LOCK.
......
I MAY NOT BE JUDGMENT ...

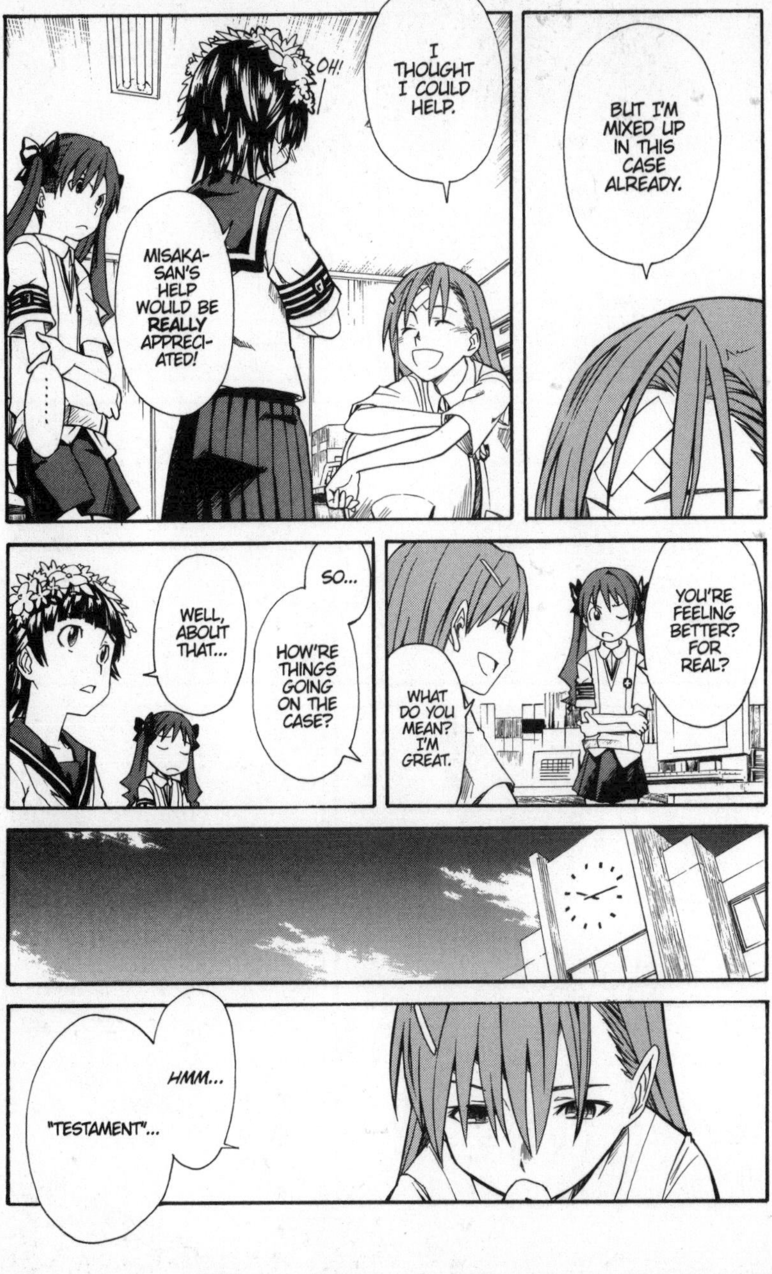
BUT I'M MIXED UP IN THIS CASE ALREADY.
I THOUGHT I COULD HELP.
OH!
MISAKA-SAN'S HELP WOULD BE REALLY APPRECIATED!
......
YOU'RE FEELING BETTER? FOR REAL?
WHAT DO YOU MEAN? I'M GREAT.
SO...
HOW'RE THINGS GOING ON THE CASE?
WELL, ABOUT THAT...
HMM...
"TESTAMENT"...

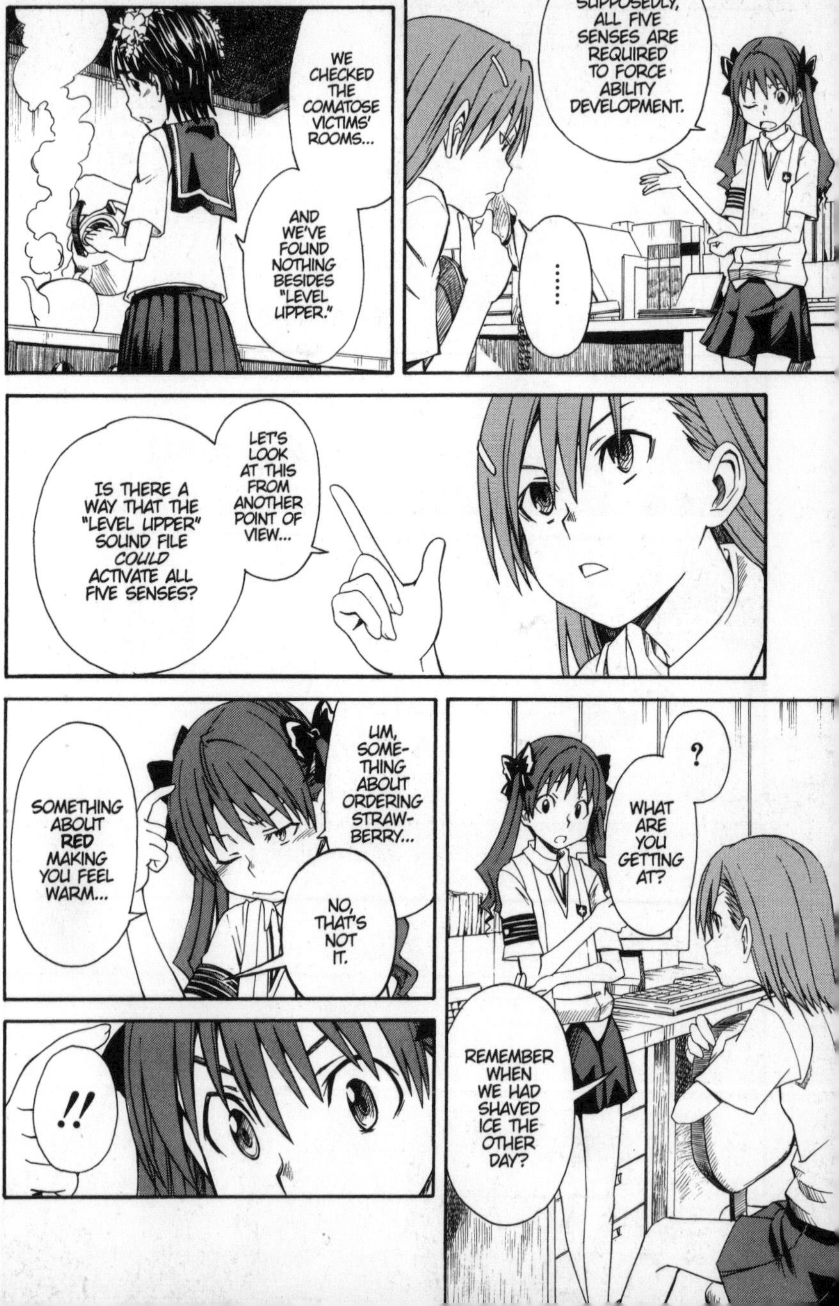
SUPPOSEDLY, ALL FIVE SENSES ARE REQUIRED TO FORCE ABILITY DEVELOPMENT.
......
WE CHECKED THE COMATOSE VICTIMS' ROOMS...
AND WE'VE FOUND NOTHING BESIDES "LEVEL UPPER."
LET'S LOOK AT THIS FROM ANOTHER POINT OF VIEW...
IS THERE A WAY THAT THE "LEVEL UPPER" SOUND FILE COULD ACTIVATE ALL FIVE SENSES?
?
WHAT ARE YOU GETTING AT?
REMEMBER WHEN WE HAD SHAVED ICE THE OTHER DAY?
UM, SOMETHING ABOUT ORDERING STRAWBERRY...
NO, THAT'S NOT IT.
SOMETHING ABOUT RED MAKING YOU FEEL WARM...
!!

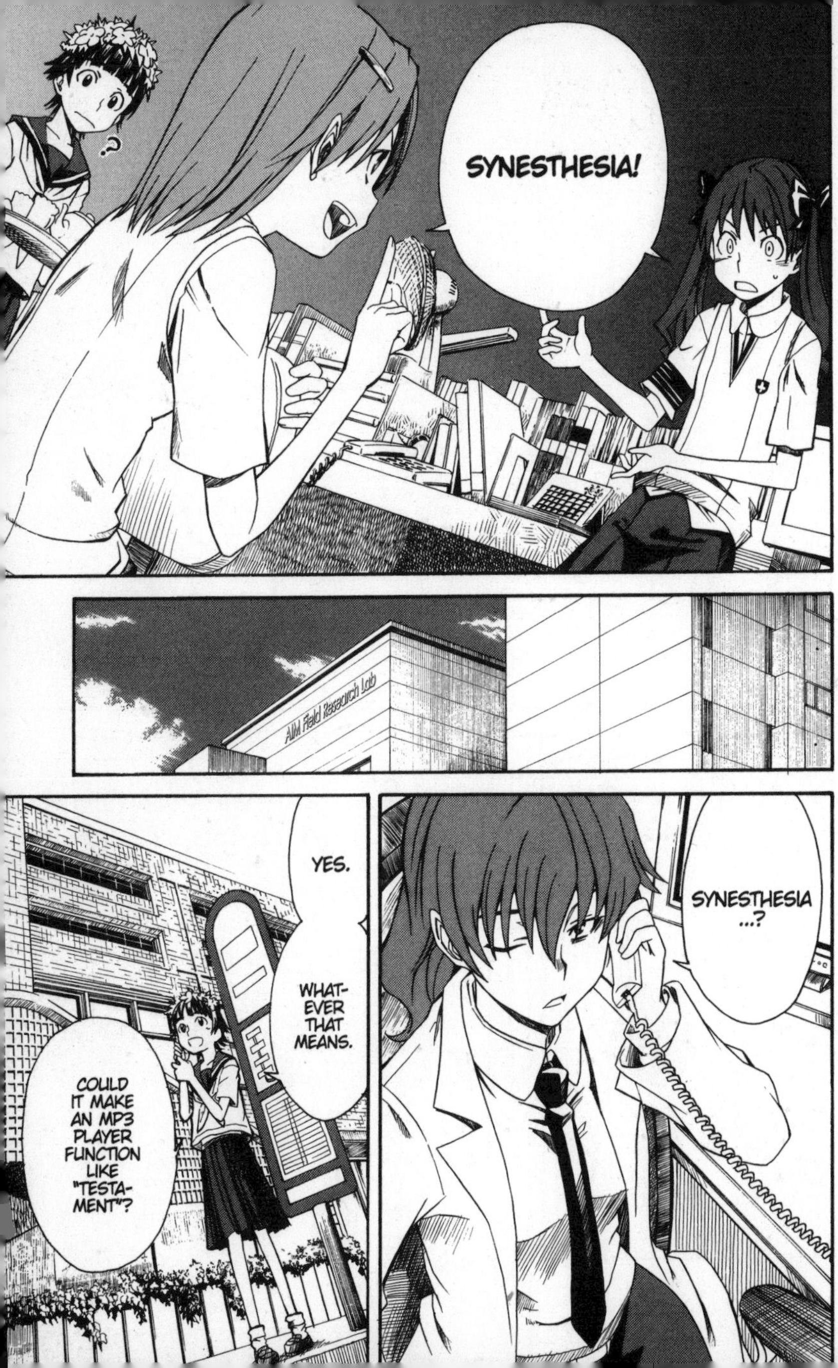
SYNESTHESIA!
AIM Field Research Lab
SYNESTHESIA ...?
YES.
WHAT-EVER THAT MEANS.
COULD IT MAKE AN MP3 PLAYER FUNCTION LIKE "TESTAMENT"?

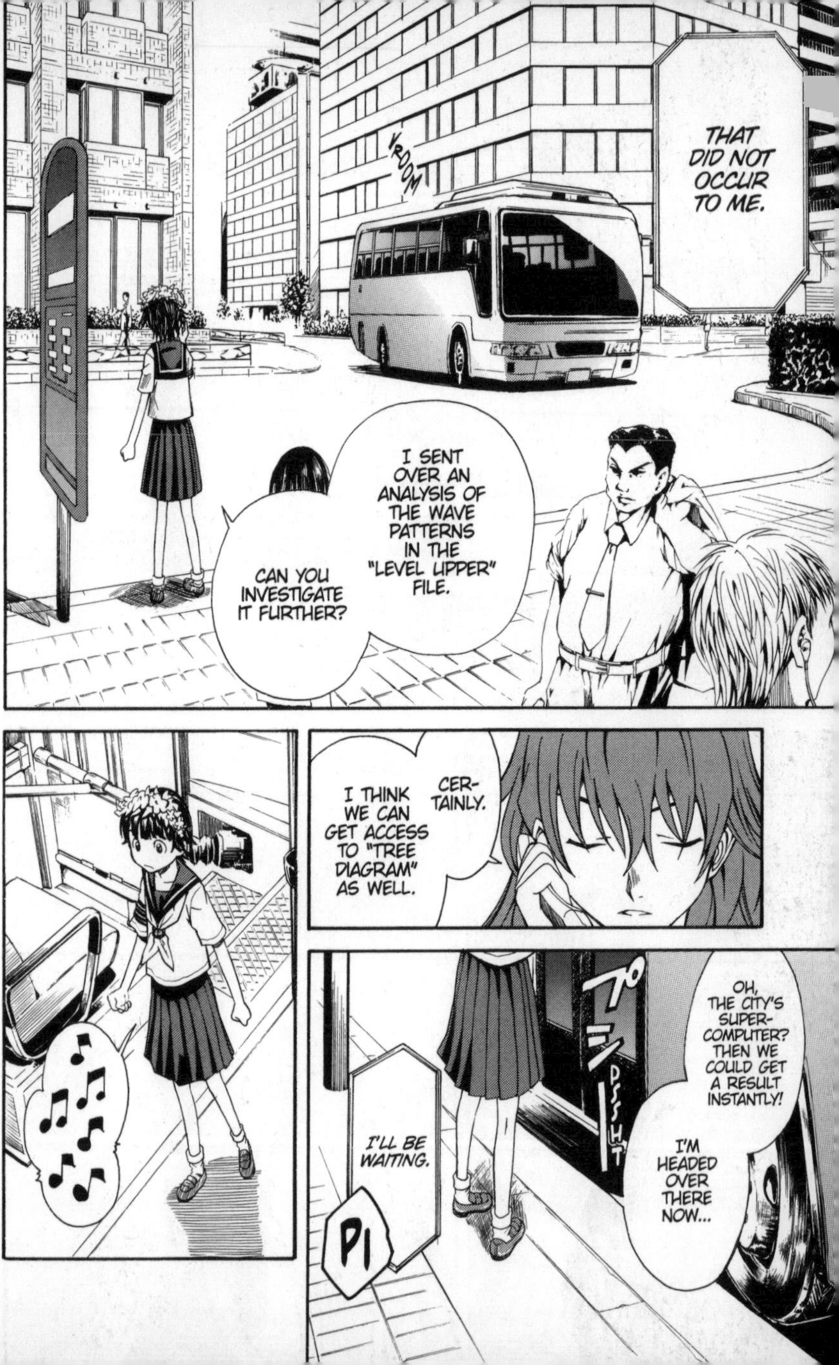
THAT DID NOT OCCUR TO ME.
VROOM
I SENT OVER AN ANALYSIS OF THE WAVE PATTERNS IN THE "LEVEL UPPER" FILE.
CAN YOU INVESTIGATE IT FURTHER?
CER-TAINLY.
I THINK WE CAN GET ACCESS TO "TREE DIAGRAM" AS WELL.
OH, THE CITY'S SUPER-COMPUTER? THEN WE COULD GET A RESULT INSTANTLY!
I'M HEADED OVER THERE NOW...
PSSHT
I'LL BE WAITING.
PI

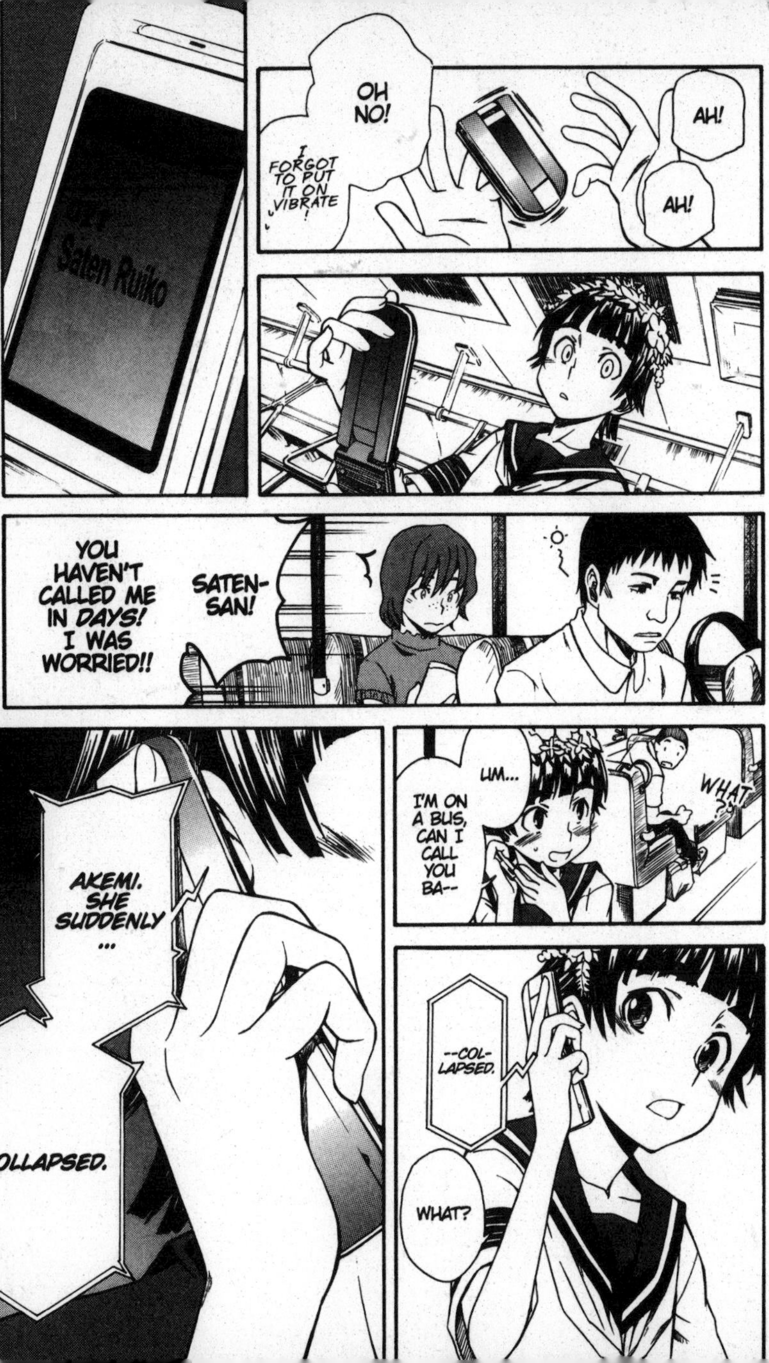
AH!
AH!
OH NO!
I FORGOT TO PUT IT ON VIBRATE!
Saten Ruiko
SATEN-SAN!
YOU HAVEN'T CALLED ME IN DAYS! I WAS WORRIED!!
UM...
I'M ON A BUS, CAN I CALL YOU BA--
WHAT?
--COL-LAPSED.
WHAT?
AKEMI. SHE SUDDENLY ...
COLLAPSED.

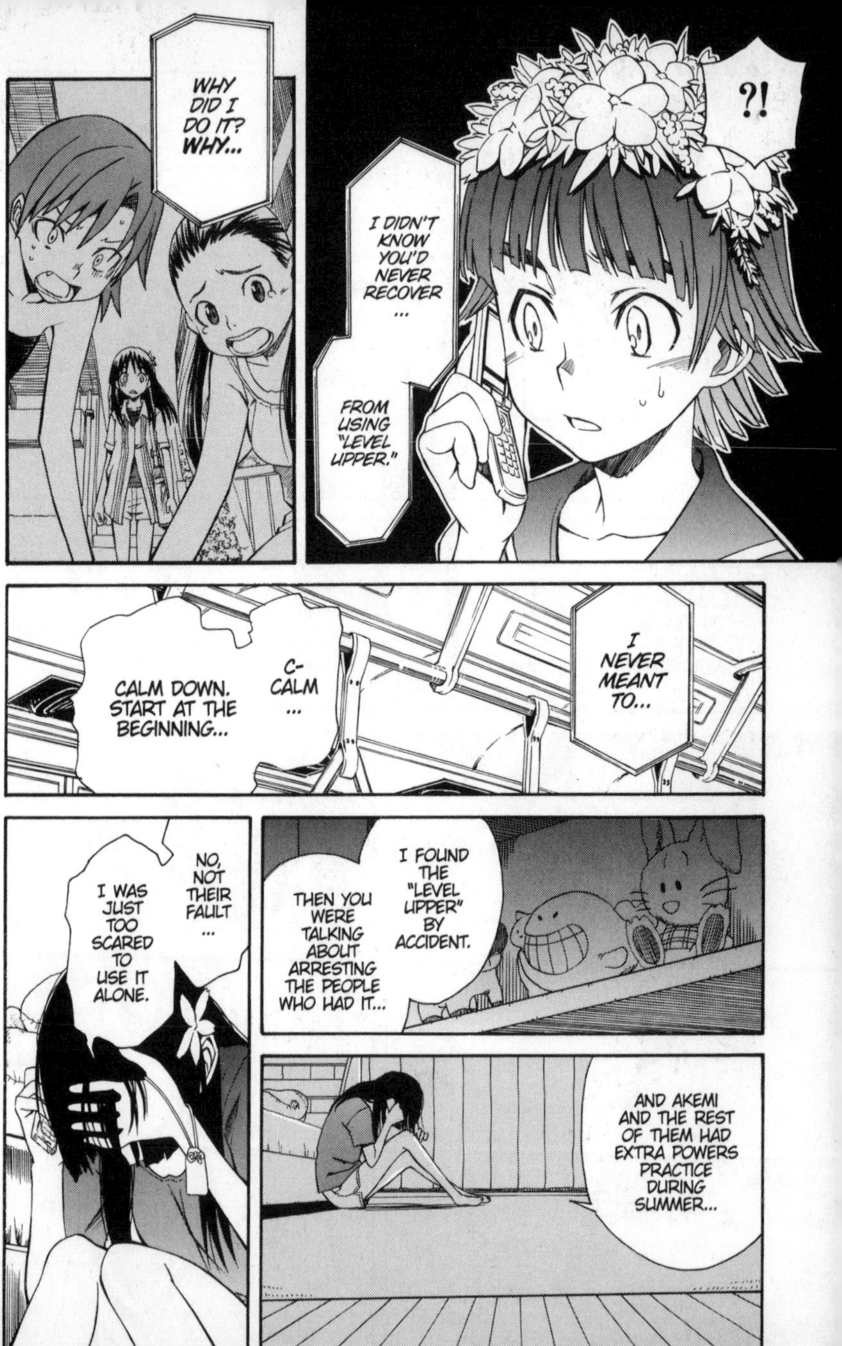
?!
I DIDN'T KNOW YOU'D NEVER RECOVER ...
FROM USING "LEVEL UPPER."
WHY DID I DO IT? WHY...
I NEVER MEANT TO...
C-CALM ...
CALM DOWN. START AT THE BEGINNING...
I FOUND THE "LEVEL UPPER" BY ACCIDENT.
THEN YOU WERE TALKING ABOUT ARRESTING THE PEOPLE WHO HAD IT...
AND AKEMI AND THE REST OF THEM HAD EXTRA POWERS PRACTICE DURING SUMMER...
NO, NOT THEIR FAULT ...
I WAS JUST TOO SCARED TO USE IT ALONE.

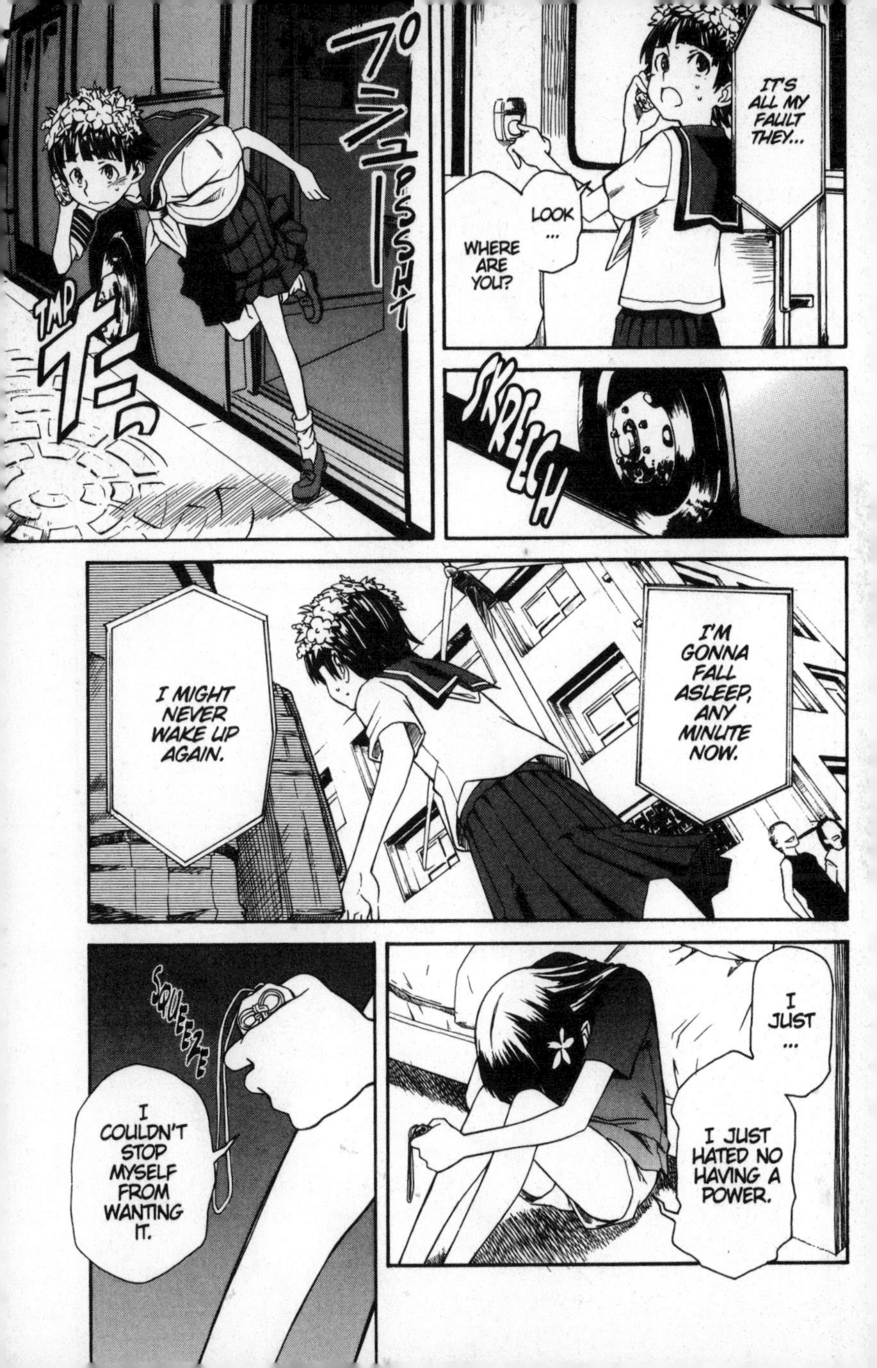
IT'S ALL MY FAULT THEY...
LOOK ...
WHERE ARE YOU?
SKREECH
PSSSHT
TMP
I'M GONNA FALL ASLEEP, ANY MINUTE NOW.
I MIGHT NEVER WAKE UP AGAIN.
I JUST ...
I JUST HATED NO HAVING A POWER.
SQUEEEZE
I COULDN'T STOP MYSELF FROM WANTING IT.

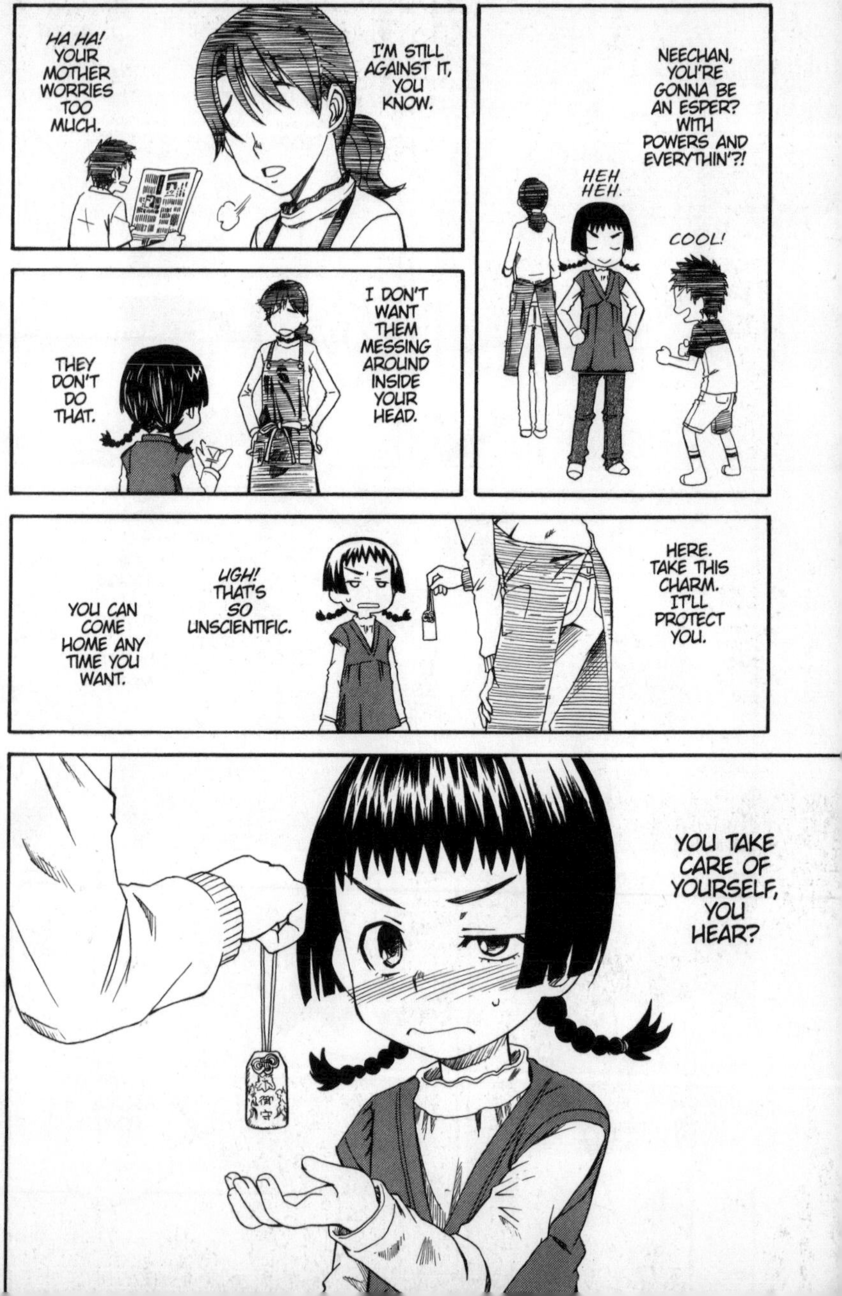
NEECHAN, YOU'RE GONNA BE AN ESPER? WITH POWERS AND EVERYTHIN'?!
HEH HEH.
COOL!
I'M STILL AGAINST IT, YOU KNOW.
HA HA! YOUR MOTHER WORRIES TOO MUCH.
I DON'T WANT THEM MESSING AROUND INSIDE YOUR HEAD.
THEY DON'T DO THAT.
HERE. TAKE THIS CHARM. IT'LL PROTECT YOU.
UGH! THAT'S SO UNSCIENTIFIC.
YOU CAN COME HOME ANY TIME YOU WANT.
YOU TAKE CARE OF YOURSELF, YOU HEAR?
御守

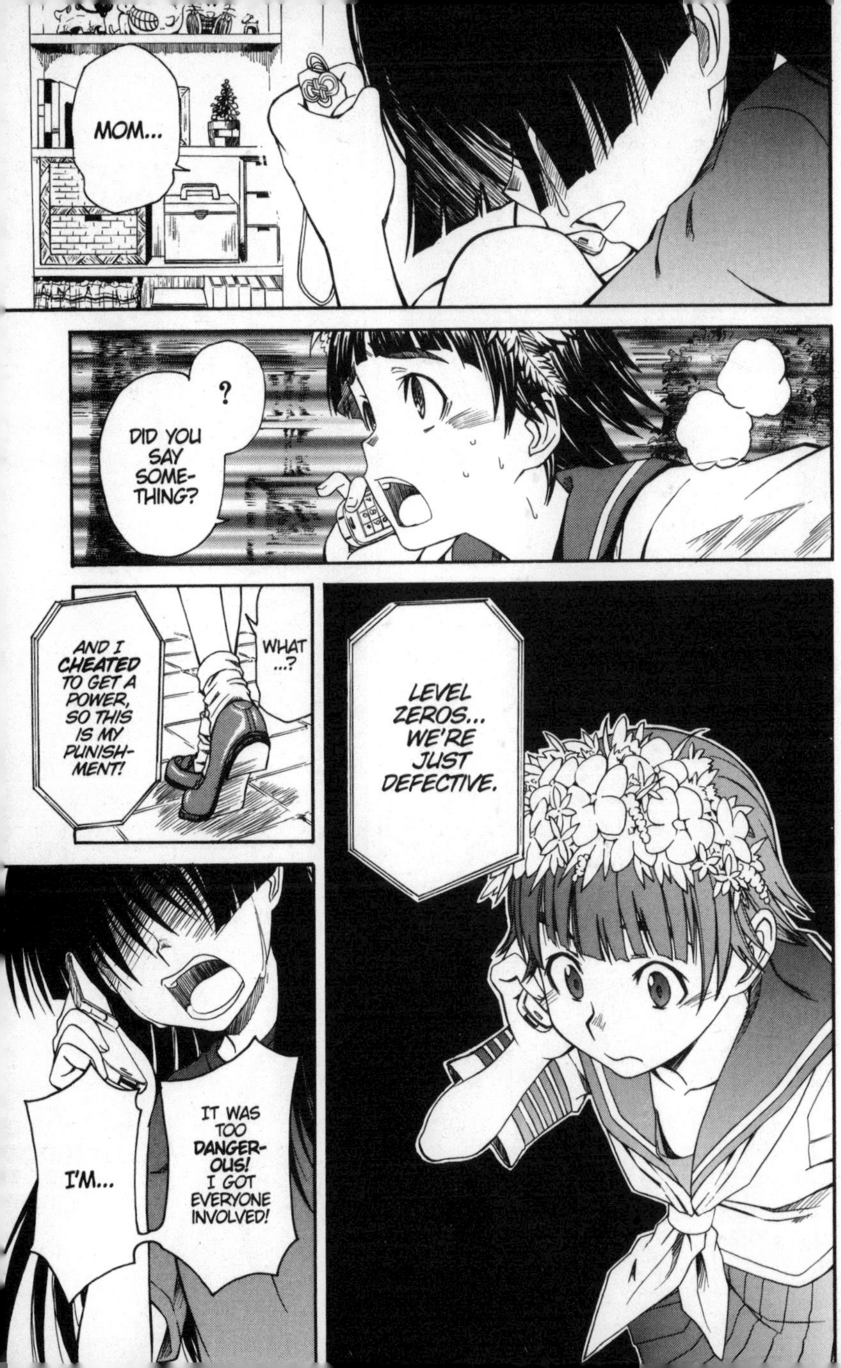
MOM...
?
DID YOU SAY SOMETHING?
LEVEL ZEROS... WE'RE JUST DEFECTIVE.
WHAT ...?
AND I CHEATED TO GET A POWER, SO THIS IS MY PUNISHMENT!
IT WAS TOO DANGEROUS! I GOT EVERYONE INVOLVED!
I'M...

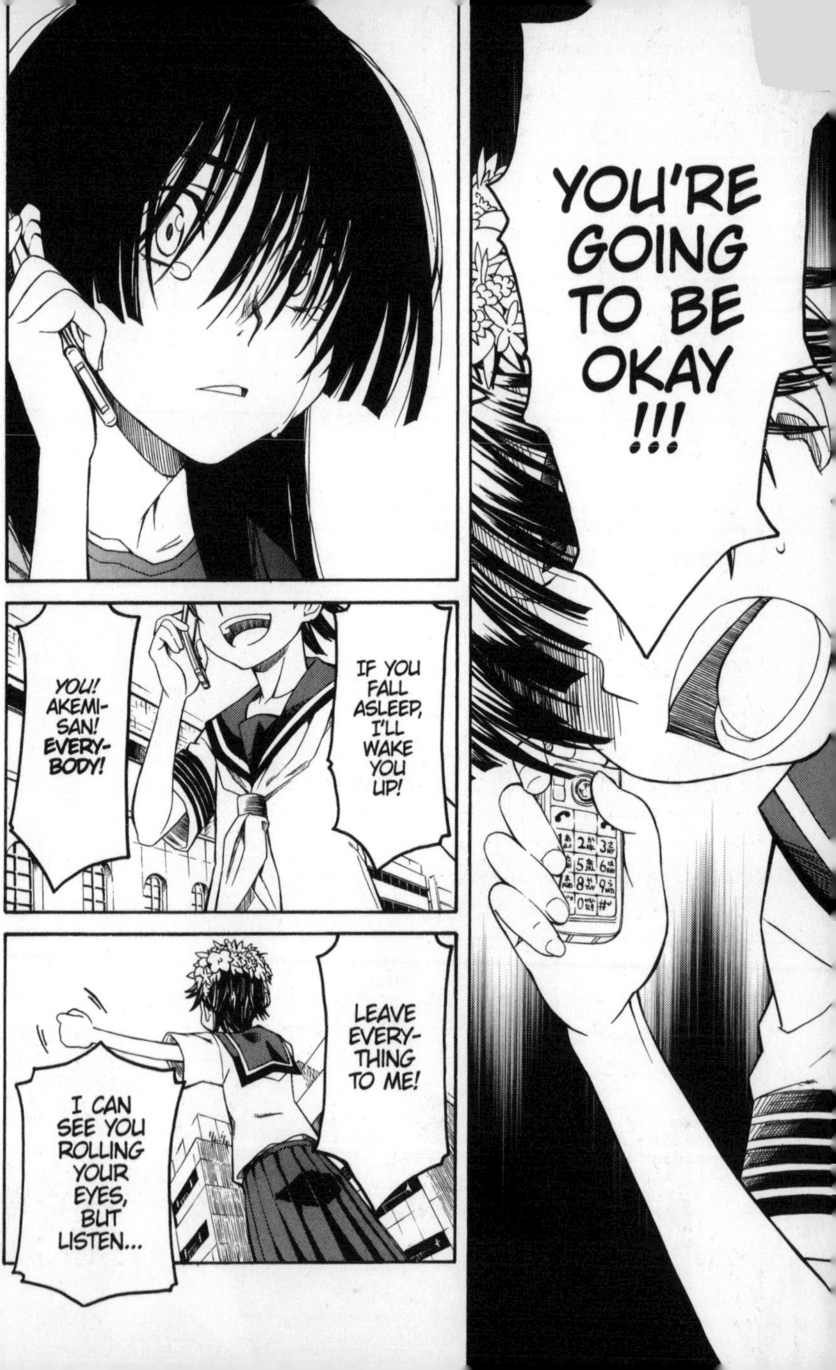
YOU'RE GOING TO BE OKAY!!!
IF YOU FALL ASLEEP, I'LL WAKE YOU UP!
YOU! AKEMI-SAN! EVERY-BODY!
LEAVE EVERY-THING TO ME!
I CAN SEE YOU ROLLING YOUR EYES, BUT LISTEN...

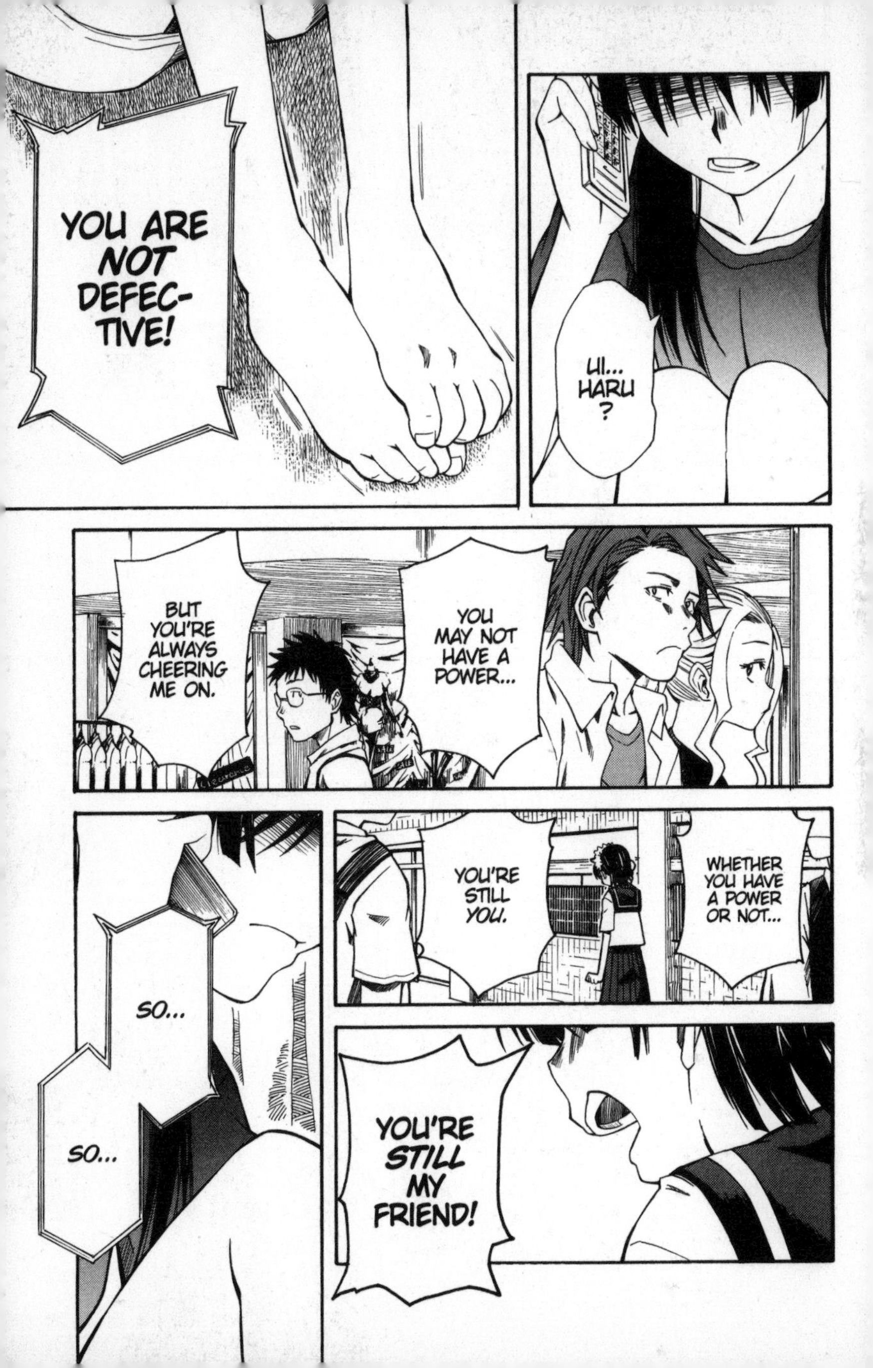
UI... HARU?
YOU ARE NOT DEFECTIVE!
YOU MAY NOT HAVE A POWER...
BUT YOU'RE ALWAYS CHEERING ME ON.
WHETHER YOU HAVE A POWER OR NOT...
YOU'RE STILL YOU.
YOU'RE STILL MY FRIEND!
SO...
SO...

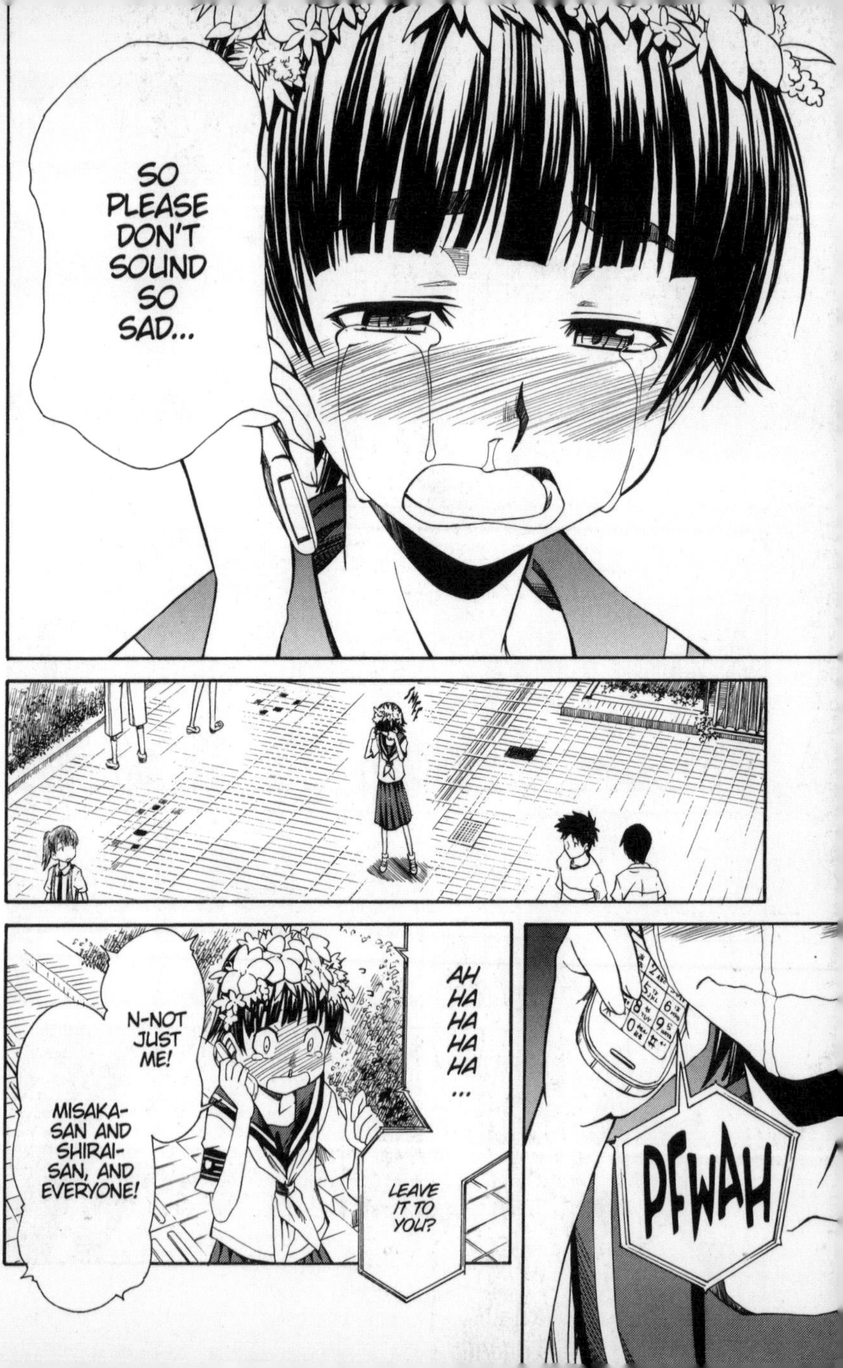
SO PLEASE DON'T SOUND SO SAD...
PFWAH
AH HA HA HA HA ...
LEAVE IT TO YOU?
N-NOT JUST ME!
MISAKA-SAN AND SHIRAI-SAN, AND EVERYONE!

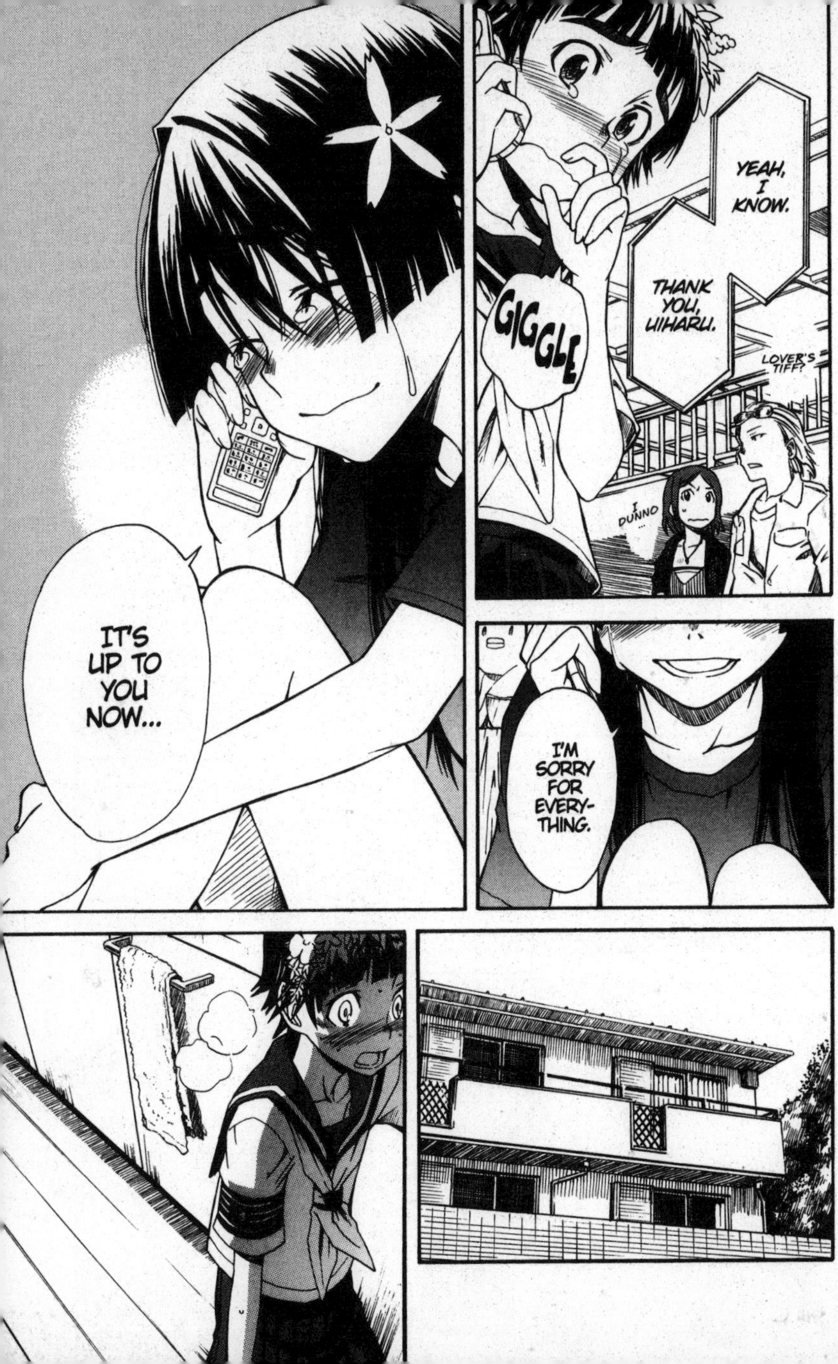
YEAH, I KNOW.
THANK YOU, UIHARU.
GIGGLE
LOVER'S TIFF?
I DUNNO...
I'M SORRY FOR EVERYTHING.
IT'S UP TO YOU NOW...

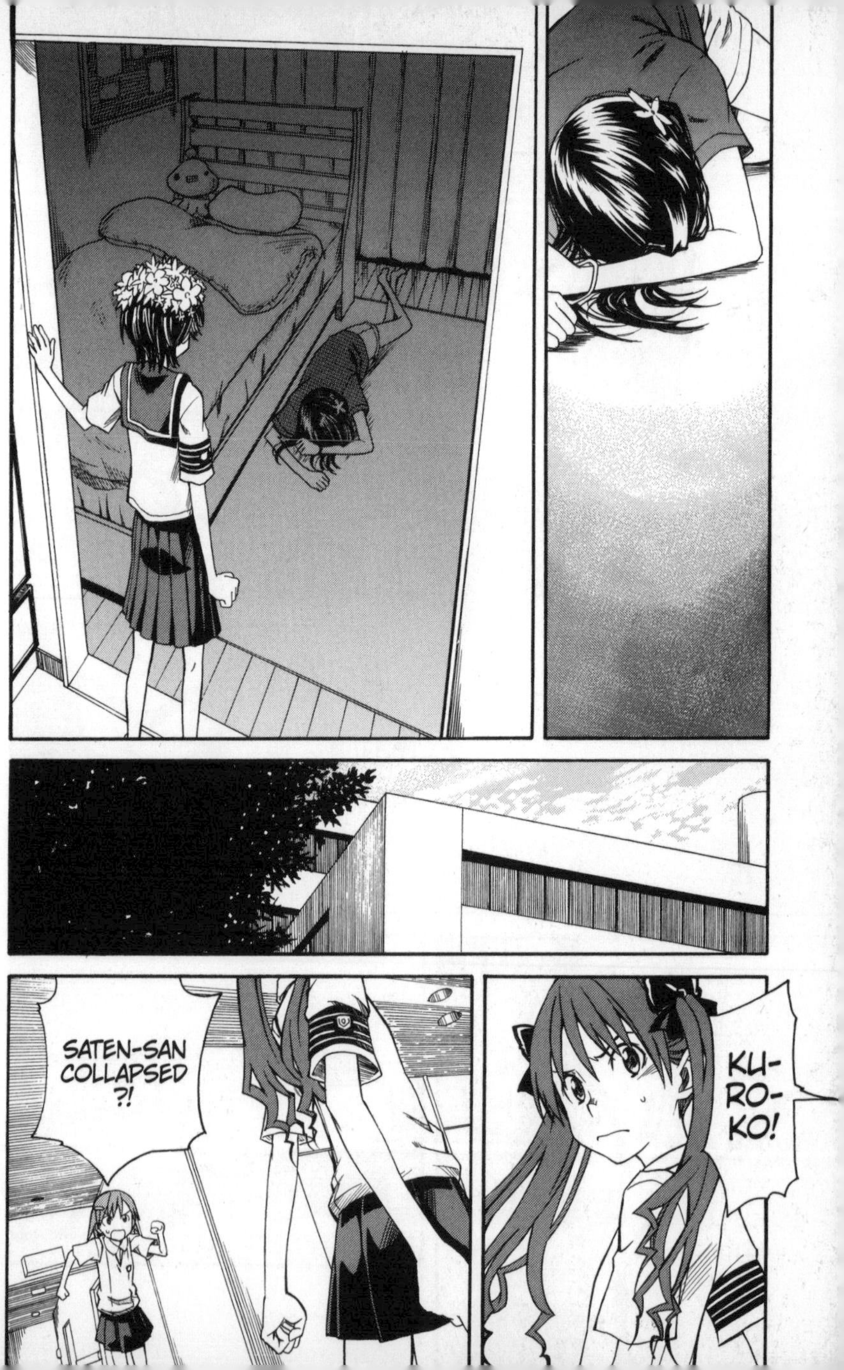
KU-RO-KO!
SATEN-SAN COLLAPSED ?!

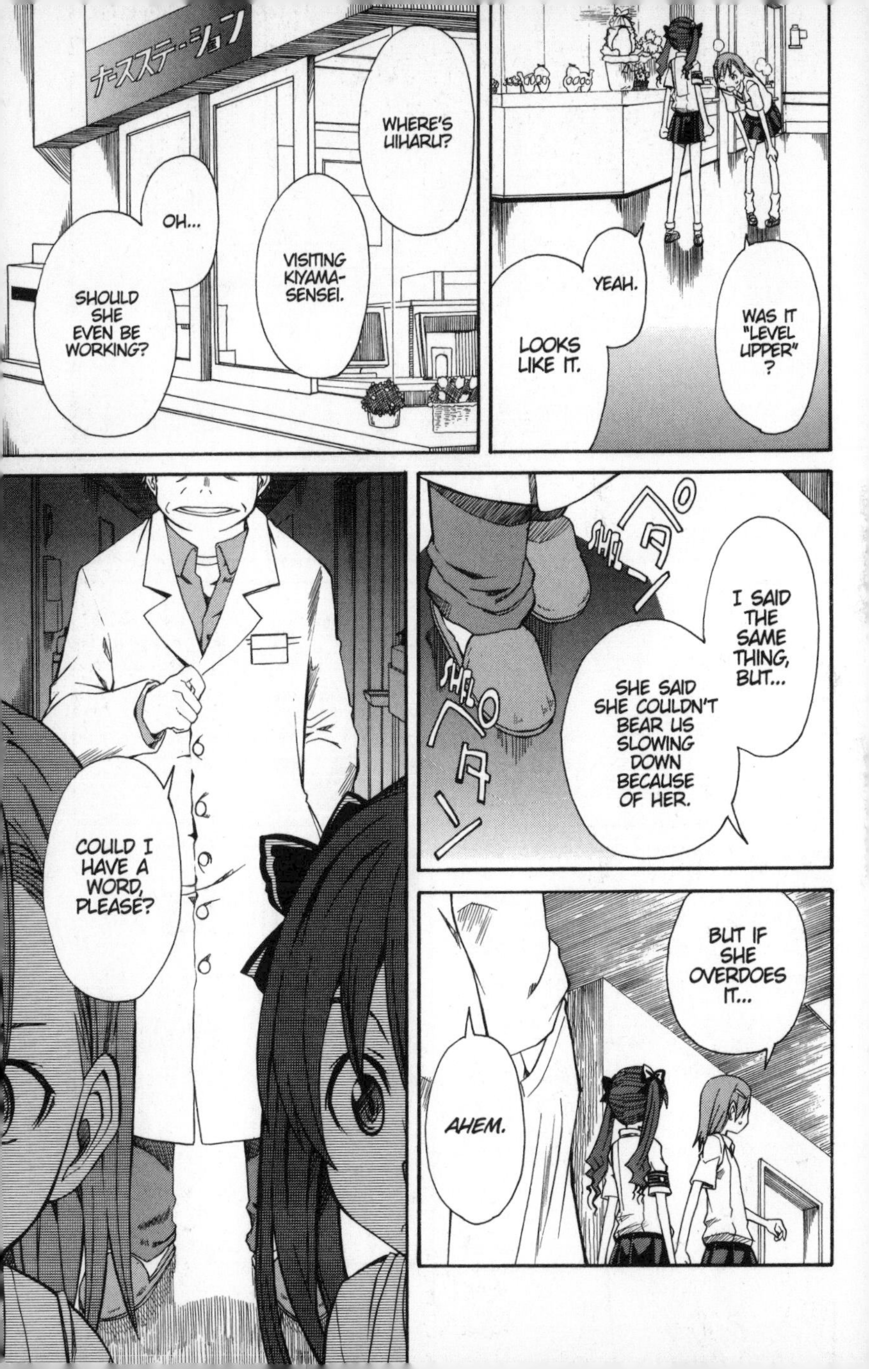
WAS IT "LEVEL UPPER"?
YEAH.
LOOKS LIKE IT.
ナースステーション
WHERE'S UIHARU?
VISITING KIYAMA-SENSEI.
OH...
SHOULD SHE EVEN BE WORKING?
I SAID THE SAME THING, BUT...
SHE SAID SHE COULDN'T BEAR US SLOWING DOWN BECAUSE OF HER.
BUT IF SHE OVERDOES IT...
AHEM.
COULD I HAVE A WORD, PLEASE?

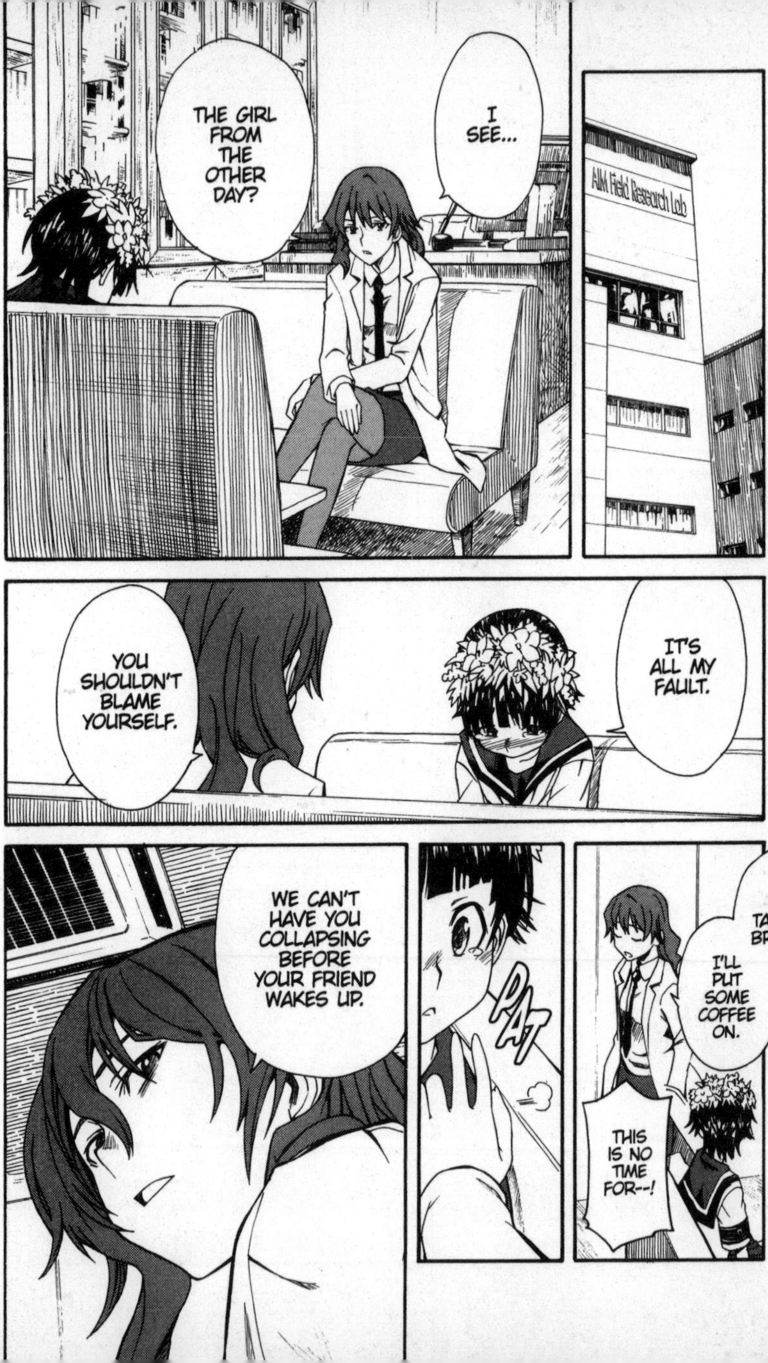
AIM Field Research Lab
I SEE...
THE GIRL FROM THE OTHER DAY?
IT'S ALL MY FAULT.
YOU SHOULDN'T BLAME YOURSELF.
TAKE A BREAK.
I'LL PUT SOME COFFEE ON.
THIS IS NO TIME FOR--!
PAT
WE CAN'T HAVE YOU COLLAPSING BEFORE YOUR FRIEND WAKES UP.

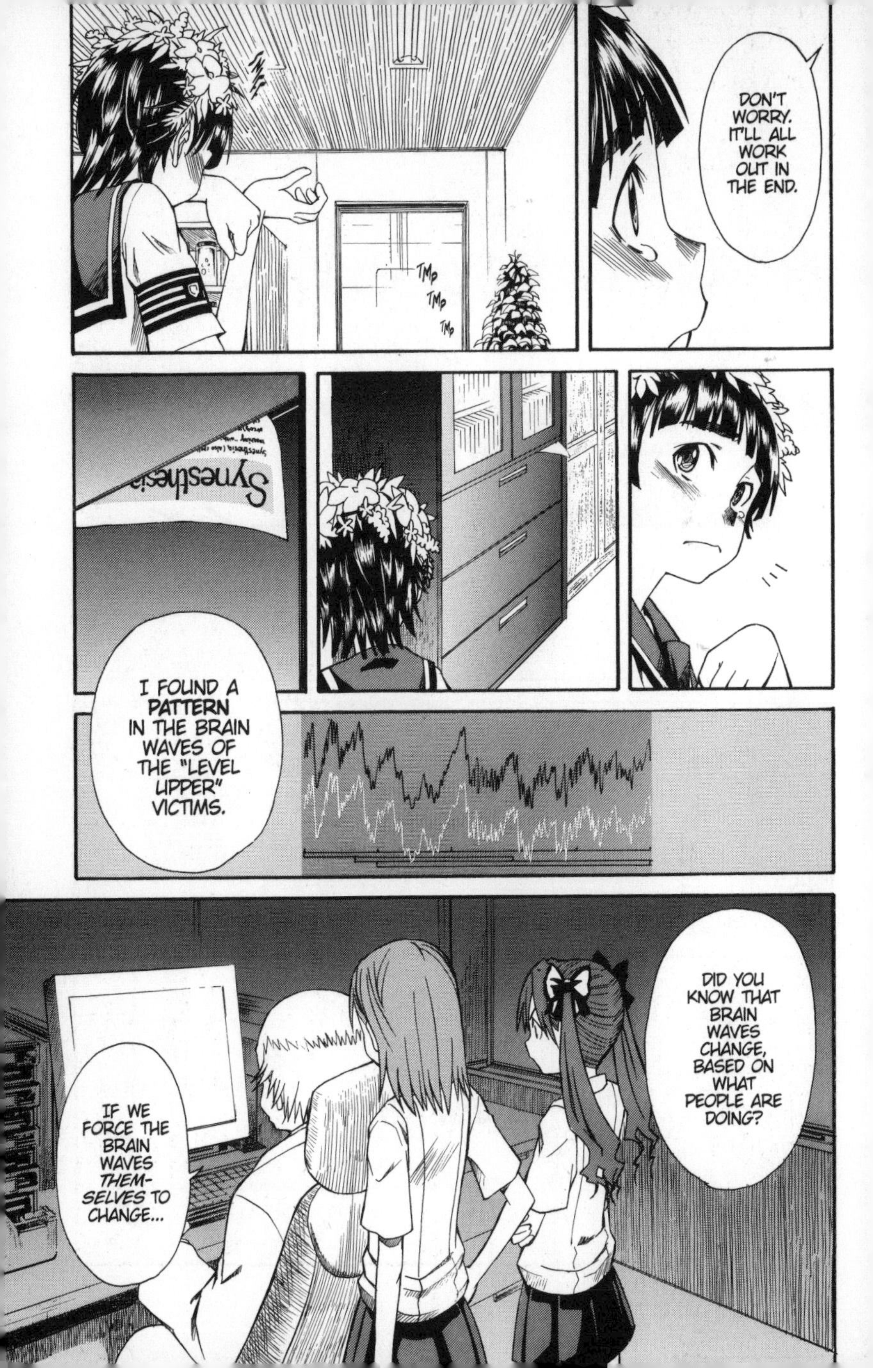
DON'T WORRY. IT'LL ALL WORK OUT IN THE END.
TMP TMP TMP
Synesthesia
I FOUND A **PATTERN** IN THE BRAIN WAVES OF THE "LEVEL UPPER" VICTIMS.
DID YOU KNOW THAT BRAIN WAVES CHANGE, BASED ON WHAT PEOPLE ARE DOING?
IF WE FORCE THE BRAIN WAVES *THEMSELVES* TO CHANGE...

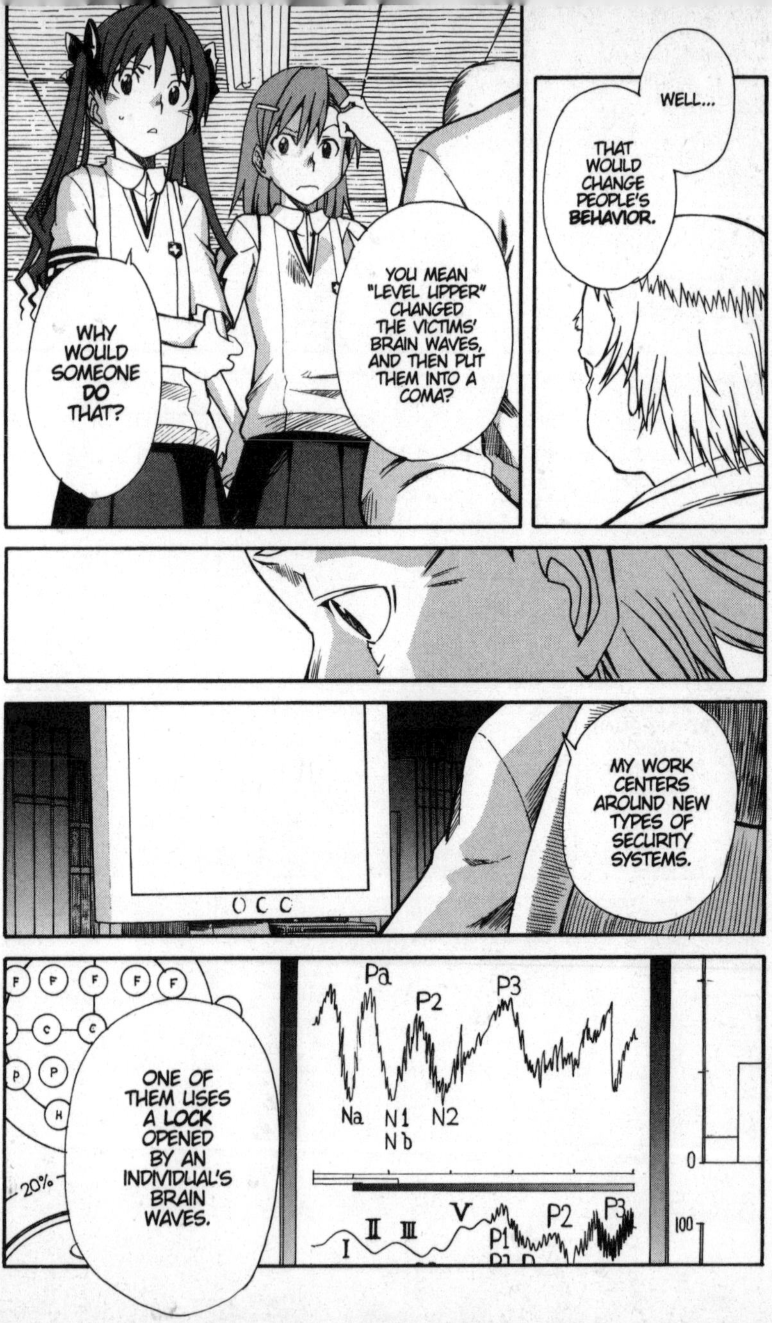
WELL...
THAT WOULD CHANGE PEOPLE'S BEHAVIOR.
YOU MEAN "LEVEL UPPER" CHANGED THE VICTIMS' BRAIN WAVES, AND THEN PUT THEM INTO A COMA?
WHY WOULD SOMEONE DO THAT?
MY WORK CENTERS AROUND NEW TYPES OF SECURITY SYSTEMS.
ONE OF THEM USES A LOCK OPENED BY AN INDIVIDUAL'S BRAIN WAVES.

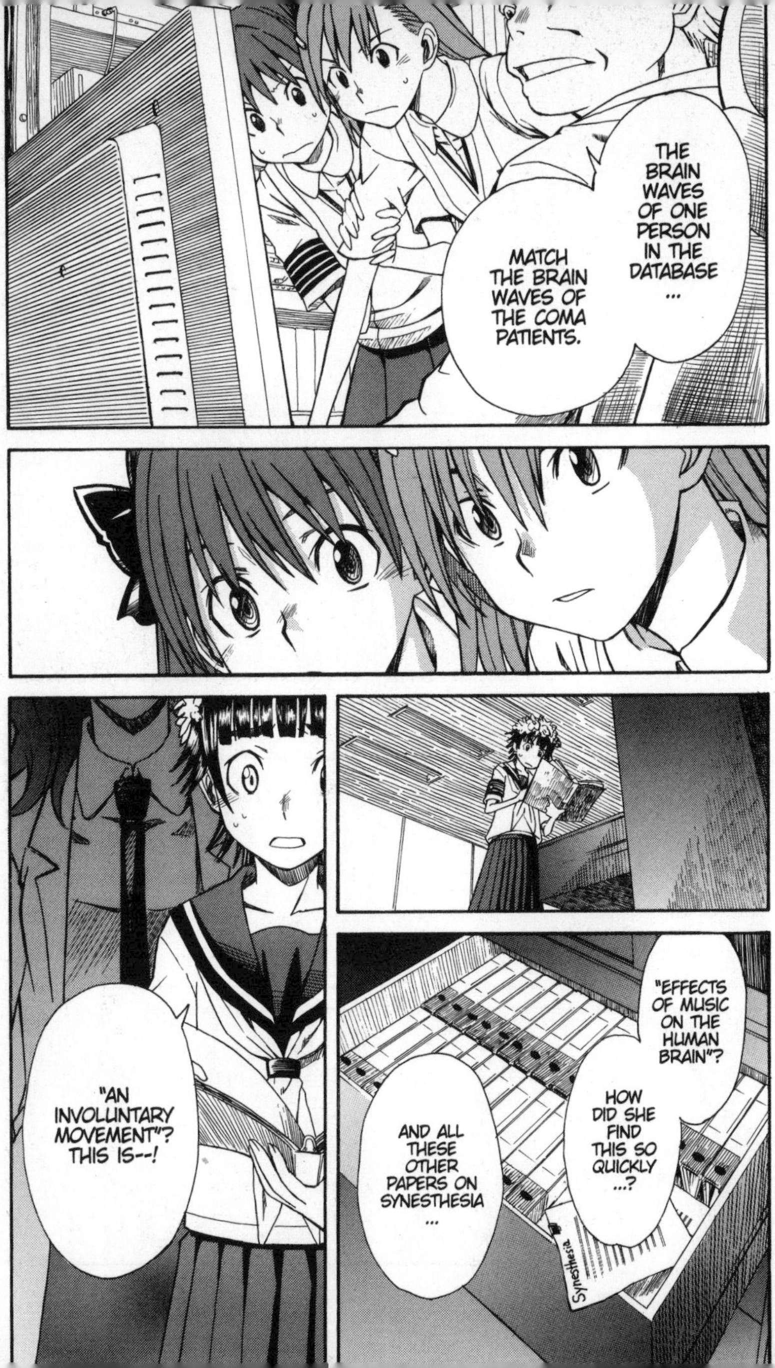
THE BRAIN WAVES OF ONE PERSON IN THE DATABASE ...
MATCH THE BRAIN WAVES OF THE COMA PATIENTS.
"EFFECTS OF MUSIC ON THE HUMAN BRAIN"?
HOW DID SHE FIND THIS SO QUICKLY ...?
AND ALL THESE OTHER PAPERS ON SYNESTHESIA ...
Synesthesia
"AN INVOLUNTARY MOVEMENT"? THIS IS--!

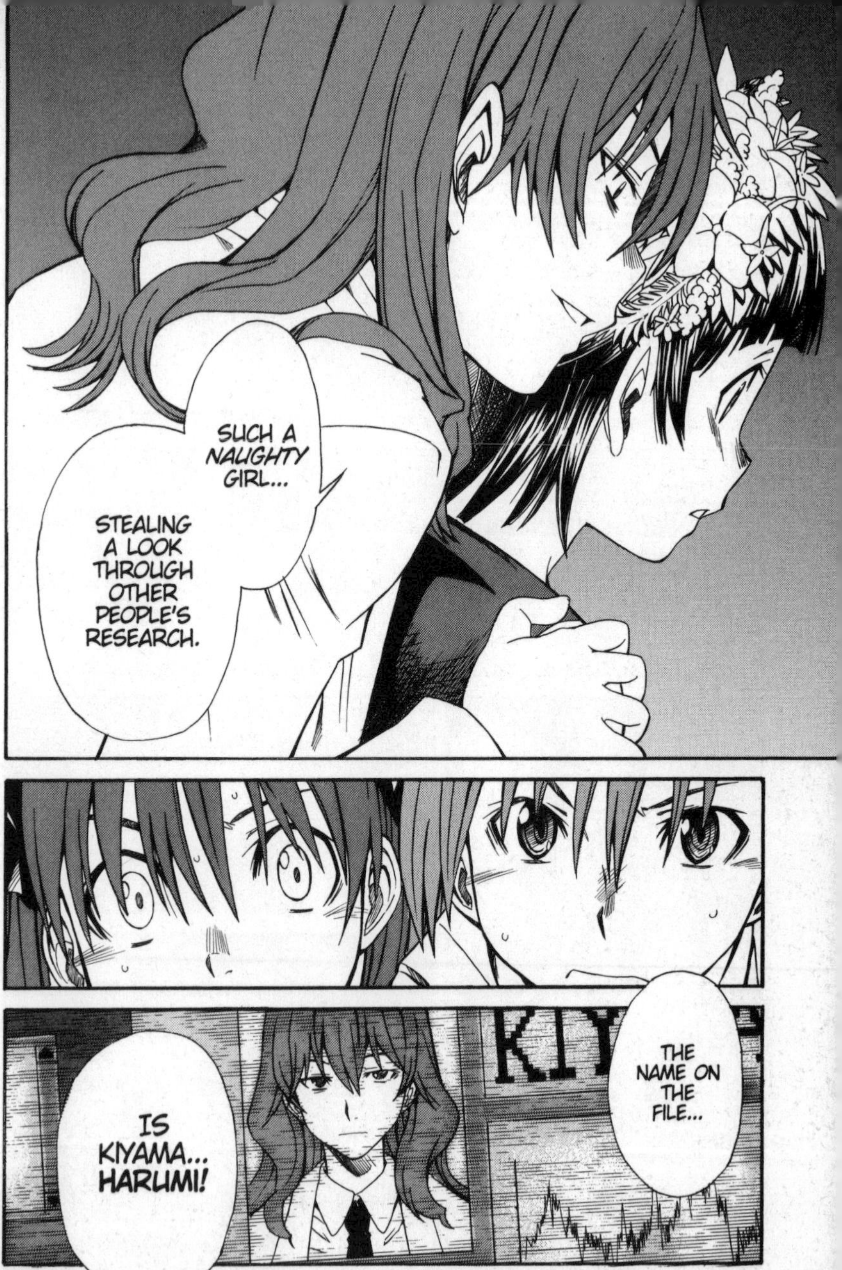
SUCH A NAUGHTY GIRL...
STEALING A LOOK THROUGH OTHER PEOPLE'S RESEARCH.
THE NAME ON THE FILE...
IS KIYAMA... **HARUMI!**

A Certain SCIENTIFIC Railgun

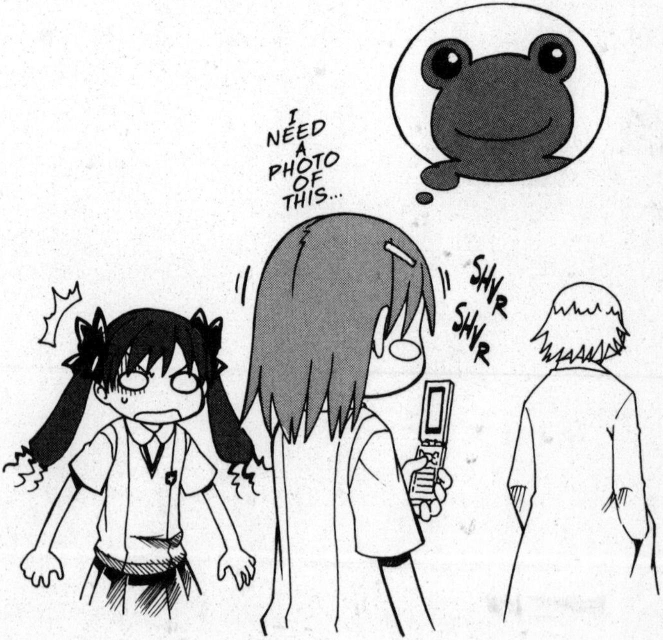
I NEED A PHOTO OF THIS...
SHVR SHVR

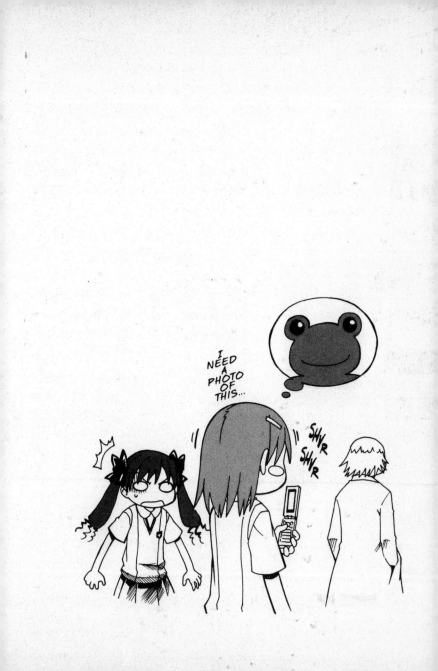

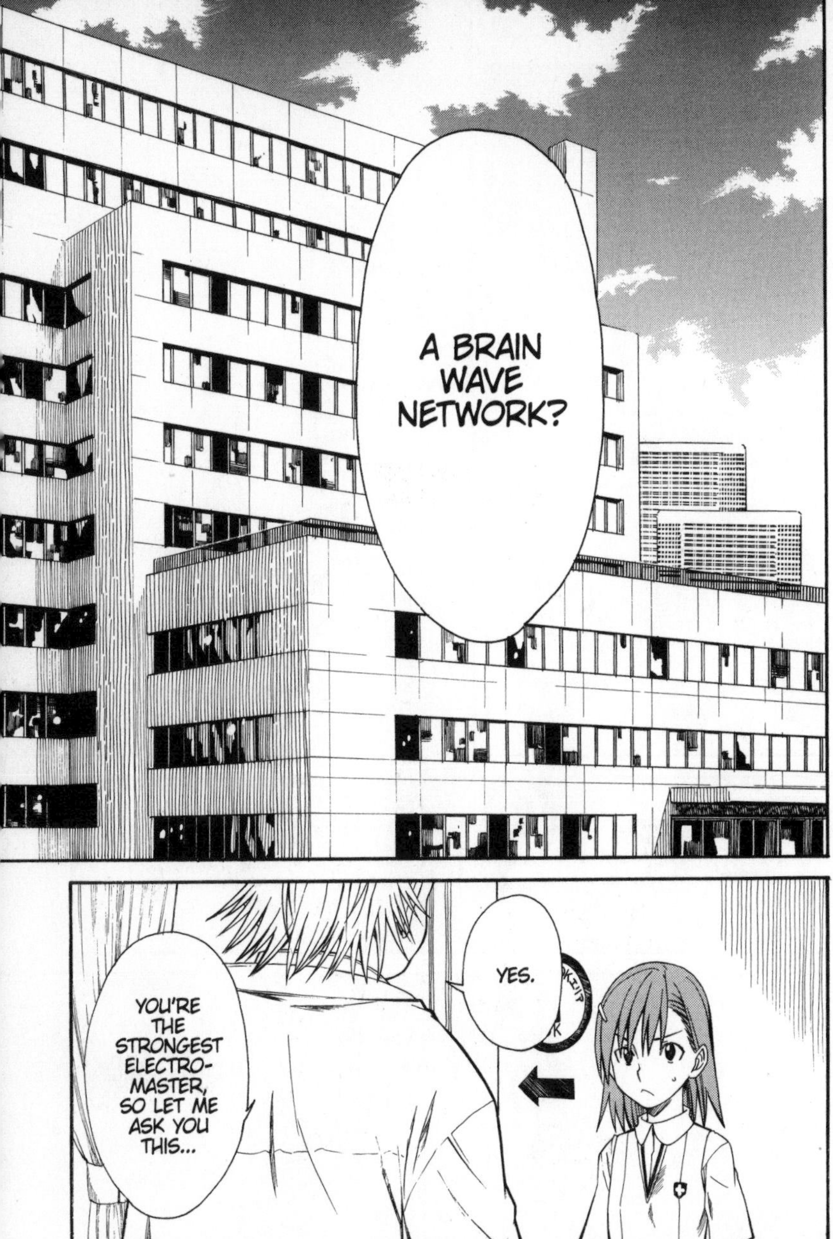
A BRAIN WAVE NETWORK?
YES.
YOU'RE THE STRONGEST ELECTRO-MASTER, SO LET ME ASK YOU THIS...

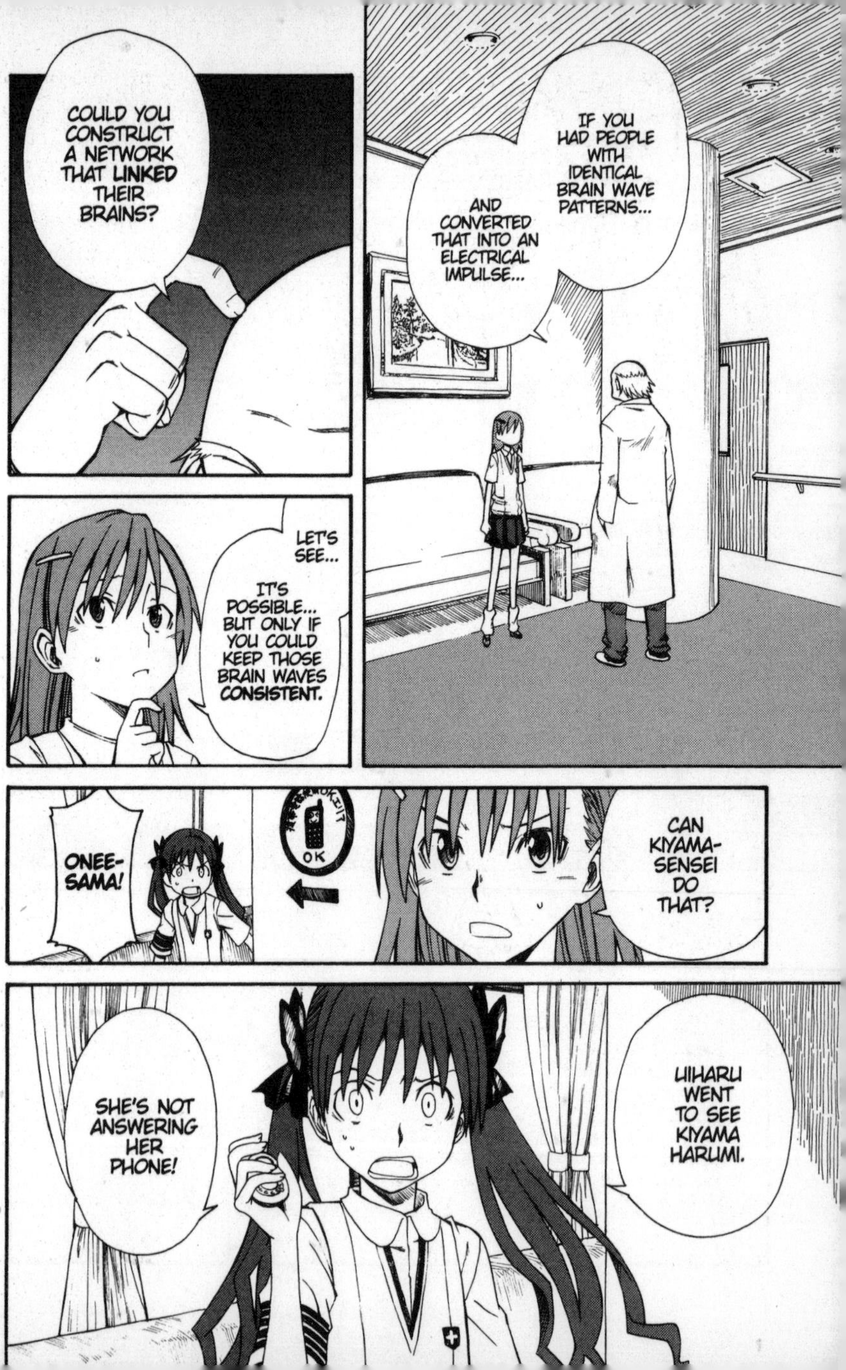
IF YOU HAD PEOPLE WITH IDENTICAL BRAIN WAVE PATTERNS...
AND CONVERTED THAT INTO AN ELECTRICAL IMPULSE...
COULD YOU CONSTRUCT A NETWORK THAT LINKED THEIR BRAINS?
LET'S SEE...
IT'S POSSIBLE... BUT ONLY IF YOU COULD KEEP THOSE BRAIN WAVES CONSISTENT.
CAN KIYAMA-SENSEI DO THAT?
OK
ONEE-SAMA!
UIHARU WENT TO SEE KIYAMA HARUMI.
SHE'S NOT ANSWERING HER PHONE!

CHAPTER 12: JULY 24 (2)

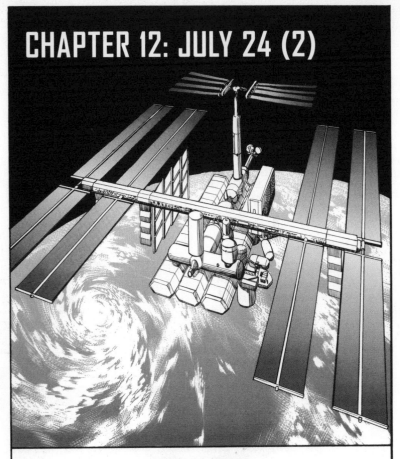

TREE DIAGRAM

* ACADEMY CITY'S SUPERCOMPUTER. IT RESIDES ON THE ORIHIME 1 SATELLITE, LAUNCHED BY ACADEMY CITY. AN ABSOLUTE SIMULATOR, IT IS THE BEST IN THE WORLD, ALMOST TWENTY-FIVE YEARS AHEAD OF ITS TIME.
* OFFICIALLY, IT WAS DESIGNED TO PROVIDE A MORE PERFECT WEATHER FORECAST. IN FACT, IT PREDICTS AN ENTIRE MONTH'S WEATHER ALL AT ONCE, AND IT SPENDS THE REST OF THE TIME PROJECTING THE RESULTS OF RESEARCH PROJECTS OCCURRING WITHIN ACADEMY CITY.
* SINCE IT CAN ACCURATELY PREDICT THE TRAJECTORIES OF EVERY MOLECULE WITHIN THE EARTH'S ATMOSPHERE, WEATHER REPORTS IN ACADEMY CITY ARE NOT PROBABILITIES, BUT SIMPLE STATEMENTS OF FACT.

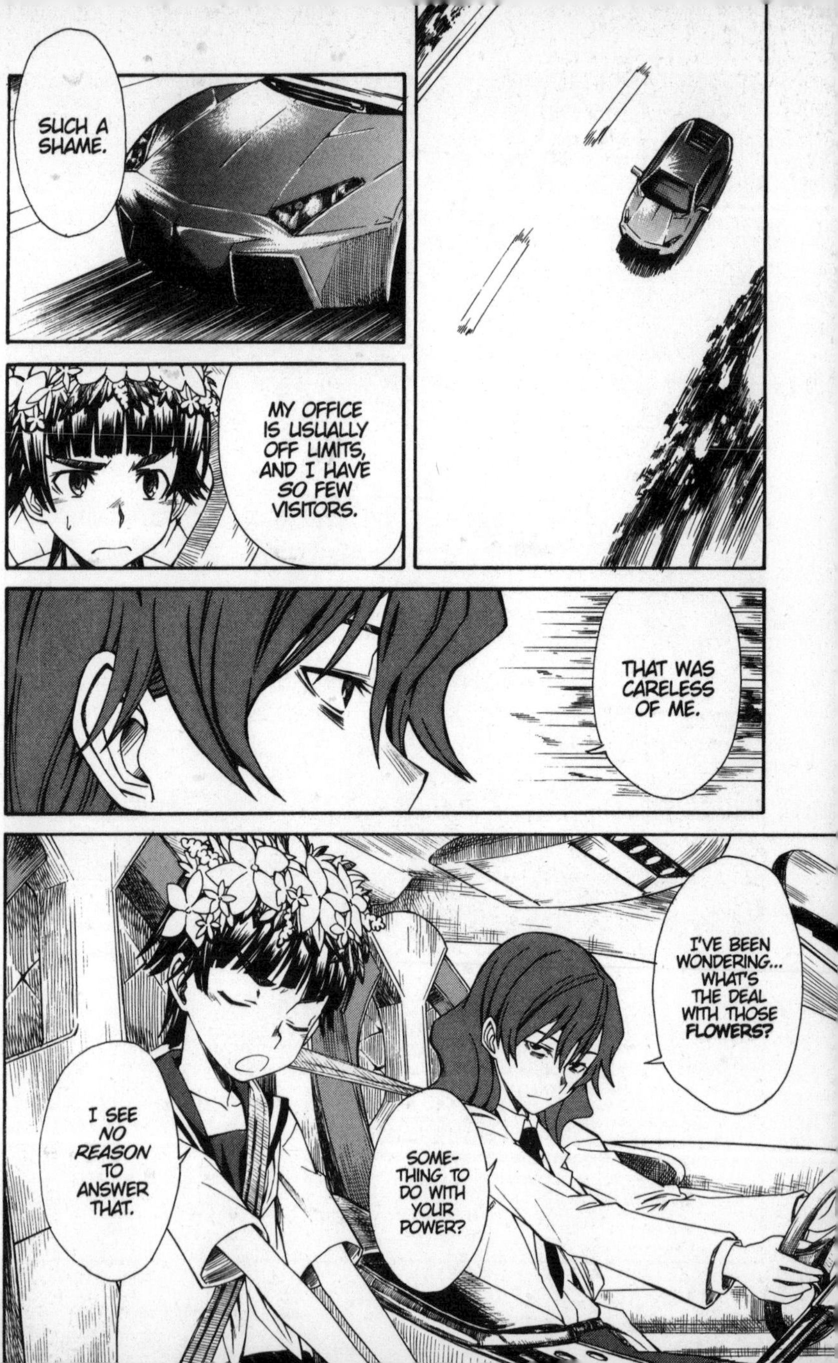
SUCH A SHAME.
MY OFFICE IS USUALLY OFF LIMITS, AND I HAVE SO FEW VISITORS.
THAT WAS CARELESS OF ME.
I'VE BEEN WONDERING... WHAT'S THE DEAL WITH THOSE FLOWERS?
SOME-THING TO DO WITH YOUR POWER?
I SEE NO REASON TO ANSWER THAT.

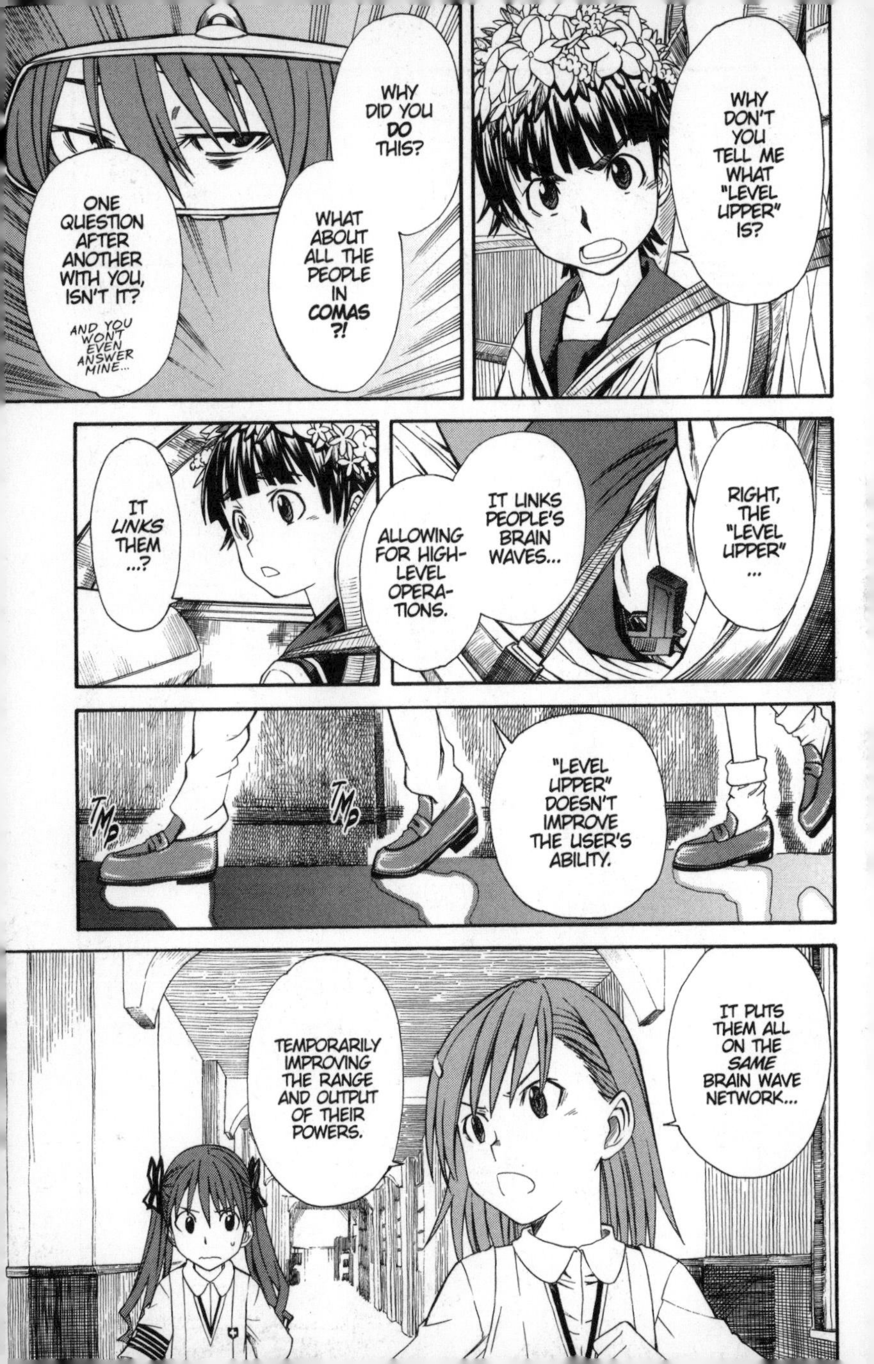
WHY DON'T YOU TELL ME WHAT "LEVEL UPPER" IS?
WHY DID YOU DO THIS?
WHAT ABOUT ALL THE PEOPLE IN COMAS?!
ONE QUESTION AFTER ANOTHER WITH YOU, ISN'T IT?
AND YOU WON'T EVEN ANSWER MINE...
RIGHT, THE "LEVEL UPPER"...
IT LINKS PEOPLE'S BRAIN WAVES...
ALLOWING FOR HIGH-LEVEL OPERATIONS.
IT LINKS THEM...?
TMP
"LEVEL UPPER" DOESN'T IMPROVE THE USER'S ABILITY.
TMP
IT PUTS THEM ALL ON THE SAME BRAIN WAVE NETWORK...
TEMPORARILY IMPROVING THE RANGE AND OUTPUT OF THEIR POWERS.

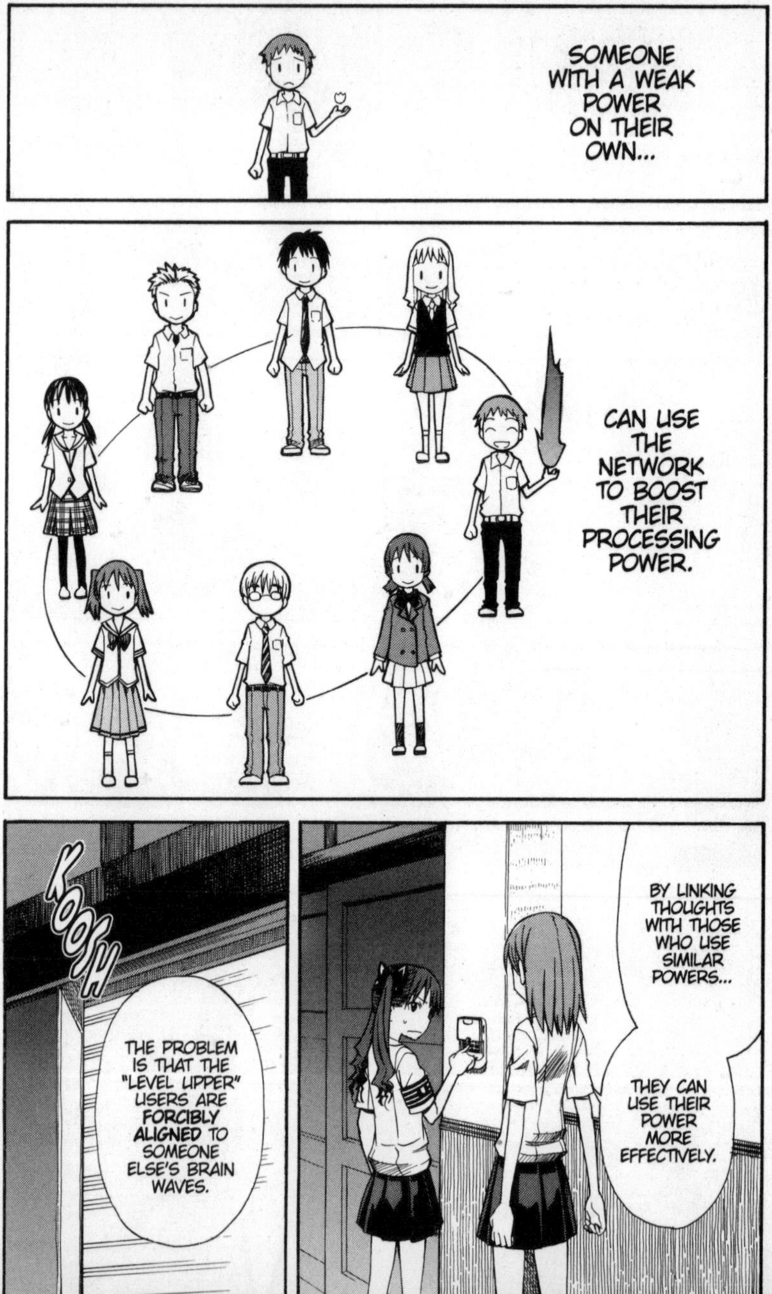
SOMEONE WITH A WEAK POWER ON THEIR OWN...
CAN USE THE NETWORK TO BOOST THEIR PROCESSING POWER.
BY LINKING THOUGHTS WITH THOSE WHO USE SIMILAR POWERS...
THEY CAN USE THEIR POWER MORE EFFECTIVELY.
KOOSH
THE PROBLEM IS THAT THE "LEVEL UPPER" USERS ARE **FORCIBLY ALIGNED** TO SOMEONE ELSE'S BRAIN WAVES.

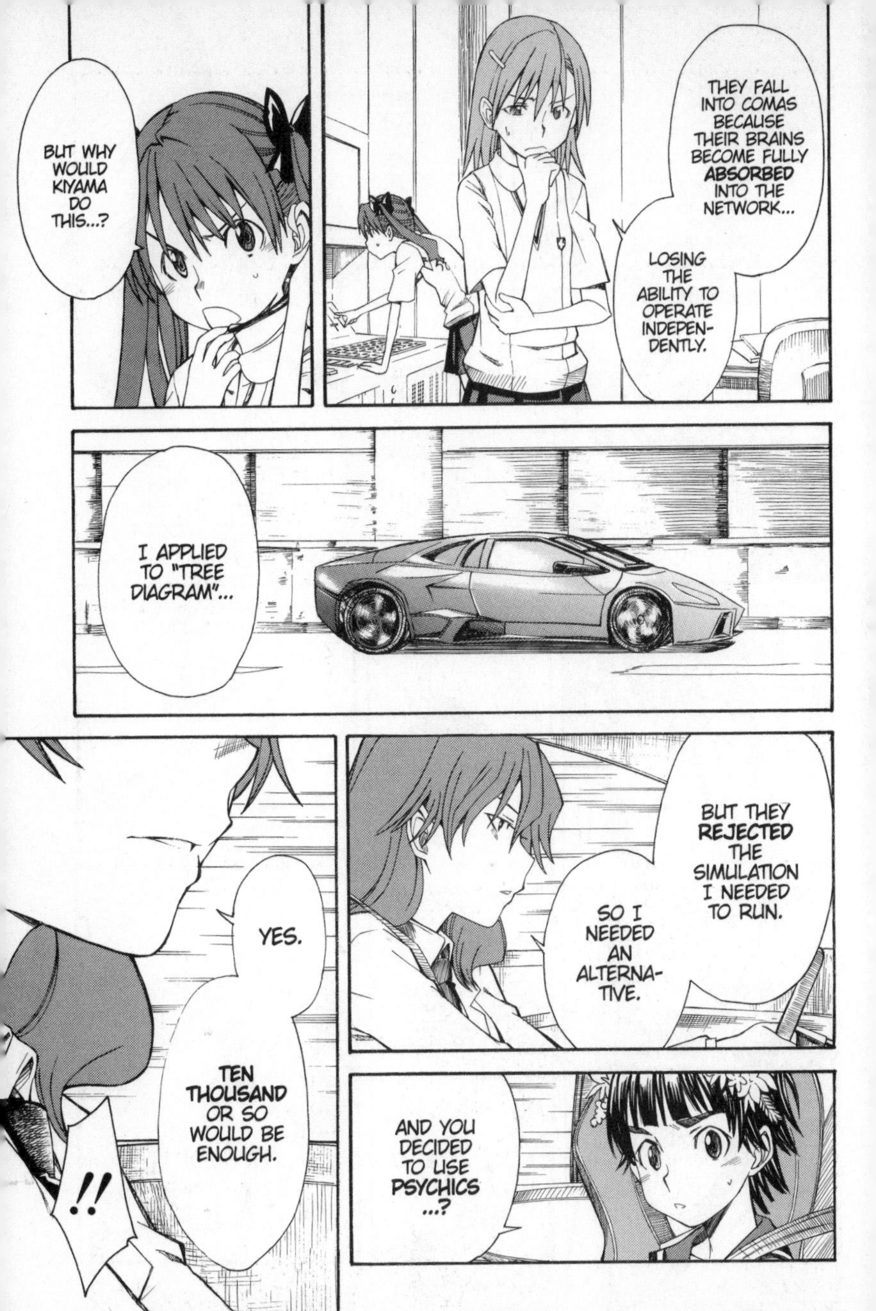
THEY FALL INTO COMAS BECAUSE THEIR BRAINS BECOME FULLY **ABSORBED** INTO THE NETWORK...
LOSING THE ABILITY TO OPERATE INDEPEN-DENTLY.
BUT WHY WOULD KIYAMA DO THIS...?
I APPLIED TO "TREE DIAGRAM"...
BUT THEY **REJECTED** THE SIMULATION I NEEDED TO RUN.
SO I NEEDED AN ALTERNA-TIVE.
AND YOU DECIDED TO USE **PSYCHICS** ...?
YES.
TEN THOUSAND OR SO WOULD BE ENOUGH.
!!

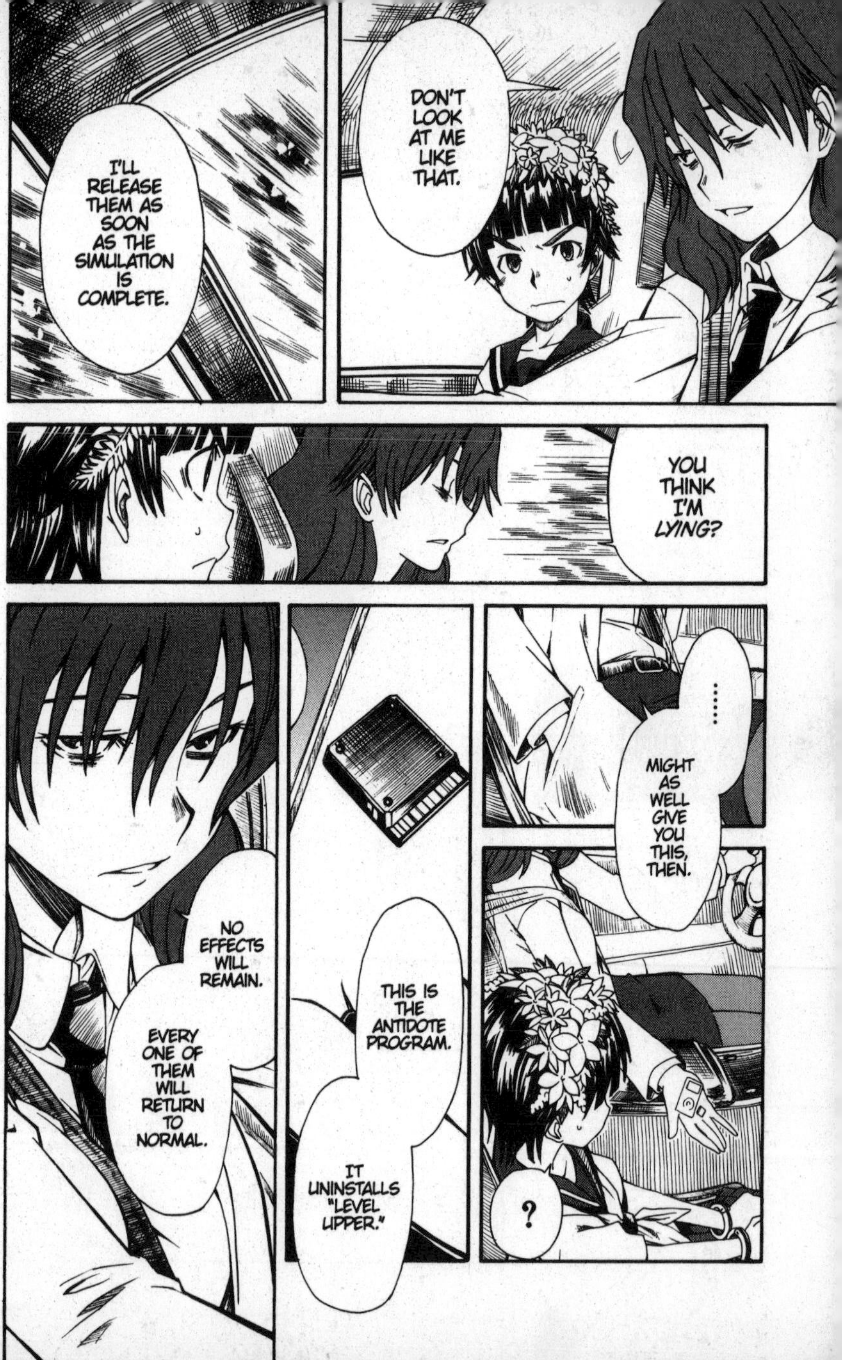
DON'T LOOK AT ME LIKE THAT.
I'LL RELEASE THEM AS SOON AS THE SIMULATION IS COMPLETE.
YOU THINK I'M *LYING?*
......
MIGHT AS WELL GIVE YOU THIS, THEN.
?
THIS IS THE ANTIDOTE PROGRAM.
IT UNINSTALLS "LEVEL UPPER."
NO EFFECTS WILL REMAIN.
EVERY ONE OF THEM WILL RETURN TO NORMAL.

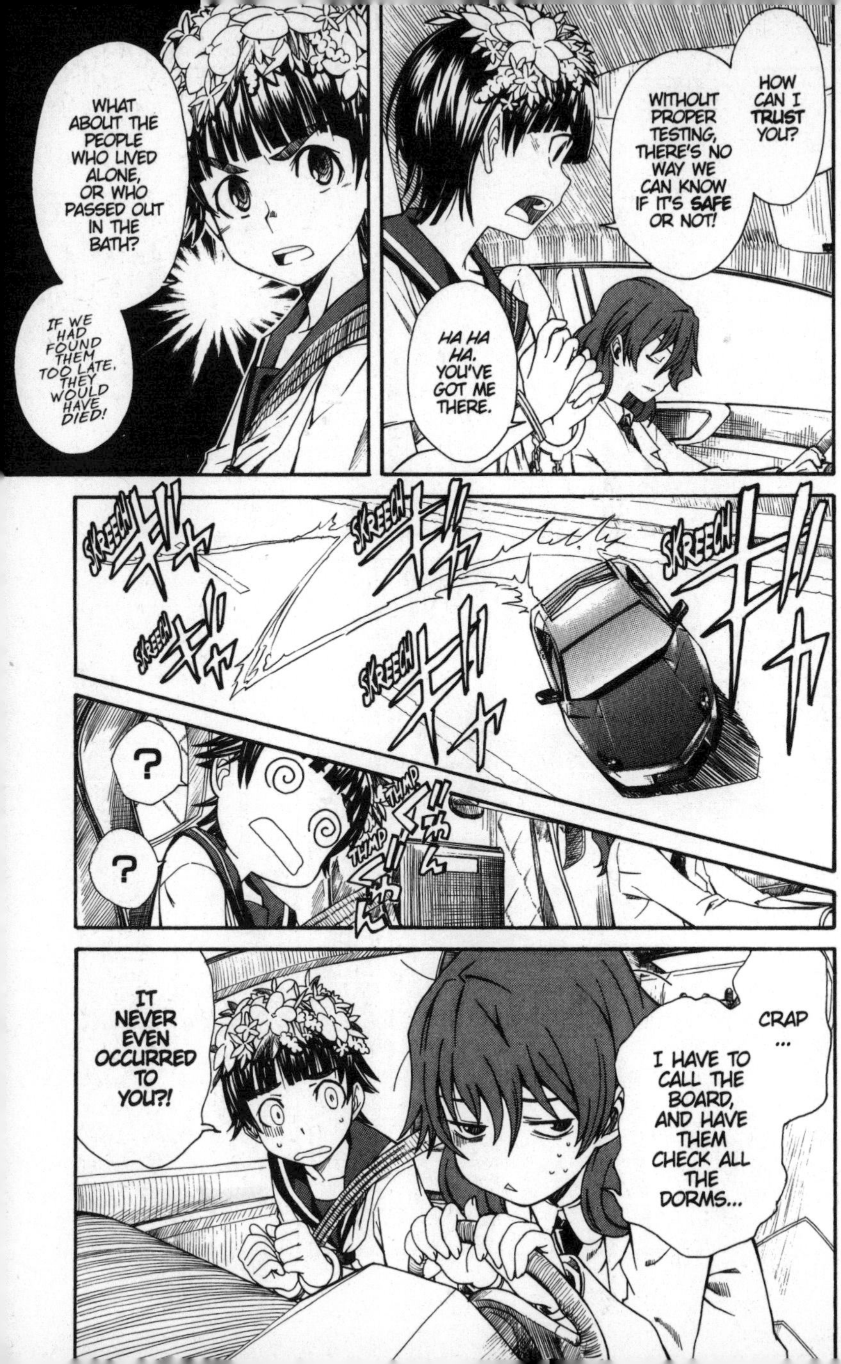
HOW CAN I TRUST YOU?
WITHOUT PROPER TESTING, THERE'S NO WAY WE CAN KNOW IF IT'S SAFE OR NOT!
HA HA HA. YOU'VE GOT ME THERE.
WHAT ABOUT THE PEOPLE WHO LIVED ALONE, OR WHO PASSED OUT IN THE BATH?
IF WE HAD FOUND THEM TOO LATE, THEY WOULD HAVE DIED!
SKREECH
SKREECH
SKREECH
SKREECH
SKREECH
?
?
THUMP
THUMP
CRAP ...
I HAVE TO CALL THE BOARD, AND HAVE THEM CHECK ALL THE DORMS...
IT NEVER EVEN OCCURRED TO YOU?!

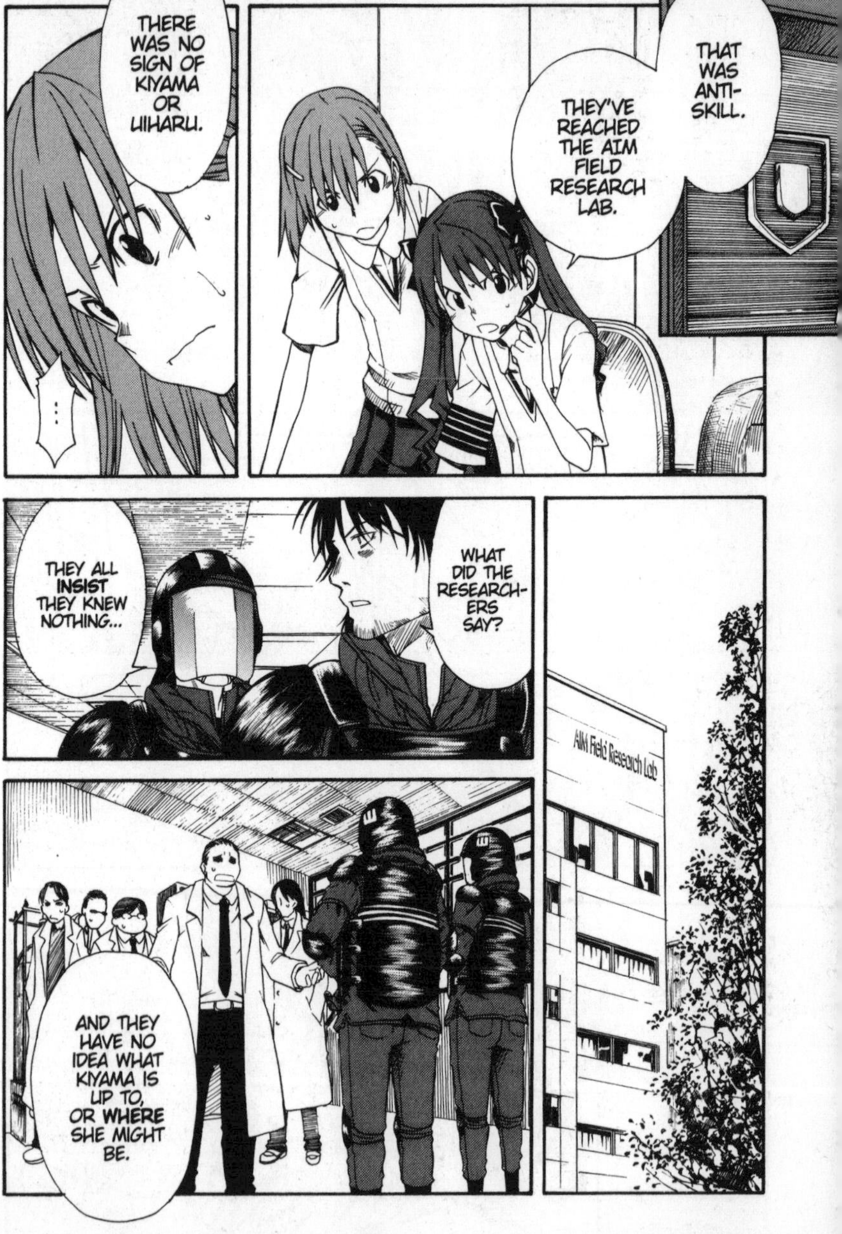
THAT WAS ANTI-SKILL.
THEY'VE REACHED THE AIM FIELD RESEARCH LAB.
THERE WAS NO SIGN OF KIYAMA OR UIHARU.
...
AIM Field Research Lab
WHAT DID THE RESEARCHERS SAY?
THEY ALL INSIST THEY KNEW NOTHING...
AND THEY HAVE NO IDEA WHAT KIYAMA IS UP TO, OR WHERE SHE MIGHT BE.

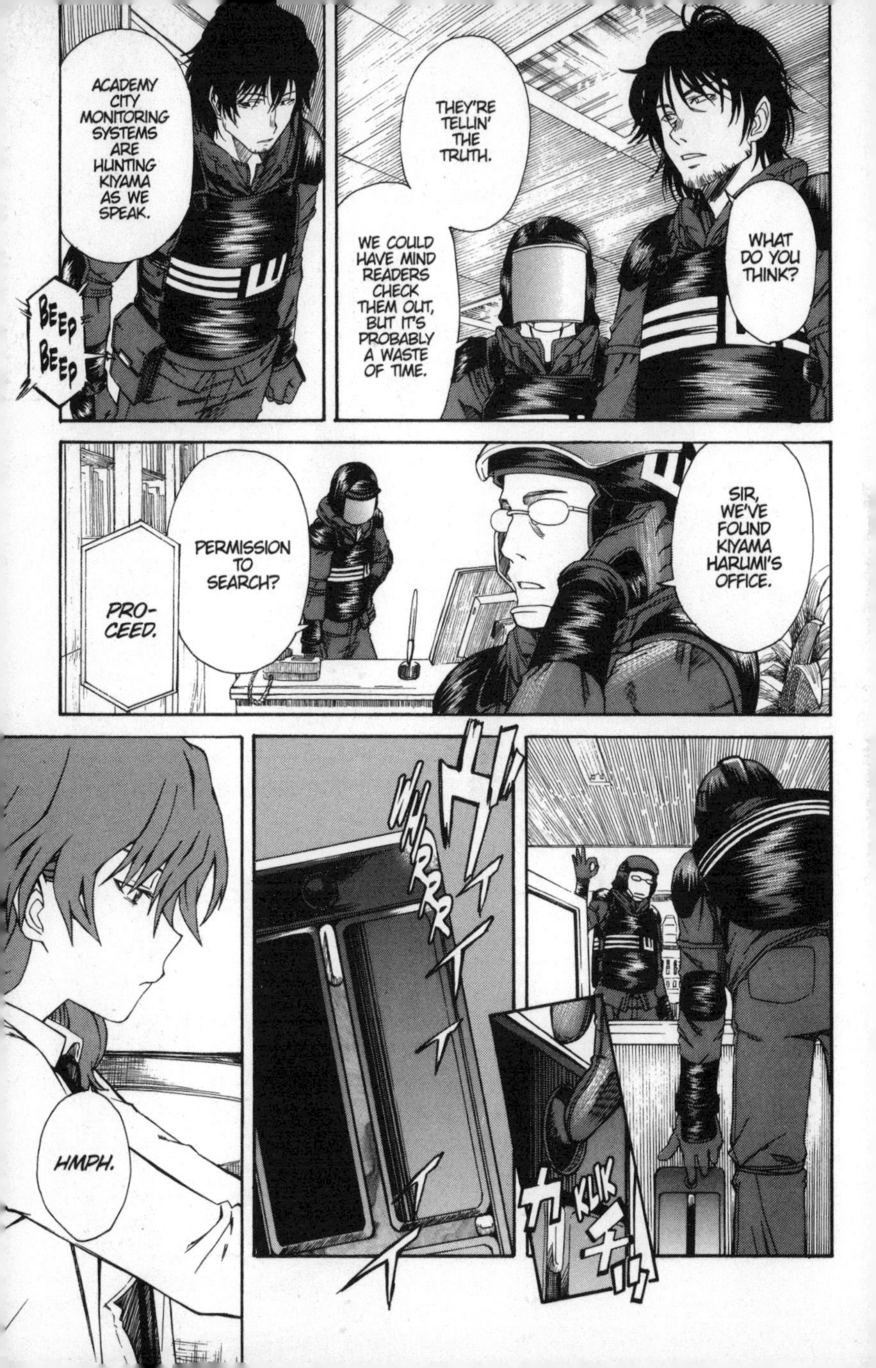
WHAT DO YOU THINK?
THEY'RE TELLIN' THE TRUTH.
WE COULD HAVE MIND READERS CHECK THEM OUT, BUT IT'S PROBABLY A WASTE OF TIME.
ACADEMY CITY MONITORING SYSTEMS ARE HUNTING KIYAMA AS WE SPEAK.
BEEP BEEP
SIR, WE'VE FOUND KIYAMA HARUMI'S OFFICE.
PERMISSION TO SEARCH?
PRO-CEED.
KLIK
WHIRRR
HMPH.

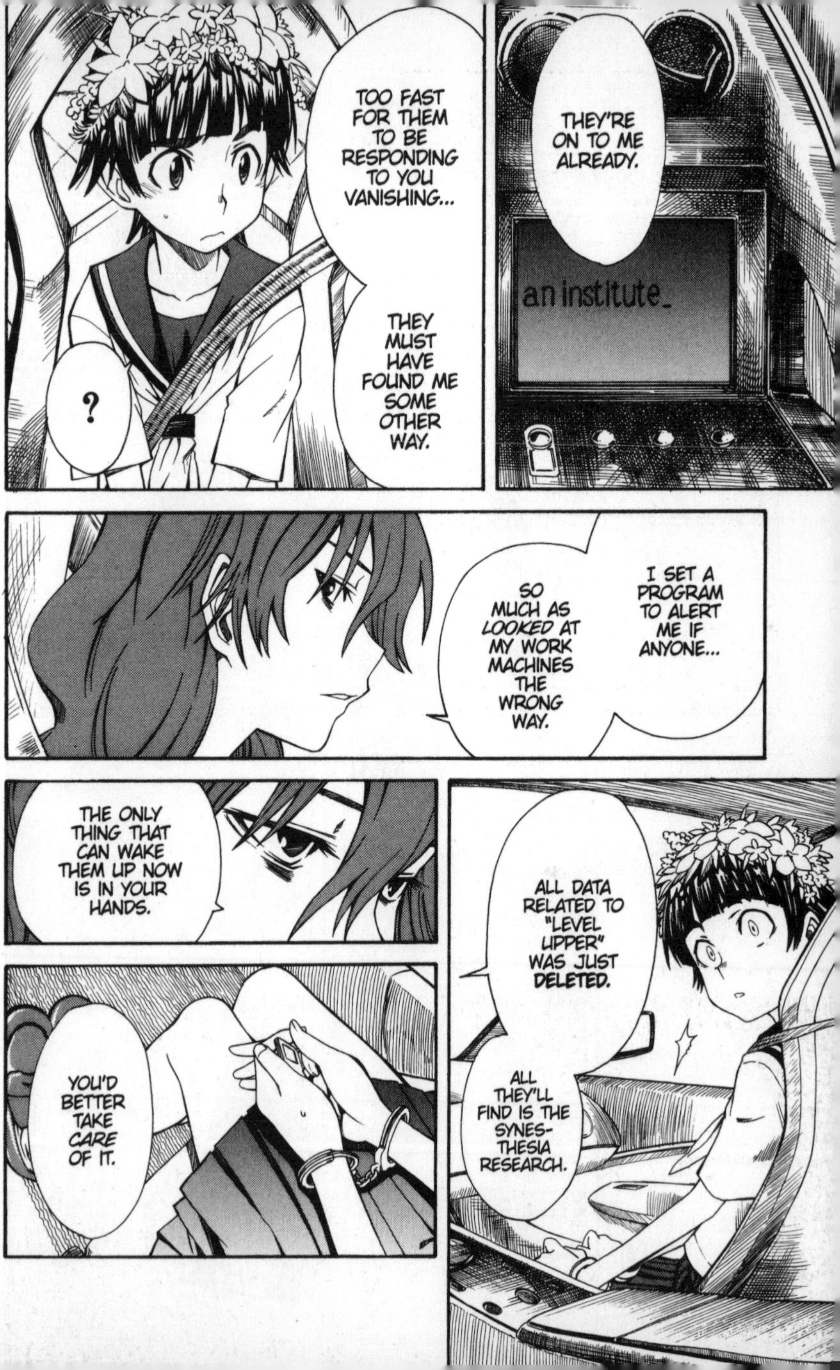
THEY'RE ON TO ME ALREADY.
an institute_
TOO FAST FOR THEM TO BE RESPONDING TO YOU VANISHING...
THEY MUST HAVE FOUND ME SOME OTHER WAY.
?
I SET A PROGRAM TO ALERT ME IF ANYONE...
SO MUCH AS *LOOKED* AT MY WORK MACHINES THE WRONG WAY.
ALL DATA RELATED TO "LEVEL UPPER" WAS JUST **DELETED.**
ALL THEY'LL FIND IS THE SYNES-THESIA RESEARCH.
THE ONLY THING THAT CAN WAKE THEM UP NOW IS IN YOUR HANDS.
YOU'D BETTER TAKE CARE OF IT.

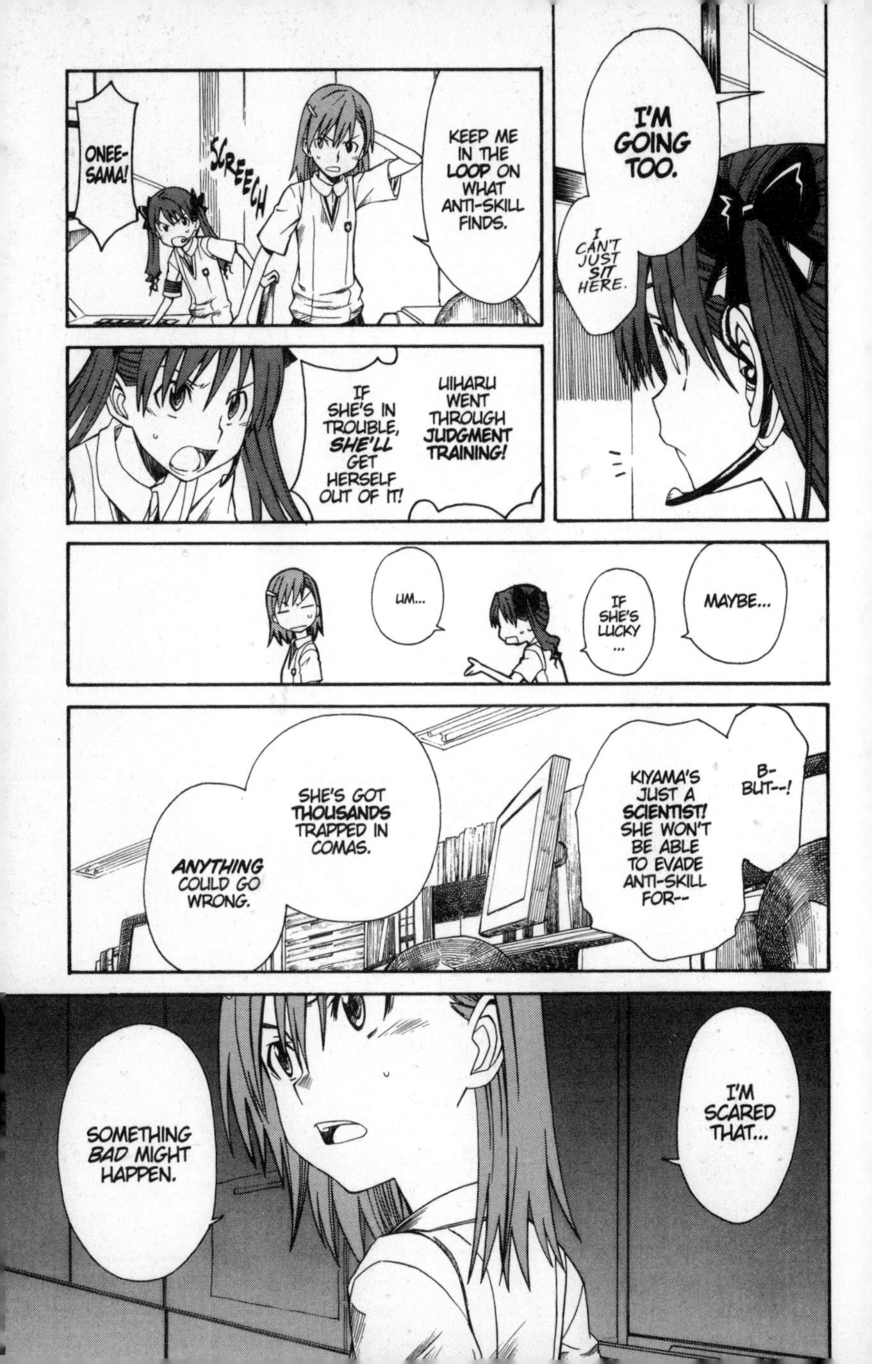
I'M GOING TOO.
I CAN'T JUST SIT HERE.
KEEP ME IN THE LOOP ON WHAT ANTI-SKILL FINDS.
SCREECH
ONEE-SAMA!
UIHARU WENT THROUGH JUDGMENT TRAINING!
IF SHE'S IN TROUBLE, SHE'LL GET HERSELF OUT OF IT!
MAYBE...
IF SHE'S LUCKY...
UM...
B-BUT--!
KIYAMA'S JUST A SCIENTIST! SHE WON'T BE ABLE TO EVADE ANTI-SKILL FOR--
SHE'S GOT THOUSANDS TRAPPED IN COMAS.
ANYTHING COULD GO WRONG.
I'M SCARED THAT...
SOMETHING BAD MIGHT HAPPEN.

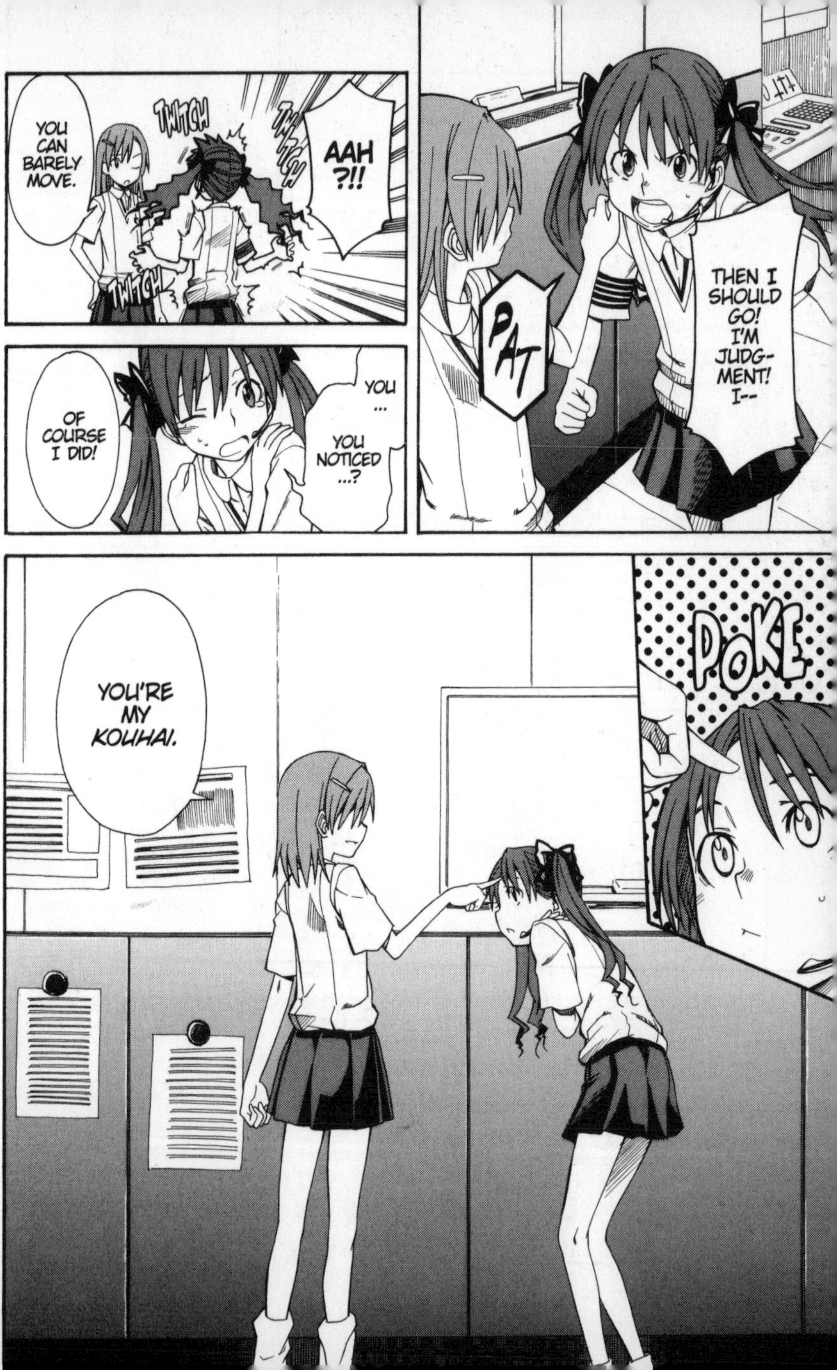
THEN I SHOULD GO! I'M JUDGMENT! I--
PAT
AAH?!!
TWITCH
TWITCH
TWITCH
YOU CAN BARELY MOVE.
YOU ... YOU NOTICED ...?
OF COURSE I DID!
POKE
YOU'RE MY KOUHAI.

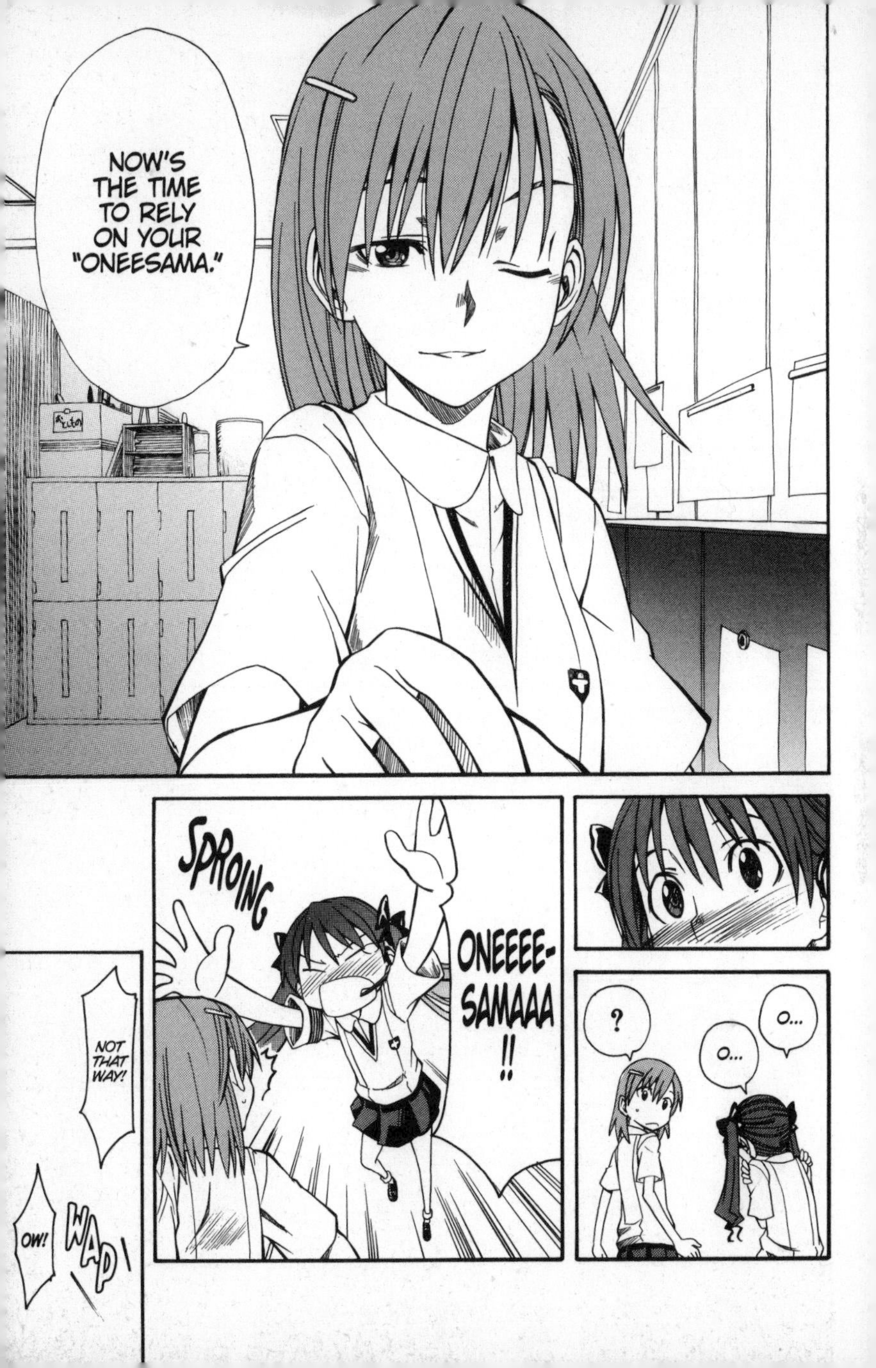
NOW'S THE TIME TO RELY ON YOUR "ONEESAMA."
O...
?
O...
SPROING
ONEEEE-SAMAAA!!
NOT THAT WAY!
WAP
OW!

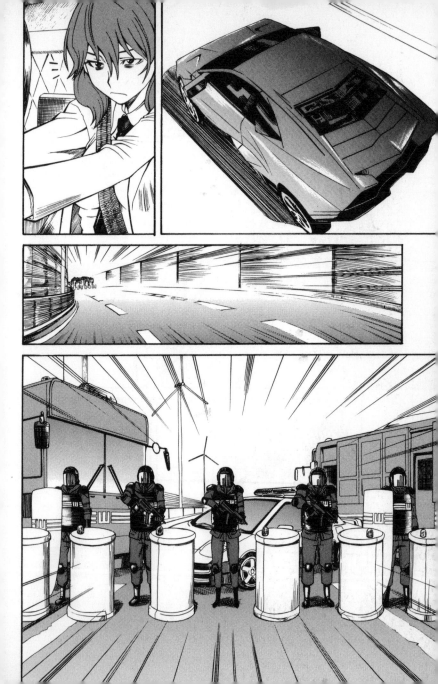

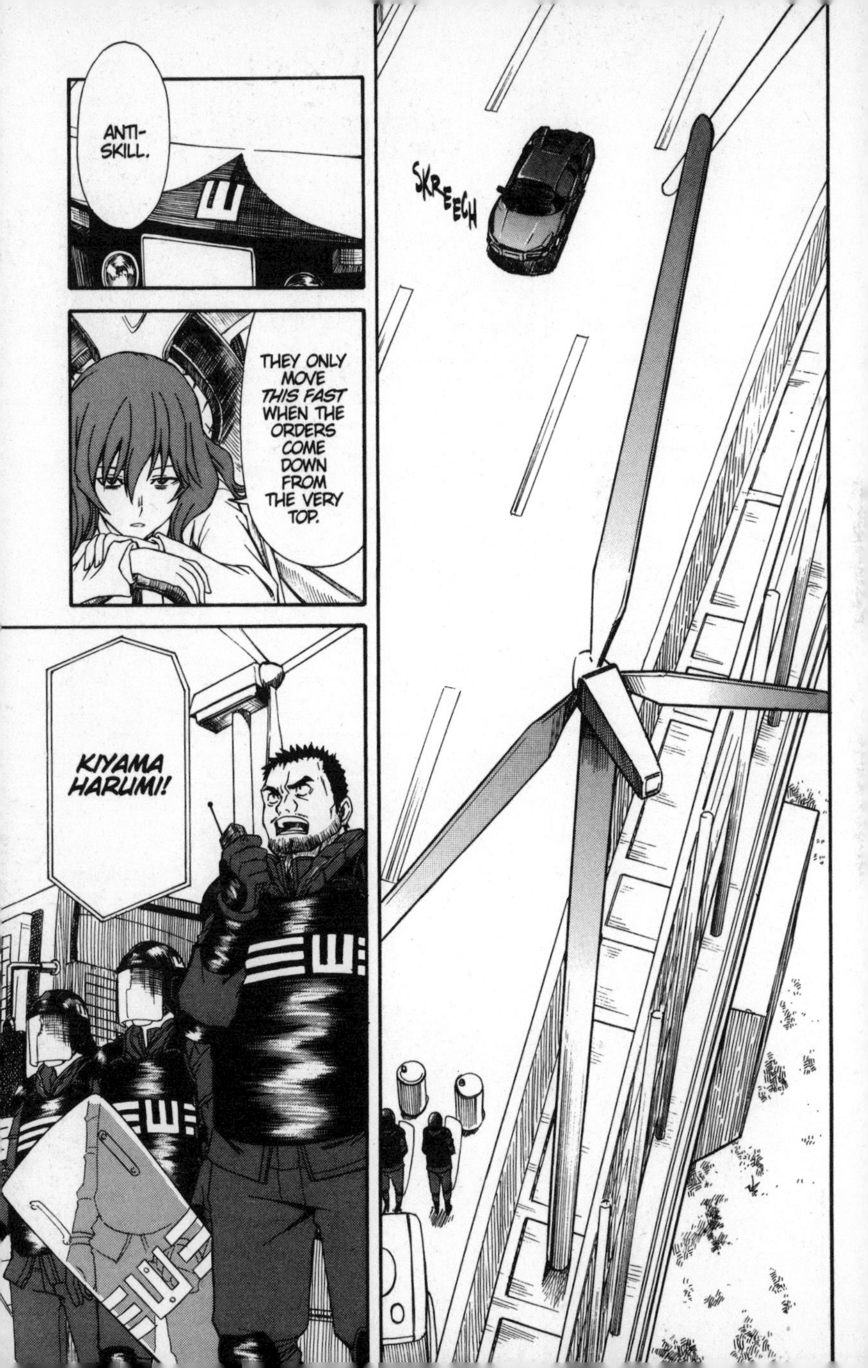
SKREEECH
ANTI-SKILL.
THEY ONLY MOVE *THIS FAST* WHEN THE ORDERS COME DOWN FROM THE VERY TOP.
KIYAMA HARUMI!

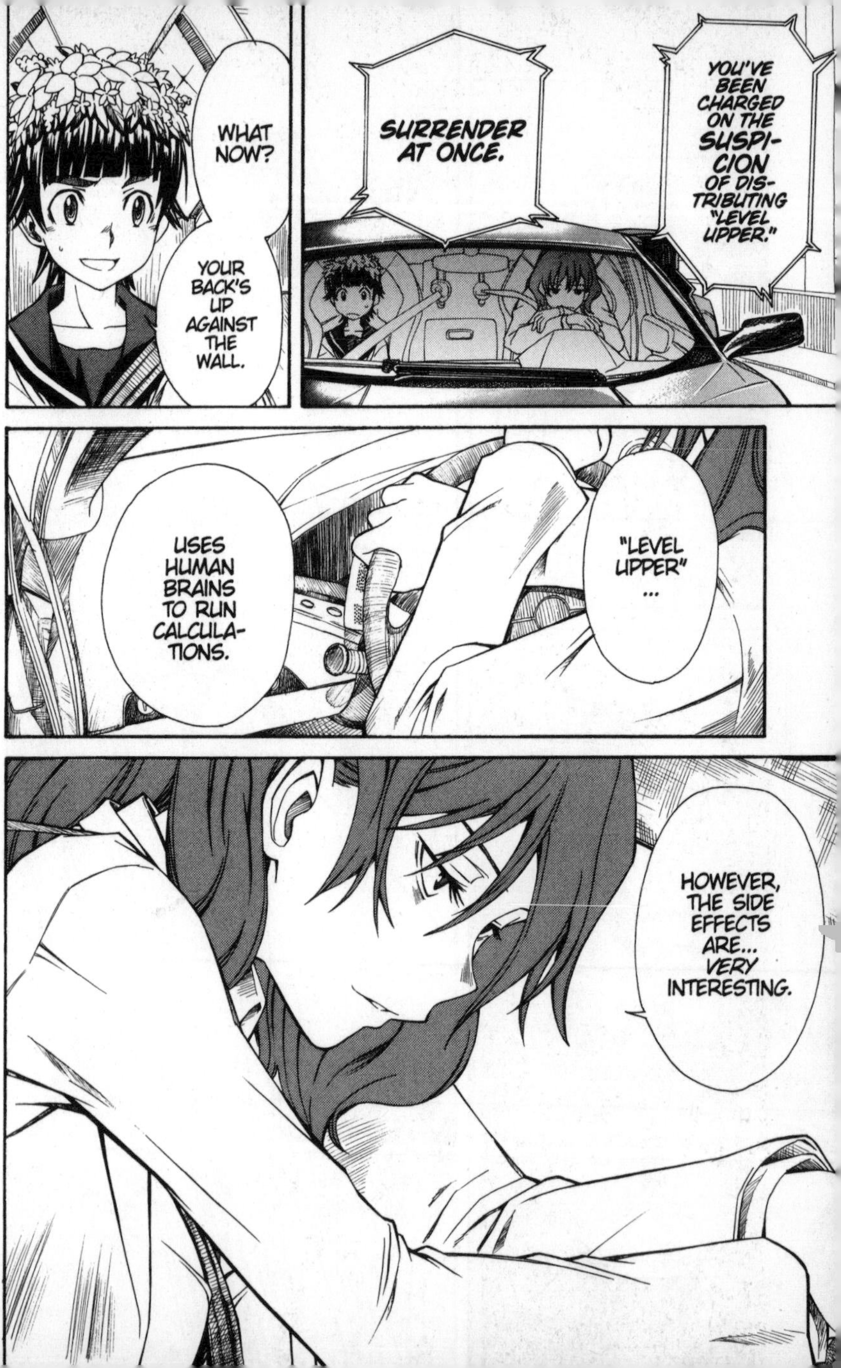

YOU'VE BEEN CHARGED ON THE SUSPICION OF DISTRIBUTING "LEVEL UPPER."
SURRENDER AT ONCE.
WHAT NOW?
YOUR BACK'S UP AGAINST THE WALL.
"LEVEL UPPER" ...
USES HUMAN BRAINS TO RUN CALCULATIONS.
HOWEVER, THE SIDE EFFECTS ARE... VERY INTERESTING.

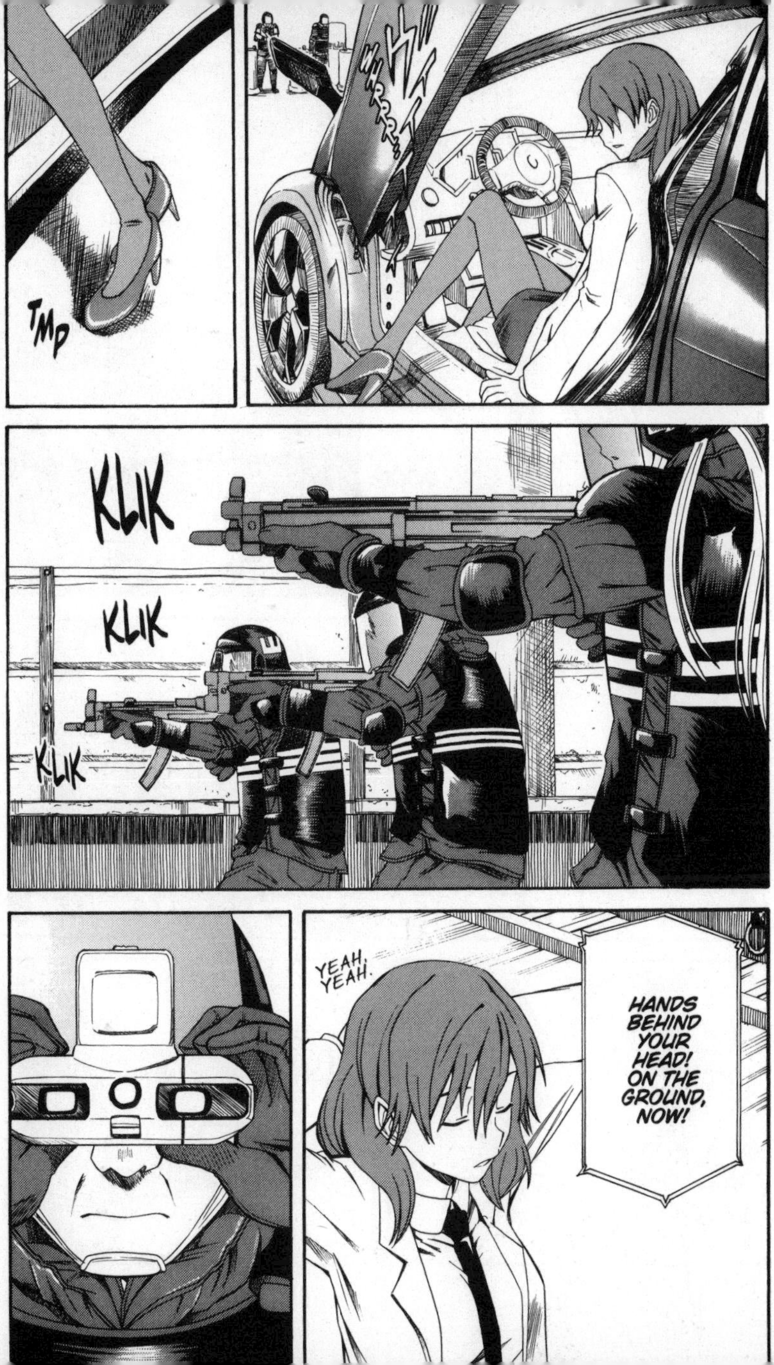
TMP
KLIK
KLIK
KLIK
HANDS BEHIND YOUR HEAD! ON THE GROUND, NOW!
YEAH, YEAH.

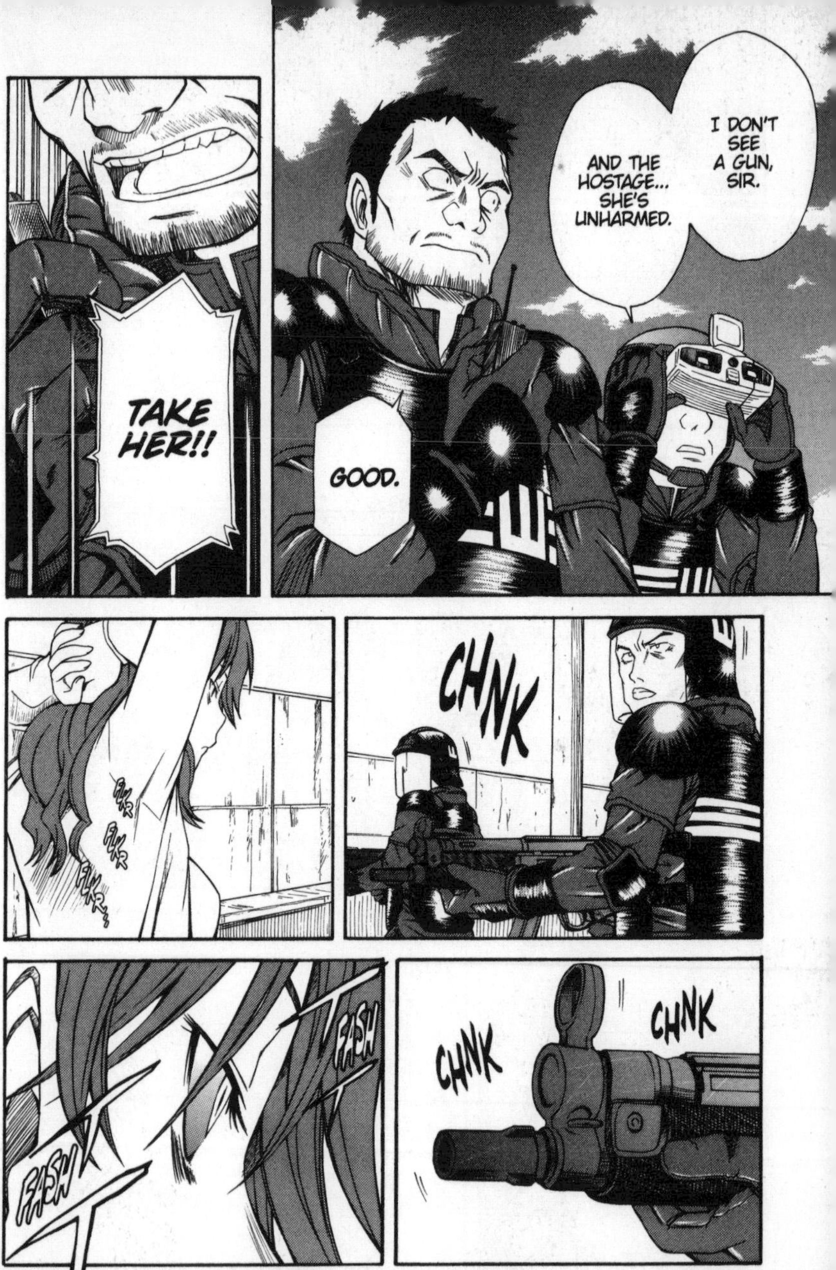
I DON'T SEE A GUN, SIR.
AND THE HOSTAGE... SHE'S UNHARMED.
GOOD.
TAKE HER!!
CHNK
FLKR
FLKR
FLKR...
CHNK
CHNK
FLASH
FLASH

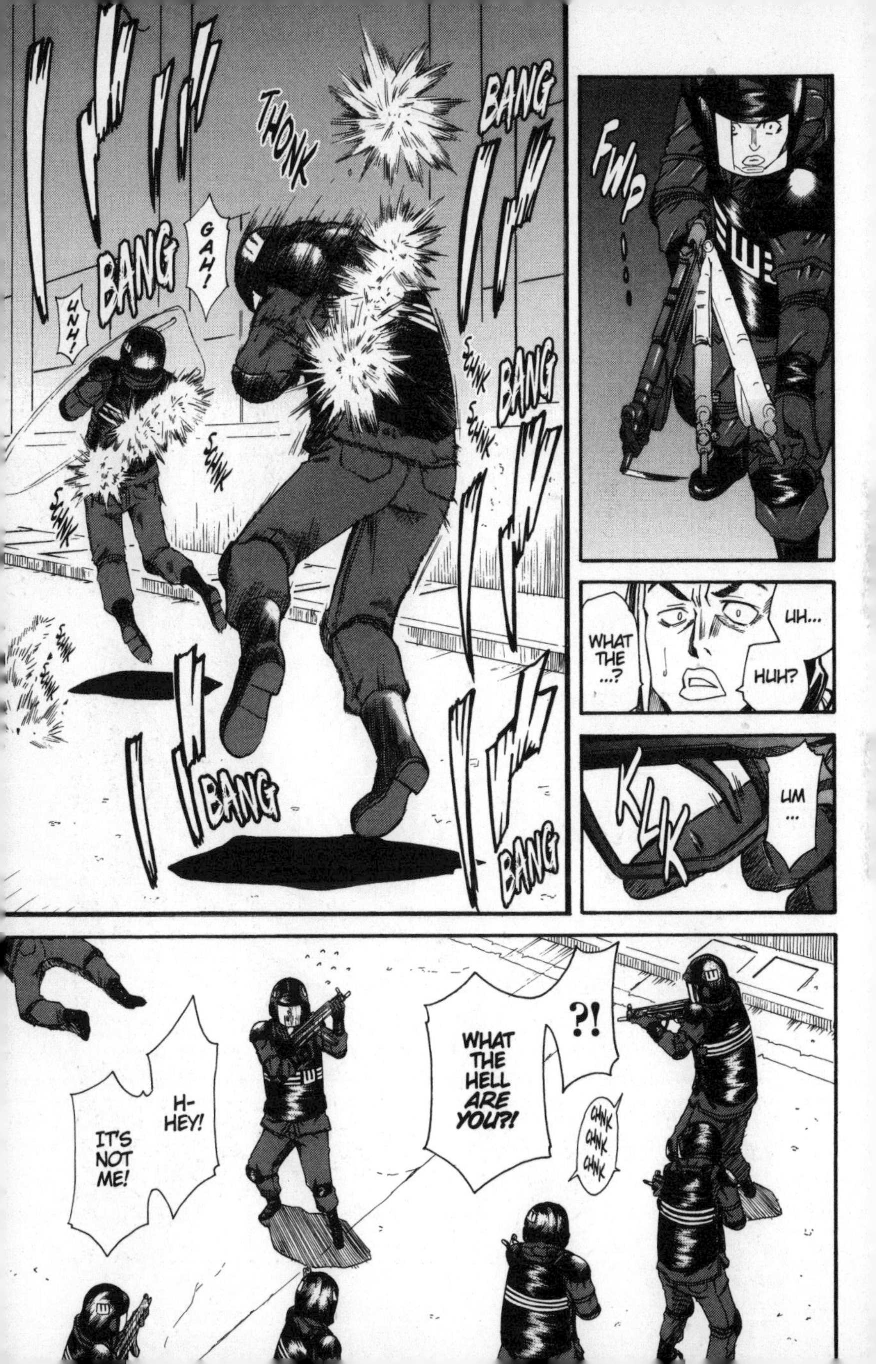
FWIP
UH... HUH?
WHAT THE ...?
KLIK
UM ...
BANG
THONK
GAH!
BANG
UNH!
SHNK SHNK
BANG
SHNK SHNK
SHNK SHNK
BANG
BANG
?!
WHAT THE HELL ARE YOU?!
CHNK CHNK CHNK
H- HEY!
IT'S NOT ME!

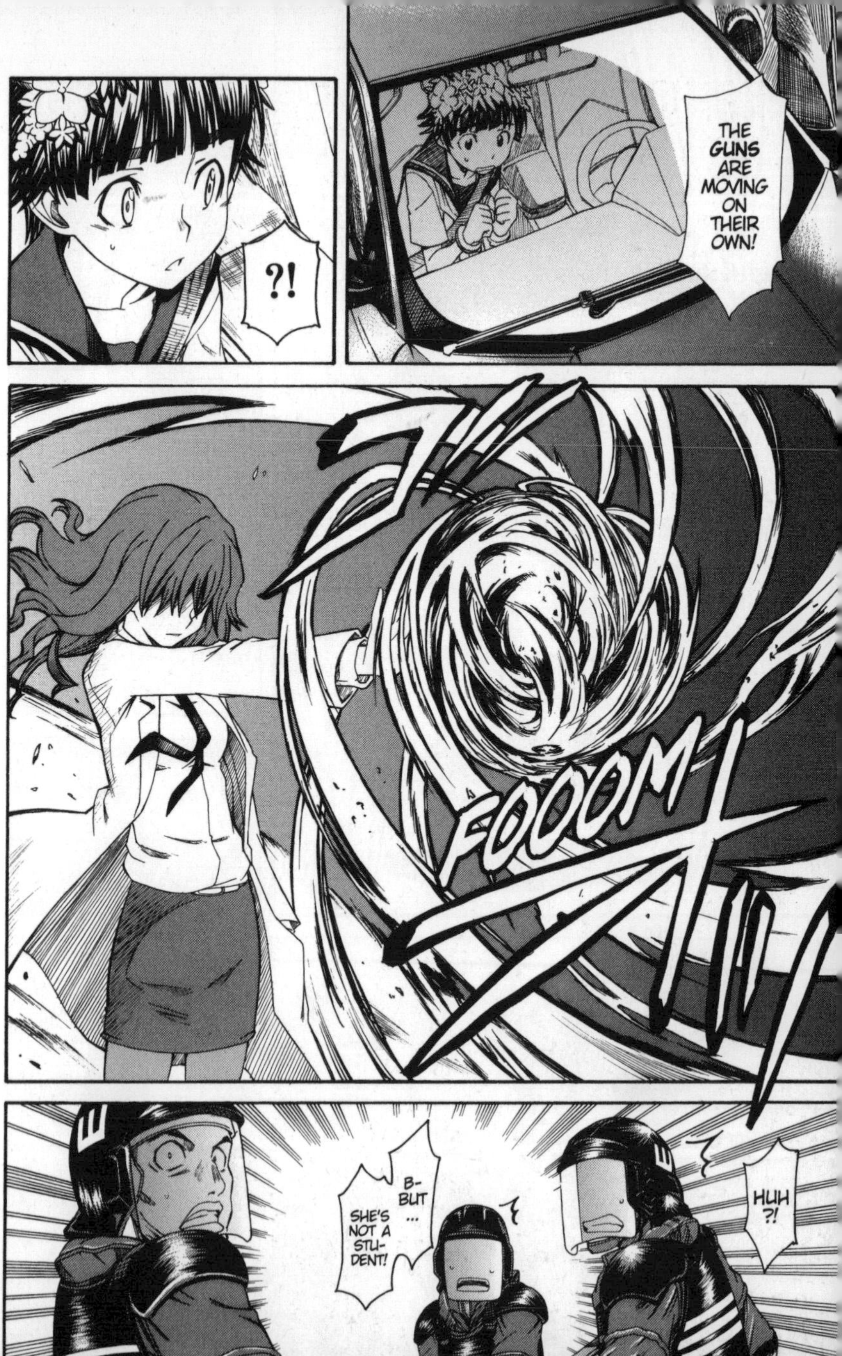
THE GUNS ARE MOVING ON THEIR OWN!
?!
FOOOM
HUH ?!
B-BUT ...
SHE'S NOT A STU-DENT!

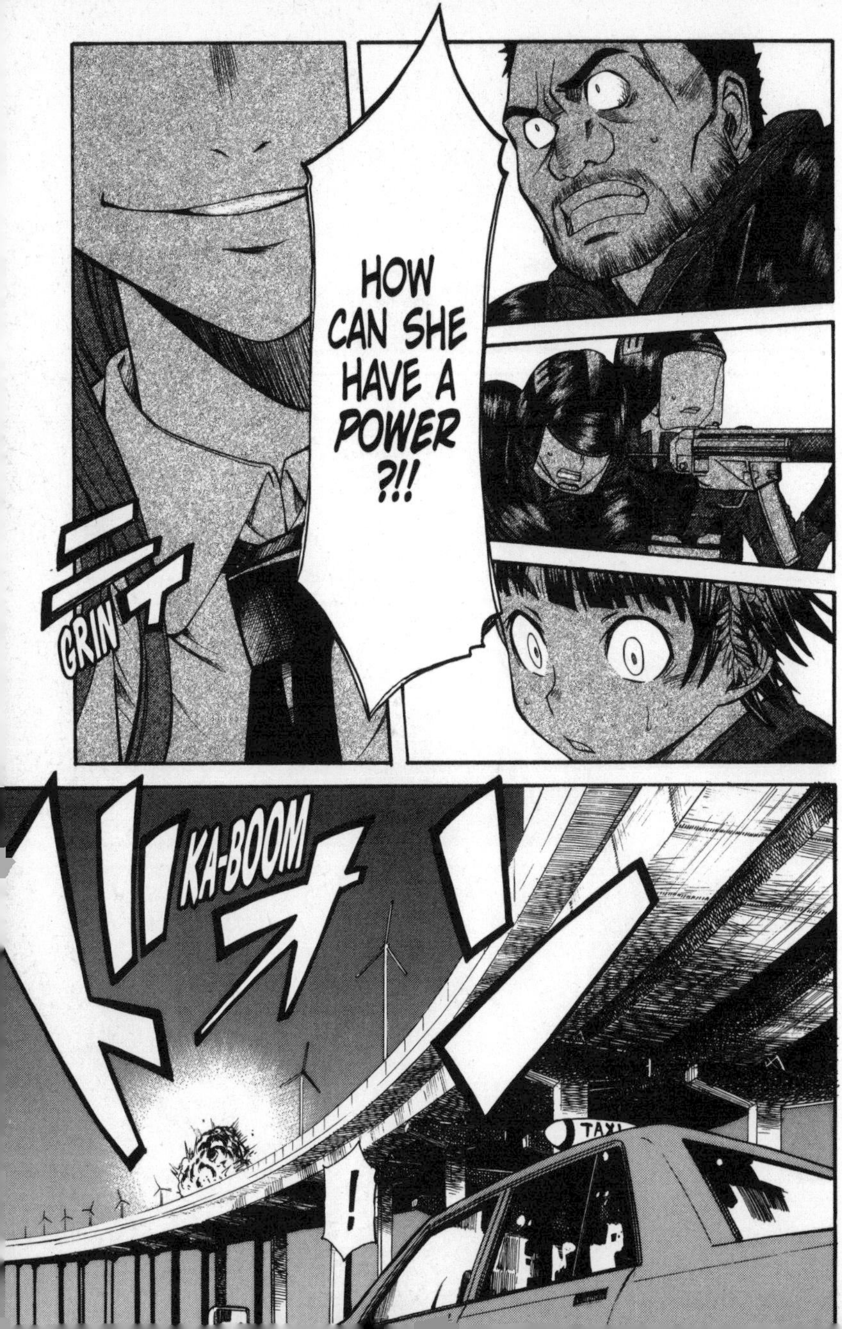
HOW CAN SHE HAVE A POWER?!!
GRIN
KA-BOOM
TAXI
!

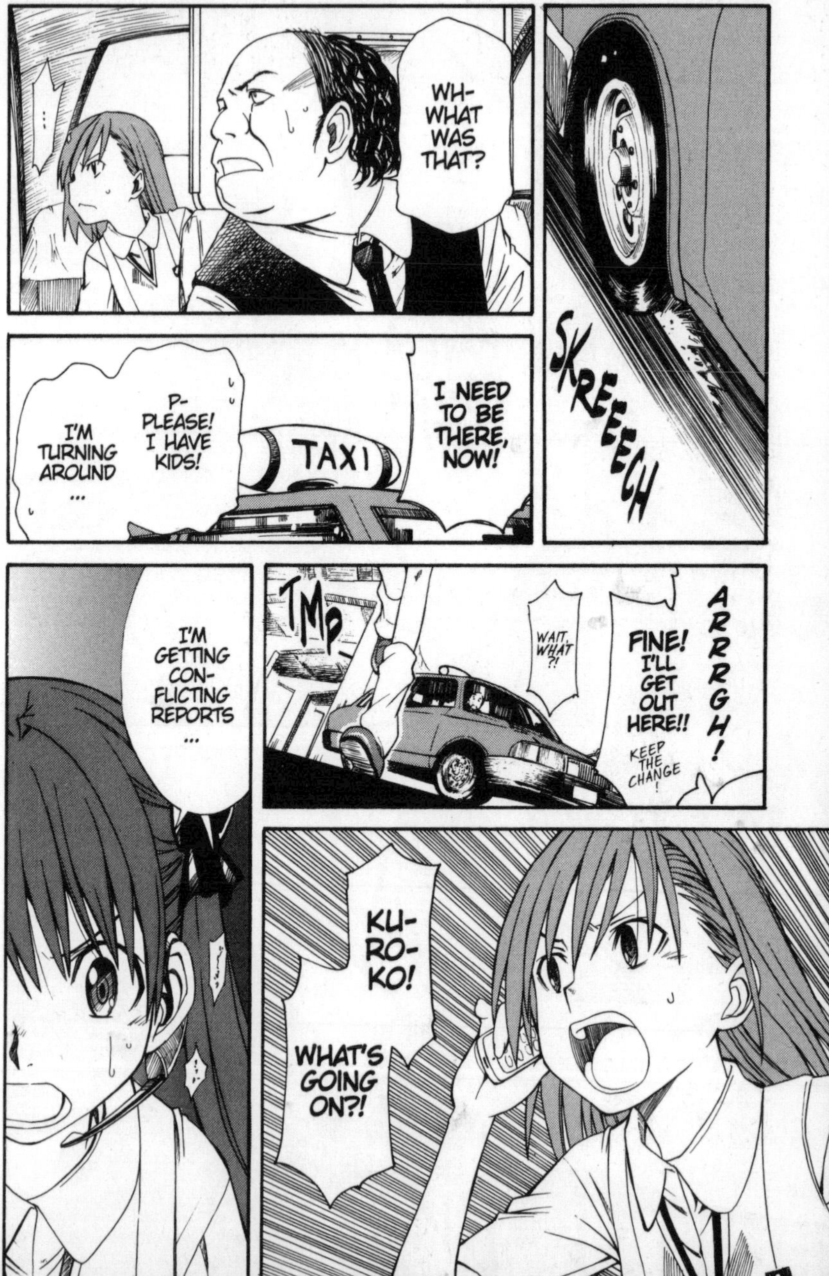
SKREEECH
WH-WHAT WAS THAT?
I NEED TO BE THERE, NOW!
TAXI
P-PLEASE! I HAVE KIDS!
I'M TURNING AROUND ...
ARRRGH!
FINE! I'LL GET OUT HERE!!
KEEP THE CHANGE!
WAIT, WHAT?!
TMP
KU-RO-KO!
WHAT'S GOING ON?!
I'M GETTING CON-FLICTING REPORTS ...

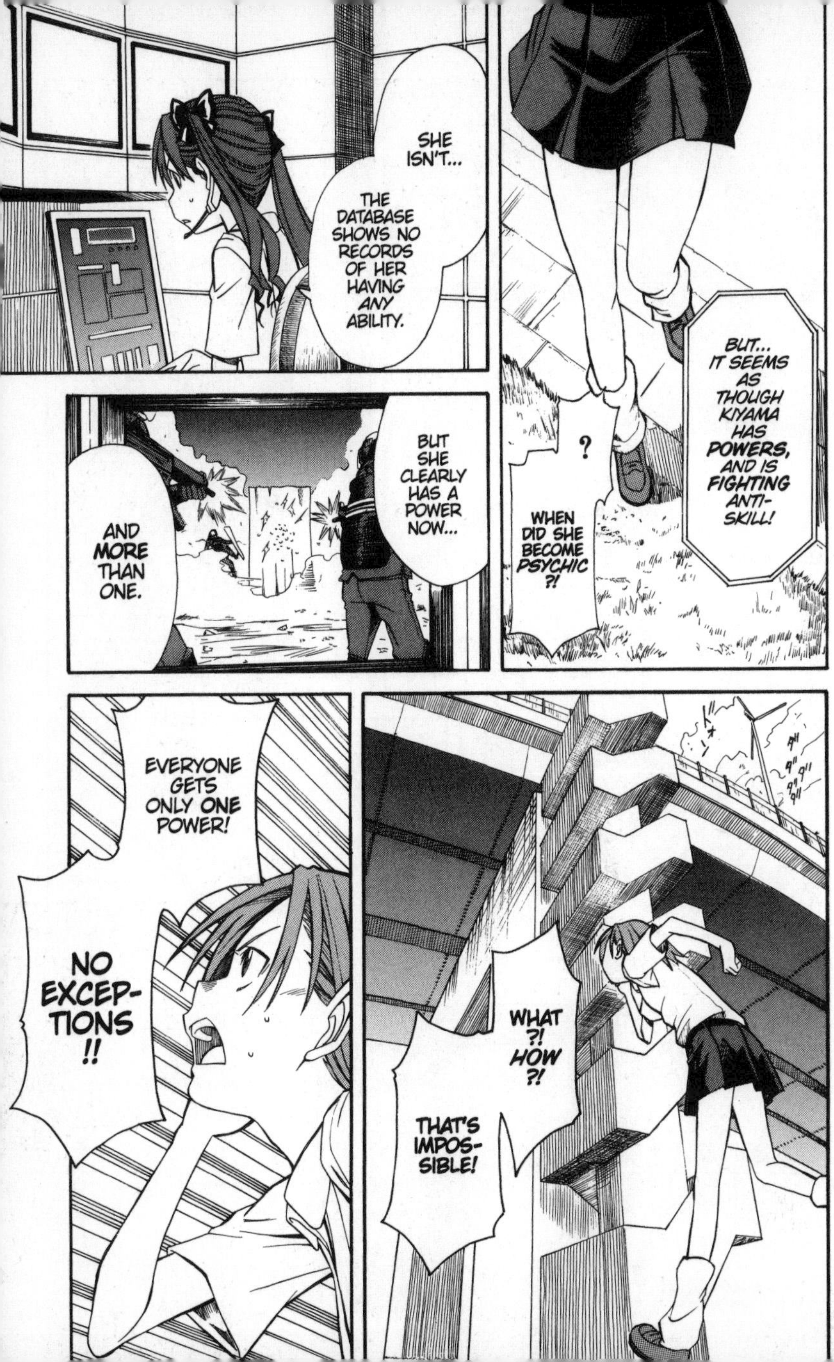
BUT... IT SEEMS AS THOUGH KIYAMA HAS POWERS, AND IS FIGHTING ANTI-SKILL!
?
WHEN DID SHE BECOME PSYCHIC ?!
SHE ISN'T...
THE DATABASE SHOWS NO RECORDS OF HER HAVING ANY ABILITY.
BUT SHE CLEARLY HAS A POWER NOW...
AND MORE THAN ONE.
WHAT ?! HOW ?!
THAT'S IMPOSSIBLE!
EVERYONE GETS ONLY ONE POWER!
NO EXCEPTIONS !!

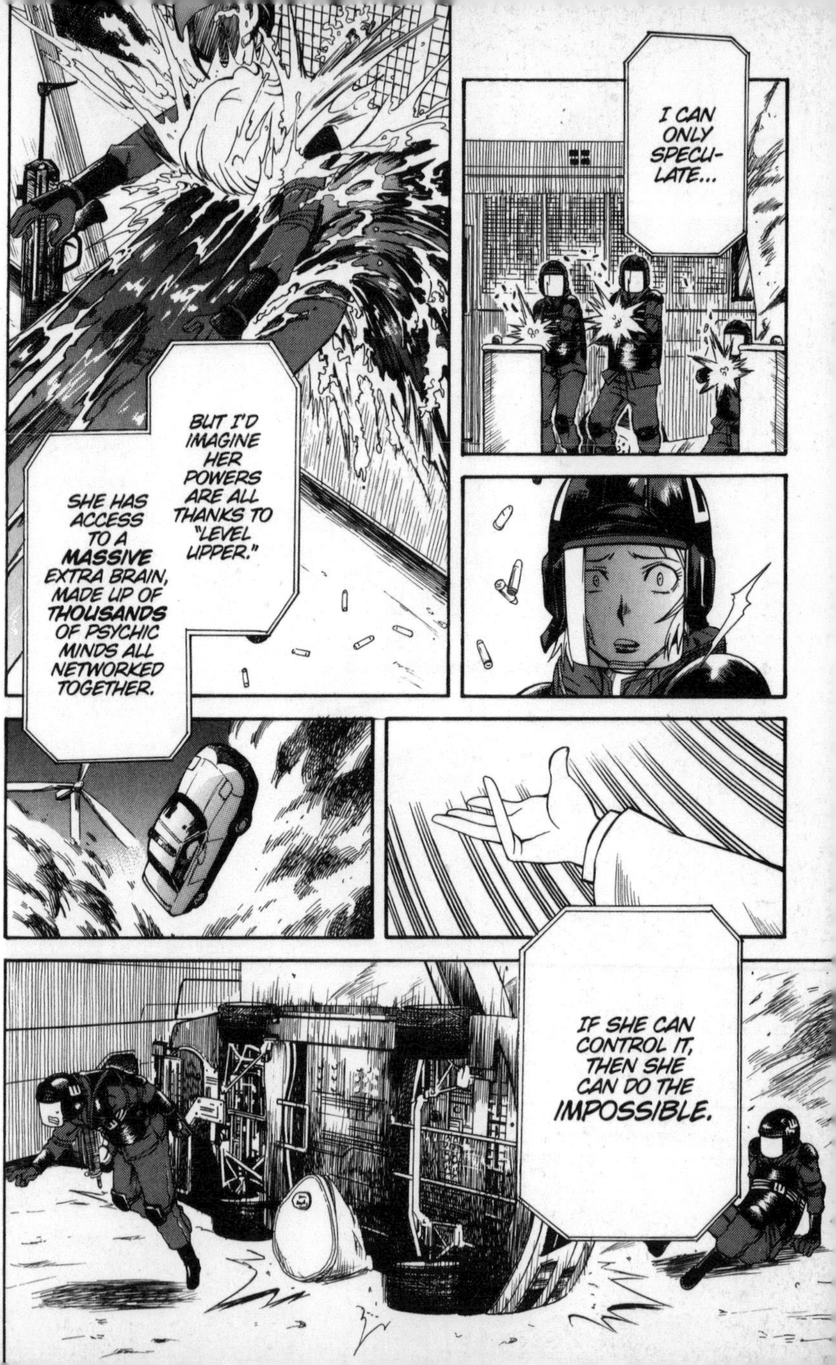
I CAN ONLY SPECU-LATE...
BUT I'D IMAGINE HER POWERS ARE ALL THANKS TO "LEVEL UPPER."
SHE HAS ACCESS TO A **MASSIVE** EXTRA BRAIN, MADE UP OF **THOUSANDS** OF PSYCHIC MINDS ALL NETWORKED TOGETHER.
IF SHE CAN CONTROL IT, THEN SHE CAN DO THE **IMPOSSIBLE.**

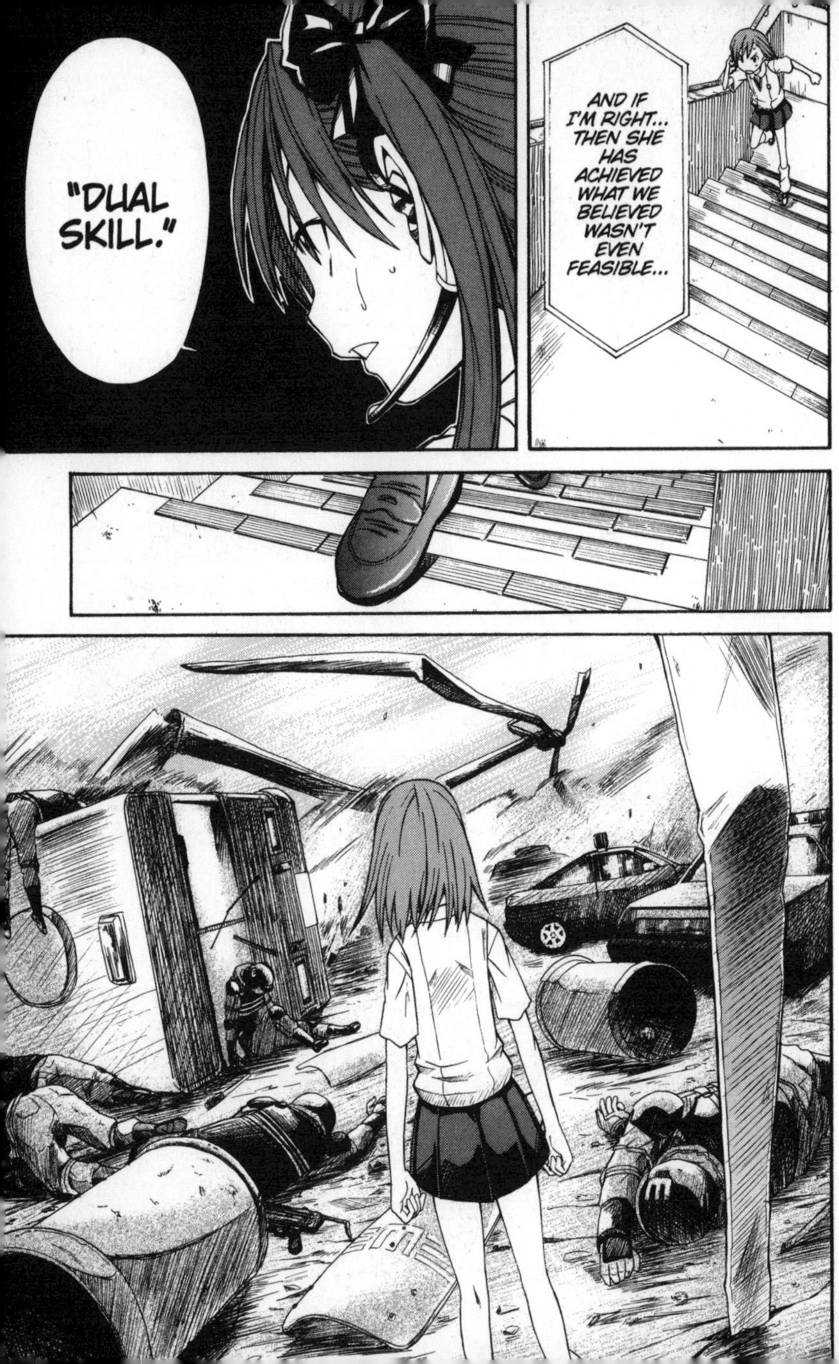
AND IF I'M RIGHT... THEN SHE HAS ACHIEVED WHAT WE BELIEVED WASN'T EVEN FEASIBLE...
"DUAL SKILL."

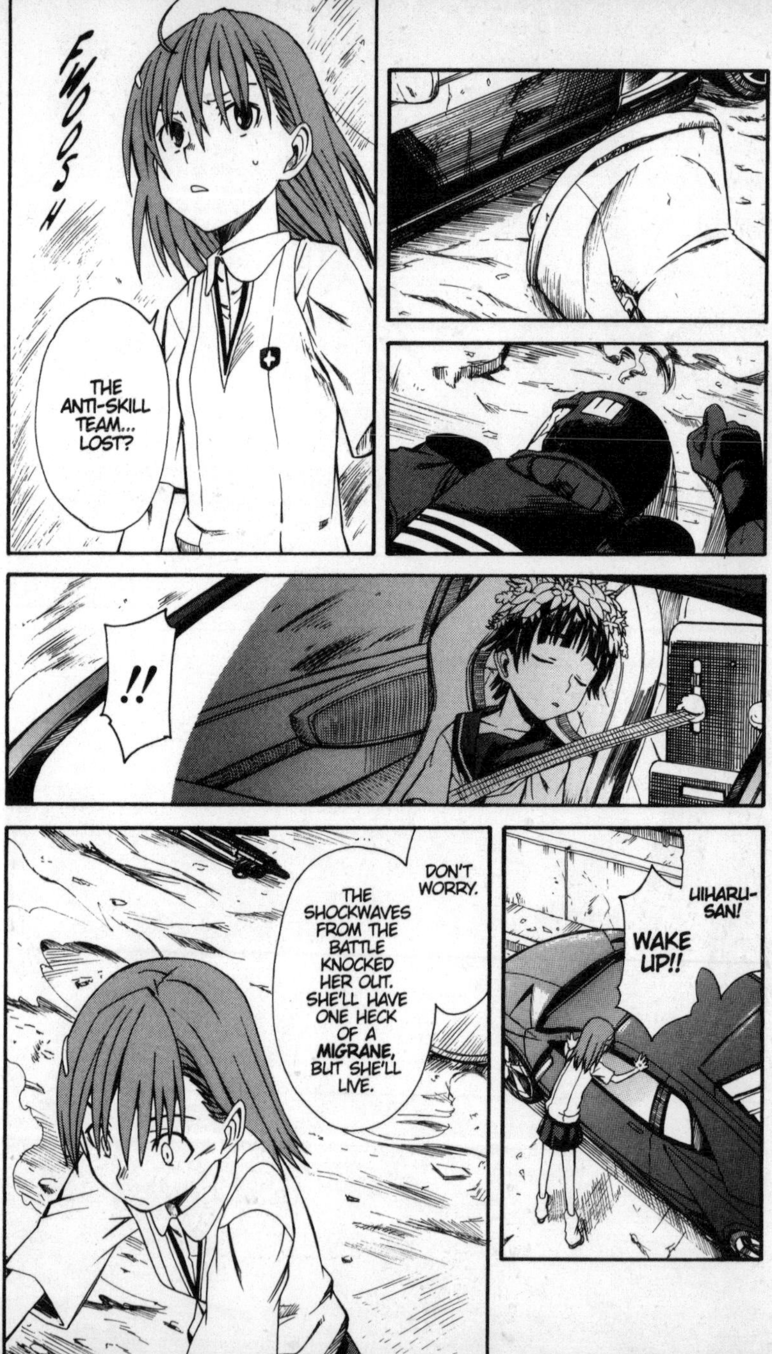
FWOOSH
THE ANTI-SKILL TEAM... LOST?
!!
UIHARU-SAN!
WAKE UP!!
DON'T WORRY.
THE SHOCKWAVES FROM THE BATTLE KNOCKED HER OUT. SHE'LL HAVE ONE HECK OF A **MIGRANE**, BUT SHE'LL LIVE.

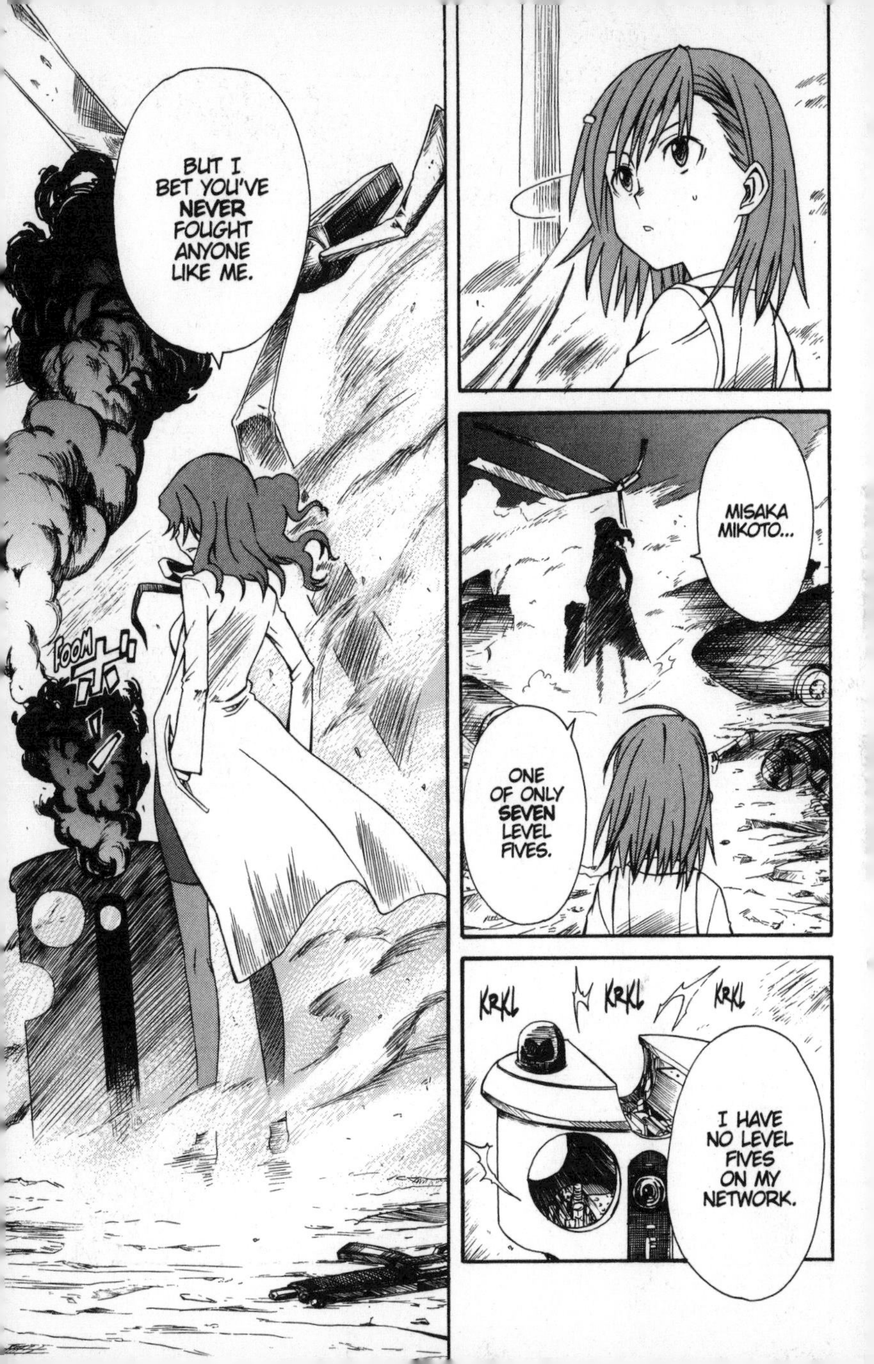
MISAKA MIKOTO...
ONE OF ONLY SEVEN LEVEL FIVES.
KRKL
KRKL
KRKL
I HAVE NO LEVEL FIVES ON MY NETWORK.
BUT I BET YOU'VE NEVER FOUGHT ANYONE LIKE ME.
FOOM

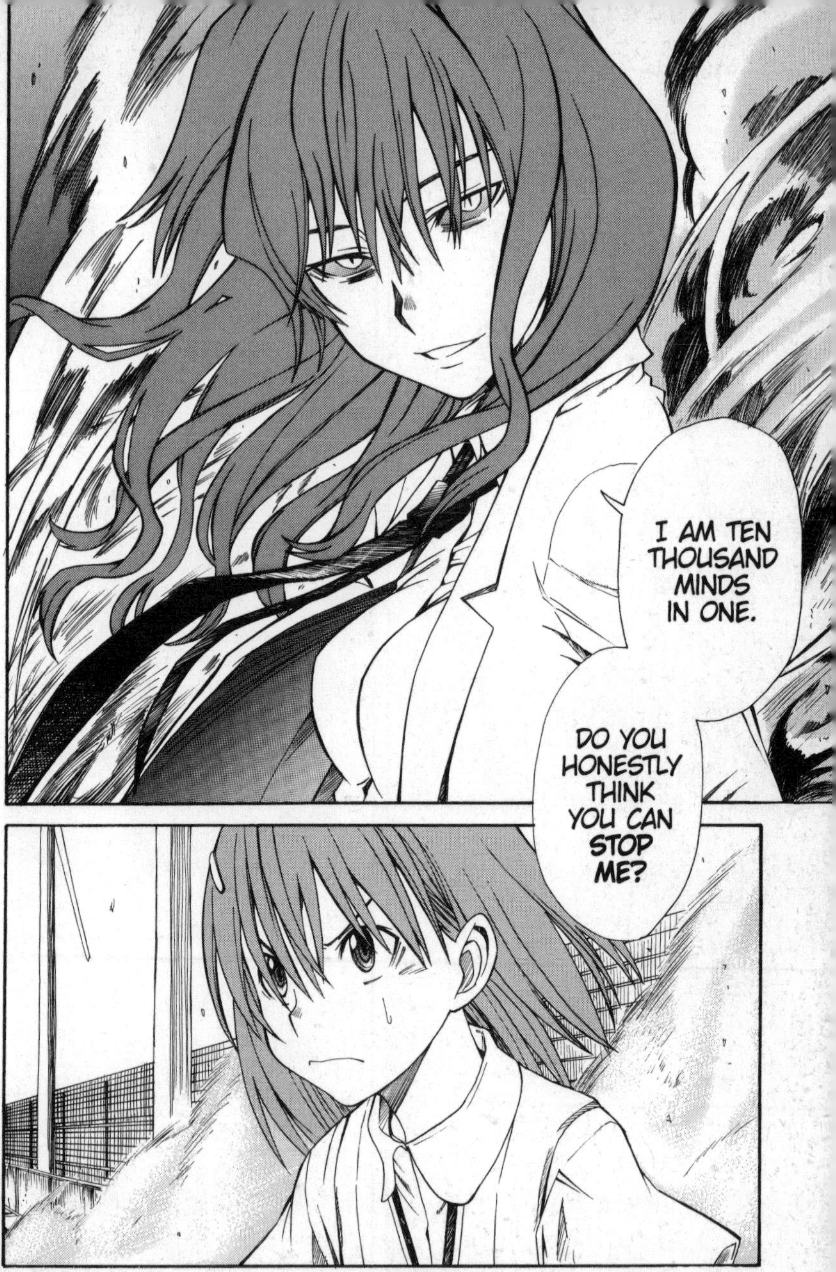
I AM TEN THOUSAND MINDS IN ONE.
DO YOU HONESTLY THINK YOU CAN STOP ME?

A Certain SCIENTIFIC Railgun

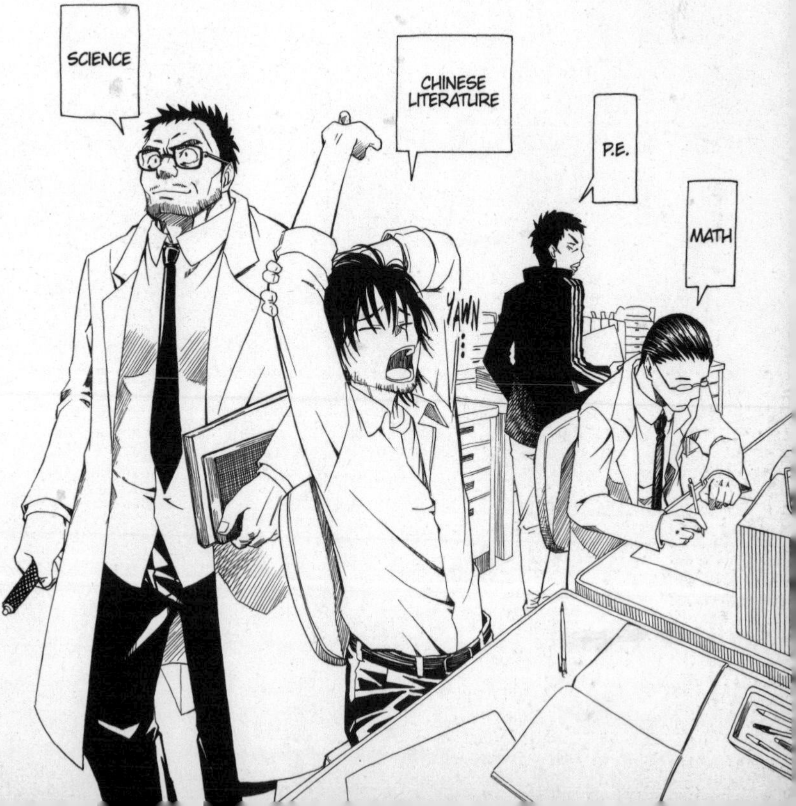
MATH
P.E.
CHINESE LITERATURE
YAWN
SCIENCE

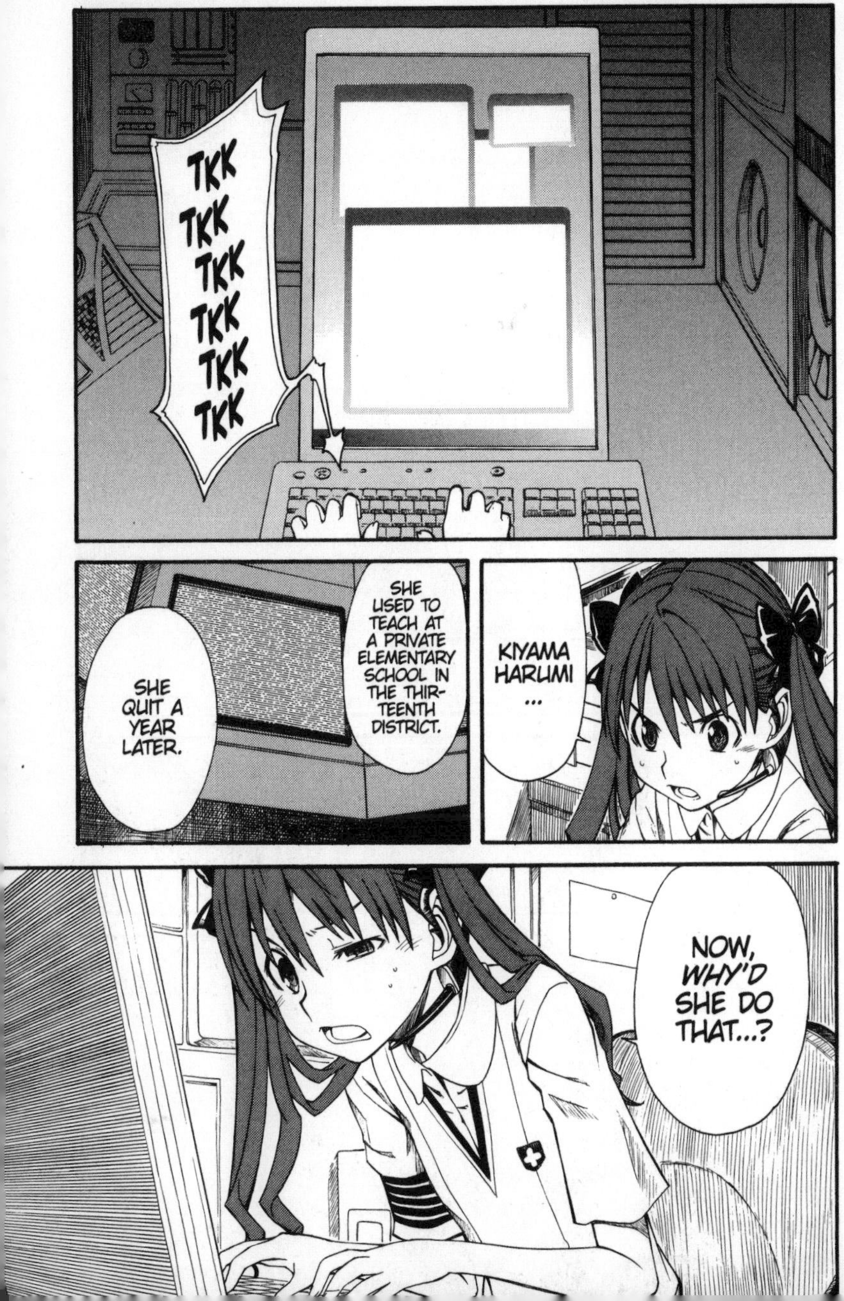
TKK TKK TKK TKK TKK TKK
KIYAMA HARUMI ...
SHE USED TO TEACH AT A PRIVATE ELEMENTARY SCHOOL IN THE THIRTEENTH DISTRICT.
SHE QUIT A YEAR LATER.
NOW, *WHY'D* SHE DO THAT...?

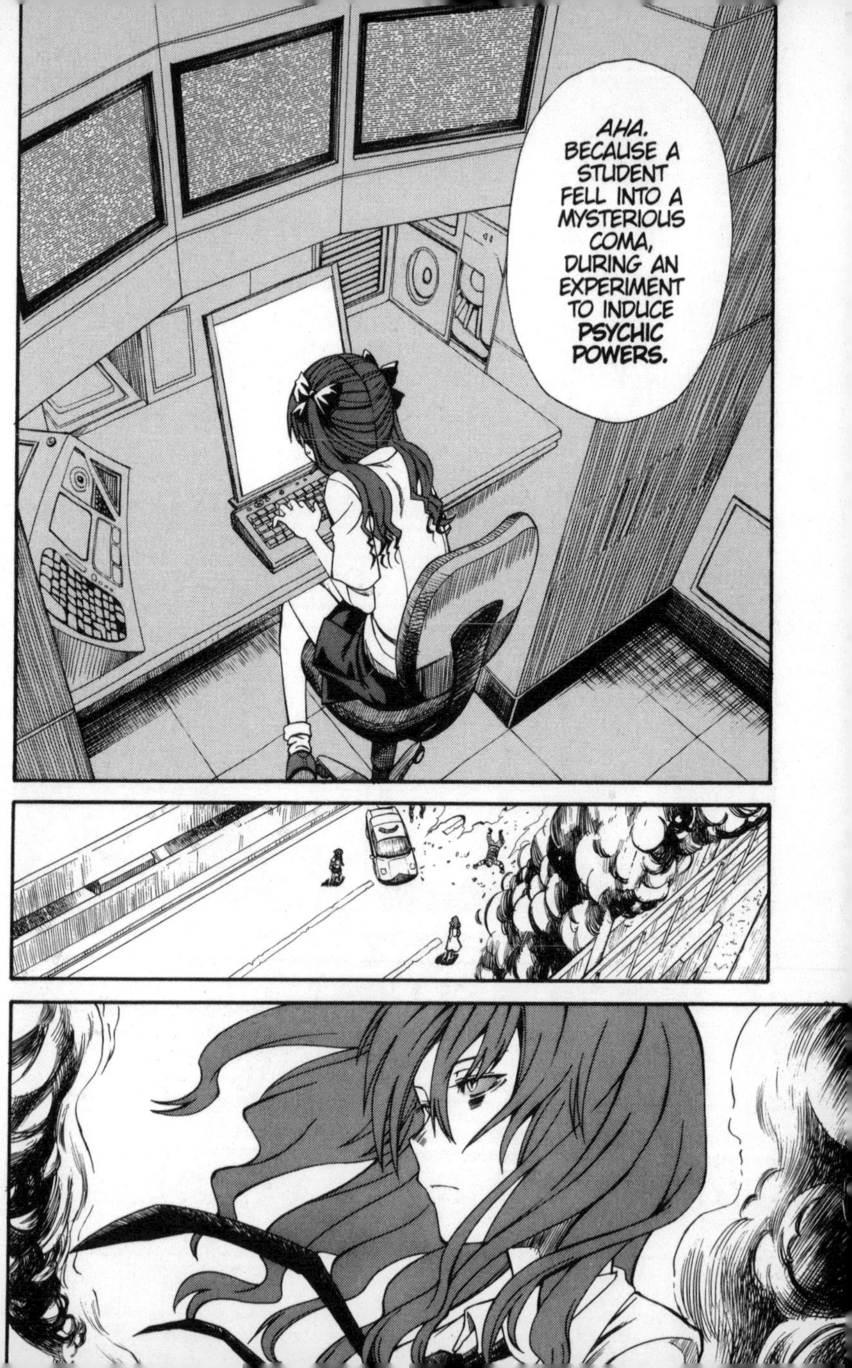
AHA. BECAUSE A STUDENT FELL INTO A MYSTERIOUS COMA, DURING AN EXPERIMENT TO INDUCE PSYCHIC POWERS.

A Certain SCIENTIFIC Railgun
CHAPTER 13: JULY 24 (3)

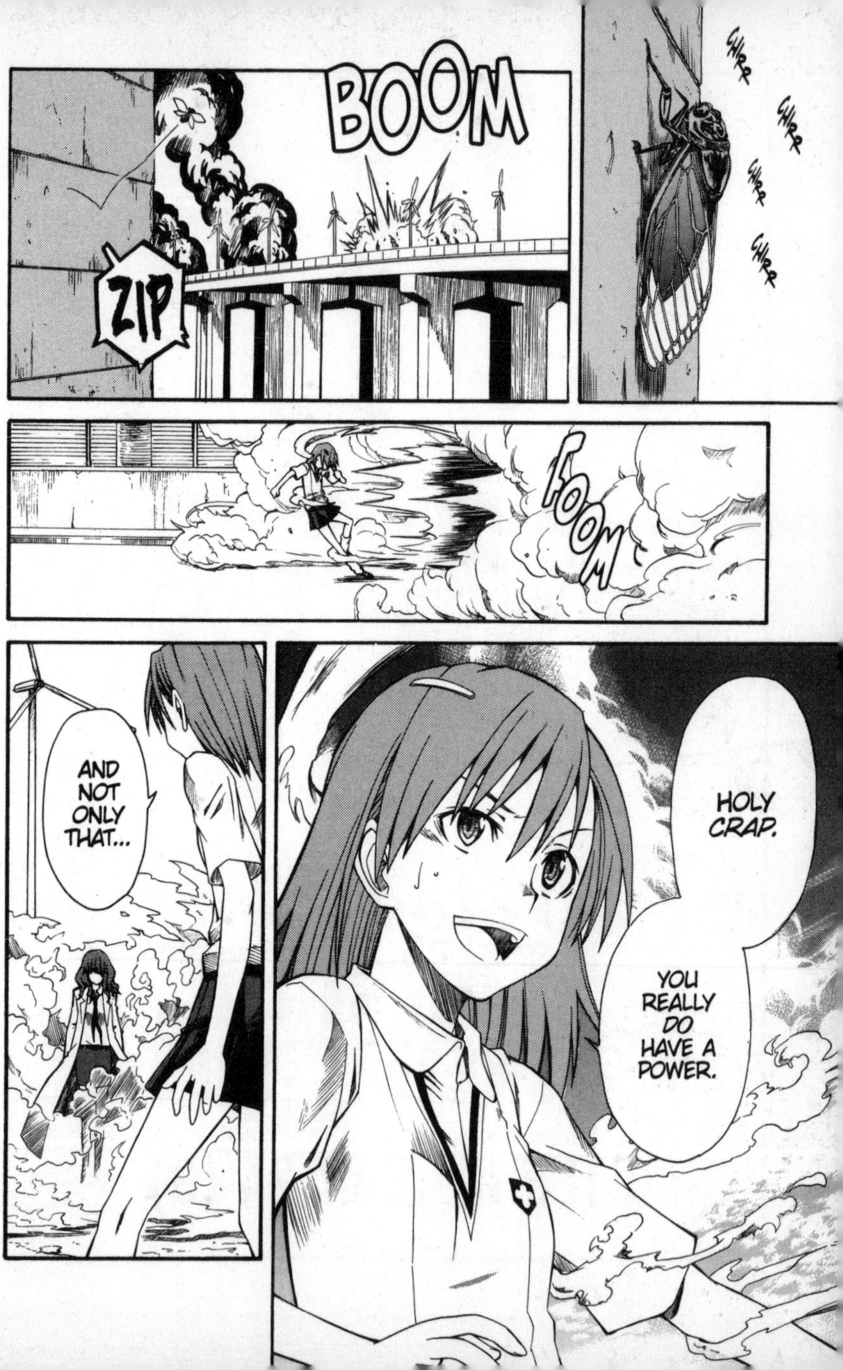
CHIRR
CHIRR
CHIRR
CHIRR
BOOM
ZIP
FOOM
HOLY CRAP.
YOU REALLY DO HAVE A POWER.
AND NOT ONLY THAT...

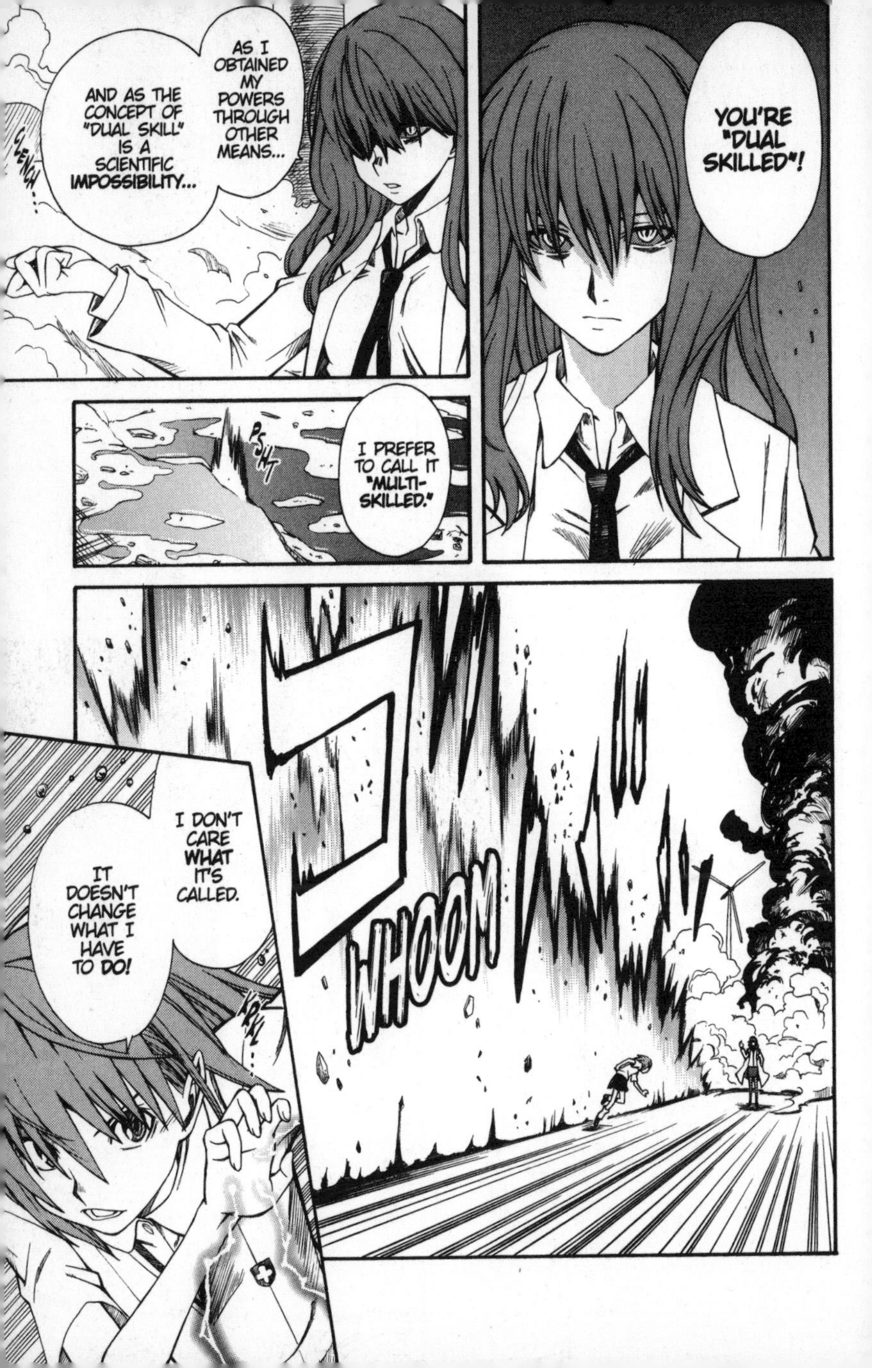

YOU'RE "DUAL SKILLED"!
AS I OBTAINED MY POWERS THROUGH OTHER MEANS...
AND AS THE CONCEPT OF "DUAL SKILL" IS A SCIENTIFIC IMPOSSIBILITY...
CLENCH...
PSHT
I PREFER TO CALL IT "MULTI-SKILLED."
WHOOM
I DON'T CARE WHAT IT'S CALLED.
IT DOESN'T CHANGE WHAT I HAVE TO DO!
KRKL

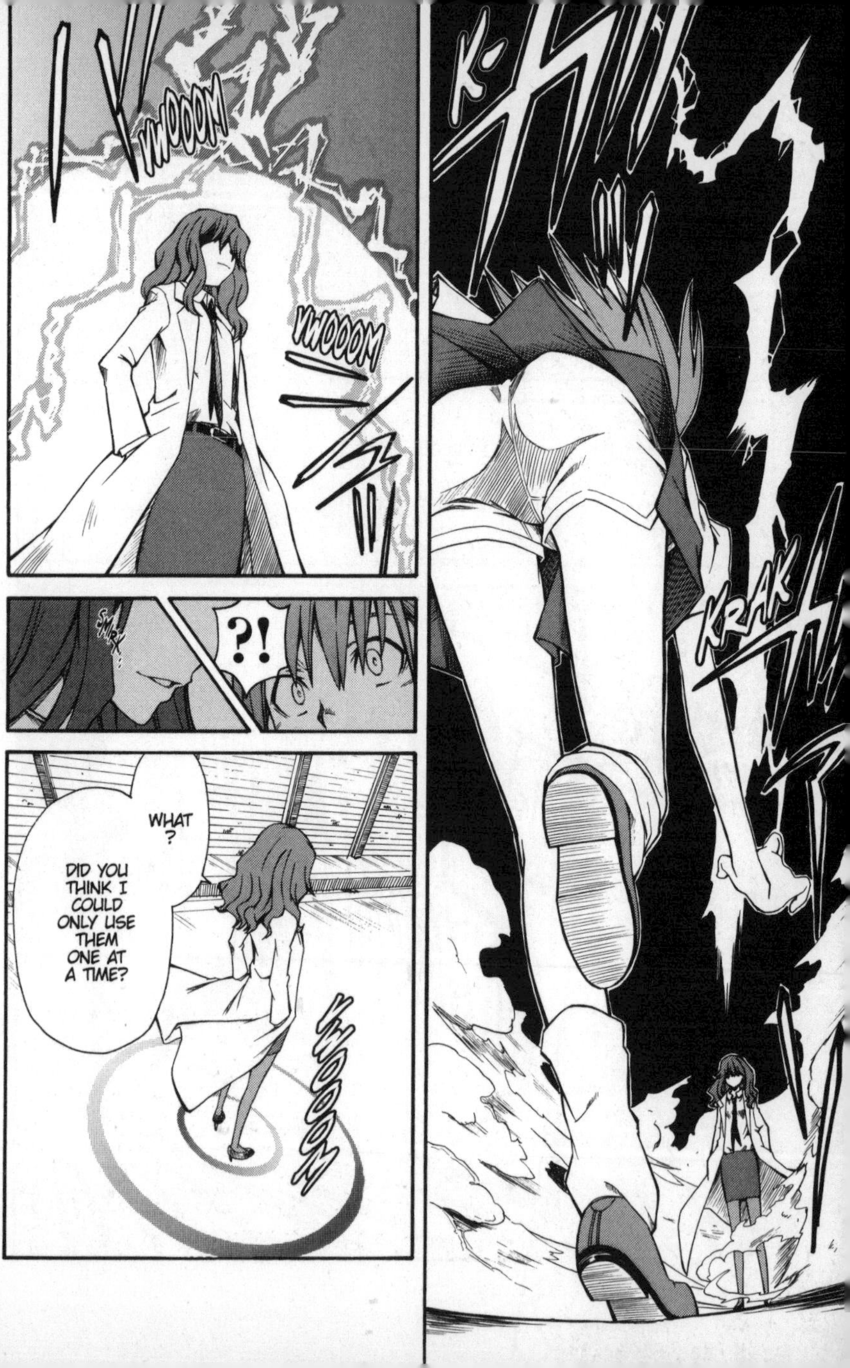
K-
KRAK
VWOOOM
VWOOOM
?!
SMIRK
WHAT?
DID YOU THINK I COULD ONLY USE THEM ONE AT A TIME?
VWOOOOM

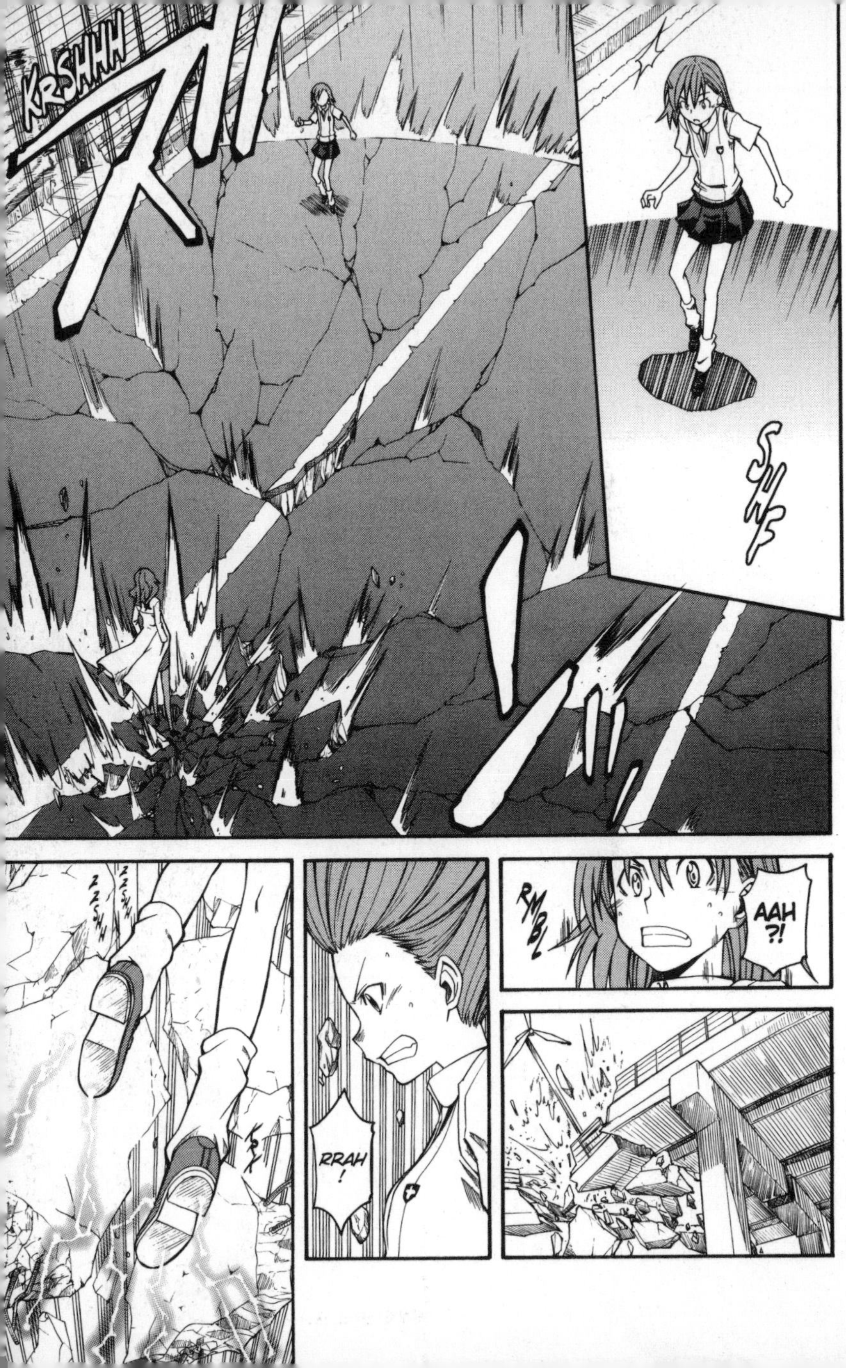
SHF
KRSHHH
RMBL
AAH ?!
RRAH !
ZZSHH
ZZSHH

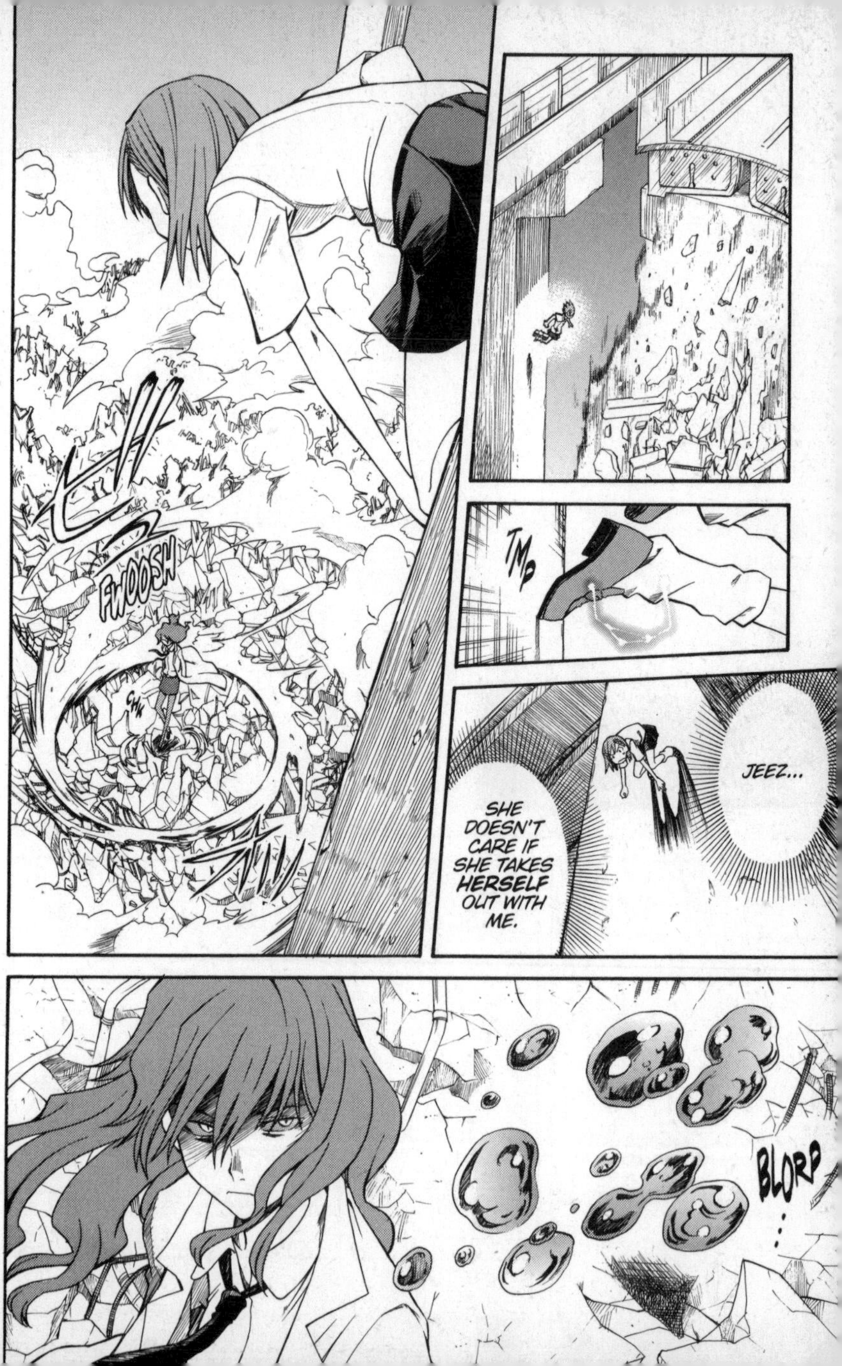
TMP
JEEZ...
SHE DOESN'T CARE IF SHE TAKES HERSELF OUT WITH ME.
FWOOSH
BLORP

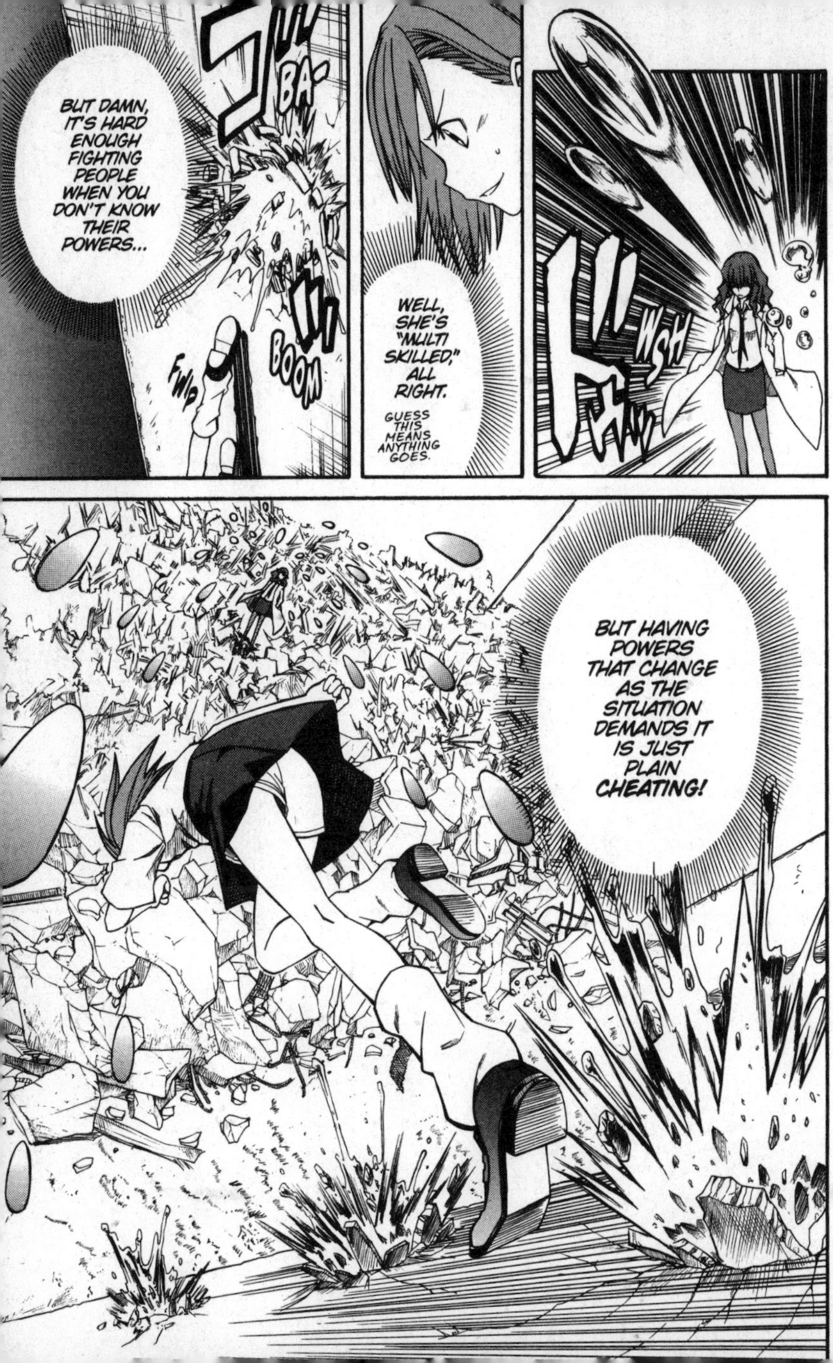
WSH
WELL, SHE'S "MULTI SKILLED," ALL RIGHT.
GUESS THIS MEANS ANYTHING GOES.
BA-
BOOM
FWIP
BUT DAMN, IT'S HARD ENOUGH FIGHTING PEOPLE WHEN YOU DON'T KNOW THEIR POWERS...
BUT HAVING POWERS THAT CHANGE AS THE SITUATION DEMANDS IT IS JUST PLAIN CHEATING!

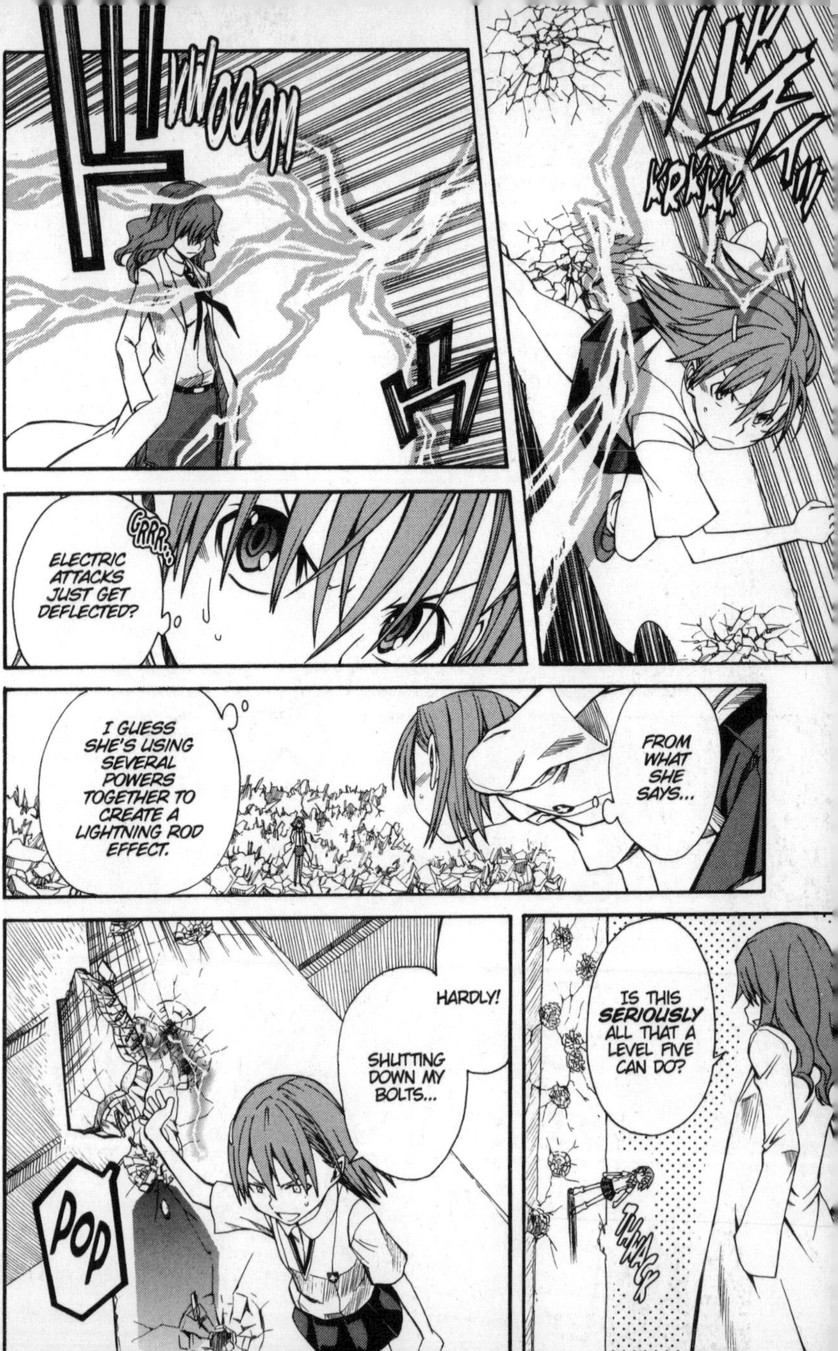
KRAKKK
VWOOOM
GRRR..
ELECTRIC ATTACKS JUST GET DEFLECTED?
FROM WHAT SHE SAYS...
I GUESS SHE'S USING SEVERAL POWERS TOGETHER TO CREATE A LIGHTNING ROD EFFECT.
IS THIS **SERIOUSLY** ALL THAT A LEVEL FIVE CAN DO?
THWACK
HARDLY!
SHUTTING DOWN MY BOLTS...
POP

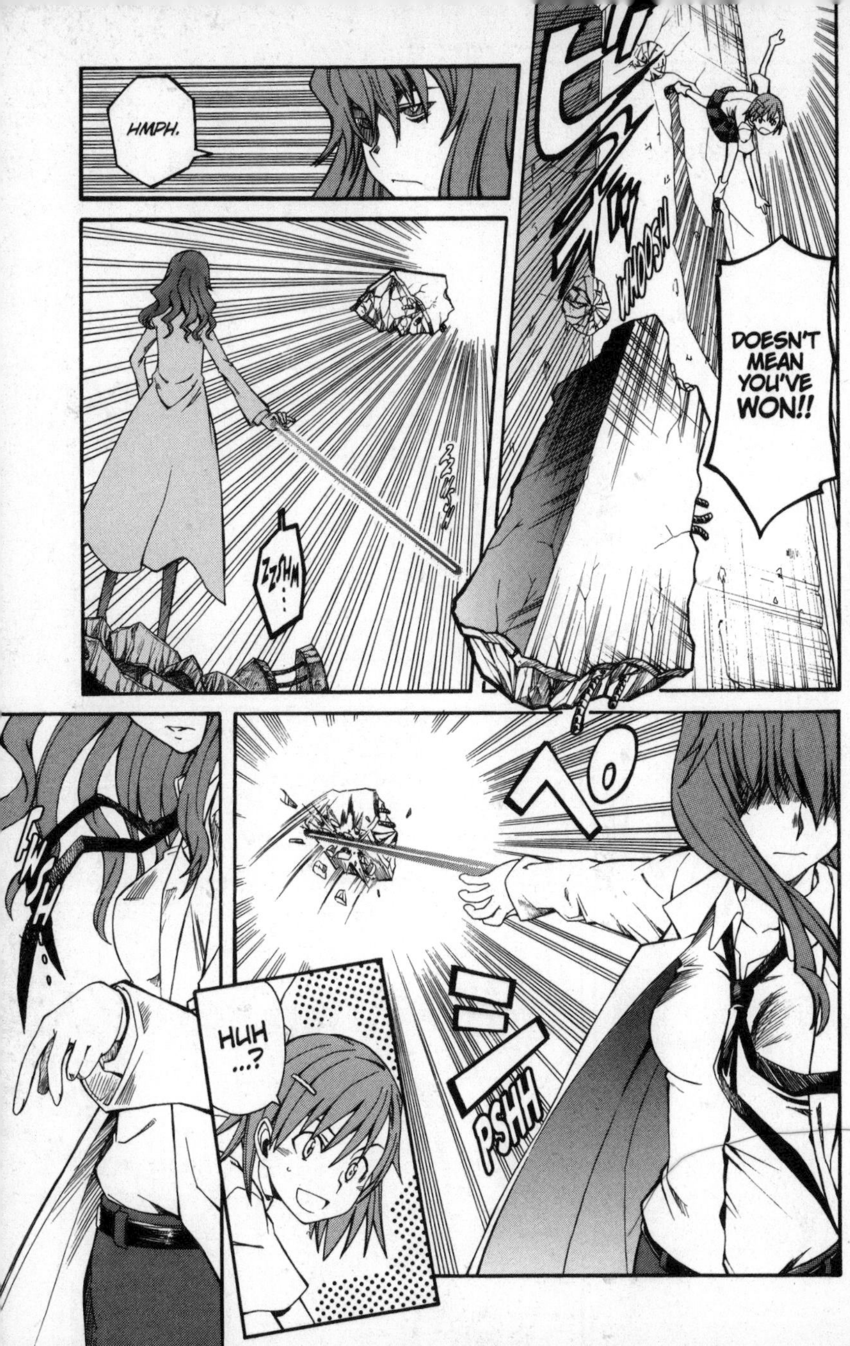
DOESN'T MEAN YOU'VE WON!!
WHOOSH
HMPH.
ZZSHM...
PSHH
HUH ...?
FWSH

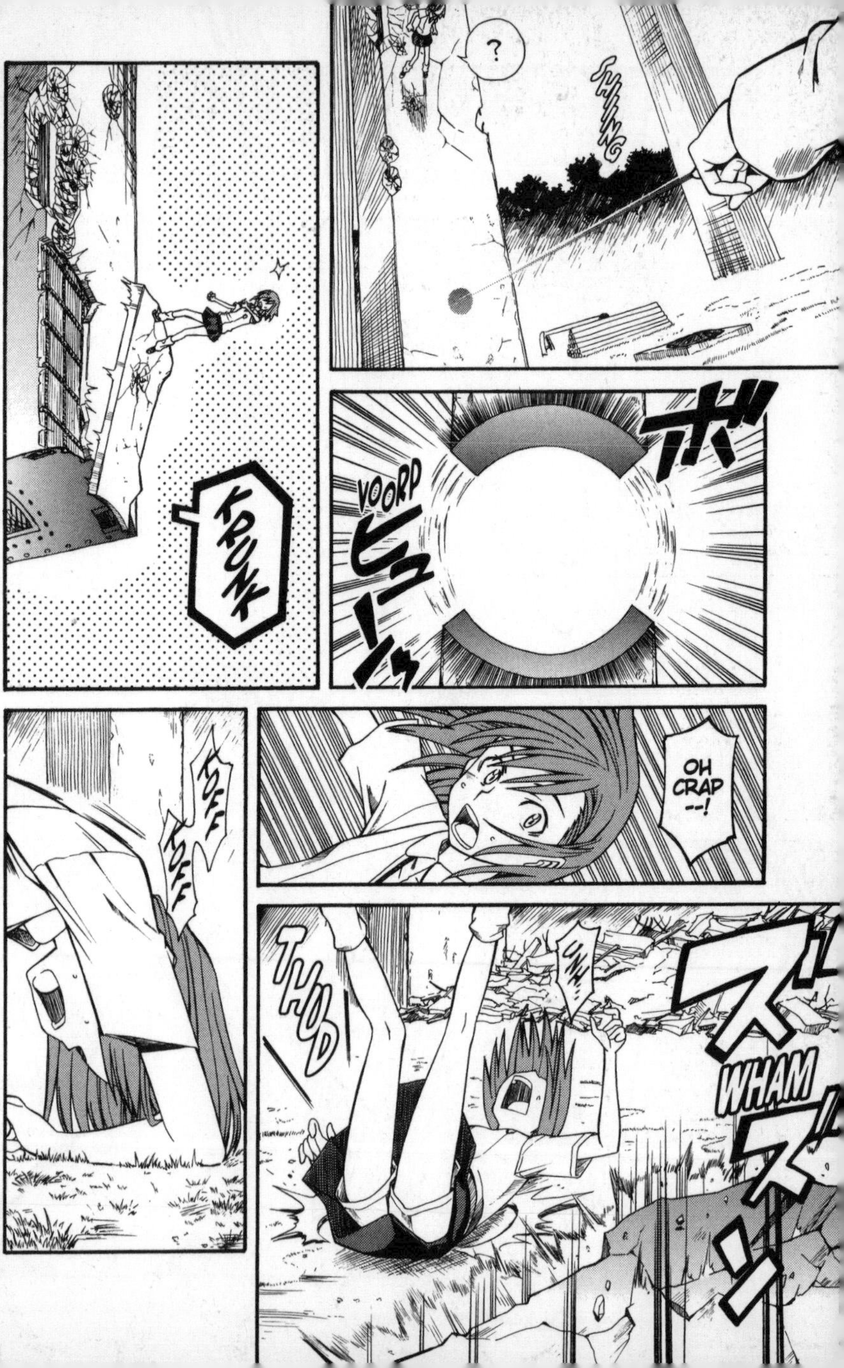
?
SHHING
ボ
VOORP
ヒューン
KRUNK
OH CRAP --!
ズズン
WHAM
UNH
THUD
KOFF
KOFF

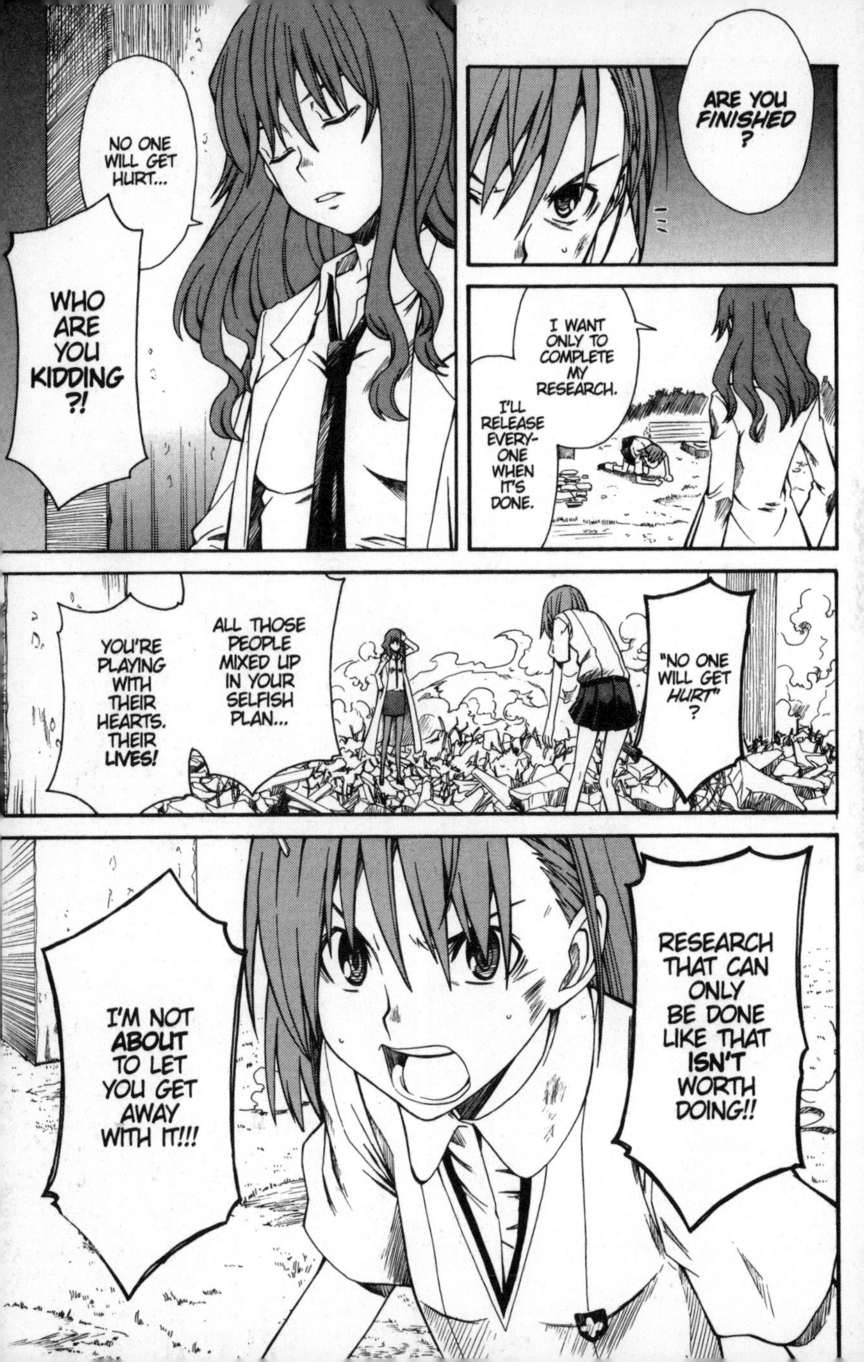
ARE YOU FINISHED?
I WANT ONLY TO COMPLETE MY RESEARCH.
I'LL RELEASE EVERY-ONE WHEN IT'S DONE.
NO ONE WILL GET HURT...
WHO ARE YOU KIDDING?!
"NO ONE WILL GET HURT"?
ALL THOSE PEOPLE MIXED UP IN YOUR SELFISH PLAN...
YOU'RE PLAYING WITH THEIR HEARTS. THEIR LIVES!
RESEARCH THAT CAN ONLY BE DONE LIKE THAT ISN'T WORTH DOING!!
I'M NOT ABOUT TO LET YOU GET AWAY WITH IT!!!

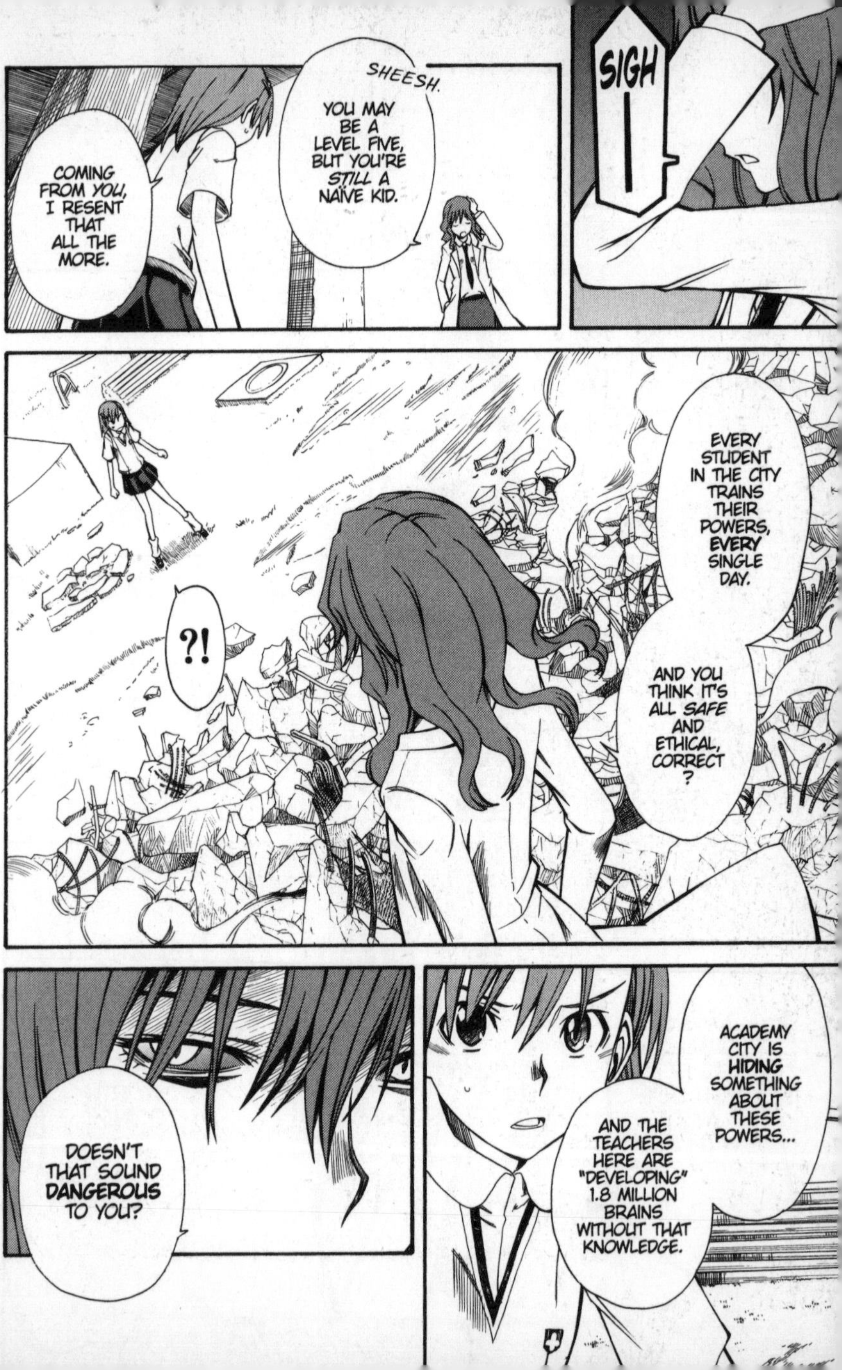
SIGH
SHEESH.
YOU MAY BE A LEVEL FIVE, BUT YOU'RE STILL A NAÏVE KID.
COMING FROM YOU, I RESENT THAT ALL THE MORE.
EVERY STUDENT IN THE CITY TRAINS THEIR POWERS, EVERY SINGLE DAY.
AND YOU THINK IT'S ALL SAFE AND ETHICAL, CORRECT?
?!
ACADEMY CITY IS HIDING SOMETHING ABOUT THESE POWERS...
AND THE TEACHERS HERE ARE "DEVELOPING" 1.8 MILLION BRAINS WITHOUT THAT KNOWLEDGE.
DOESN'T THAT SOUND DANGEROUS TO YOU?

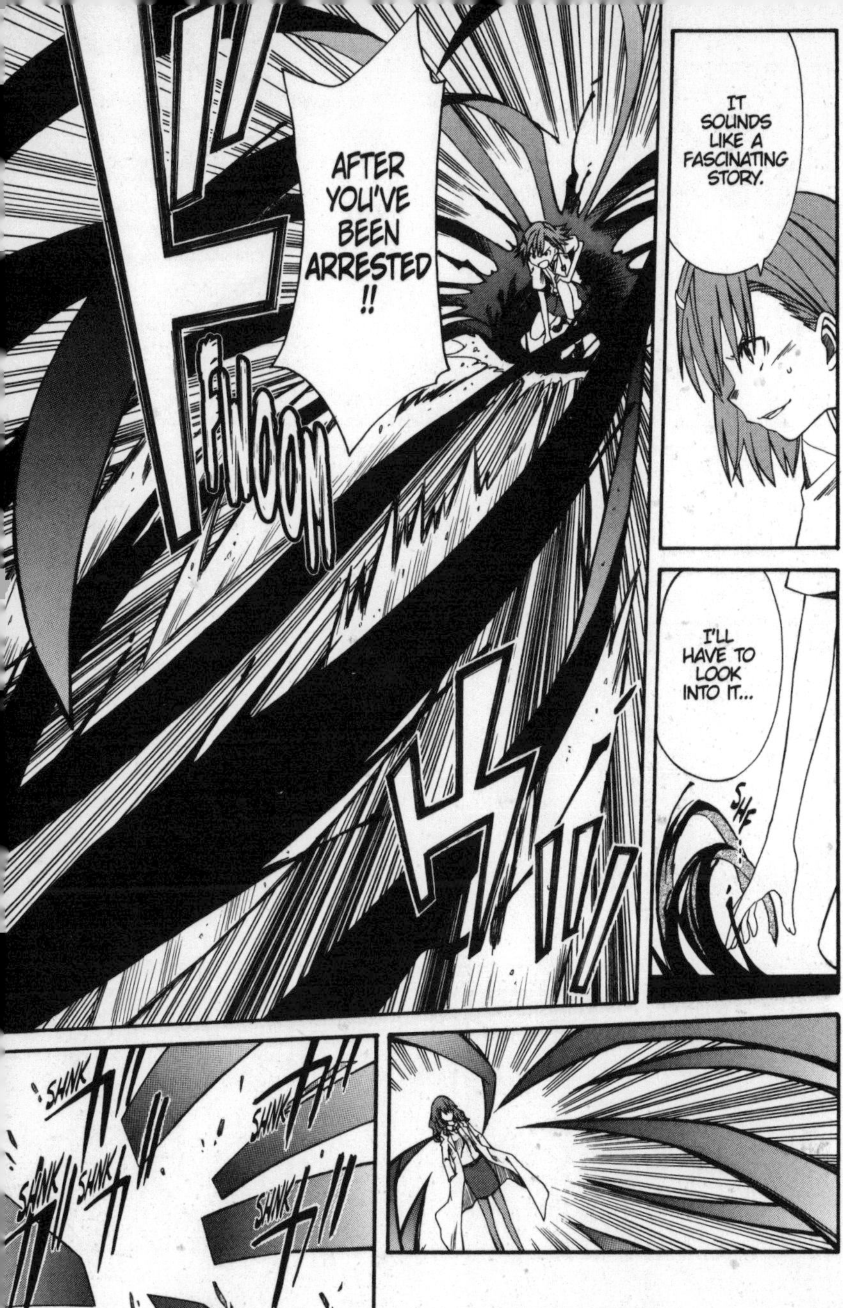
IT SOUNDS LIKE A FASCINATING STORY.
I'LL HAVE TO LOOK INTO IT...
SHF
AFTER YOU'VE BEEN ARRESTED !!
FWOOM
SHINK
SHINK
SHINK
SHINK
SHINK

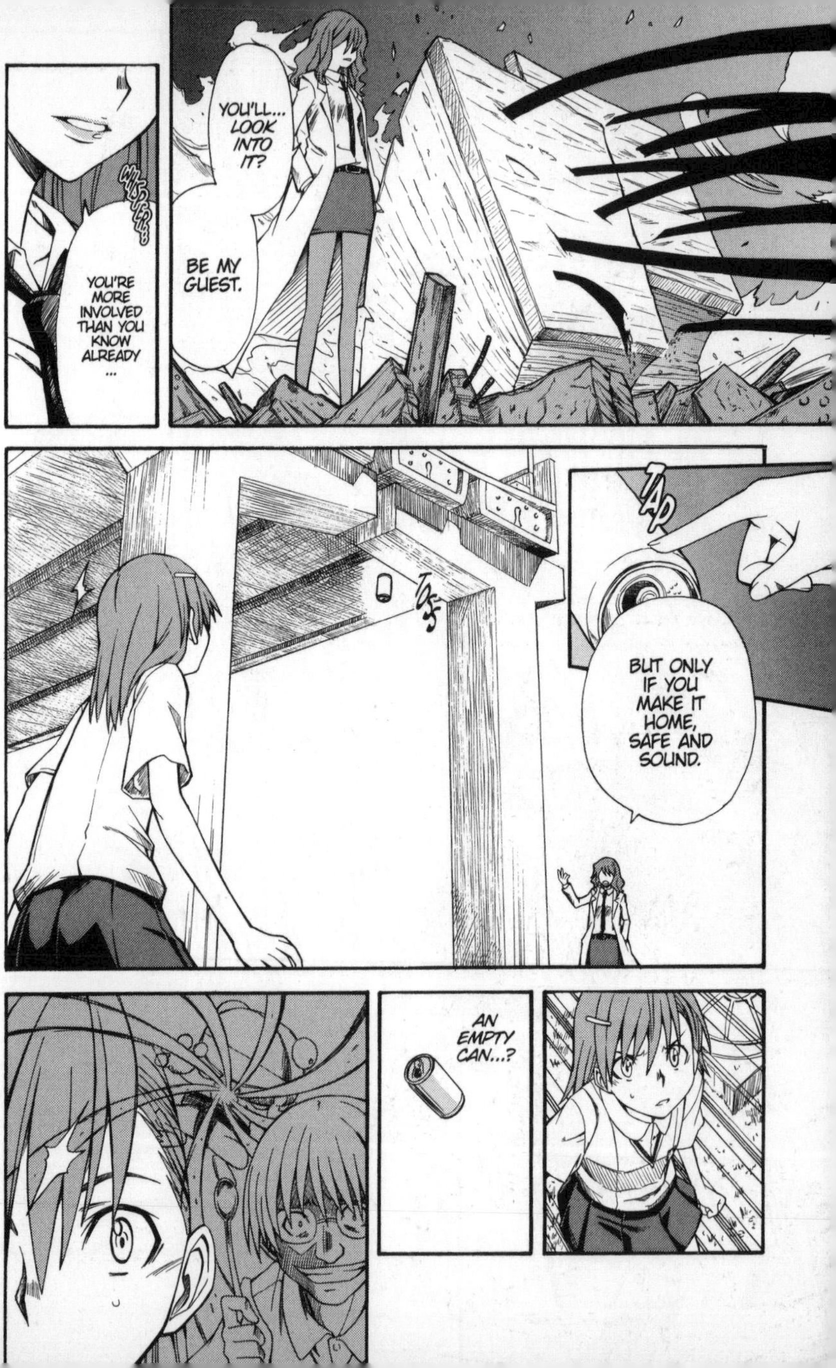
YOU'LL... LOOK INTO IT?
BE MY GUEST.
WHISPER
YOU'RE MORE INVOLVED THAN YOU KNOW ALREADY ...
TAP
TOSS
BUT ONLY IF YOU MAKE IT HOME, SAFE AND SOUND.
AN EMPTY CAN...?

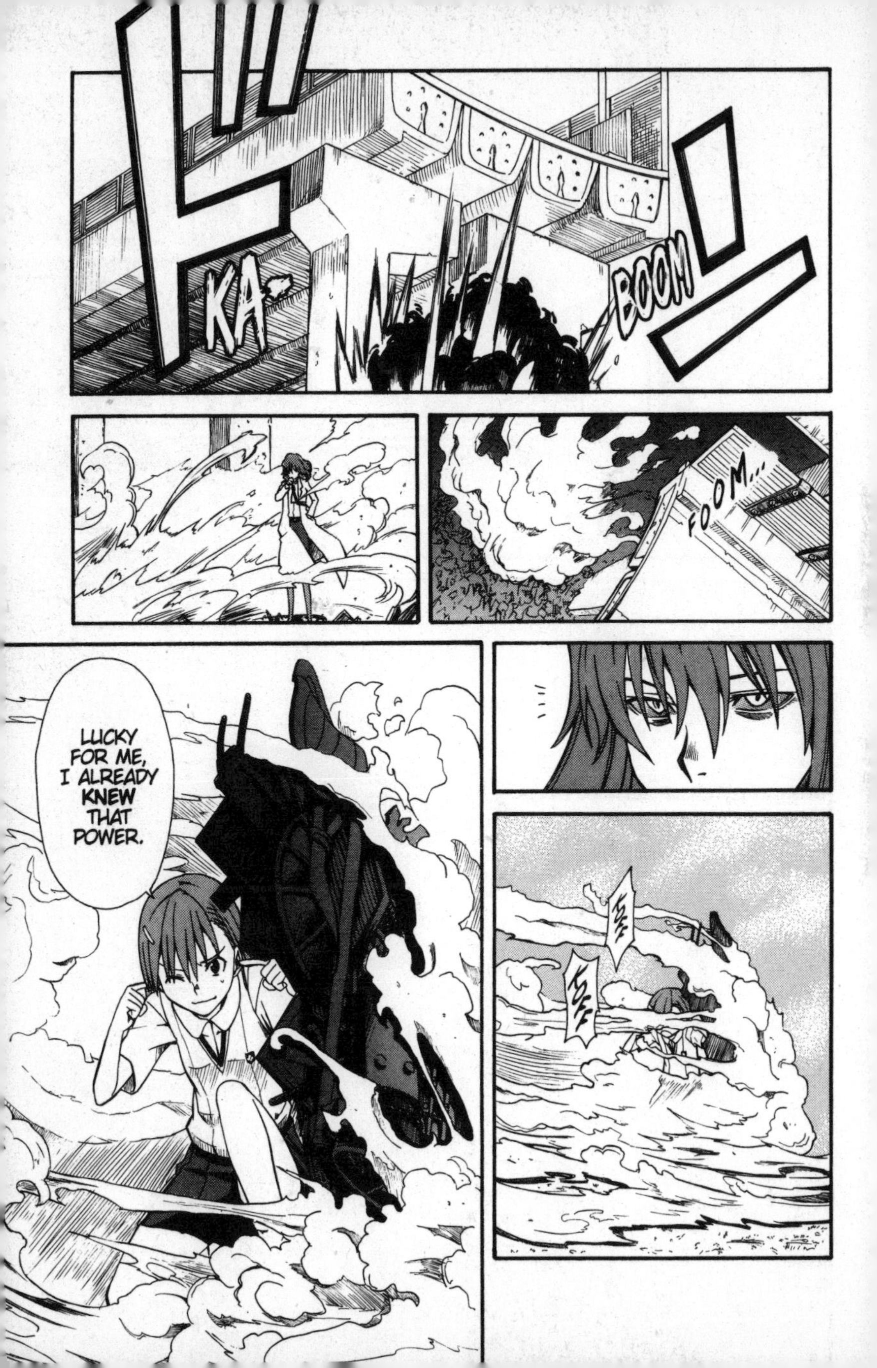
KA
BOOM
FOOM...
LUCKY FOR ME, I ALREADY KNEW THAT POWER.

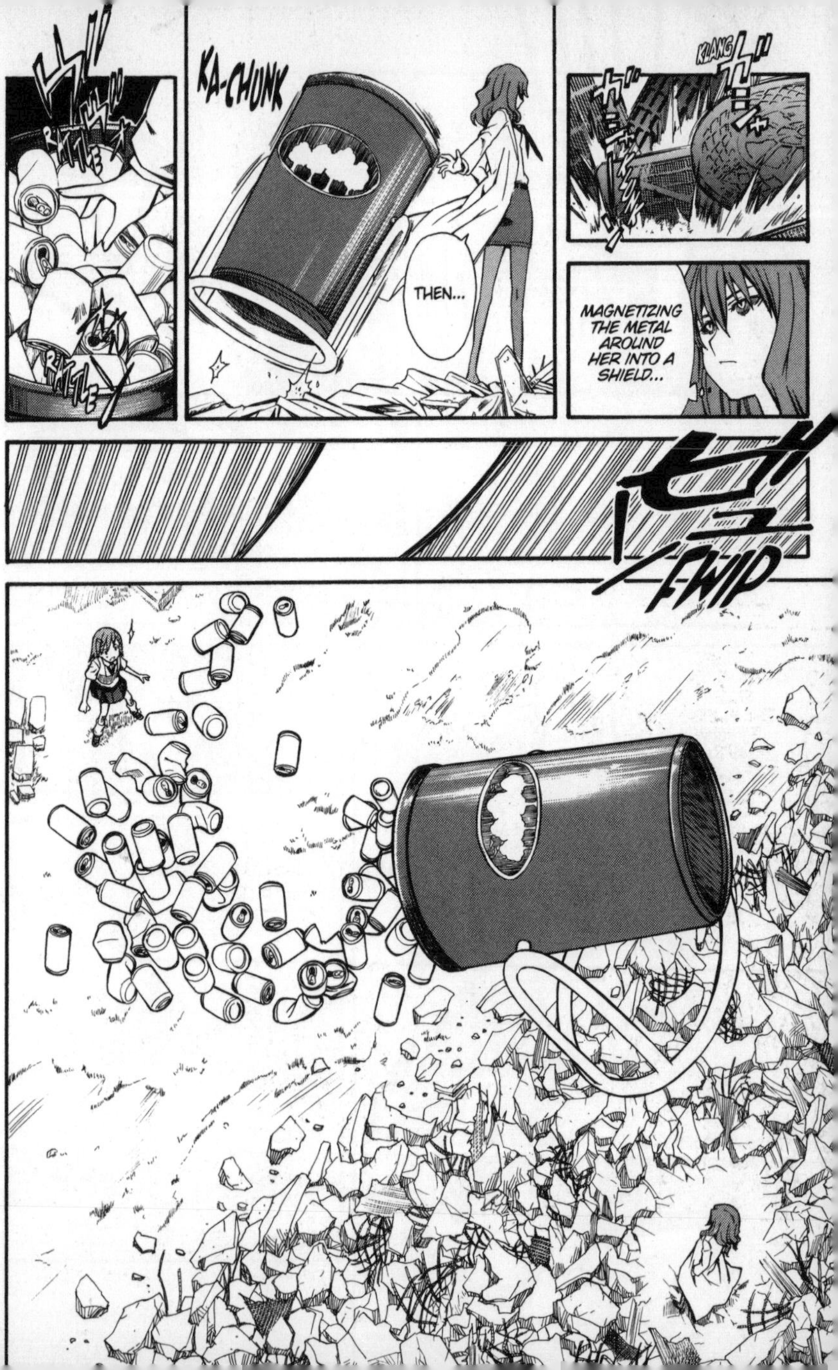
KLANG
MAGNETIZING THE METAL AROUND HER INTO A SHIELD...
KA-CHUNK
THEN...
RATTLE
RATTLE
FWIP

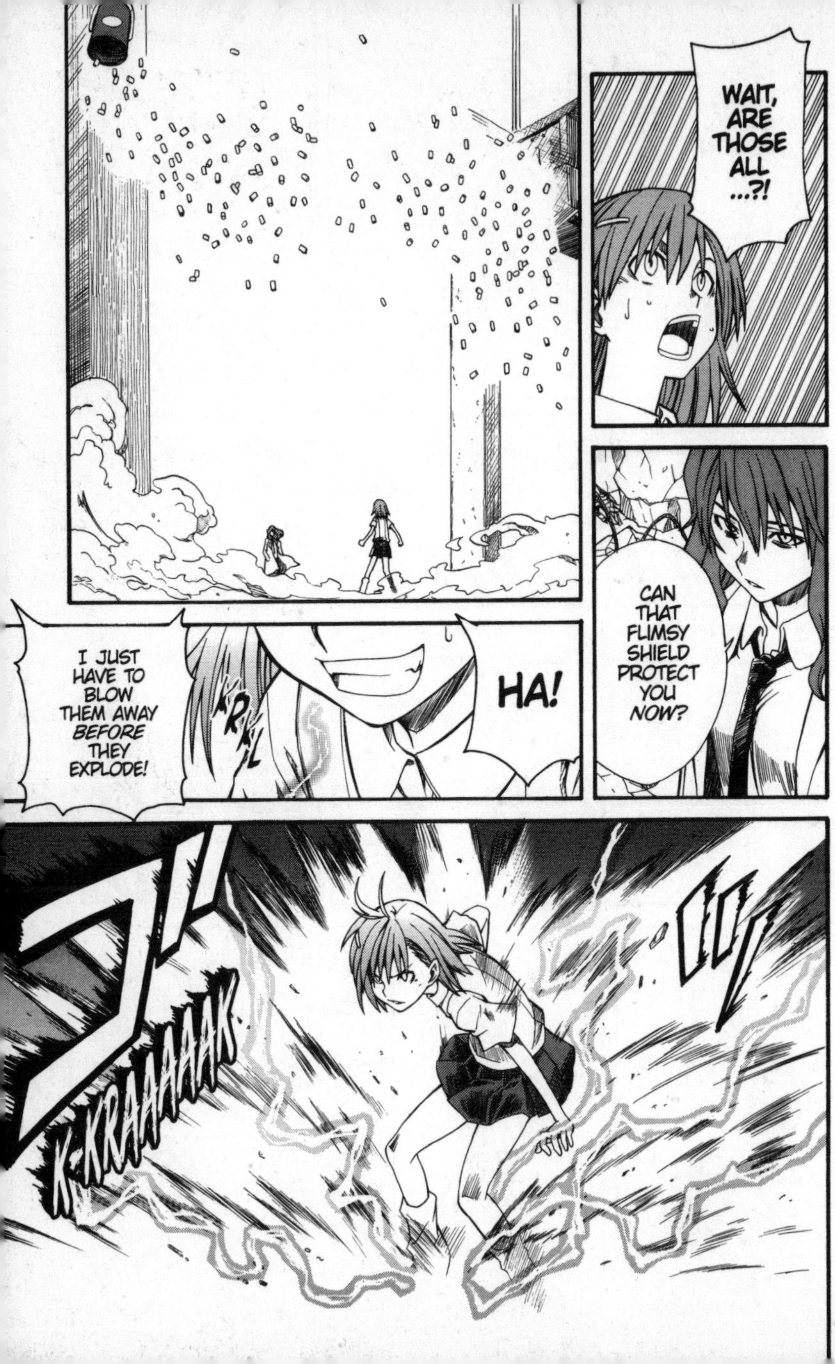
WAIT, ARE THOSE ALL ...?!
CAN THAT FLIMSY SHIELD PROTECT YOU *NOW?*
HA!
I JUST HAVE TO BLOW THEM AWAY *BEFORE* THEY EXPLODE!
K-KRAAAAAK

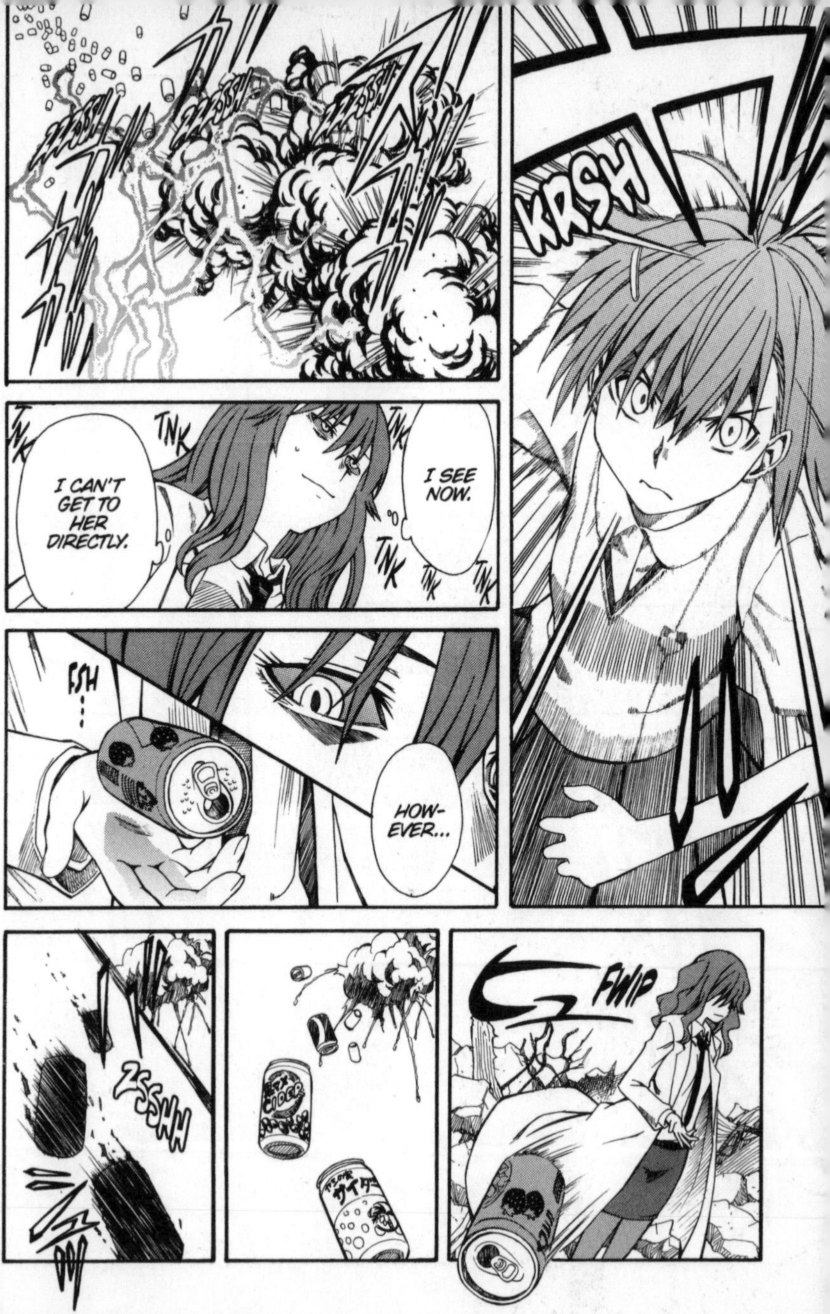
KRSH
TNK
I SEE NOW.
TNK
TNK
TNK
TNK
I CAN'T GET TO HER DIRECTLY.
TNK
HOW-EVER...
FSH...
FWIP
CIDER
ZSSHH

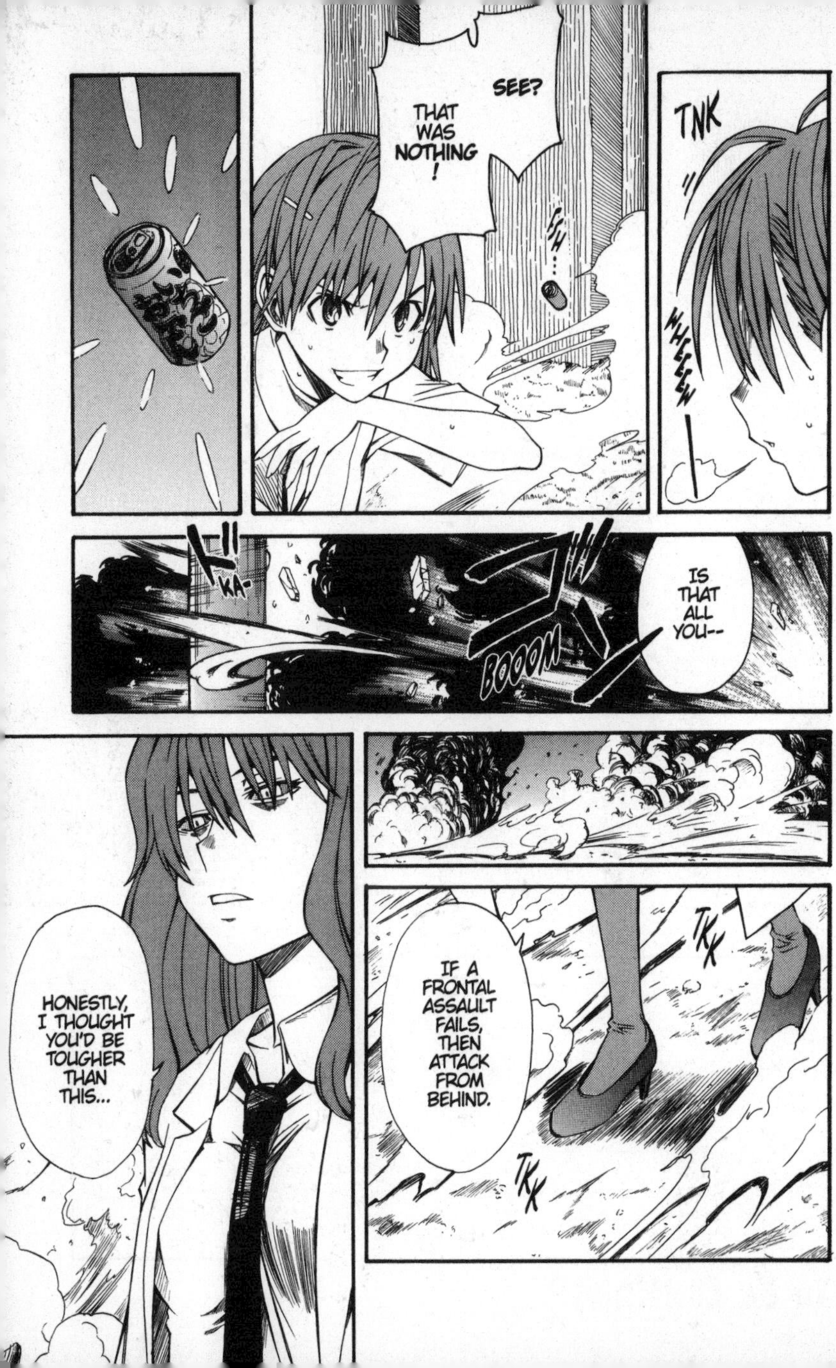
TNK
WHEEEW
SEE?
THAT WAS NOTHING!
FSH...
IS THAT ALL YOU--
BOOOM
KA-
IF A FRONTAL ASSAULT FAILS, THEN ATTACK FROM BEHIND.
TKK
TKK
HONESTLY, I THOUGHT YOU'D BE TOUGHER THAN THIS...

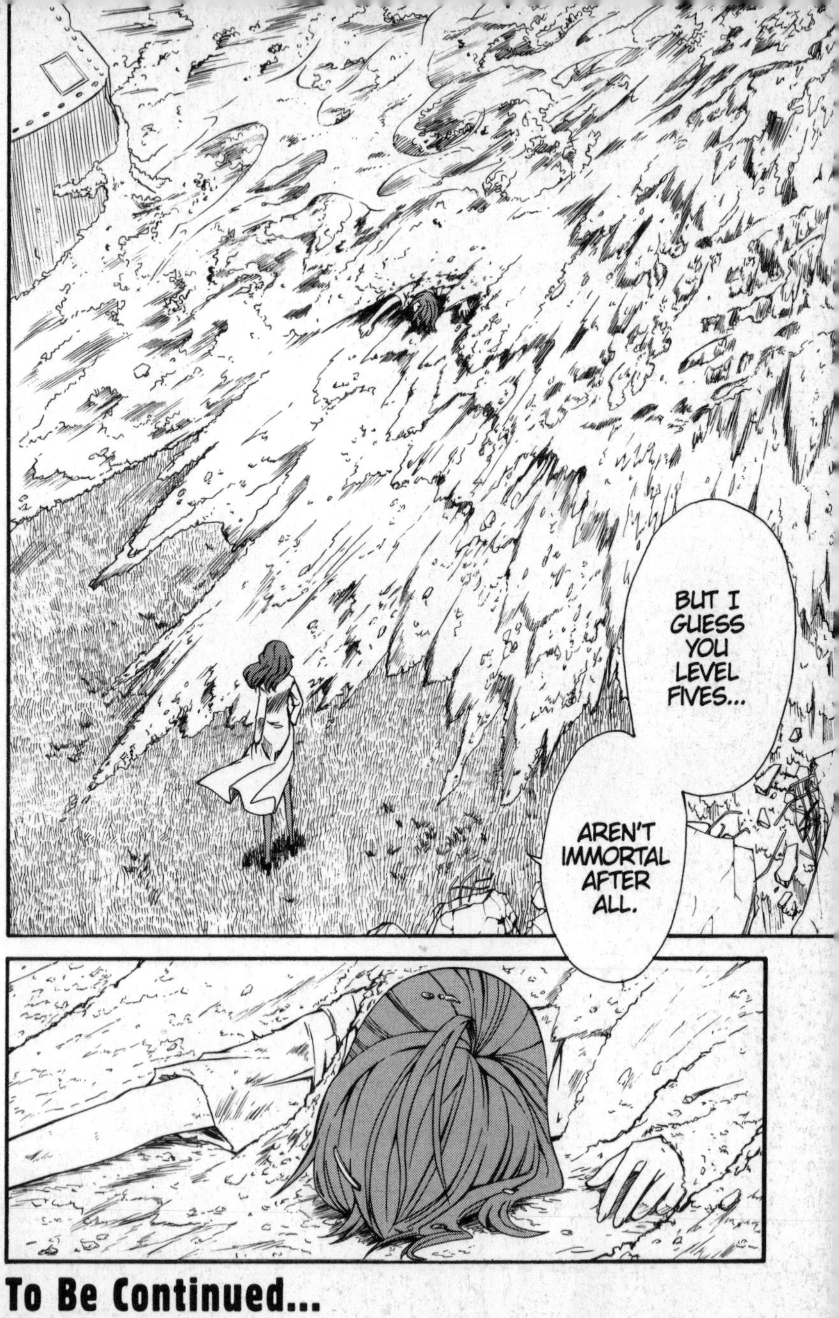
BUT I GUESS YOU LEVEL FIVES...
AREN'T IMMORTAL AFTER ALL.

To Be Continued...

A Certain SCIENTIFIC Railgun

ガンガンサイドよりお祝いメッセージ
the Gangan Side

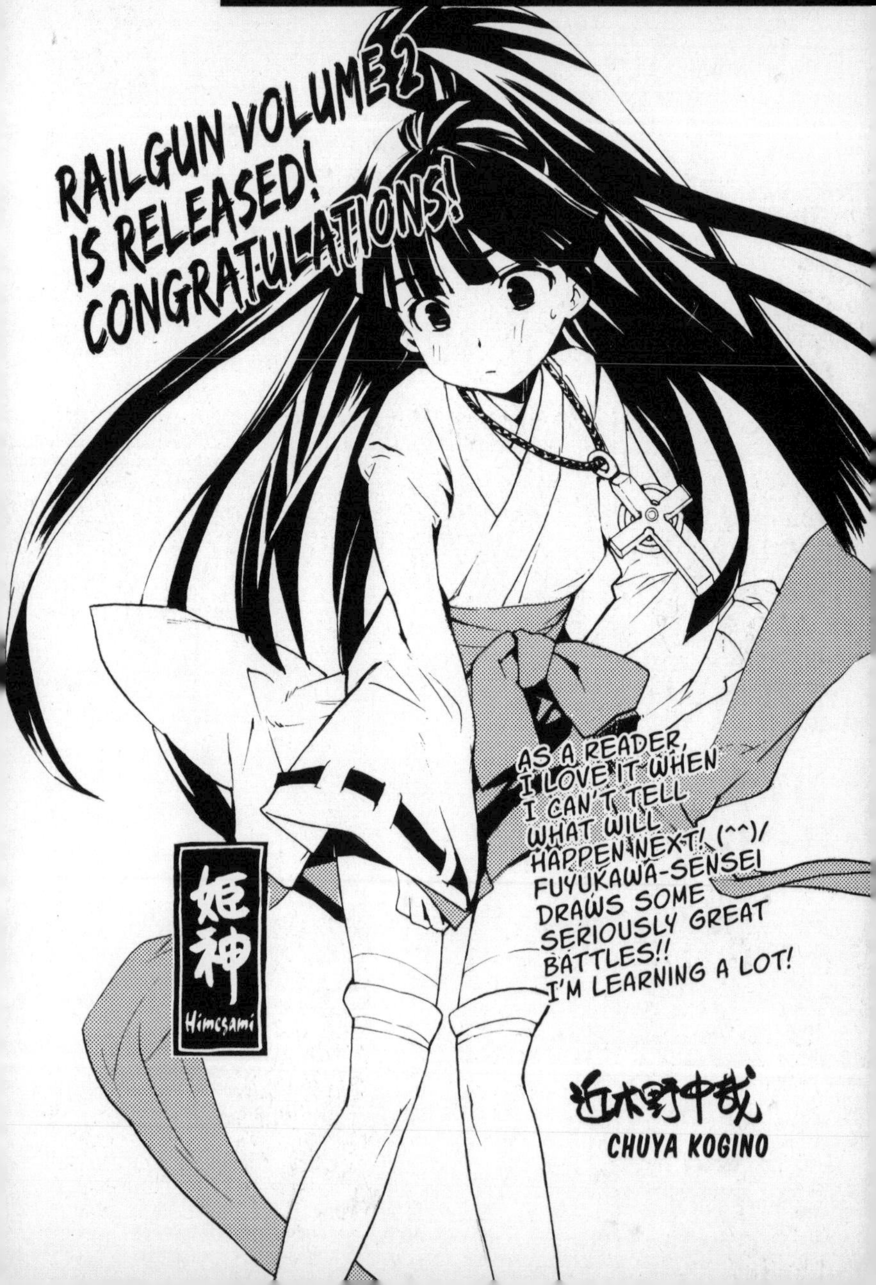
RAILGUN VOLUME 2 IS RELEASED! CONGRATULATIONS!
AS A READER, I LOVE IT WHEN I CAN'T TELL WHAT WILL HAPPEN NEXT! (^^)/ FUYUKAWA-SENSEI DRAWS SOME SERIOUSLY GREAT BATTLES!! I'M LEARNING A LOT!
姫神
Himegami
近木野中哉
CHUYA KOGINO

Cheers from the original side 原作サイドよりお祝いメッセージ

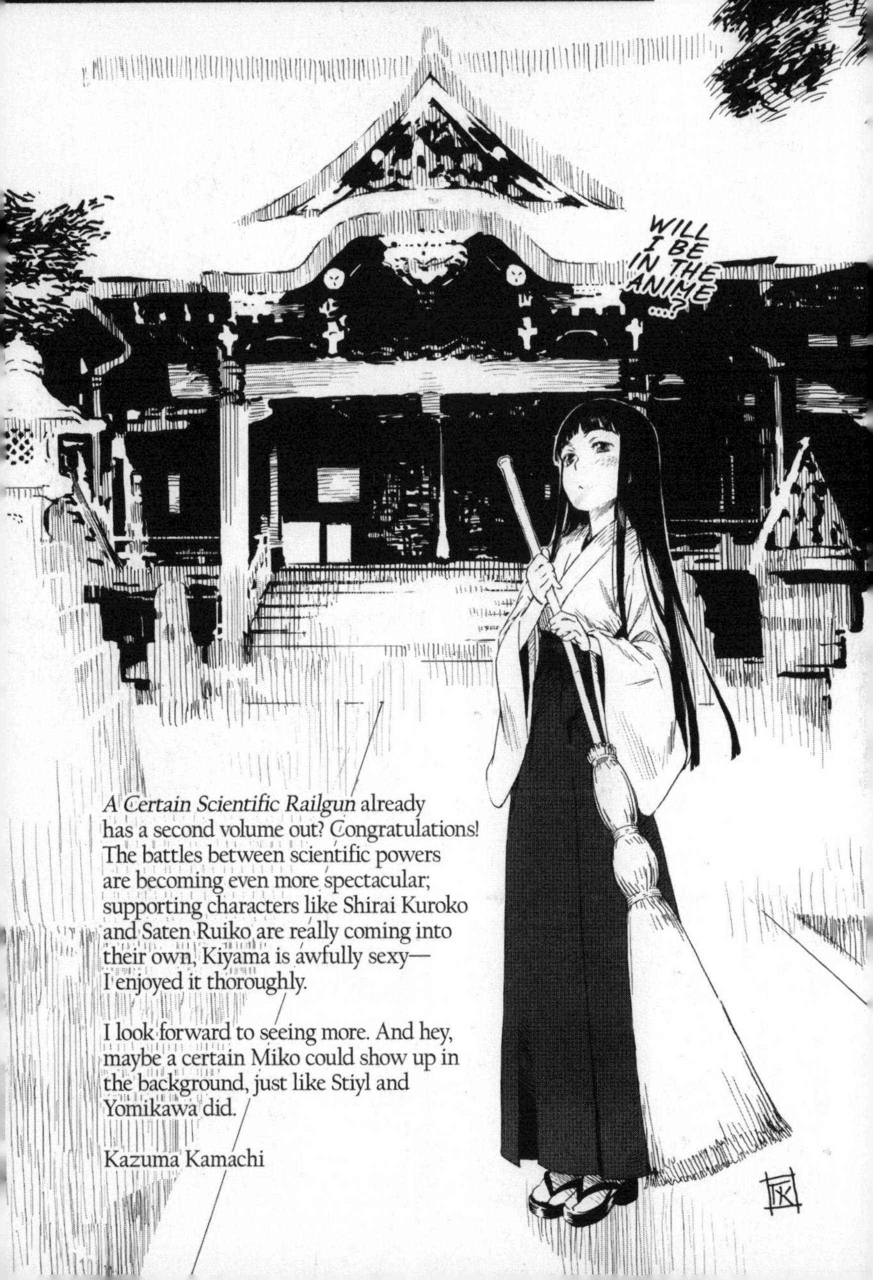
WILL I BE IN THE ANIME ...?

A Certain Scientific Railgun already has a second volume out? Congratulations! The battles between scientific powers are becoming even more spectacular; supporting characters like Shirai Kuroko and Saten Ruiko are really coming into their own, Kiyama is awfully sexy—I enjoyed it thoroughly.

I look forward to seeing more. And hey, maybe a certain Miko could show up in the background, just like Stiyl and Yomikawa did.

Kazuma Kamachi

Kiyama's Diary ①

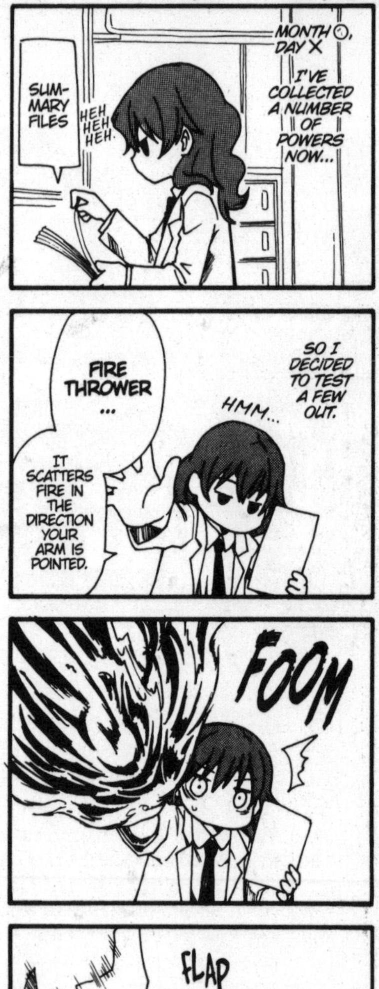
MONTH ○, DAY X
I'VE COLLECTED A NUMBER OF POWERS NOW...
SUMMARY FILES
HEH HEH HEH.
SO I DECIDED TO TEST A FEW OUT.
HMM...
FIRE THROWER ...
IT SCATTERS FIRE IN THE DIRECTION YOUR ARM IS POINTED.
FOOM
FLAP
FLAP
NO! NOT MY DATA!!

Kiyama's Diary ②

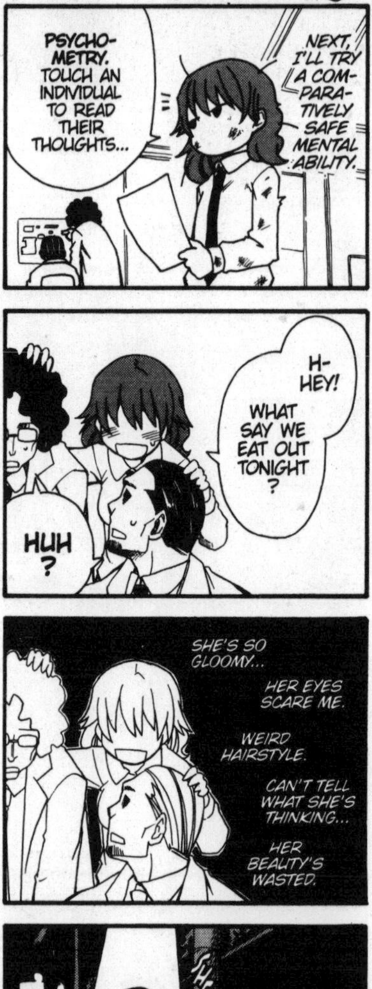
NEXT, I'LL TRY A COMPARATIVELY SAFE MENTAL ABILITY.
PSYCHOMETRY. TOUCH AN INDIVIDUAL TO READ THEIR THOUGHTS...
H-HEY!
WHAT SAY WE EAT OUT TONIGHT?
HUH?
SHE'S SO GLOOMY...
HER EYES SCARE ME.
WEIRD HAIRSTYLE.
CAN'T TELL WHAT SHE'S THINKING...
HER BEAUTY'S WASTED.

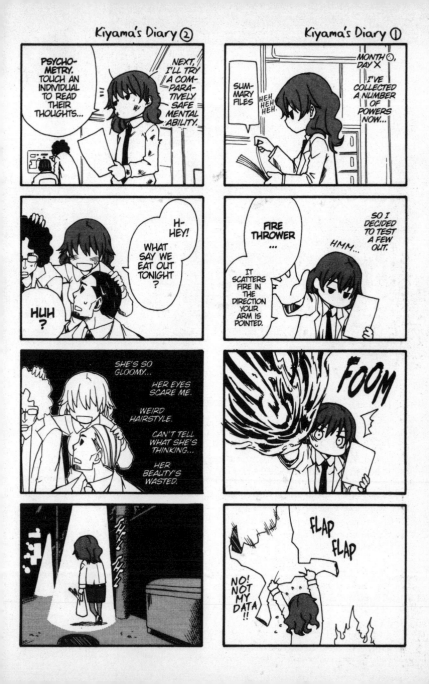

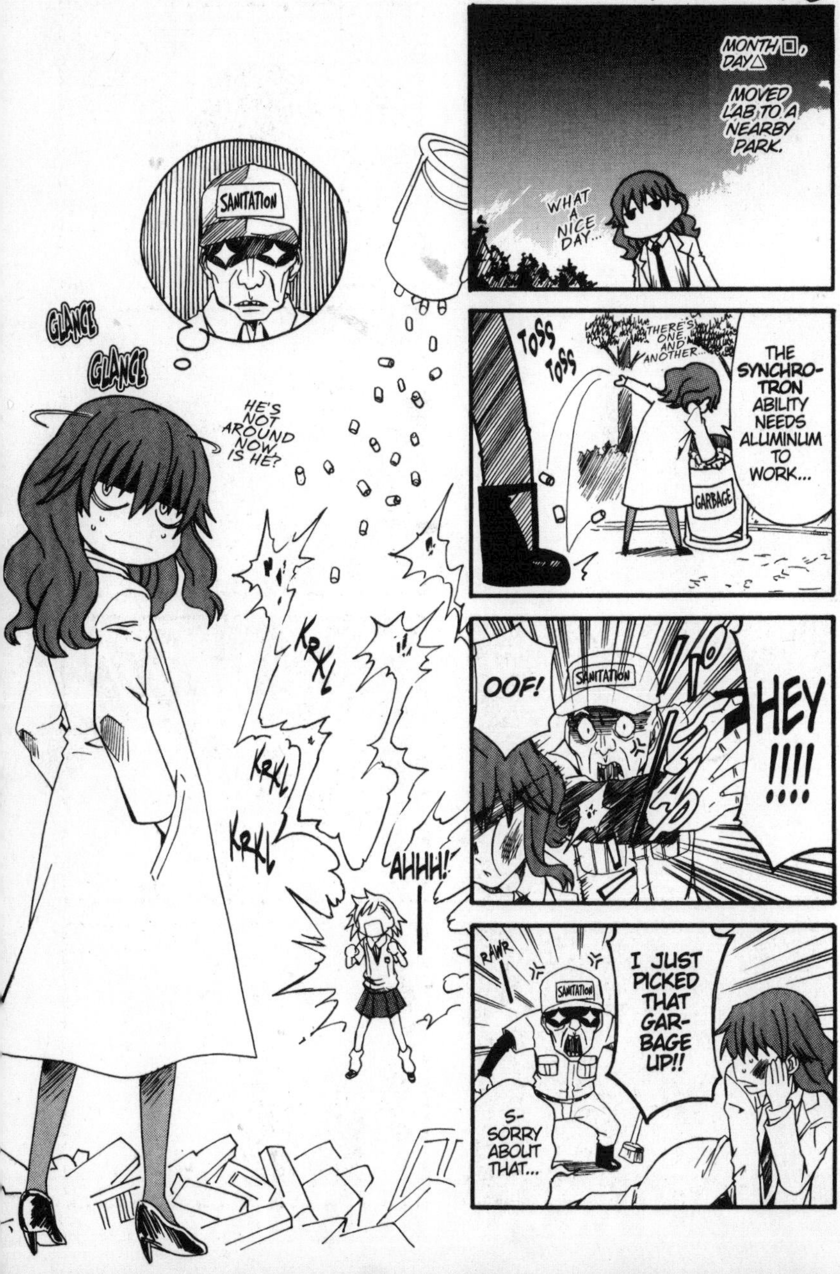
MONTH □, DAY △
MOVED LAB TO A NEARBY PARK.
WHAT A NICE DAY...
THE SYNCHRO-TRON ABILITY NEEDS ALUMINUM TO WORK...
THERE'S ONE AND ANOTHER...
TOSS TOSS
HEY!!!!
SANITATION
OOF!
I JUST PICKED THAT GAR-BAGE UP!!
SANITATION
RAWR
S-SORRY ABOUT THAT...
SANITATION
GARBAGE
GLANCE
GLANCE
HE'S NOT AROUND NOW, IS HE?
KRKL
KRKL
KRKL
AHHH!

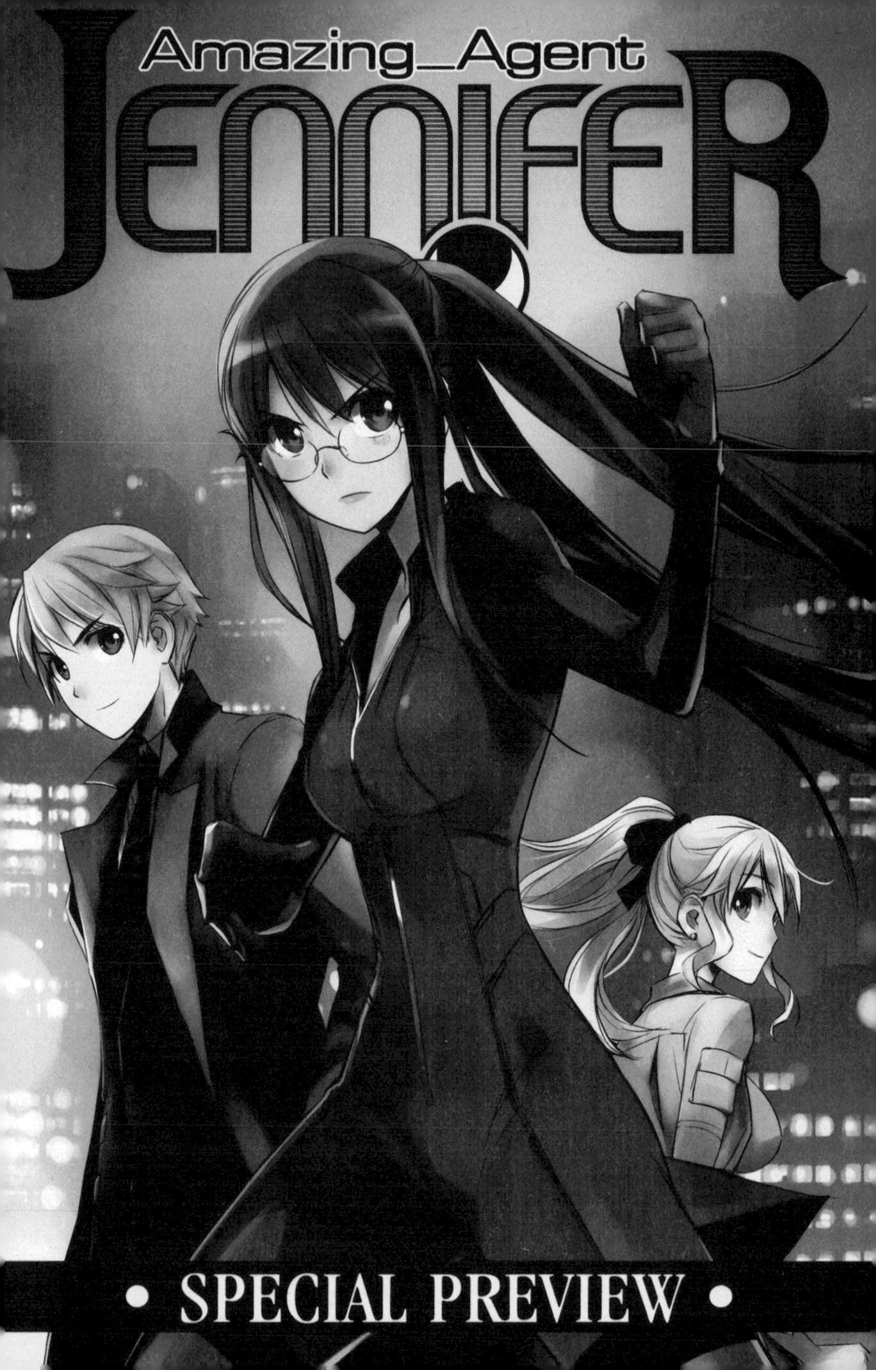
Amazing_Agent
JENNIFER
• SPECIAL PREVIEW •

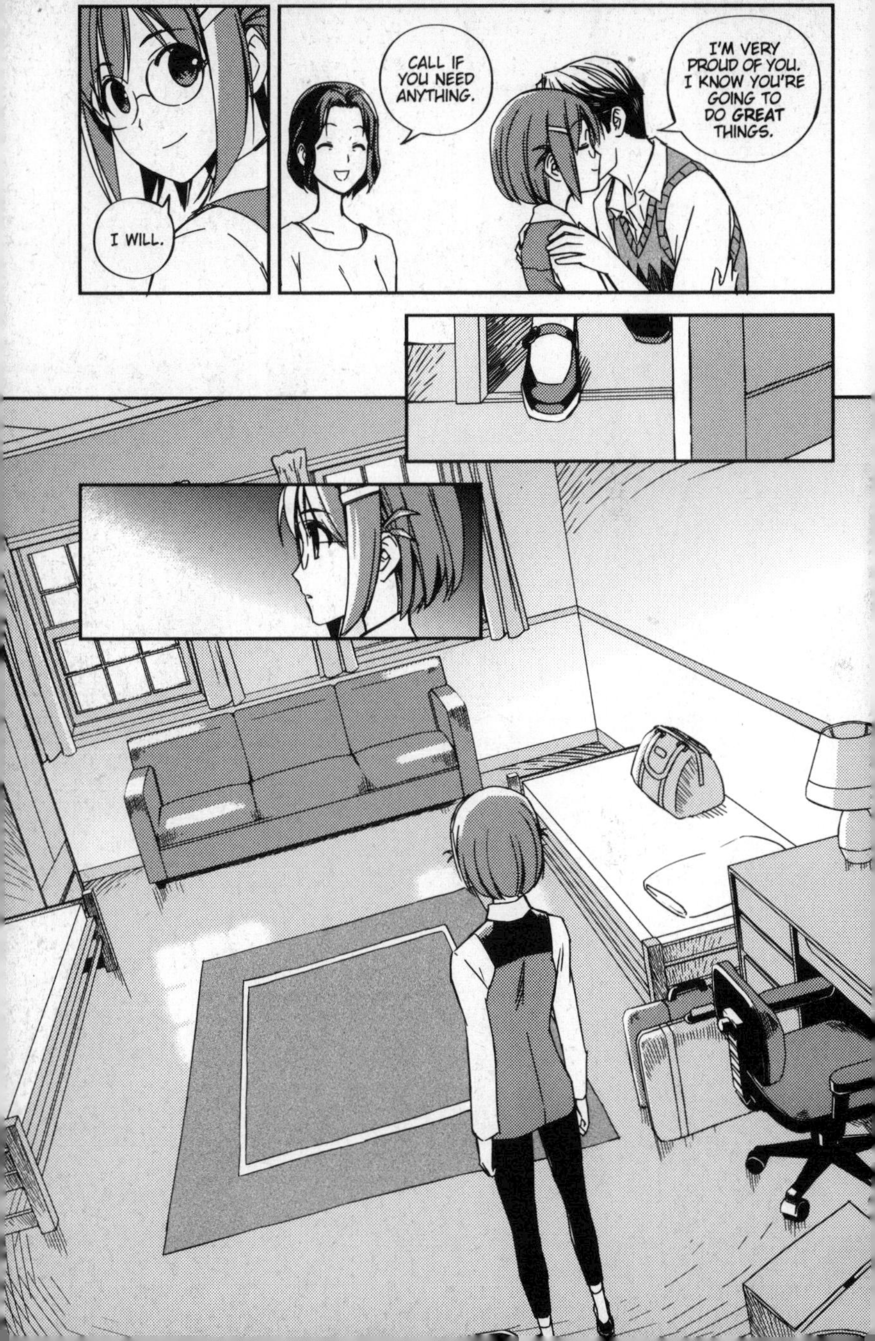
I'M VERY PROUD OF YOU. I KNOW YOU'RE GOING TO DO GREAT THINGS.
CALL IF YOU NEED ANYTHING.
I WILL.

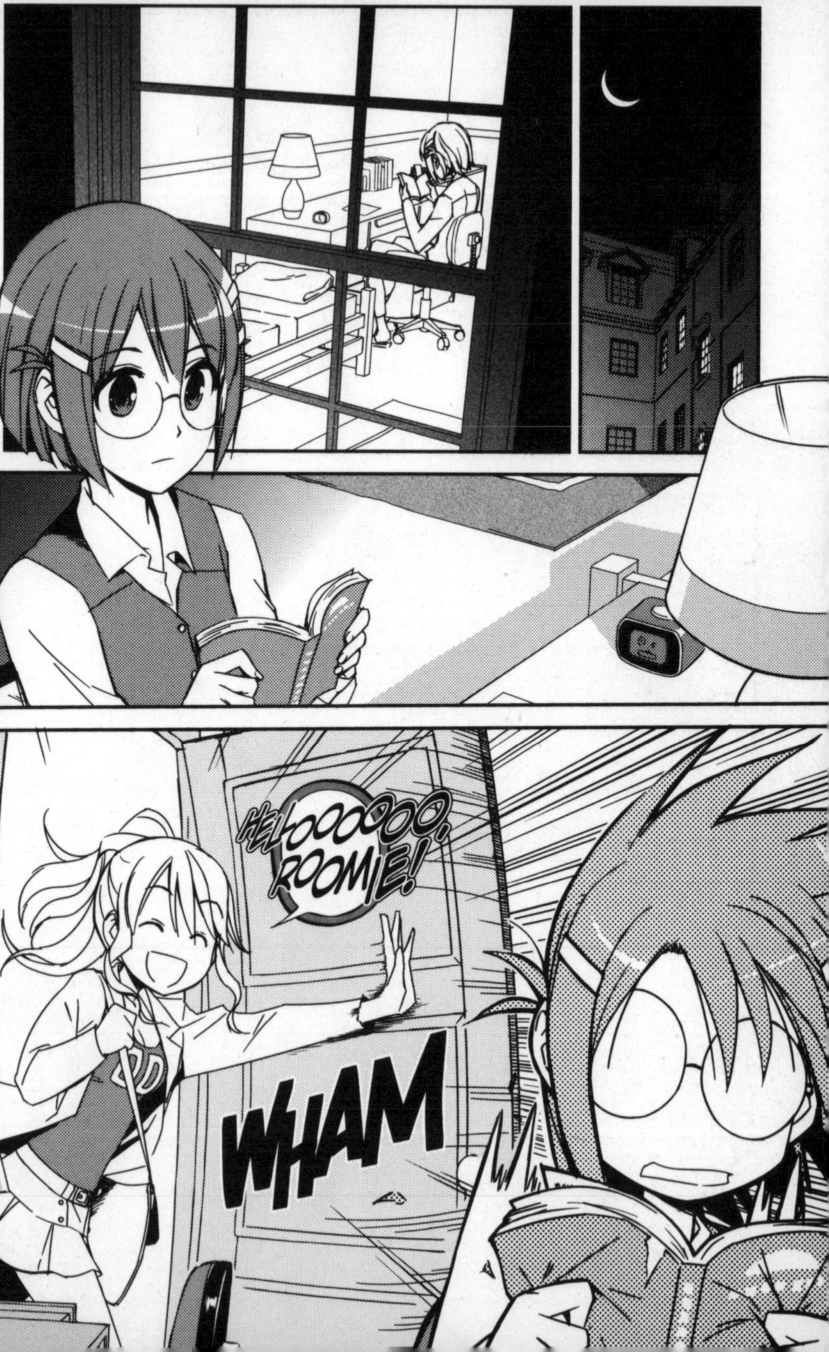
HELLOOOOOO, ROOMIE!
WHAM

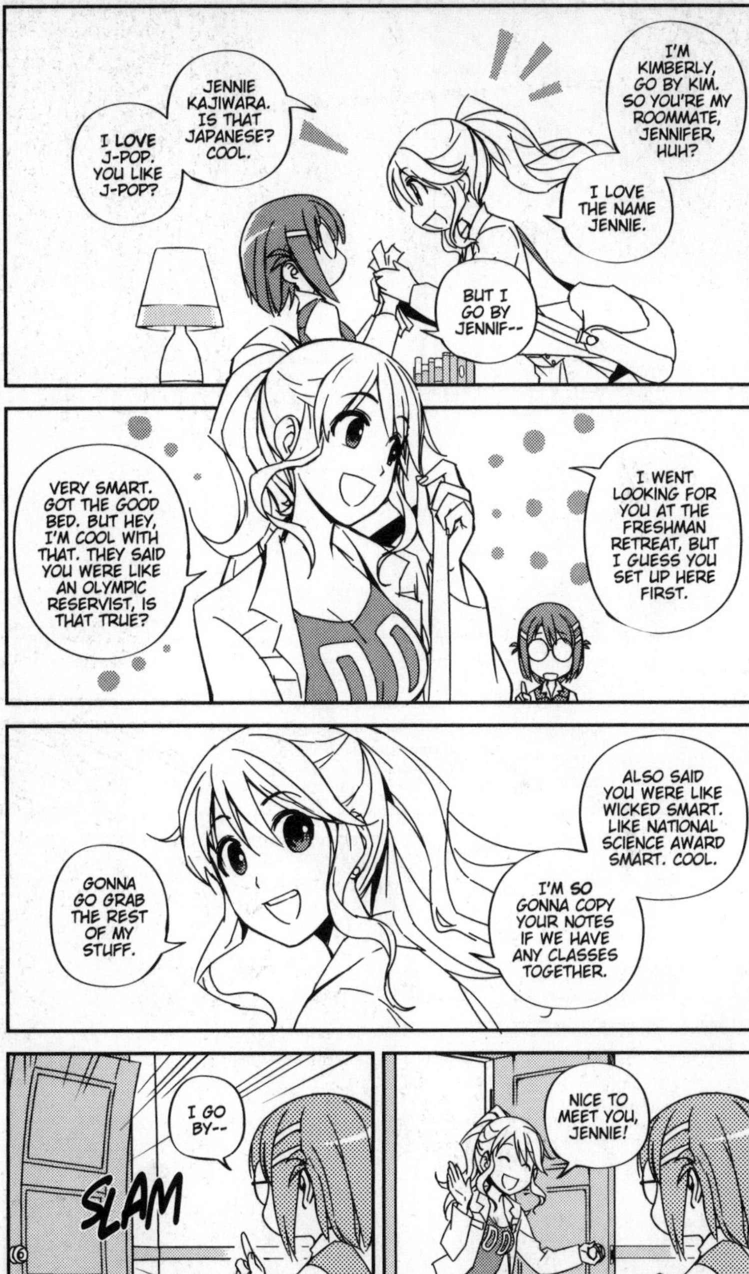
I'M KIMBERLY, GO BY KIM. SO YOU'RE MY ROOMMATE, JENNIFER, HUH?
I LOVE THE NAME JENNIE.
BUT I GO BY JENNIF--
JENNIE KAJIWARA. IS THAT JAPANESE? COOL.
I LOVE J-POP. YOU LIKE J-POP?
I WENT LOOKING FOR YOU AT THE FRESHMAN RETREAT, BUT I GUESS YOU SET UP HERE FIRST.
VERY SMART. GOT THE GOOD BED. BUT HEY, I'M COOL WITH THAT. THEY SAID YOU WERE LIKE AN OLYMPIC RESERVIST, IS THAT TRUE?
ALSO SAID YOU WERE LIKE WICKED SMART. LIKE NATIONAL SCIENCE AWARD SMART. COOL.
I'M SO GONNA COPY YOUR NOTES IF WE HAVE ANY CLASSES TOGETHER.
GONNA GO GRAB THE REST OF MY STUFF.
NICE TO MEET YOU, JENNIE!
I GO BY--
SLAM

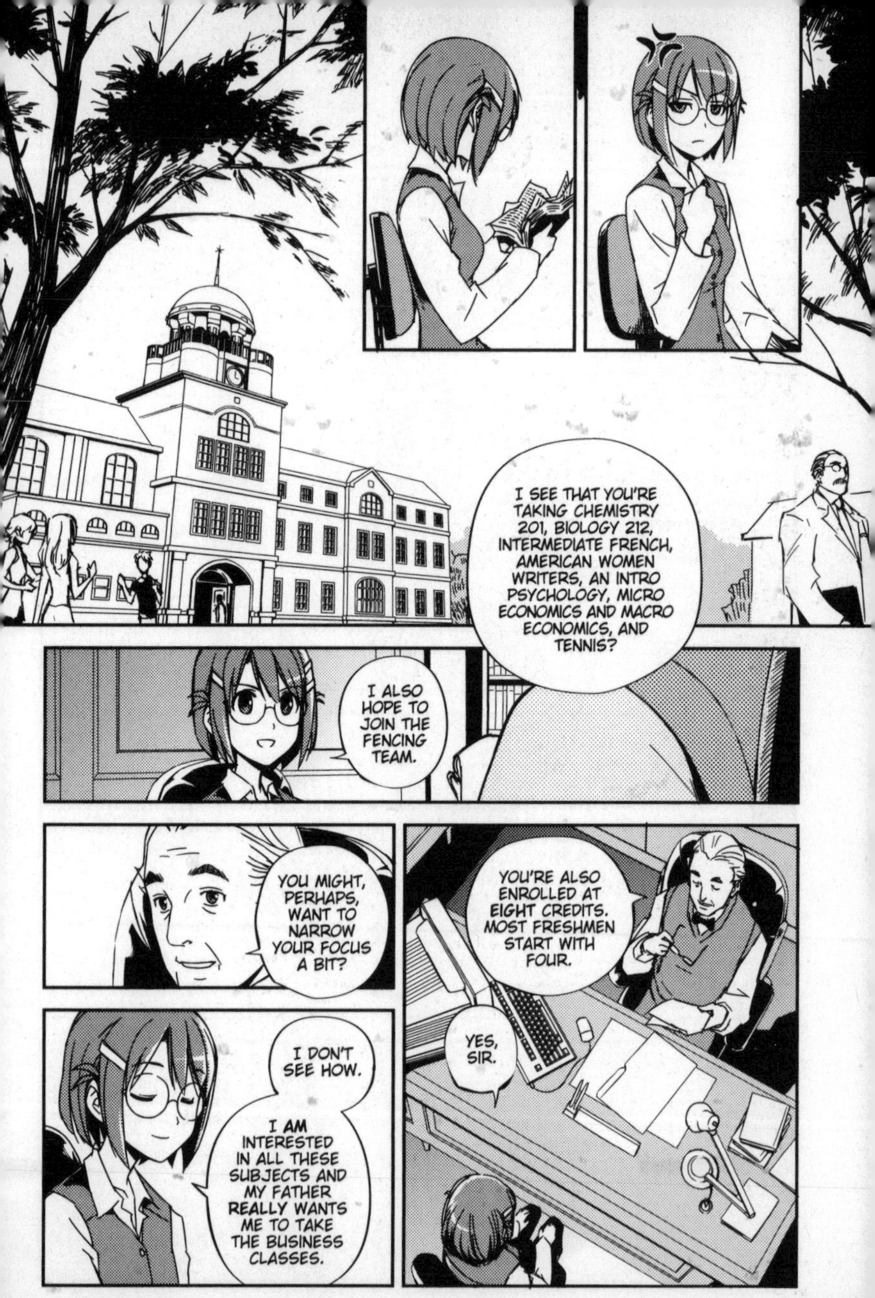
I SEE THAT YOU'RE TAKING CHEMISTRY 201, BIOLOGY 212, INTERMEDIATE FRENCH, AMERICAN WOMEN WRITERS, AN INTRO PSYCHOLOGY, MICRO ECONOMICS AND MACRO ECONOMICS, AND TENNIS?
I ALSO HOPE TO JOIN THE FENCING TEAM.
YOU'RE ALSO ENROLLED AT EIGHT CREDITS. MOST FRESHMEN START WITH FOUR.
YES, SIR.
YOU MIGHT, PERHAPS, WANT TO NARROW YOUR FOCUS A BIT?
I DON'T SEE HOW.
I AM INTERESTED IN ALL THESE SUBJECTS AND MY FATHER REALLY WANTS ME TO TAKE THE BUSINESS CLASSES.

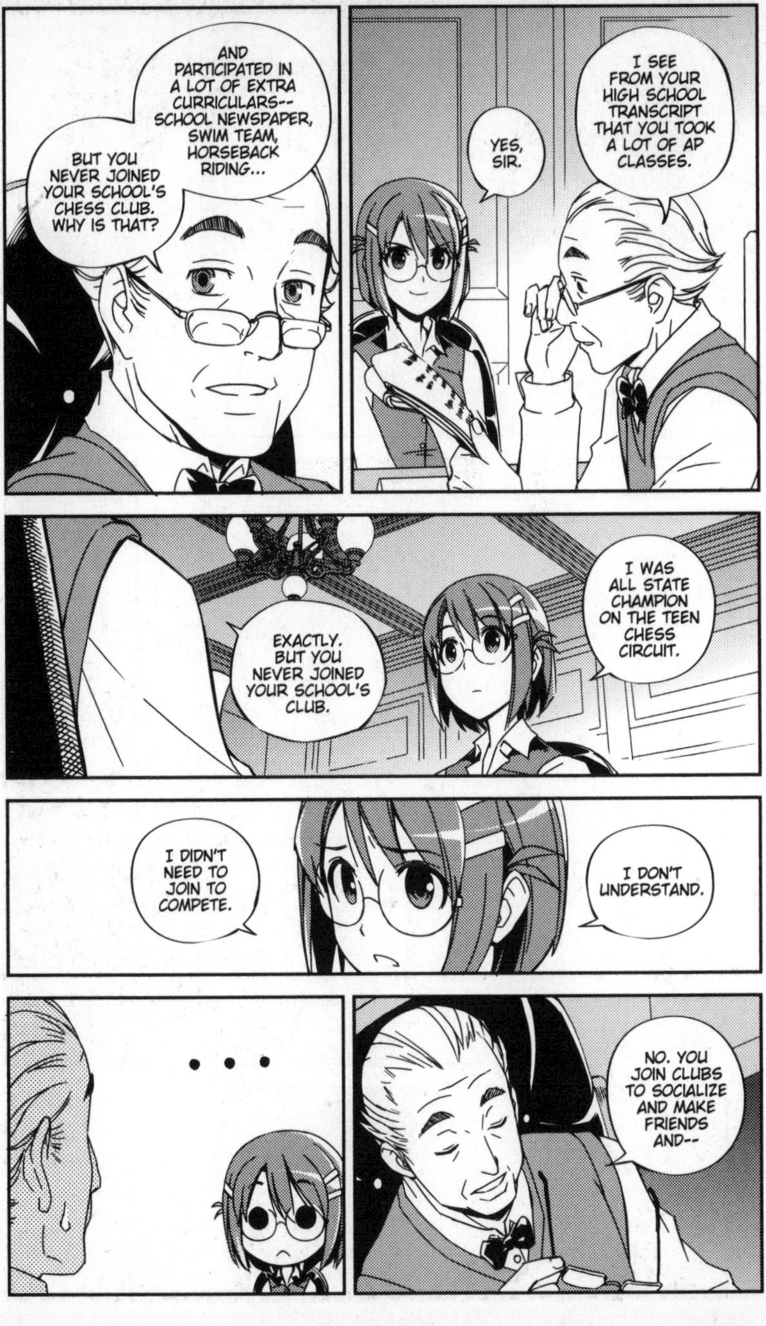
I SEE FROM YOUR HIGH SCHOOL TRANSCRIPT THAT YOU TOOK A LOT OF AP CLASSES.
YES, SIR.
AND PARTICIPATED IN A LOT OF EXTRA CURRICULARS--SCHOOL NEWSPAPER, SWIM TEAM, HORSEBACK RIDING...
BUT YOU NEVER JOINED YOUR SCHOOL'S CHESS CLUB. WHY IS THAT?
I WAS ALL STATE CHAMPION ON THE TEEN CHESS CIRCUIT.
EXACTLY. BUT YOU NEVER JOINED YOUR SCHOOL'S CLUB.
I DON'T UNDERSTAND.
I DIDN'T NEED TO JOIN TO COMPETE.
NO. YOU JOIN CLUBS TO SOCIALIZE AND MAKE FRIENDS AND--
• • •

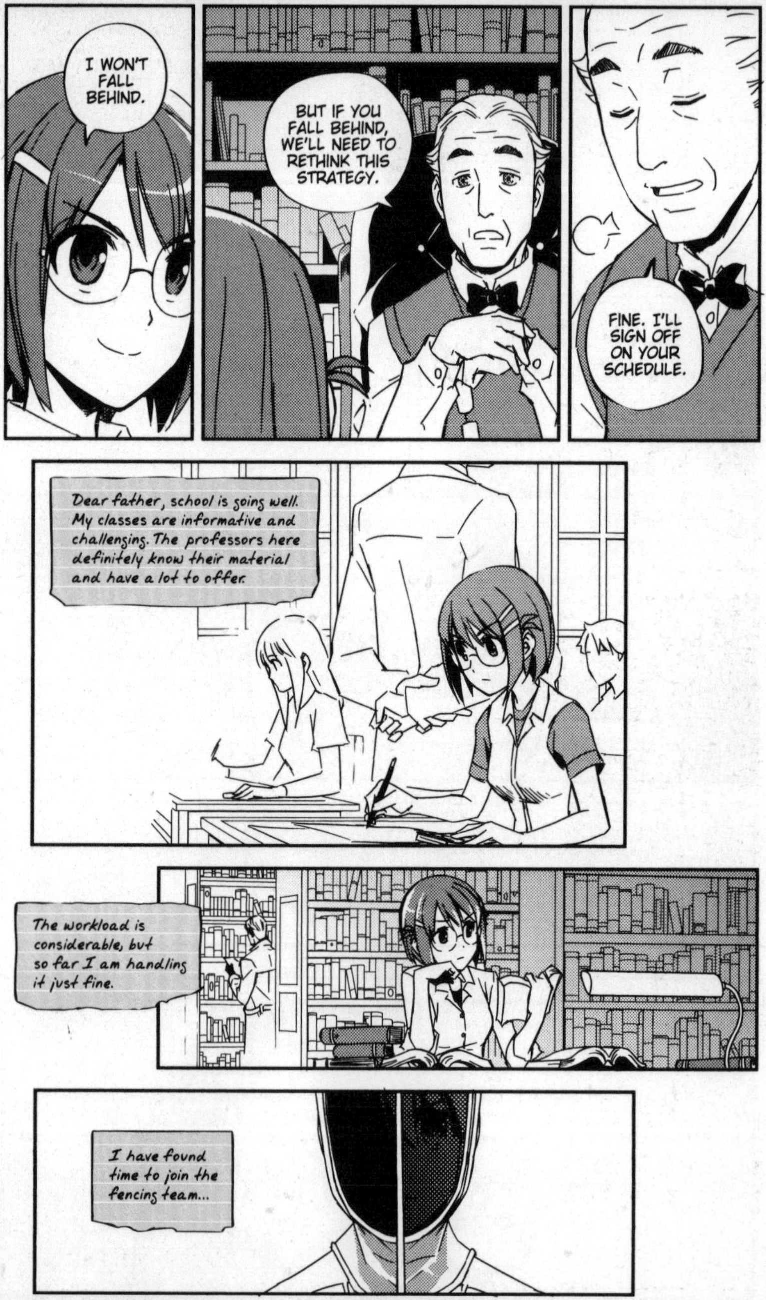
FINE. I'LL SIGN OFF ON YOUR SCHEDULE.
BUT IF YOU FALL BEHIND, WE'LL NEED TO RETHINK THIS STRATEGY.
I WON'T FALL BEHIND.
Dear father, school is going well. My classes are informative and challenging. The professors here definitely know their material and have a lot to offer.
The workload is considerable, but so far I am handling it just fine.
I have found time to join the fencing team...

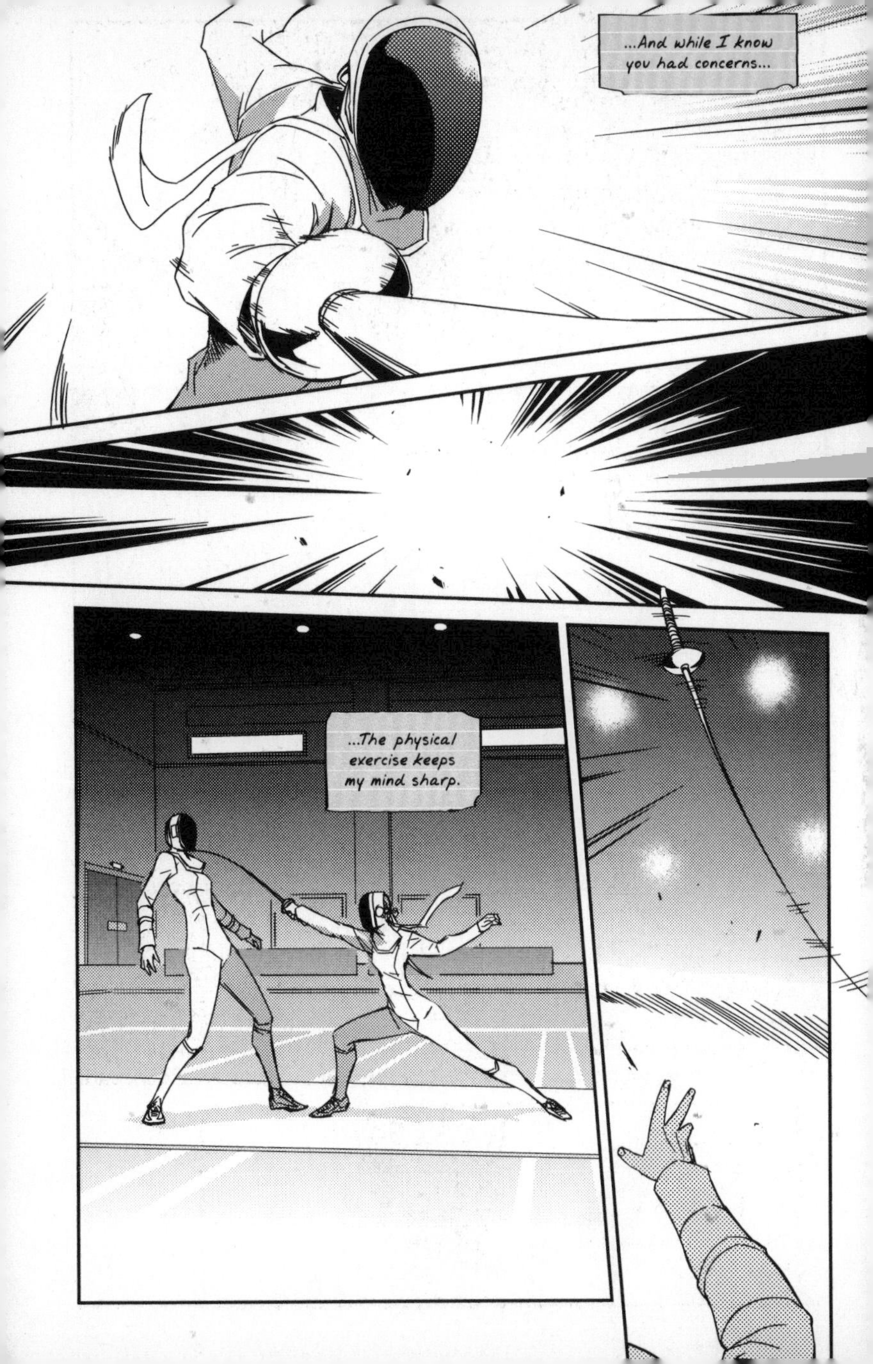
...And while I know you had concerns...
...The physical exercise keeps my mind sharp.

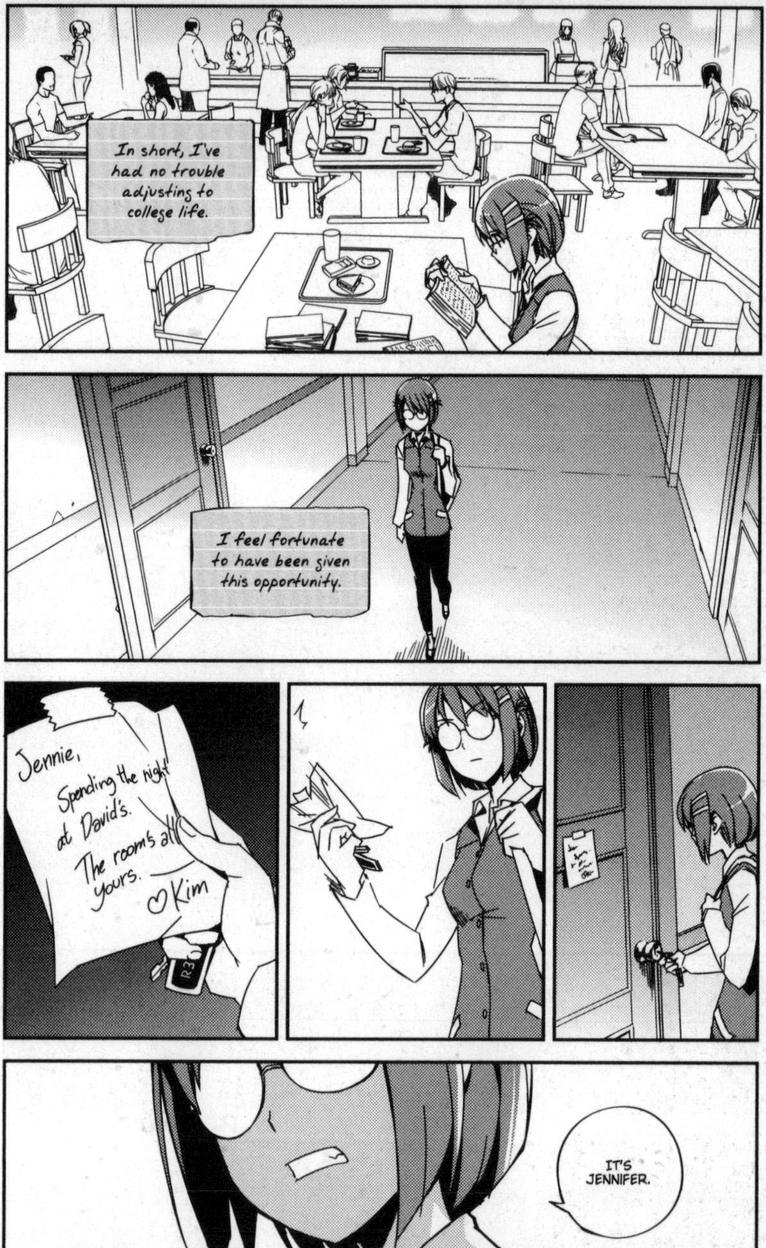
In short, I've had no trouble adjusting to college life.
I feel fortunate to have been given this opportunity.
Jennie, Spending the night at David's. The room's all yours. Kim
IT'S JENNIFER.

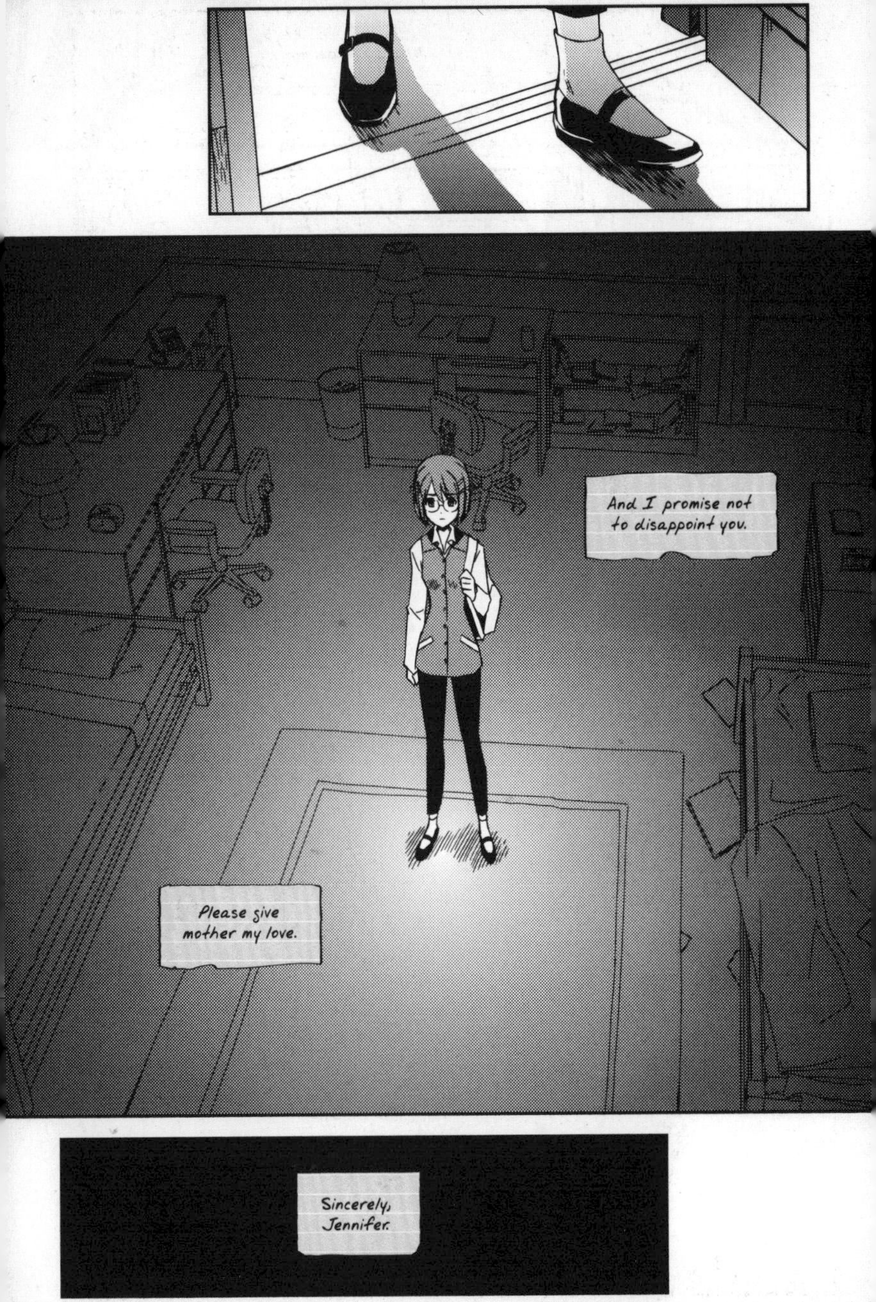
And I promise not to disappoint you.
Please give mother my love.
Sincerely, Jennifer.

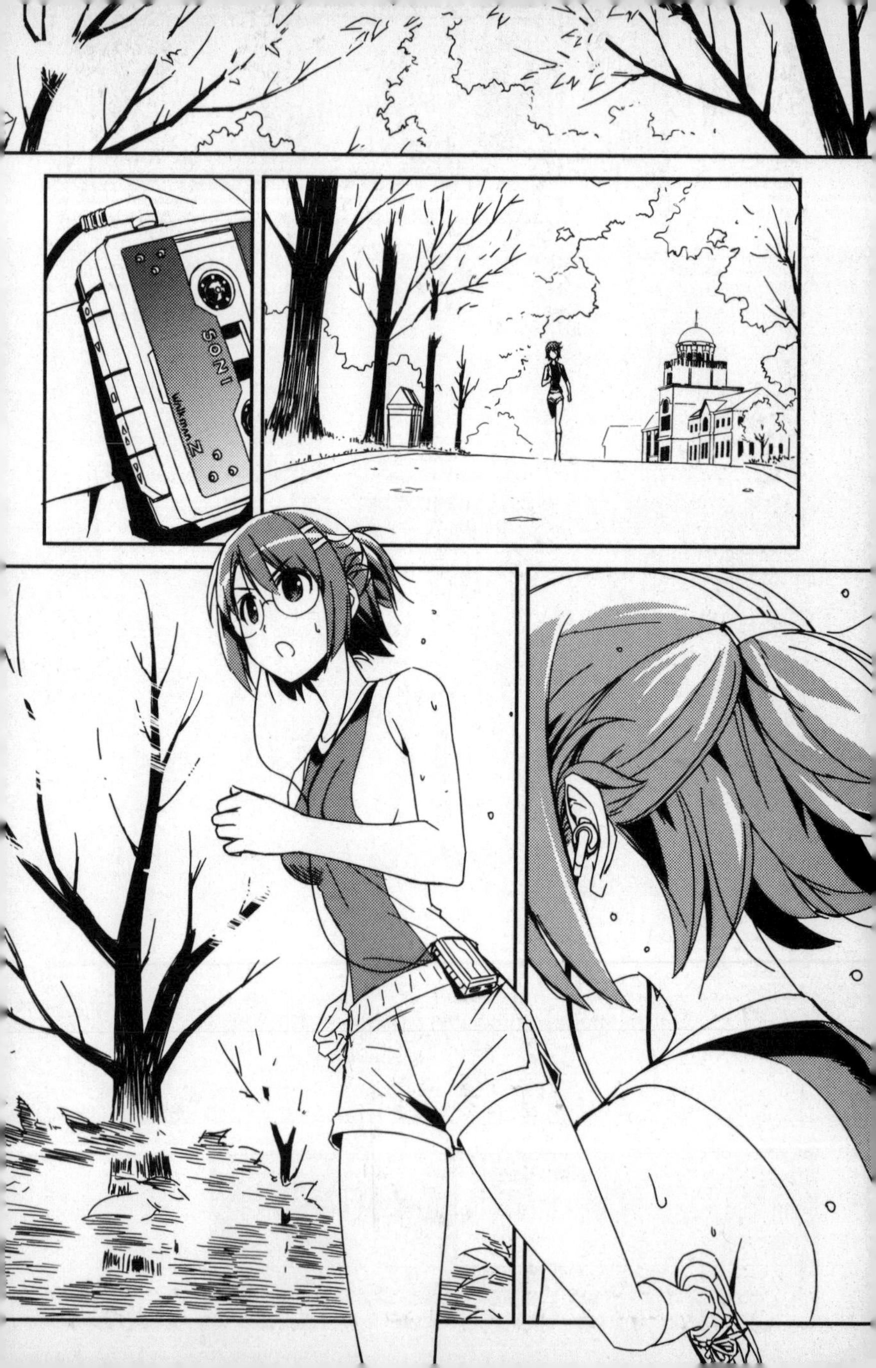
SONI
Walkman Z

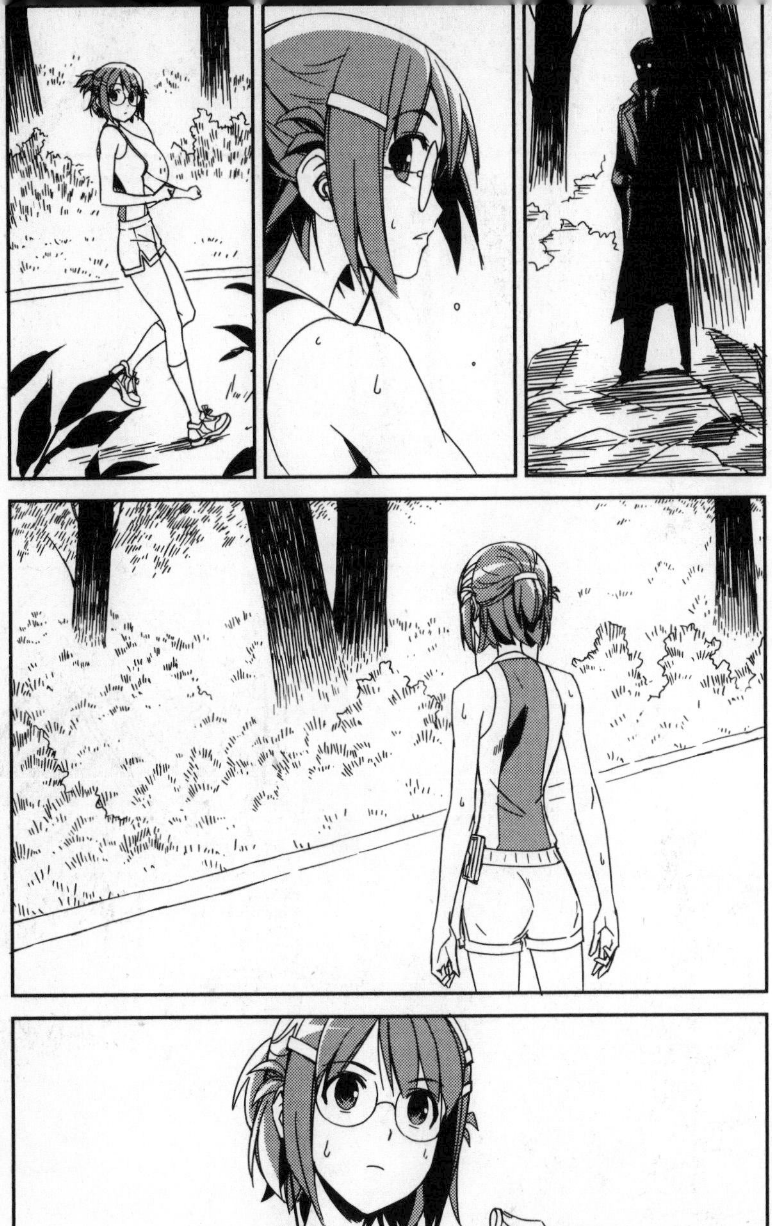

CONTINUED IN AMAZING AGENT JENNIFER VOL. 1!